1984–85

FACT BOOK

on Higher Education

ACE Board of Directors

1984–85 FACT BOOK on Higher Education

Compiled by
CECILIA A. OTTINGER

American Council on Education • Macmillan Publishing Company
NEW YORK

Collier Macmillan Publishers
LONDON

The American Council on Education/Macmillan Series in Higher Education

Macmillan Publishing Company
A Division of Macmillan, Inc.
866 Third Avenue, New York, N. Y. 10022

Collier Macmillan Canada, Inc.

ISSN 0363–6720

Printed in the United States of America

printing number
1 2 3 4 5 6 7 8 9 10

Contents

I. Demographic and Economic Data

II. Enrollment Data

III. Data on Institutions

IV. Data on Faculty and Staff

V. Student Data

VI. Earned Degrees Data

Foreword

It was about twenty-five years ago that the Committee on Statistical Information and Research of the American Council on Education approved my proposal for the development and distribution of a loose-leaf *Fact Book on Higher Education*. The first pages were distributed October 3, 1958.

At that time, the existing quantifiable data about higher education were subject to widespread suspicion or even, in many cases, outright rejection. All too often data collected were not only inadequate but were not made available until the time of their usefulness was past.

It had become increasingly apparent that data had to be improved in quality and in speed of dissemination. In addition, the data had to be presented in a clear and understandable form to be of maximum use to decision makers.

In general, data were presented on each page in two ways: a diagram showing trends for several years, and a table showing the actual data. Thus, comparisons among sets of data were easily made, and trends were readily noted. Eventually, over 200 pages developed and as most of them were updated each year the effort became, in effect, a "book" a year.

In later years a quarterly, then an annual publication, replaced the loose-leaf method of distribution. The page format has, however, remained essentially unchanged during the twenty-five years.

With convenience of use, ease of understanding, faster availability, and increased accuracy, the use of data in the decision-making process has now become commonplace.

Elmer D. West
Director/Editor for the
Fact Book on Higher Education
1958–1964

Introduction

In compiling this latest edition of the *Fact Book on Higher Education,* we have sought to continue *Fact Book*'s long tradition of condensing pertinent data from many sources into useful figures and tables that emphasize both trends and baseline information related to higher education.

As with other editions, *Fact Book* is based on the latest available data from more than thirty documentary sources; no new data gathering is performed. Government sources for national data include: the National Center for Education Statistics, the U. S. Bureau of the Census, the Office of Civil Rights, the Bureau of Labor Statistics of the U. S. Department of Labor, the U. S. Department of Commerce, the National Science Foundation, and Committees of the U. S. Congress. Notably, an increasing number of tables contained in this volume are based on unpublished tabulations of government data that are otherwise available only on data tapes.

Fact Book is divided into sections containing information on: demographic and economic trends significant to higher education; enrollments; institutions; faculty and staff; students; and earned degrees. This year, for the first time, detailed highlights appear at the beginning of each section. In addition, because of the special interest in statistical data on the status of women and minorities in higher education, highlights have been abstracted for these groups on the following pages.

Elmer West's comments, in the Foreword, remind us that *Fact Book* has been published by the American Council on Education for twenty-five years, beginning in 1958. We are pleased to continue this tradition. His comments also emphasize the importance of making data available in a convenient form. Cecilia Ottinger, the research analyst who most ably pulled together the information for this volume, would welcome questions or suggestions from *Fact Book* readers on the information that has been presented.

Elaine El-Khawas
Vice President for
Policy Analysis
and Research

Highlights on the Status of Minorities in Higher Education

Population

- In 1980 and 1981, approximately 16 percent of the college-age population (18–24 years old) were minorities.
- In 1980, minorities comprised 16 percent of all full-time enrollees; blacks represented 10 percent of this population and other minorities made up 6 percent.

Income and Employment

- There were sizable differences in the 1981 median incomes for families according to race:

  white families, $23,517,
  Hispanic families, $16,401, and
  black families, $13,266.

- The 1981, median income for all minority families was $14,598.
- Median income also varied considerably on the basis of sex and level of education attained:

  black males 25 years and older with a high school education, $12,349,
  black females 25 years and older with a high school education, $7,332,
  black males 25 years and older with 5 or more years of college, $21,666, and
  black females 25 years and older with 5 or more years of college, $16,522.

- In 1980, minorities comprised 12.2 percent of the total U.S. labor force; 47 percent of the minority labor force were women and 53 percent were men; in the overall U.S. labor force, 58 percent were male and 42 percent were female.
- The 1982 unemployment rate for whites was 8.6 percent while for blacks and Hispanics the unemployment rate was 18.9 percent and 13.8 percent, respectively.

Enrollment

- There were 1.1 million minorities enrolled full-time in higher education institutions in 1980; this represents 16 percent of the total full-time enrollment. In 1972, minorities were 12 percent of all full-time enrollees.
- In 1979, there were 3.9 million families with one or more college-age members (18–24 years old) attending college full-time.
- The percentage of those families with incomes $15,000 and over by race and ethnicity in 1979 were:

  white families, 80 percent,
  Hispanic families, 46 percent, and
  black families, 41 percent.

- The percentage of those families with incomes under $15,000 by race and ethnicity in 1979 were:

  white families, 20 percent,
  Hispanic families, 54 percent, and
  black families, 59 percent.

1982 Freshmen Characteristics

- The racial/ethnic backgrounds of males in the freshman class of 1982 were:

  89.0 percent white,
  7.6 percent black,
  1.8 percent Mexican American or Puerto Rican,
  1.0 percent American Indian, and
  1.5 percent of other racial/ethnic backgrounds.

- The racial/ethnic backgrounds of females in the freshman class of 1982 were:

  87.5 percent white,
  9.4 percent black,
  1.8 percent Mexican American and Puerto Rican,
  1.3 percent Asian,
  1.3 percent of other racial/ethnic backgrounds, and
  0.9 percent American Indian.

Earned Degrees

Bachelor's Degrees

- In academic year 1980–81, minorities earned 12 percent (116,046) of all bachelor's degrees awarded.
- Bachelor's degrees awarded by race/ethnicity for 1981 were:

  whites, 804,659 (85.3 percent),
  blacks, 60,589 (6.4 percent),
  Hispanics, 33,066 (3.5 percent),
  Asians, 18,807 (2.0 percent),
  American Indians, 3,584 (0.4 percent), and
  nonresident aliens, 22,615 (2.4 percent).

Master's Degrees

- In 1981, minorities earned 10.8 percent of master's degrees awarded. More than half (53.7 percent) of the master's degrees awarded to minorities were to blacks.

- Among minorities, women were more likely to have earned a master's degree than their male counterparts (56 percent of women vs. 44 percent of men).

- The majority of minorities who earned master's degrees in 1981 were awarded degrees in the field of education (41.8 percent). The next two most likely academic areas were business (16.2 percent) and public affairs (9.7 percent).

First Professional Degrees

- In 1981, over half of all minorities earning professional degrees (50.2 percent) had earned a degree in the field of law. Medicine was the second most likely field in which minorities earned a first professional degree (28.1 percent).

- Among minorities, women earned 34.1 percent of first professional degrees in 1981 while men were awarded 65.9 percent.

Doctorates

- In academic year 1980–81, 2,751 doctorates were earned by minorities. Blacks and Asians were the most likely of all minorities to have earned doctorates. Of all the doctorates awarded to minorities, blacks had earned 46 percent of the doctorates and another 32 percent were earned by Asians.

- During academic year 1980–81, a larger proportion of doctorates was awarded to minority men than to minority women (63 percent vs. 37 percent, respectively).

- In 1981, 56 percent of all doctorates awarded to minority women were earned by blacks.

- The largest proportion of doctorates awarded to blacks, Hispanics, and American Indians were in the field of education (33 percent). Asians were more likely to have earned a doctorate in the field of engineering. Twenty-two percent of Asians had earned a doctorate in engineering.

Highlights on the Status of Women in Higher Education

Demographic and Economic Data

- In 1981, 51 percent of the total U. S. population were women (118 million).
- The total college-age population (18–24 years old) in 1981 was 30.4 million; women comprised 49 percent of this population while men represented 51 percent.
- Median incomes in 1981 varied considerably on the basis of sex and level of education attained:

  males 25 years and over with a high school education, $16,989,
  males 25 years and over with five or more years of college, $27,339,
  females 25 years and over with a high school education, $6,495, and
  females 25 years and over with five or more years of college, $15,386.
- Women had an annual unemployment rate of 9.4 percent in 1982 while for men the rate was 9.9 percent.
- In 1980, women were 42 percent of the total U. S. labor force; this is an increase over 1970, when women made up 37 percent of the labor force.

Enrollment Data

- Women comprised 52 percent of 1982 college enrollees; in 1972, only 42 percent of college students were women.
- For the fall of 1982, 6.4 million women were enrolled in all institutions compared to approximately 6.0 million men. Women were less likely than men to attend full-time (54 percent of women vs. 62 percent of men) and were more likely to attend part-time (46 percent of women vs. 38 percent of men).
- The opening fall enrollment for four-year institutions in 1982 was 7.5 million, of which 3.8 million were men and 3.7 million were women.
- In the fall of 1982, 56 percent of the students enrolled in two-year institutions were women while men were 45 percent of the populaton. From 1972–1982, the number of women attending two-year institutions increased 117 percent.
- Equal proportions of men and women were enrolled in graduate school as of 1981.

Freshmen Characteristics

- Almost one-quarter of entering female freshmen in 1982 had a high school average of "A" or better in comparison to 17.5 percent of their male counterparts.
- Business was the most probable major field of study for women freshmen in 1982 (25.7 percent). This is up from the proportion who indicated this area in 1972 (13.7 percent). Other popular majors include: health professions (13.3 percent) and the social sciences (5.5 percent).

Faculty and Staff

- In the fall of 1981, there were 401,581 full-time faculty members. Almost three-quarters of the full-time faculty were males (73.2 percent) and 27 percent were females.
- Forty-five percent of women who were full-time faculty members in 1981 held tenure in comparison to 65 percent of their male counterparts.
- In 1982, there were 244 women college presidents; 152 were at four-year institutions and 92 held the position at two-year institutions.
- Between 1975–1982, the number of women college presidents increased approximately 65 percent.

Earned Degrees

All Levels

- Slightly larger proportions of men had earned degrees in academic year 1980–1981 than women (51.8 percent of men vs. 48.2 percent of women).
- The number of degrees earned by women during the 1970–71 to 1980–81 decade increased 37.6 percent; this was a considerable increase in comparison to male rates of degree attainment during this decade with an increase of 1.8 percent.

Bachelor's Degrees

- During academic year 1980–81, 935,140 students had earned their bachelor's degrees. Equal proportions of these degrees had been awarded to men and women (50 percent, respectively).
- From 1970–71 to 1980–81, the number of bachelor's degrees earned by women increased. In 1971,

367,687 had been awarded a bachelor's degree in comparison to 465,257 in 1981.

Master's Degrees

- In academic year 1980–81, a total of 295,739 master's degrees had been earned. Women were awarded 50.3 percent of the master's degrees in 1981 while men were awarded 49.7 percent of these degrees.
- The increase from 1970–71 to 1980–81 in the total number of master's degrees awarded was 27.8 percent. For women the increase was 60.1 percent while the increase for men during this decade was 6.1 percent.

First Professional Degrees

- In academic year 1980–81, there were 71,956 first professional degrees awarded by institutions of higher education. Almost three-quarters of the first professional degrees were earned by men (74 percent) and 27 percent were awarded to women.
- The number of first professional degrees awarded to women increased considerably during the 1971–1981 decade. In 1981, 19,614 first professional degrees had been awarded to women while in 1971 only 2,479 of these degrees were awarded to women.

Doctorates

- There were 32,958 doctorates earned in academic year 1980–81. Slightly more than 3 of 10 doctorates were earned by women (31.8 percent) and 68 percent were earned by men.

Field of Study

- In 1981, women had been awarded 25 percent of all the degrees in medicine (M.D.'s); in 1971, women were awarded only 9 percent of the medical degrees.
- During academic year 1980–81, 5,460 degrees were awarded in the field of dentistry; 86 percent of these degrees were earned by men and 14 percent by women.
- Between the years 1971 and 1981, the number of dentistry degrees earned by women increased from 46 in 1971 to 788 in 1981.
- In 1981, women were awarded 37 percent of the bachelor's degrees in business in comparison to 1971, when women were awarded 13 percent of these degrees.

Demographic and Economic Data Highlights

Population

- The total U. S. population in 1981 was approximately 230 million. Forty-nine percent of the population were men (112 million) and 51 percent (118 million) were women.
- Twelve percent (27 million) of the U. S. population in 1981 was black.
- Between 1970–1981 the U. S. population increased 12 percent.
- In 1980, the proportion of the U. S. resident population residing in each region was:

  Southeast region, 24 percent,
  Great Lake region, 19 percent,
  Mideast region, 19 percent,
  Far West region, 14 percent,
  Southwest region, 9 percent,
  Plains region, 7 percent,
  New England region, 5 percent, and
  Mountain region, 3 percent.

- The regions with the largest resident population growth in the 1970–80 decade were the Rocky Mountain region with a 31 percent increase followed by the Southwest with a 29 percent increase in resident population.
- In 1980, 65 percent of all households were comprised of married couples.
- Over half (66.3 percent) of the U. S. population over 25 years of age had a high school education. Approximately 16 percent of this same population had completed four or more years of college.
- The total college age population (18–24 years old) in 1981 was 30 million; this population is projected to decline by 1 million in 1985.

Income

- The median income for all families in 1981 was $22,388.
- There were sizable differences in 1981 median incomes for families according to race:

  white families, $23,517,
  Hispanic families, $16,401, and
  black families, $13,266.

- Median incomes also varied considerably on the basis of sex and level of education attained:

  males 25 years and over with a high school education, $16,989,
  males 25 years and over with five or more years of college, $27,339,
  females 25 years and over with a high school education, $6,495, and
  females 25 years and over with five or more years of college, $15,386.

- Slightly more than half of the families of college freshmen had incomes over $25,000 in 1981.

Institutional Finances

- The costs of instruction made up 32 percent of all institutional spending in academic year 1980–81.
- Grants and gifts made up only 4.8 percent of institutional revenues in 1980–81. This proportion has shown little change in recent years.
- In 1982–83, $24.2 billion of state tax funds were appropriated to institutions of higher education for operating expenses. In 1980–81, $20.9 billion was appropriated for this purpose.

Employment

- The total U. S. labor force in 1982 was approximately 112 million. This is up from 89 million in 1972 and 110 million in 1981.
- In 1982, 9.7 percent of the civilian labor force was unemployed.
- The 1982 unemployment rate for whites was 8.6 percent while for blacks and Hispanics the unemployment rate was 18.9 percent and 13.8 percent, respectively.
- The manufacturing industry employed the largest percentage of all employed persons in 1980 (22.3 percent). The professional and related services industry employed 20.3 percent of the working force.
- Public administration (e.g., judicial and legislative employees) employed the smallest percentage of all employed persons (5.4 percent).

1 U. S. Population, by Sex and Race, Selected Years, 1900–2050

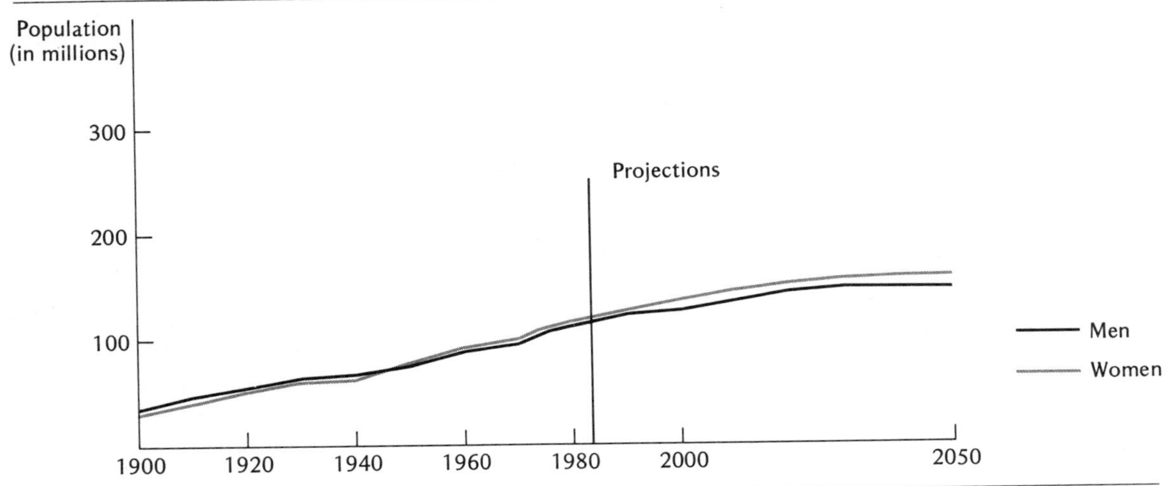

Year	U. S. Population[a] (in thousands)					Percentage of Total Population			
	Both Sexes	Men	Women	Negro[b]	65 & Over	Men	Women	Negro[b]	65 & Over
1900	76,094	38,867	37,227	9,194	3,099	51	49	12	4
1910	92,407	47,554	44,853	10,270	3,986	51	49	11	4
1920	106,461	54,291	52,170	10,951	4,929	51	49	10	5
1930	123,077	62,297	60,780	12,518	6,705	51	49	10	5
1940	132,122	66,352	65,770	13,494	9,031	50	50	10	7
1950	152,271	75,849	76,422	16,288	12,397	50	50	11	8
1960	180,671	89,320	91,352	20,648	16,675	49	51	11	9
1965	194,303	95,609	98,694	23,098	18,451	49	51	12	9
1970[c]	205,052	100,354	104,698	22,801	20,107	49	51	11	10
1975[c]	215,973	105,366	110,607	24,778	22,696	49	51	11	10
1976[c]	218,035	106,309	111,727	25,157	23,278	49	51	12	11
1977[c]	220,239	107,335	112,905	25,559	23,892	49	51	12	11
1978[c]	222,585	108,424	114,161	25,984	24,502	49	51	12	11
1979[c]	225,055	109,584	115,472	26,417	25,134	49	51	12	11
1980[c]	227,658	110,834	116,824	26,850	25,708	49	51	12	11
1981[c]	229,807	111,876	117,931	27,291	26,253	49	51	12	11
	Middle Series Projections[d]								
1982	231,997	112,924	119,073	27,737	26,833	49	51	12	12
1983	234,193	113,977	120,216	28,187	27,427	49	51	12	12
1984	236,413	115,045	121,368	28,645	28,035	49	51	12	12
1985	238,648	116,123	122,525	29,107	28,673	49	51	12	12
1990	249,731	121,497	128,234	31,452	31,799	49	51	13	13
1995	259,631	126,314	133,317	33,693	34,006	49	51	13	13
2000	267,990	130,379	137,611	35,795	35,036	49	51	13	13
2010	283,141	137,765	145,376	40,059	39,269	49	51	14	14
2020	296,339	144,061	152,278	44,167	51,386	49	51	15	17
2030	304,330	147,378	156,952	47,546	64,344	48	52	16	21
2040	307,952	148,504	159,448	50,223	66,642	48	52	16	22
2050	308,856	148,772	160,084	52,146	67,060	48	52	17	22

na: Not available in source.

a Except as footnoted otherwise, figures are estimates and projections of the total population as of July 1. The population of Alaska and Hawaii is excluded prior to 1950; armed forces overseas are excluded prior to 1940.

b Figures from 1900 through 1950 are for "nonwhite" population; figures for 1960 and 1965 are for "Negro" population; figures beginning 1970 are for "Black" population. In 1960 the "Negro" population represented 92 percent of the total nonwhite population.

c Figures from 1970 through 1981 reflect revisions based on the 1980 Census.

d Middle series projections are based on a fertility rate of 1.9 lifetime births per woman. Projections reflect the 1980 Census.

Sources: U. S. Bureau of the Census, *Current Population Reports,* Series P-25 (Washington: GPO), No. 311, July 1965; No. 519, April 1974, table 1; No. 917, July 1982, table 1; No. 922, October 1982, tables 1–3; and unpublished data.

2 Resident Population, by Region and State, Selected Years, 1965–1990

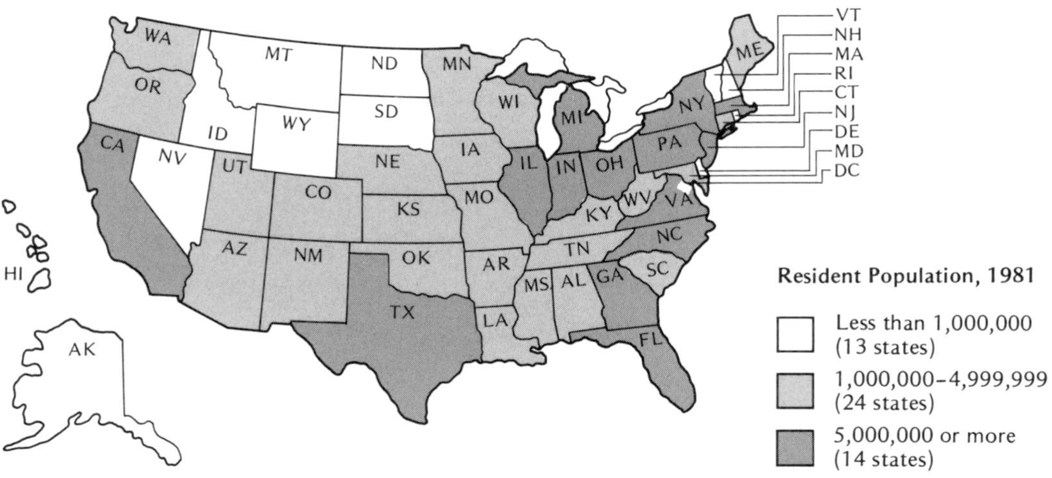

Region and State	Resident Population[a] (in thousands) 1965	1970	1980	1981[b]	1985[c]	1990[c]
50 States & D. C.	**193,460**	**203,302**	**226,505**	**229,348**	**232,371**	**243,004**
New England	**11,329**	**11,847**	**12,348**	**12,448**	**13,141**	**13,703**
Connecticut	2,857	3,032	3,108	3,136	3,345	3,489
Maine	997	994	1,125	1,131	1,143	1,192
Massachusetts	5,502	5,689	5,737	5,774	6,186	6,415
New Hampshire	676	738	921	937	939	1,007
Rhode Island	893	950	947	955	1,000	1,040
Vermont	404	445	511	515	528	560
Mideast	**41,025**	**42,442**	**42,237**	**42,383**	**44,401**	**45,569**
Delaware	507	548	595	597	648	684
D. C.	797	757	638	633	694	693
Maryland	3,600	3,924	4,216	4,259	4,721	5,048
New Jersey	6,767	7,171	7,364	7,421	7,964	8,344
New York	17,734	18,241	17,557	17,598	18,288	18,528
Pennsylvania	11,620	11,801	11,867	11,875	12,086	12,272
Southeast	**41,857**	**43,825**	**55,346**	**53,538**	**53,479**	**56,455**
Alabama	3,443	3,444	3,890	3,920	3,842	3,967
Arkansas	1,894	1,923	2,286	2,293	2,292	2,390
Florida	5,954	6,791	9,740	10,147	10,335	11,305
Georgia	4,332	4,588	5,464	5,565	5,638	6,006
Kentucky	3,140	3,221	3,661	3,665	3,647	3,796
Louisiana	3,496	3,645	4,204	4,295	4,090	4,245
Mississippi	2,246	2,217	2,521	2,536	2,471	2,545
North Carolina	4,863	5,084	5,874	5,952	6,026	6,332
South Carolina	2,494	2,591	3,119	3,170	3,164	3,346
Tennessee	3,798	3,926	4,591	4,624	4,552	4,755
Virginia	4,411	4,651	5,346	5,425	5,585	5,899
West Virginia	1,860	1,744	1,950	1,946	1,837	1,869
Great Lakes	**36,225**	**41,795**	**41,668**	**41,667**	**43,372**	**44,847**
Illinois	10,081	11,110	11,418	11,444	11,688	12,015
Indiana	4,662	5,195	5,490	5,485	5,621	5,804
Michigan	7,823	8,882	9,258	9,215	9,866	10,302
Ohio	9,706	10,657	10,797	10,793	11,251	11,570
Wisconsin	3,952	4,418	4,705	4,740	4,946	5,156

(*Continued on next page*)
For footnotes and sources, see next page.

3 Resident Population, by Region and State, Selected Years, 1965–1990—*Continued*

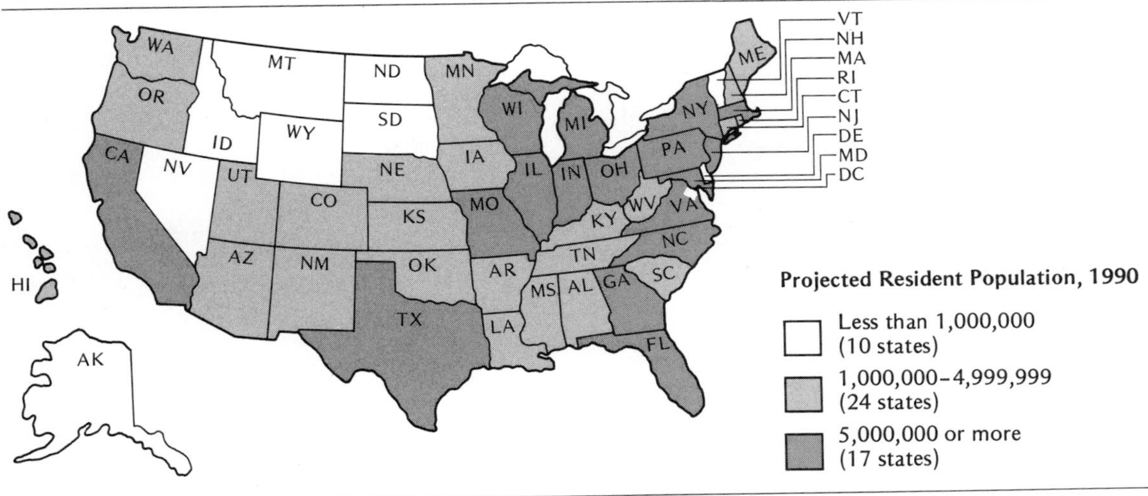

Region and State	1965	1970	1980	1981[b]	1985[c]	1990[c]
	Resident Population[a] (in thousands)					
Plains	**15,395**	**16,237**	**17,183**	**17,279**	**17,495**	**18,016**
Iowa	2,758	2,825	2,913	2,914	2,930	2,988
Kansas	2,179	2,249	2,363	2,385	2,370	2,429
Minnesota	3,414	3,806	4,077	4,113	4,209	4,382
Missouri	4,320	4,678	4,917	4,940	5,051	5,226
Nebraska	1,411	1,485	1,570	1,577	1,628	1,679
North Dakota	632	618	653	660	631	633
South Dakota	681	666	690	690	676	679
Southwest	**14,161**	**16,550**	**21,271**	**21,952**	**21,088**	**22,509**
Arizona	1,302	1,775	2,718	2,791	2,771	3,031
New Mexico	951	1,017	1,300	1,333	1,262	1,322
Oklahoma	2,328	2,559	3,025	3,104	2,976	3,116
Texas	9,580	11,199	14,228	14,724	14,079	15,040
Rocky Mountains	**4,317**	**5,008**	**6,552**	**6,735**	**6,532**	**6,958**
Colorado	1,754	2,210	2,889	2,976	3,007	3,237
Idaho	667	713	944	958	926	982
Montana	675	694	787	795	793	821
Utah	891	1,059	1,461	1,516	1,398	1,493
Wyoming	330	332	471	490	408	425
Far West	**21,483**	**27,038**	**32,596**	**33,336**	**32,866**	**34,948**
Alaska	226	303	400	416	419	441
California	15,717	19,971	23,669	24,212	24,081	25,588
Hawaii	633	770	965	979	1,000	1,062
Nevada	285	489	799	846	709	764
Oregon	1,769	2,092	2,633	2,663	2,610	2,781
Washington	2,853	3,413	4,130	4,220	4,047	4,312

a The U. S. totals shown here will not agree with total U. S. population shown elsewhere because the latter includes estimates for U. S. armed forces overseas. All data are estimates as of July 1. Details may not add to totals because of rounding.

b Provisional estimates.

c Census Series IIA projections, which assume a fertility rate of 2.1 births per woman and the continuation from 1975 to 2000 of interstate migration patterns observed for the period 1965–75.

Sources: U. S. Bureau of the Census, *Current Population Reports,* Series P-25 (Washington: GPO), No. 460, June 1971, table 1; No. 727, July 1978, table 3; No. 794, March 1979, table 1; No. 876, February 1980, table 1; Series P-20, No. 374, September 1982, table 2–3.

4 College-Age Population, by Sex and Race, Selected Years, 1950–2050

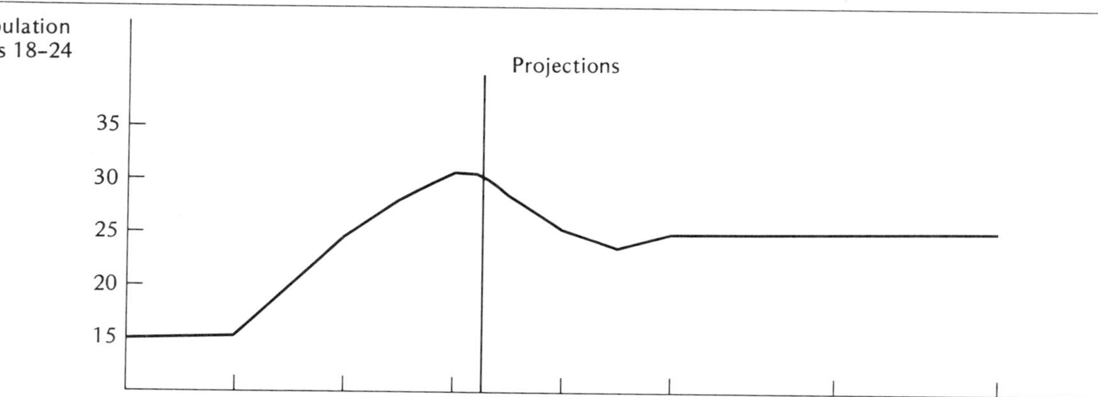

Year	All Races Total	All Races Men	All Races Women	Black & Other Races Total	Black & Other Races Men	Black & Other Races Women	Black Total	Black Men	Black Women
	Population, Ages 18–24[a] (in thousands)								
1950	16,075	8,009	8,067	1,889	898	992	b	b	b
1960	16,128	8,093	8,034	1,959	946	1,013	1,798	863	935
1970	24,712	12,451	12,261	3,180	1,551	1,630	2,829	1,374	1,455
1975	28,005	14,137	13,868	4,015	1,964	2,051	3,510	1,711	1,799
1976	28,645	14,465	14,180	4,162	2,039	2,122	3,622	1,768	1,854
1977	29,174	14,733	14,441	4,318	2,120	2,199	3,747	1,831	1,916
1978	29,662	14,961	14,661	4,459	2,191	2,268	3,858	1,886	1,972
1979	30,048	15,186	14,861	4,592	2,260	2,332	3,956	1,936	2,019
1980	30,337	15,343	14,994	4,745	2,341	2,404	4,038	1,981	2,057
1981	30,436	15,421	15,015	4,859	2,413	2,446	4,119	2,033	2,086
	Series II Projections[c]								
1982	30,344	15,395	14,950	4,929	2,457	2,472	4,177	2,072	2,105
1983	30,055	15,260	14,795	4,967	2,482	2,485	4,205	2,094	2,111
1984	29,476	14,973	14,503	4,941	2,471	2,470	4,176	2,084	2,092
1985	28,715	14,587	14,127	4,874	2,439	2,435	4,110	2,053	2,056
1990	25,777	13,115	12,663	4,622	2,313	2,309	3,809	1,908	1,901
1995	23,684	12,058	11,625	4,420	2,214	2,206	3,543	1,778	1,765
2000	24,590	12,523	12,067	4,761	2,386	2,375	3,803	1,909	1,894
2025	25,447	12,970	12,477	5,861	2,949	2,912	4,565	2,299	2,266
2050	25,659	13,079	12,580	6,426	3,237	3,189	4,811	2,424	2,387

a Total population, including armed forces overseas as of July 1.

b Source does not estimate population for "Negro" or "Black," only for "nonwhite."

c Series II projections use a fertility assumption of 1.9 lifetime births per woman. Projections reflect the results of the 1980 Census.

Sources: U. S. Bureau of the Census, *Current Population Reports,* Series P-25 (Washington: GPO), No. 311, p. 22; No. 519, table 1; No. 704, table 8; No. 800, table 1; No. 870, table 1; No. 917, table 1; No. 922, table 2.

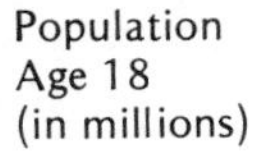

18-Year-Olds, by Sex and Race, Selected Years, 1950–2050

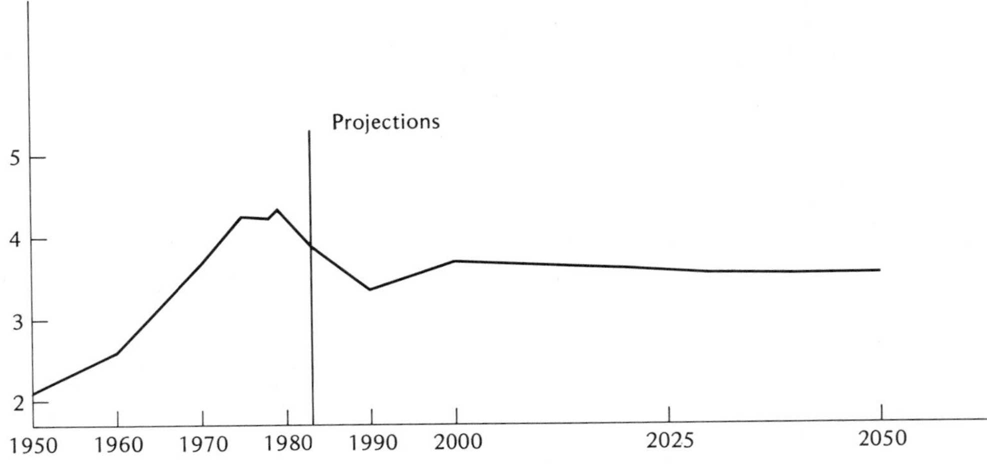

Population, Age 18[a] (in thousands)

	All Races			Black & Other Races			Black		
Year	**Total**	**Men**	**Women**	**Total**	**Men**	**Women**	**Total**	**Men**	**Women**
1950	2,164	1,090	1,074	271	133	138	b	b	b
1960	2,613	1,323	1,289	312	155	157	288	143	145
1970	3,781	1,914	1,868	512	254	259	463	229	234
1975	4,256	2,159	2,097	641	320	321	568	283	285
1976	4,266	2,164	2,101	646	323	323	570	284	286
1977	4,257	2,159	2,099	666	332	333	586	292	294
1978	4,247	2,157	2,090	670	335	335	588	292	295
1979	4,316	2,196	2,121	689	345	344	600	299	300
1980	4,256	2,165	2,090	697	350	347	601	300	300
1981	4,234	2,156	2,078	706	356	350	605	303	302
				Series II Projections[c]					
1982	4,185	2,134	2,052	706	357	350	603	303	300
1983	4,012	2,043	1,969	685	345	340	583	292	291
1984	3,772	1,922	1,849	653	329	324	553	277	275
1985	3,655	1,864	1,792	634	319	315	534	268	266
1990	3,429	1,751	1,678	628	317	311	514	259	256
1995	3,329	1,701	1,628	623	314	308	500	252	248
2000	3,758	1,921	1,837	745	377	368	618	312	306
2025	3,673	1,877	1,796	851	431	420	668	337	331
2050	3,647	1,864	1,783	916	464	452	688	347	340

a Total population, including armed forces overseas as of July 1.

b Source does not estimate population for "Negro" or "Black," only "Nonwhite."

c Series II projections use a fertility assumption of 1.9 lifetime births per woman. Projections reflect the results of the 1980 Census.

Sources: U. S. Bureau of the Census, *Current Population Reports,* Series P-25 (Washington: GPO), No. 311, p. 22; No. 519, table 1; No. 704, table 8; No. 721, table 1; No. 800, table 1; No. 870, table 1; No. 917, table 1; No. 922, table 2.

6 Population, Ages 18–24, by State, Selected Years, 1965–1990

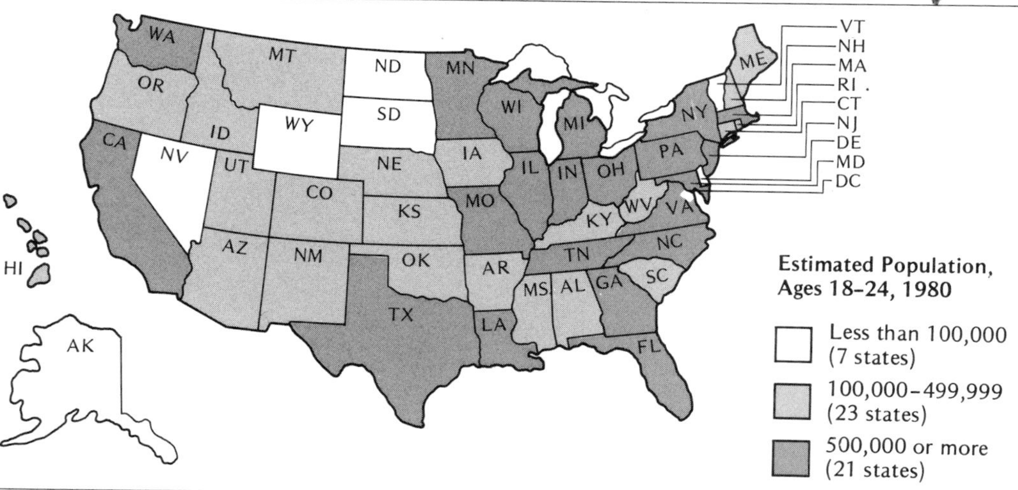

Region and State	Population, Ages 18–24[a] (in thousands)					
	1965	1970	1978[b]	1980[p]	1985[c]	1990[c]
50 States & D. C.	**19,758**	**23,698**	**28,699**	**29,227**	**27,608**	**24,904**
New England	**1,101**	**1,373**	**1,603**	**1,642**	**1,578**	**1,369**
Connecticut	265	326	394	406	391	334
Maine	104	111	136	139	135	120
Massachusetts	523	671	784	791	756	648
New Hampshire	70	85	112	117	112	102
Rhode Island	97	124	114	122	119	106
Vermont	42	55	62	67	65	59
Mideast	**3,880**	**4,596**	**5,227**	**5,242**	**5,136**	**4,480**
Delaware	51	63	83	83	81	72
D. C.	88	110	102	99	95	85
Maryland	381	459	569	584	591	526
New Jersey	619	728	862	886	902	798
New York	1,675	1,982	2,186	2,172	2,134	1,853
Pennsylvania	1,066	1,257	1,425	1,418	1,333	1,146
Southeast	**4,785**	**5,324**	**6,488**	**6,526**	**6,355**	**5,896**
Alabama	387	403	479	490	451	410
Arkansas	208	211	266	257	257	237
Florida	580	714	1,033	1,066	1,100	1,044
Georgia	529	588	686	702	700	663
Kentucky	346	392	454	462	437	400
Louisiana	384	444	550	557	522	474
Mississippi	259	262	313	313	304	285
North Carolina	598	677	768	746	740	690
South Carolina	328	352	413	407	405	382
Tennessee	428	470	556	551	531	487
Virginia	557	615	758	765	714	647
West Virginia	181	195	212	210	194	177
Great Lakes	**3,609**	**4,587**	**5,515**	**5,530**	**5,113**	**4,523**
Illinois	974	1,220	1,459	1,481	1,368	1,218
Indiana	483	607	712	715	665	592
Michigan	796	1,032	1,274	1,263	1,185	1,058
Ohio	978	1,215	1,429	1,419	1,301	1,151
Wisconsin	378	504	641	652	594	504

(Continued on next page)
For footnotes and sources, see next page.

7 Population, Ages 18–24, by State, Selected Years, 1965–1990—*Continued*

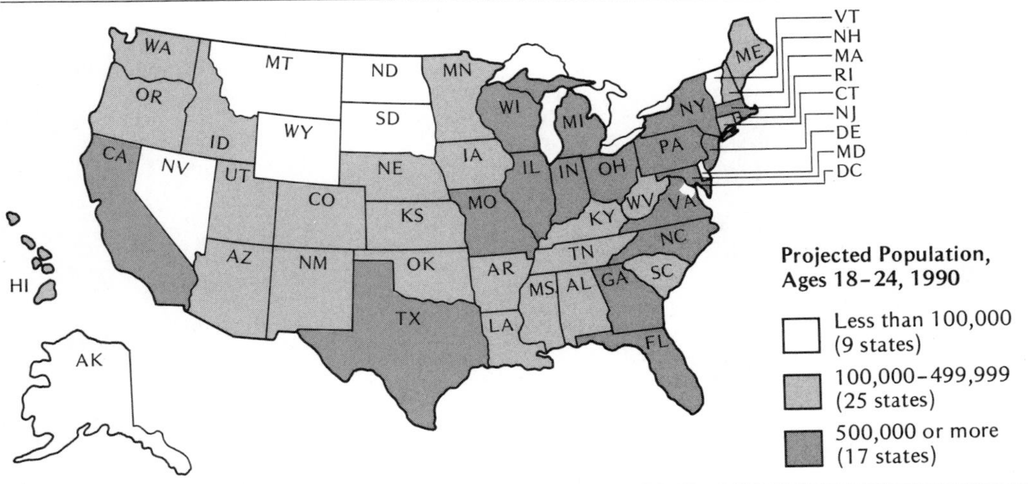

Region and State	1965	1970	1978[b]	1980[p]	1985[c]	1990[c]
	Population, Ages 18–24[a] (in thousands)					
Plains	**1,538**	**1,858**	**2,253**	**2,298**	**2,035**	**1,766**
Iowa	253	309	366	364	334	284
Kansas	235	274	312	328	274	241
Minnesota	332	433	560	568	505	429
Missouri	435	522	627	643	579	514
Nebraska	145	171	209	212	190	167
North Dakota	70	73	87	92	75	64
South Dakota	68	75	92	91	78	67
Southwest	**1,712**	**2,012**	**2,615**	**2,754**	**2,552**	**2,418**
Arizona	167	211	310	329	336	325
New Mexico	114	120	173	182	161	145
Oklahoma	265	301	362	376	339	316
Texas	1,166	1,380	1,770	1,867	1,716	1,632
Rocky Mountains	**492**	**629**	**861**	**913**	**826**	**776**
Colorado	210	292	390	420	388	359
Idaho	70	80	116	118	110	104
Montana	70	77	104	104	94	83
Utah	111	143	195	206	185	186
Wyoming	31	37	56	65	49	44
Far West	**2,635**	**3,316**	**4,139**	**4,326**	**4,013**	**3,676**
Alaska	40	46	68	63	67	63
California	1,933	2,447	3,026	3,140	2,929	2,673
Hawaii	98	109	144	146	137	129
Nevada	48	53	86	101	87	81
Oregon	196	238	309	324	296	274
Washington	320	424	506	552	497	456

a Data are resident population which excludes armed forces abroad. Figures for 1970 are as of April 1; for 1980, as of November; for other years, as of July 1.

b Estimates based on the relationships between Census Bureau estimates for 1978 population, ages 18–20, and estimates for 1976 population, ages 18–24. Results of these estimates were then adjusted to agree with national totals for 1978 population, ages 18–24, less an estimate for armed forces abroad.

c Estimates for ages 18–24 based on Census Series IIA projections for the age group 15–24. Series IIA assumes interstate migration will continue 1965–75 trends throughout the period 1975–2000. Census figures have been adjusted to represent ages 18–24 by applying to each state's 15–24 age group a percentage that the 18–24 age group represents of the 15–24 group for the year indicated. The percentage applied is the national figure for that year modified slightly for regional differences based on 1970 census data.

p Census Bureau projections.

Sources: U. S. Bureau of the Census, *Current Population Reports,* Series P-25 (Washington: GPO), No. 375, pp. 42–49; No. 626, table 2; No. 646, table 1; No. 704, table 8; No. 794, table 1; No. 796, table 6; No. 800, table 1; No. 879, table 1. U. S. Bureau of the Census, *1970 Census of Population PC(V2)* (Washington: GPO, 1971), Reports 1–52.

8 Households by Region and State, 1965, 1970, 1975, 1980

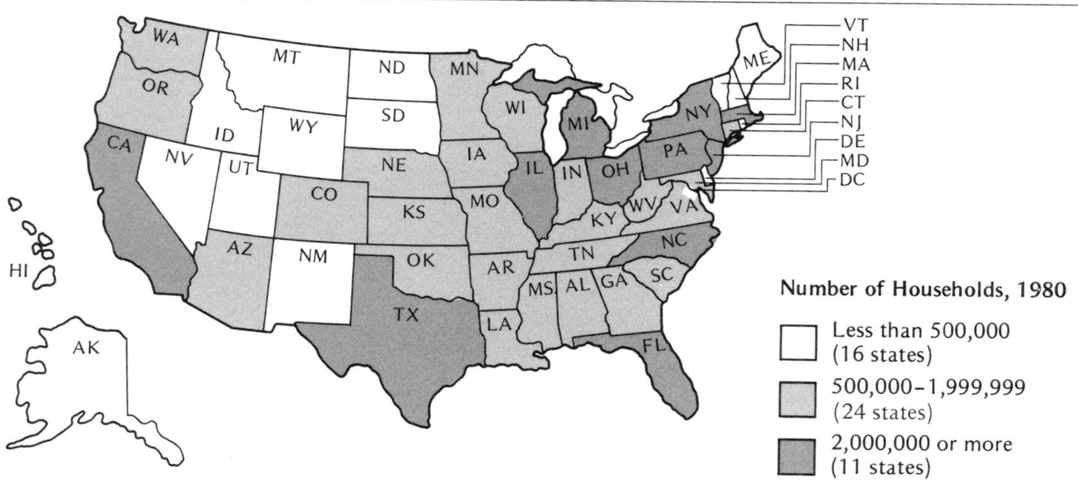

Households by Region and State

Region and State	All Households[a] (in thousands) 1965	1970	1975	1980[c]	Husband-Wife Households[b] as a Percentage of All Households 1965	1970	1975	1980[c]
50 States & D. C.	**57,300**	**63,450**	**71,535**	**80,434**	**73**	**69**	**66**	**65**
New England	**3,280**	**3,645**	**4,044**	**4,360**	**72**	**69**	**66**	**59**
Connecticut	829	933	1,029	1,094	74	71	68	59
Maine	284	303	347	397	73	71	68	63
Massachusetts	1,588	1,760	1,936	2,027	70	67	64	57
New Hampshire	198	225	267	324	73	72	69	63
Rhode Island	266	292	312	339	70	68	65	59
Vermont	115	132	153	179	73	70	68	61
Mideast	**12,404**	**13,440**	**14,474**	**15,022**	**71**	**67**	**64**	**58**
Delaware	141	165	188	207	75	72	68	61
D. C.	260	263	272	253	51	43	39	30
Maryland	971	1,175	1,335	1,466	76	71	67	59
New Jersey	1,983	2,218	2,416	2,551	75	71	68	61
New York	5,609	5,914	6,268	6,332	69	65	61	54
Pennsylvania	3,440	3,705	3,995	4,213	73	69	66	62
Southeast	**11,852**	**13,371**	**15,714**	**18,531**	**74**	**71**	**67**	**62**
Alabama	960	1,034	1,167	1,342	75	71	68	64
Arkansas	570	615	716	821	74	71	69	65
Florida	1,825	2,285	3,004	3,743	71	68	65	60
Georgia	1,200	1,369	1,580	1,872	74	70	67	61
Kentucky	897	984	1,107	1,264	75	72	69	66
Louisiana	977	1,052	1,189	1,421	72	69	65	61
Mississippi	605	637	721	831	73	69	66	62
North Carolina	1,334	1,510	1,756	2,047	76	73	69	63
South Carolina	661	734	872	1,031	74	71	67	64
Tennessee	1,098	1,213	1,382	1,615	76	72	69	64
Virginia	1,201	1,391	1,615	1,857	75	72	68	62
West Virginia	524	547	605	687	74	71	69	66
Great Lakes	**11,253**	**12,382**	**13,489**	**14,670**	**74**	**71**	**68**	**61**
Illinois	3,224	3,502	3,753	4,051	72	69	65	58
Indiana	1,456	1,609	1,759	1,936	76	73	70	64
Michigan	2,380	2,653	2,933	3,193	76	72	69	61
Ohio	3,000	3,289	3,550	3,837	75	72	68	63
Wisconsin	1,193	1,329	1,494	1,653	75	72	69	64

(*Continued on next page*)
For footnotes and sources, see next page.

9 Households, by Region and State, 1965, 1970, 1975, 1980—*Continued*

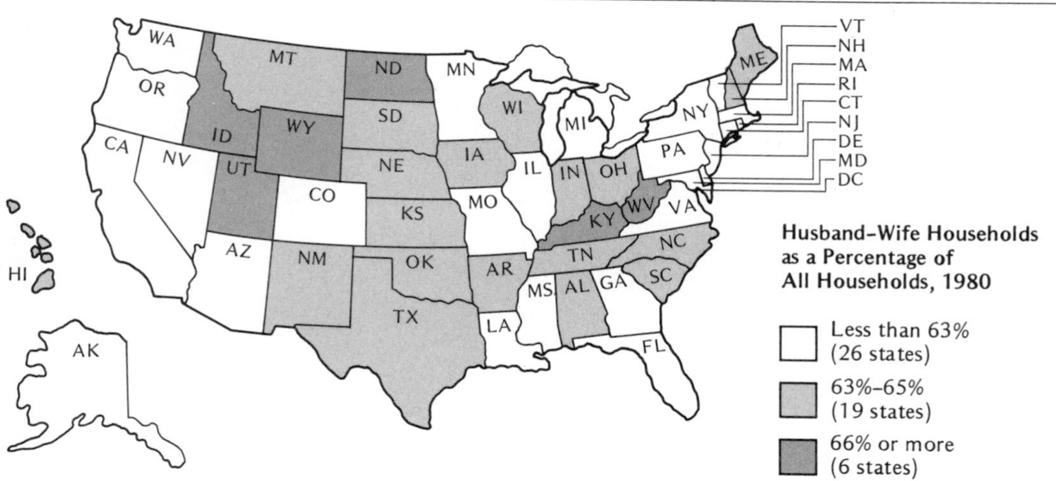

Households by Region and State

Region and State	All Households[a] (in thousands) 1965	1970	1975	1980[c]	Husband-Wife Households[b] as a Percentage of All Households 1965	1970	1975	1980[c]
Plains	**4,815**	**5,155**	**5,676**	**6,206**	**73**	**71**	**68**	**63**
Iowa	848	896	979	1,056	74	72	69	65
Kansas	698	727	798	870	74	72	68	63
Minnesota	1,035	1,154	1,292	1,442	73	71	68	62
Missouri	1,412	1,521	1,652	1,792	71	69	66	62
Nebraska	445	474	528	572	74	71	68	63
North Dakota	181	182	204	230	76	72	70	66
South Dakota	196	201	223	244	76	72	69	64
Southwest	**4,578**	**5,113**	**6,061**	**7,466**	**74**	**71**	**68**	**63**
Arizona	443	539	726	963	74	72	68	62
New Mexico	267	289	357	444	76	72	68	63
Oklahoma	784	851	962	1,114	72	70	67	64
Texas	3,084	3,434	4,016	4,945	74	72	68	63
Rocky Mountains	**1,379**	**1,530**	**1,864**	**2,282**	**74**	**72**	**68**	**63**
Colorado	588	691	863	1,059	72	70	66	59
Idaho	206	219	264	323	77	74	72	67
Montana	212	217	253	286	72	70	67	64
Utah	273	298	358	448	78	76	72	70
Wyoming	100	105	126	166	75	72	70	66
Far West	**7,737**	**8,814**	**10,213**	**11,897**	**69**	**66**	**62**	**57**
Alaska	64	79	104	132	73	76	71	62
California	5,807	6,574	7,584	8,634	68	65	61	56
Hawaii	170	203	252	293	72	73	68	64
Nevada	134	160	207	305	69	68	63	56
Oregon	622	692	814	993	73	70	67	56
Washington	940	1,106	1,252	1,540	71	69	65	60

a Data for 1965 and 1975 are estimates as of July 1; data for 1970 are census data as of April 1. Totals vary from figures on the next page because of the difference in dates.

b A "husband-wife" household is one which is maintained by a married couple.

c Provisional data.

Sources:

1 U. S. Bureau of the Census, *Statistical Abstract of the United States, 1967* (Washington: GPO), p. 39.

2 U. S. Bureau of the Census, *Current Population Reports,* Series P-25 (Washington: GPO), No. 710, October 1977, table 1; No. 807, July 1979, table 1.

3 U. S. Bureau of the Census, *1980 Census of Population and Housing, Provisional Estimates of Social, Economic and Housing Characteristics,* PHC 80-S1-1, March 1982, table P-1.

10 Households and Families, Selected Years, 1940–1990

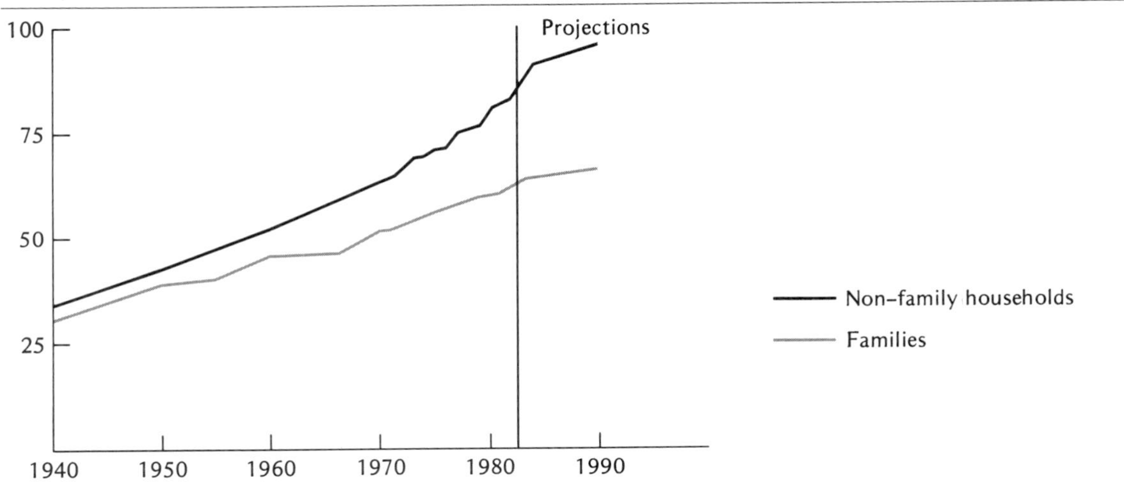

Number of Households and Families

Year	Households[a] (in thousands) Total	Average Population per Household: All Ages	Under 18 Years	18 Years and Over	Families[b] (in thousands) Total	Average Population per Family: All Ages	Under 18 Years	18 Years and Over
1940	34,949	3.67	1.14	2.53	32,166	3.76	1.24	2.52
1950	43,554	3.37	1.06	2.31	39,303	3.54	1.17	2.37
1955	47,874	3.33	1.14	2.19	41,951	3.59	1.30	2.29
1960	52,799	3.33	1.21	2.12	45,111	3.67	1.41	2.26
1965	57,436	3.29	1.21	2.09	47,956	3.70	1.44	2.26
1970	63,401	3.14	1.09	2.05	51,456	3.58	1.34	2.25
1971	64,778	3.11	1.07	2.04	52,227	3.57	1.32	2.25
1972	66,676	3.06	1.03	2.03	53,296	3.53	1.29	2.25
1973	68,251	3.01	1.00	2.02	54,373	3.48	1.25	2.23
1974	69,859	2.97	.96	2.00	55,053	3.44	1.21	2.23
1975	71,120	2.94	.93	2.01	55,712	3.42	1.18	2.23
1976	72,867	2.89	.89	2.00	56,245	3.39	1.15	2.23
1977	74,142	2.86	.87	1.99	56,710	3.37	1.13	2.24
1978	76,030	2.81	.83	1.98	57,215	3.33	1.10	2.23
1979	77,330	2.78	.81	1.97	57,804	3.31	1.08	2.23
1980	80,776	2.76	.79	1.97	59,550	3.29	1.05	2.23
1981	82,368	2.73	.76	1.96	60,309	3.27	1.03	2.23
1982	83,527	2.72	.75	1.97	61,019	3.25	1.01	2.24
Series II Projections[c]								
1985 B	88,565	2.58	.70	1.88	64,299	3.10	.96	2.15
A	89,705	2.55	.69	1.86	64,343	3.08	.96	2.13
C	88,514	2.58	.70	1.88	63,262	3.13	.97	2.16
1990 B	96,653	2.47	.67	1.80	68,619	3.01	.93	2.07
A	98,950	2.41	.65	1.76	68,816	2.97	.93	2.04
C	96,792	2.47	.67	1.80	67,325	3.04	.95	2.09

Note: Figures show estimates and projections of civilian population of the U.S. plus members of the armed forces in the U.S. living off-post or with their families on-post. All other members of the armed forces are excluded. Alaska and Hawaii are included beginning in 1960. Data for 1940 and 1955 are estimates as of April 1. Data for other years prior to 1980 are estimates as of March 1. Data after 1980 are projections as of July 1.

a A household consists of all the persons who occupy a housing unit.

b A family consists of two or more persons related by blood, marriage, or adoption and residing together.

c Three series of projections are shown for each year. Series B is based on 1964–1978 trends in marital status and householder proportions. Series A is based on Series B and is calculated to provide an adequate upper range of variation. Series C is based on 1974–1978 trends for 1980 and on 1966–1980 trends for the other years.

Sources:

1 U. S. Bureau of the Census, *Current Population Reports,* Series P-20 (Washington: GPO), No. 357, October 1980; No. 376, October 1982.

2 U. S. Bureau of the Census, *Current Population Reports,* Series P-25 (Washington: GPO), No. 805, May 1979, tables 1, 3.

11 Births and Birth Rates; Deaths and Death Rates; Selected Years, 1910–1982

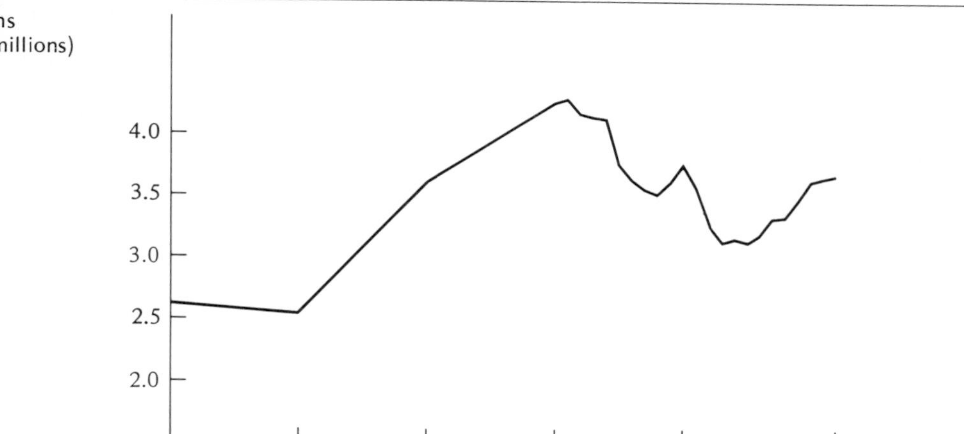

Year	Births[ab]	Deaths[ac]	Birth Rate[a]	Death Rate[a]
1910	2,777	697	30.1	14.7
1920	2,950	1,118	27.7	13.0
1930	2,618	1,327	21.3	11.3
1940	2,559	1,417	19.4	10.8
1950	3,632	1,452	24.1	9.6
1960	4,258	1,712	23.7	9.5
1961	4,268	1,702	23.3	9.3
1962	4,167	1,757	22.4	9.5
1963	4,098	1,814	21.7	9.6
1964	4,027	1,798	21.0	9.4
1965	3,760	1,828	19.4	9.4
1966	3,606	1,863	18.4	9.5
1967	3,521	1,851	17.8	9.4
1968	3,502	1,930	17.5	9.7
1969	3,600	1,922	17.8	9.5
1970	3,731	1,921	18.4	9.5
1971	3,556	1,921	17.2	9.3
1972	3,258	1,962	15.6	9.4
1973	3,137	1,975	14.9	9.4
1974	3,160	1,934	14.9	9.2
1975	3,144	1,893	14.8	8.9
1976	3,168	1,909	14.8	8.9
1977	3,327	1,900	15.0	8.7
1978	3,333	1,928	15.1	8.6
1979	3,494	1,914	15.6	8.5
1980[d]	3,612	1,986	15.8	8.7
1981[d]	3,646	1,987	15.9	8.7
1982[d]	3,655	1,965	15.9	8.6

a Number of births and number of deaths for all years exclude armed forces abroad. Alaska is reported beginning 1959; Hawaii, beginning 1960.

b Live births. Data through 1959 have been adjusted for underregistration.

c Excludes fetal deaths. Prior to 1933 not all states are represented.

d Provisional data.

Sources:

1 U. S. Bureau of the Census, *Historical Statistics of the United States, Colonial Times to 1957* (Washington: GPO, 1960), pp. 22, 23, 27.

2 U. S. Bureau of the Census, *Statistical Abstract of the United States* (Washington: GPO), *1963,* p. 52; *1973,* p. 51.

3 National Center for Health Statistics, *Monthly Vital Statistics Reports* (Washington: GPO), Vol. 25, No. 10, No. 11, No. 12; Vol. 27, No. 11 Supplement, No. 12; Vol. 28, No. 1 Supplement; Vol. 29, No. 12.

4 National Center for Health Statistics (Washington, 1983), unpublished data.

12 Educational Attainment of the Population 25 Years Old and Over, 1980

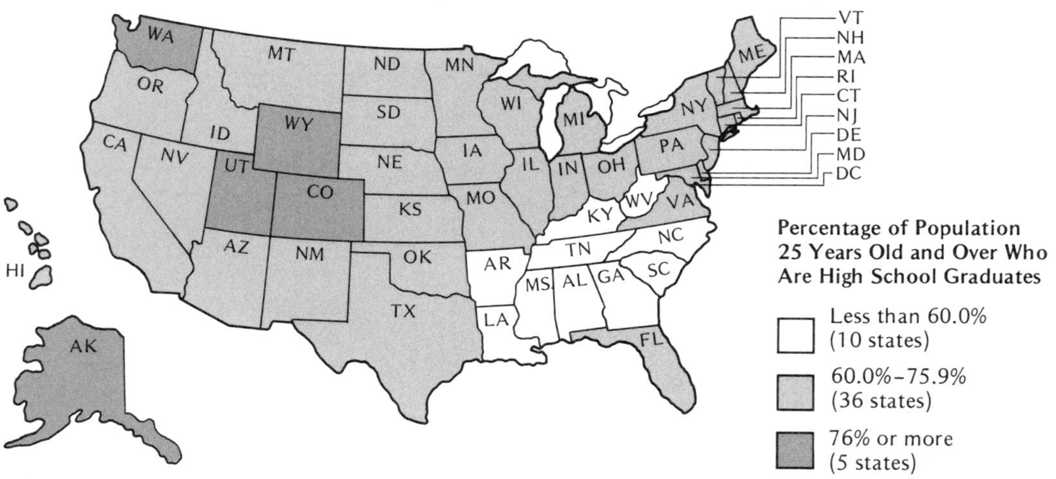

Region and State	Population 25 Years Old and Over	Highest Level of Education Completed (Percent)					Percentage High School Graduates
			High School		College		
		0–8 Yrs.	1–3 Yrs.	4 Yrs.	1–3 Yrs.	4 Yrs. or More	
Total U. S.	**132,775,652**	**18.3**	**15.3**	**34.4**	**15.7**	**16.3**	**66.3**
New England							
Connecticut	1,899,279	16.0	13.5	33.6	15.7	21.2	70.5
Maine	661,929	17.0	14.5	39.0	15.5	14.0	68.5
Massachusetts	3,463,235	13.6	13.7	37.1	15.6	20.0	72.7
New Hampshire	541,913	14.9	13.1	36.8	16.8	18.4	72.0
Rhode Island	574,890	20.5	18.8	32.8	12.6	15.3	60.7
Vermont	295,009	17.1	12.4	35.6	15.3	19.6	70.5
Mideast							
Delaware	344,358	15.2	16.9	37.3	14.3	16.3	67.8
D. C.	398,312	15.9	16.1	25.8	14.1	28.1	68.0
Maryland	2,497,823	17.4	15.9	32.2	14.7	19.8	66.7
New Jersey	4,501,658	17.6	14.6	36.0	13.2	18.6	67.0
New York	10,713,565	18.4	15.4	33.4	14.1	18.7	66.2
Pennsylvania	7,239,323	18.2	17.2	40.0	10.8	13.8	64.5
Southeast							
Alabama	2,216,888	24.4	18.8	31.6	12.5	12.7	56.7
Arkansas	1,336,869	27.4	17.7	34.2	11.0	9.7	54.9
Florida	6,245,990	17.5	15.3	35.2	17.3	14.7	67.2
Georgia	3,085,410	24.1	19.4	28.4	12.8	15.3	56.5
Kentucky	2,086,555	32.8	15.3	30.0	10.9	11.0	51.9
Louisiana	2,281,086	24.4	17.6	31.8	12.8	13.4	58.0
Mississippi	1,368,171	26.6	18.3	28.6	13.5	13.0	55.1
North Carolina	3,401,805	24.1	20.6	27.7	14.2	13.4	55.3
South Carolina	1,732,387	25.3	20.7	26.5	13.3	14.2	54.0
Tennessee	2,691,400	27.6	17.0	31.7	11.7	12.0	55.4
Virginia	3,131,138	21.5	16.0	28.7	14.7	19.1	62.5
West Virginia	1,147,016	27.5	15.9	36.0	10.1	10.5	56.6
Great Lakes							
Illinois	6,674,165	19.5	15.5	35.8	14.7	14.5	65.0
Indiana	3,134,984	16.8	17.3	41.6	11.9	12.4	65.9
Michigan	5,253,518	14.8	17.0	37.5	15.5	15.2	68.2
Ohio	6,289,826	15.0	17.6	39.6	13.0	14.8	67.4
Wisconsin	2,705,702	17.9	12.1	40.6	14.5	14.9	70.0

For source, see next page.

Educational Attainment of the Population 25 Years Old and Over, 1980—*Continued*

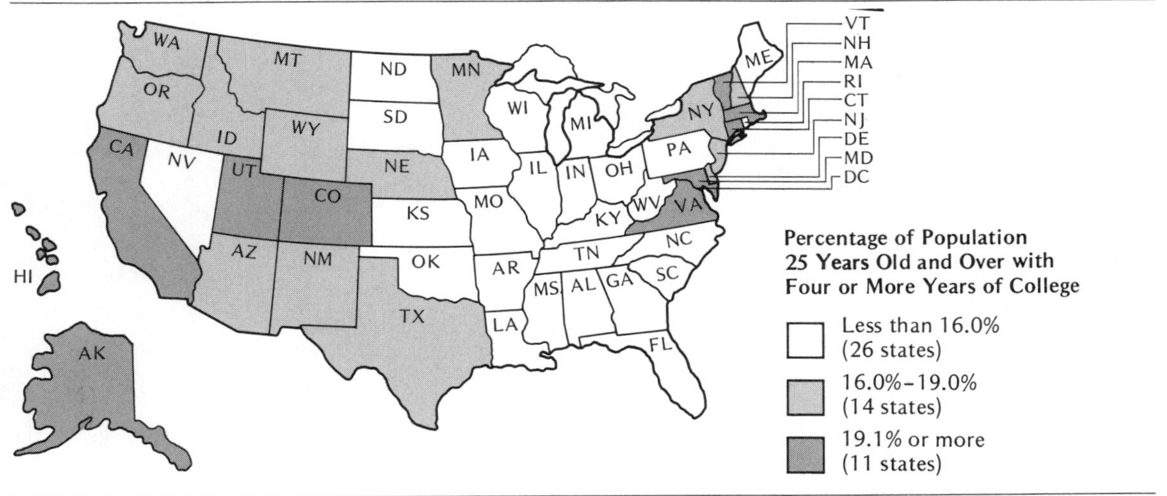

Region and State	Population 25 Years Old and Over	Highest Level of Education Completed (Percent)					Percentage High School Graduates
			High School		College		
		0–8 Yrs.	1–3 Yrs.	4 Yrs.	1–3 Yrs.	4 Yrs. or More	
Plains							
Iowa	1,699,965	17.0	11.8	42.5	14.6	14.1	71.2
Kansas	1,388,068	15.1	12.6	39.2	17.4	15.7	72.3
Minnesota	2,345,433	17.3	10.3	38.3	17.4	16.7	72.4
Missouri	2,918,069	22.0	14.2	36.2	13.6	14.0	63.7
Nebraska	911,944	14.5	11.7	40.4	17.3	16.1	73.8
North Dakota	364,536	24.7	8.9	31.4	19.9	15.1	66.5
South Dakota	389,907	21.9	9.6	36.3	18.0	14.2	68.5
Southwest							
Arizona	1,557,807	14.5	13.1	34.3	21.3	16.8	72.3
New Mexico	706,660	18.2	13.6	34.3	16.6	17.3	68.2
Oklahoma	1,768,185	17.9	15.3	34.6	16.5	15.7	66.7
Texas	7,938,271	21.6	17.0	28.7	16.7	16.0	61.4
Rocky Mountains							
Colorado	1,663,192	11.0	10.9	33.7	21.4	23.0	78.1
Idaho	514,236	13.5	13.7	35.7	21.0	16.1	72.8
Montana	450,771	13.5	11.1	38.3	19.8	17.3	75.4
Utah	704,541	7.2	12.5	35.8	24.2	20.3	80.3
Wyoming	255,044	9.9	12.3	40.1	20.5	17.2	77.8
Far West							
Alaska	211,391	8.7	8.5	38.1	22.4	22.4	82.8
California	14,029,451	14.2	12.2	31.0	22.8	19.8	73.6
Hawaii	546,825	16.5	10.1	34.6	18.5	20.3	73.4
Nevada	479,353	9.6	14.8	40.1	20.4	15.1	75.5
Oregon	1,579,498	11.8	13.4	37.5	20.1	17.2	74.7
Washington	2,438,501	10.8	12.2	37.7	20.5	18.8	77.0

Source: U. S. Bureau of the Census, *Provisional Estimates of Social, Economic, and Housing Characteristics, 1980.* Census of Population and Housing, U. S. Government Printing Office, Washington, D. C., 1982, pp. 14–19.

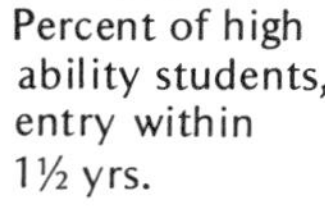

14 College Participation Rates of 1972 and 1980 High School Graduates by Socioeconomic Status, Level of Ability, and Time of Entry

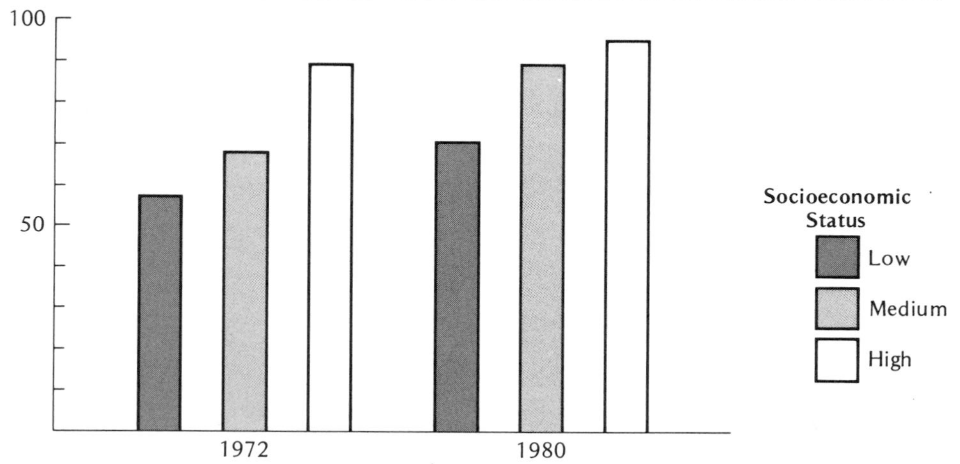

	Low Socioeconomic Status (percent)	Medium Socioeconomic Status (percent)	High Socioeconomic Status (percent)
Low Ability			
1972			
Immediate Entry	13.2	14.9	30.1
Entry within 1½ Years	15.5	17.3	34.3
1980			
Immediate Entry	13.6	16.5	31.1
Entry within 1½ Years	16.2	32.0	53.5
Medium Ability			
1972			
Immediate Entry	23.5	35.3	61.3
Entry within 1½ Years	25.3	39.3	67.3
1980			
Immediate Entry	31.2	13.5	67.7
Entry within 1½ Years	45.6	60.0	38.3
High Ability			
1972			
Immediate Entry	53.4	63.3	34.3
Entry within 1½ Years	66.7	67.5	39.5
1980			
Immediate Entry	55.6	75.7	30.3
Entry within 1½ Years	70.0	89.4	95.0

Source: Special tabulations by ACE's Division of Policy Analysis and Research from unpublished tables from the National Center for Education Statistics, Division of Multi-level Education Statistics, Longitudinal Studies Branch.

Notes: The socioeconomic status (SES) index is a composite of five equally weighted standardized components: father's education, mother's education, family income, father's occupation, and household items. The terms high, medium, and low refer to the upper, middle two, and lower quartiles of the weighted SES composite index classification.

In 1972, academic achievement was determined from test scores in four areas: vocabulary, reading, mathematics, and letter groups. The mean of the four standarized test scores served as a general academic achievement composite. In 1980, three of these four tests were employed—a letter-test was not given—to develop a similar composite. In some instances, the 1972 and 1980 tests were identical (e.g., the senior vocabulary and reading tests), in others only subsets of items were identical. The weighted distributions of 1972 and 1980 composite scores were used to group students into academic achievement quartiles. The "medium" category combines the middle two quartiles.

15 Median Incomes, by Sex, Race, and Educational Attainment, 1981

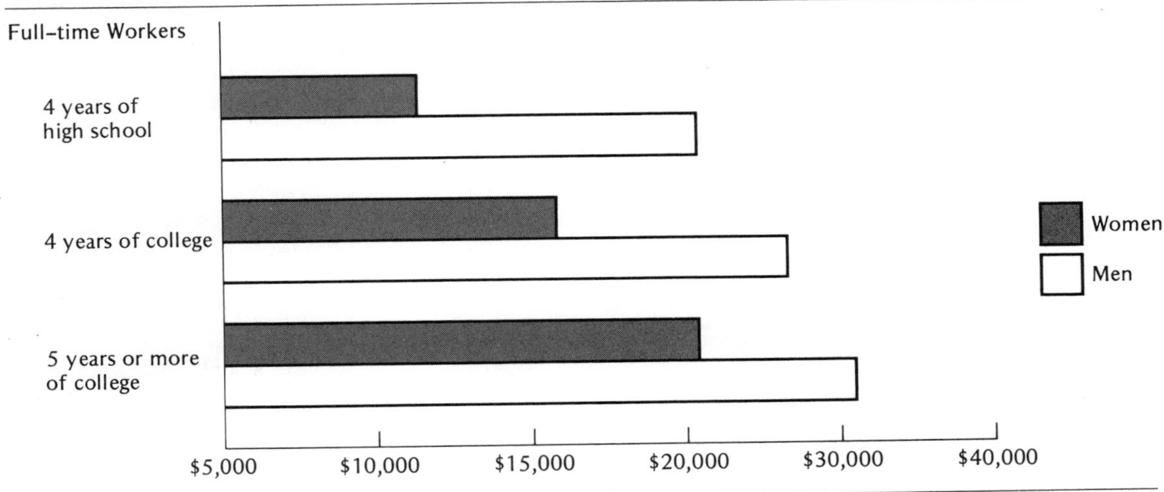

Race and Years of School Completed	Median 1981 Income of Men: All Men	Men: Year-round, Full-time Workers	Women: All Women	Women: Year-round, Full-time Workers
All Races, 25 years old and over				
5 or more years of college	27,339	30,434	15,386	20,148
4 years of college	23,640	26,394	10,497	16,322
1–3 years of college	19,504	22,565	8,257	14,343
4 years of high school	16,989	20,598	6,495	12,332
1–3 years of high school	11,936	16,938	4,655	10,043
8 or less years of elem. school	7,123	12,866	3,657	8,419
White, 25 years old and over				
5 or more years of college	27,655	30,801	15,315	20,189
4 years of college	24,257	26,864	10,291	16,463
1–3 years of college	20,116	23,129	8,018	14,613
4 years of high school	17,548	20,968	6,347	12,455
1–3 years of high school	12,561	17,795	4,684	10,271
8 or less years of elem. school	7,674	13,157	3,740	8,486
Black, 25 years old and over				
5 or more years of college	21,666	24,042	16,522	19,395
4 years of college	17,523	19,892	12,278	14,955
1–3 years of college	14,657	17,436	10,173	13,208
4 years of high school	12,349	16,014	7,332	11,527
1–3 years of high school	8,546	12,445	4,563	9,176
8 or less years of elem. school	5,375	11,464	3,441	7,880

Source: U. S. Bureau of the Census, *Current Population Reports,* Series P-60 (Washington: GPO), No. 137, March 1983, table 47.

16 Estimated Lifetime Income of Males and Females by Educational Attainment, Selected Years, 1956–1979

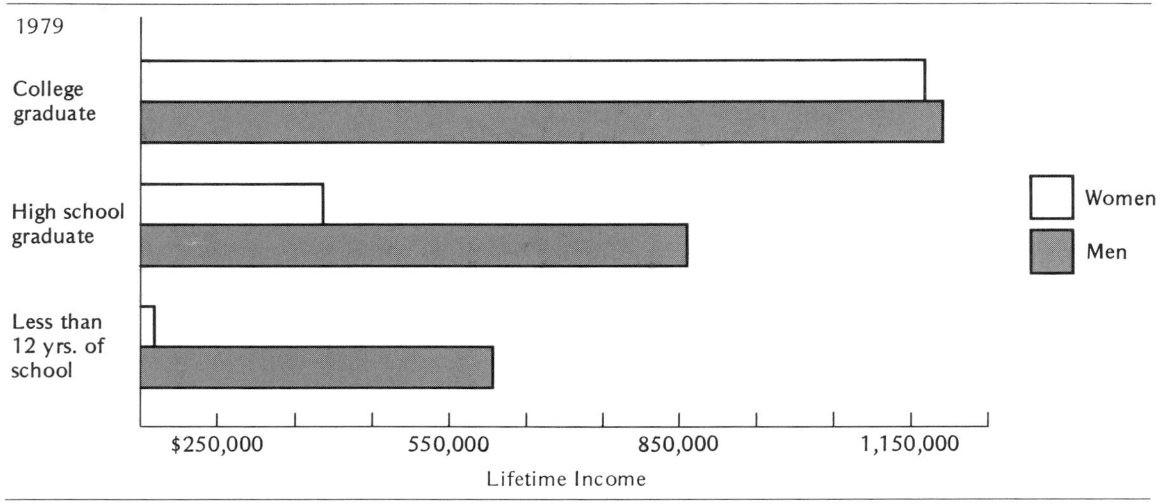

	Estimated Lifetime Income of			Difference between Lifetime Income of: Persons with Less than 12 Yrs. of School and High School Graduates		Difference between Lifetime Income of: High School Graduates and College Graduates	
Year	Persons with Less than 12 Yrs. of School	High School Graduates	College Graduates	Amount	As Percentage of Persons with Less than 12 Yrs. of School Income	Amount	As Percentage of High School Graduates Income
			Males from Age 18 to Age 64				
1956	159,174	215,775	325,276	56,601	36	109,501	51
1961	182,525	241,199	379,662	58,674	32	138,463	57
1966	221,759	303,284	473,292	81,525	37	170,008	56
1971	277,791	383,988	613,560	106,197	38	229,572	60
1972	305,071	420,828	655,474	115,757	38	234,646	56
1979*	601,000	861,000	1,190,000	260,000	43	329,000	38
			Males from Age 25 to Age 64				
1956	146,059	199,463	310,597	53,404	37	111,134	56
1961	168,967	224,626	360,951	55,659	33	136,325	61
1966	203,248	282,456	450,868	79,208	39	168,412	60
1971	259,182	360,277	589,558	101,095	39	229,281	64
1972	284,185	393,151	627,296	108,966	38	234,145	60
1979*	563,000	803,000	1,165,000	240,000	43	362,000	45
			Females from Age 18 to Age 64				
1979*	211,000	381,000	523,000	170,000	80	142,000	37
			Females from Age 25 to Age 64				
1979*	188,000	330,000	474,000	142,000	76	144,000	44

Source: U. S. Bureau of the Census, *Current Population Reports,* Series P-60 (Washington: GPO), No. 92, March 1974, p. 24; P-60, No. 139, February 1983, tables 1 and 2.

* The 1979 figures are based on an assumption of a 0 percent productivity rate and are in constant 1981 dollars.

17 Families, by Income Range and by Race, Selected Years, 1950–1981

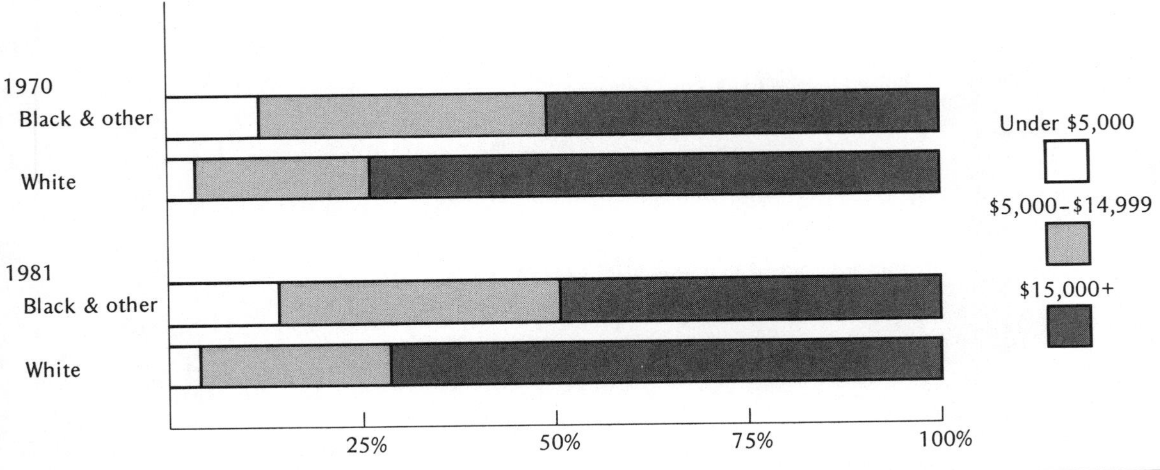

Year	Percentage of Families[a] with Income[b] of (in constant 1981 dollars): Under $5,000	$5,000–$9,999	$10,000–$14,999	$15,000–$19,999	$20,000–$24,999	$25,000 & Above	Median Income (in constant 1981 dollars)
All Families							
1950	15.9	20.7	63.5				12,539
1955	12.5	15.6	22.0	23.3	10.3	16.3	15,006
1960	10.0	14.3	16.5	23.1	11.5	24.5	17,259
1965	7.2	12.5	14.0	20.7	11.5	34.1	20,054
1970	5.2	10.3	12.1	17.6	10.7	44.2	23,111
1975	4.5	11.4	12.7	12.9	13.2	45.2	23,183
1980	5.6	11.1	12.7	12.7	12.7	45.2	23,204
1981	5.8	11.5	13.6	12.6	12.6	44.0	22,388
White Families							
1950	13.9	19.6	66.4				13,016
1955	10.6	14.5	21.9	24.4	10.9	17.7	15,668
1960	8.2	13.2	16.2	24.0	12.0	26.2	17,919
1965	6.2	11.1	13.3	21.2	11.9	36.3	20,901
1970	4.3	9.3	11.5	17.7	10.8	46.4	23,975
1975	3.6	10.2	12.3	12.7	13.6	47.6	24,110
1980	4.5	9.7	12.3	12.8	13.0	47.8	24,176
1981	4.5	10.3	13.1	12.6	13.0	46.5	23,517
Black Families and Families of Other Races							
1950	36.9	33.2	29.9				7,061
1955	30.3	26.3	23.5	13.2	3.8	2.9	8,641
1960	26.0	24.7	19.2	15.1	6.3	8.7	9,919
1965	17.2	25.2	20.7	16.0	7.4	17.1	11,510
1970	12.5	19.0	17.9	16.9	9.1	24.6	15,262
1975	11.2	20.7	15.9	14.2	10.8	27.2	15,751
1980	13.8	20.3	15.4	12.2	10.6	27.7	15,279
1981	14.8	20.0	16.2	12.3	9.8	26.8	14,598

a Data refer to families only: a group of two or more persons related by blood, marriage, or adoption, and residing together; all such persons are considered as members of the same family. Excluded are "unrelated individuals," i.e., persons 14 years old and over who are not living with relatives.

b Total money income before deductions for taxes, etc.

Source: U. S. Bureau of the Census, *Current Population Reports,* Series P-60 (Washington: GPO), No. 137, March 1983, table 15.

18 Median Income of Families and Individuals, by Race, Selected Years, 1950–1981 (in current dollars)

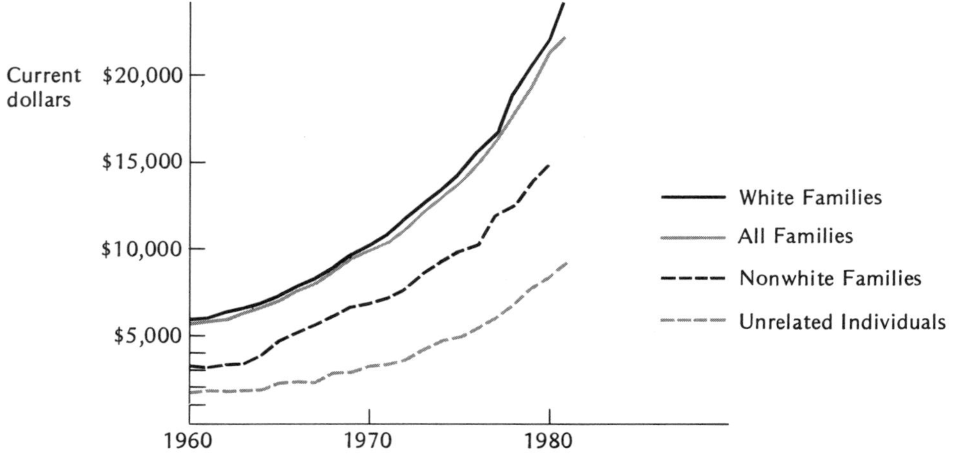

Year	Median Income[a] (in current dollars)			
	Families[b]			Unrelated Individuals[c]
	All	White	Nonwhite	
1950	3,319	3,445	1,869	1,045
1952	3,890	4,114	2,338	1,409
1954	4,167	4,338	2,416	1,222
1955	4,418	4,613	2,544	1,317
1956	4,780	5,002	2,632	1,426
1958	5,087	5,300	2,715	1,486
1960	5,620	5,835	3,230	1,720
1961	5,735	5,981	3,191	1,754
1962	5,956	6,237	3,328	1,753
1963	6,249	6,548	3,465	1,800
1964	6,569	6,858	3,838	1,983
1965	6,957	7,251	3,993	2,153
1966	7,532	7,825	4,691	2,290
1967	7,933	8,234	5,094	2,379
1968	8,632	8,937	5,590	2,786
1969	9,433	9,794	6,191	2,931
1970	9,867	10,236	6,516	3,137
1971	10,285	10,672	6,714	3,316
1972	11,116	11,549	7,106	3,521
1973	12,051	12,595	7,596	4,134
1974[d]	12,902	13,408	8,578	4,603
1975	13,719	14,268	9,321	4,882
1976	14,958	15,537	9,821	5,375
1977	16,009	16,740	10,142	5,907
1978	17,640	18,368	11,754	6,705
1979	19,587	20,439	12,404	7,537
1980	21,023	21,904	13,843	8,296
1981	22,388	23,517	14,598	9,138

a Total money income before deductions for taxes, etc.

b A group of two or more persons related by blood, marriage, or adoption and residing together; all such persons are considered as members of the same family.

c Persons 15 years old and over (other than inmates of institutions) who are not living with any relatives.

d Data for 1974 have been revised as a result of the adoption of new improved computing procedures by the Census Bureau in 1976.

Source: U. S. Bureau of the Census, *Current Population Reports,* Series P-60 (Washington: GPO), No. 101, January 1976, pp. 19, 20; No. 103, September 1976, pp. 15, 18; No. 118, March 1979, table 10; No. 123, June 1980, table 11; No. 125, tables 4, 6; No. 137, March 1983, table 14.

19 Median Income of Families, by Race, Selected Years, 1950–1981 (in 1981 dollars)

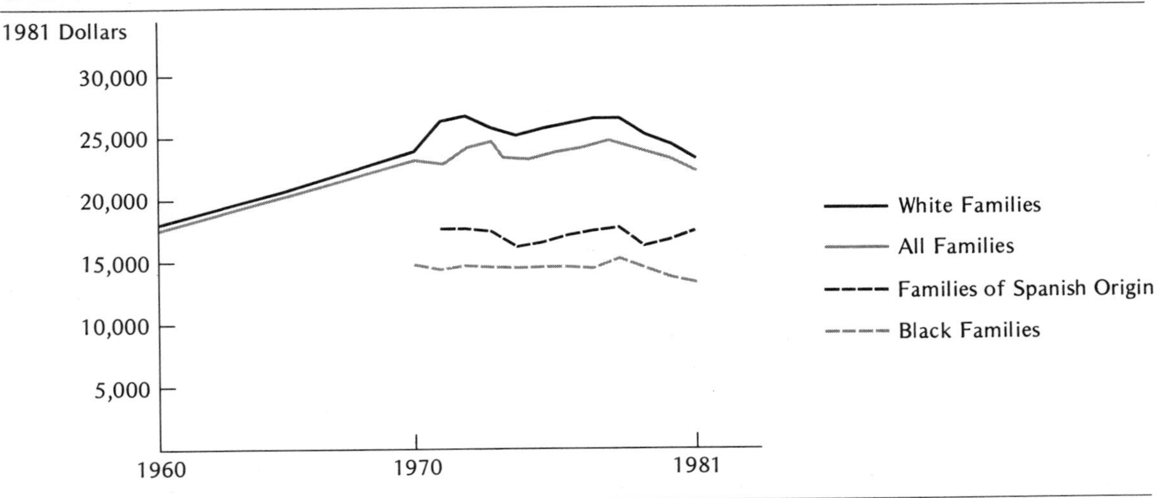

Year	Median Income[a] (in 1981 dollars)			
	Families[b]			
	All	White	Black	Spanish Origin
1950	12,539	13,016	na	na
1955	15,006	15,668	na	na
1960	17,259	17,919	na	na
1965	20,054	20,901	na	na
1970	23,111	23,975	14,707	na
1971	23,097	23,966	14,462	na
1972	24,166	25,107	14,922	17,790
1973	24,663	25,777	14,877	17,836
1974[c]	23,795	24,728	14,765	17,594
1975	23,183	24,110	14,835	16,140
1976	23,898	24,823	14,766	16,390
1977	24,027	25,124	14,352	17,141
1978	24,591	25,606	15,166	17,518
1979	24,542	25,610	14,502	17,754
1980	23,204	24,176	13,989	16,242
1981	22,388	23,517	13,266	16,401

a Total money income before deductions for taxes, etc.

b A group of two or more persons related by blood, marriage, or adoption and residing together; all such persons are considered as members of the same family.

c Data for 1974 have been revised as a result of the adoption of new improved computing procedures by the Census Bureau in 1976.

Source: U. S. Bureau of the Census, *Current Population Reports,* Series P-60 (Washington: GPO), No. 125, October 1980, table 4; No. 137, March 1983, table 15.

20 Median Family Income by Region and State, 1969 and 1979

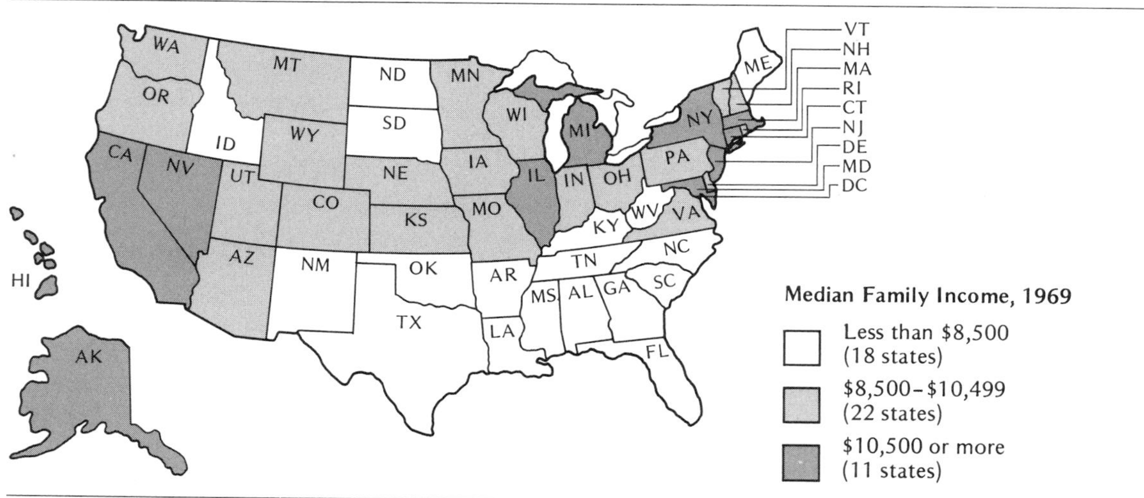

Region and State	Median Family Income 1969	1979
50 States & D. C.	**10,999**	**19,908**
New England	**10,617**	**na**
Connecticut	11,811	23,038
Maine	8,205	16,208
Massachusetts	10,835	21,329
New Hampshire	9,698	19,796
Rhode Island	9,736	19,441
Vermont	8,929	17,549
Mideast	*	*
Delaware	10,211	20,658
D. C.	9,583	18,839
Maryland	11,063	22,850
New Jersey	11,407	22,830
New York	10,617	20,385
Pennsylvania	9,558	20,259
Southeast	*	*
Alabama	7,266	16,602
Arkansas	6,273	14,356
Florida	8,267	17,558
Georgia	8,167	17,403
Kentucky	7,441	16,399
Louisiana	7,530	17,822
Mississippi	6,071	14,922
North Carolina	7,774	17,042
South Carolina	7,621	17,340
Tennessee	7,447	16,245
Virginia	9,049	20,423
West Virginia	7,415	17,621
Great Lakes	**10,563**	**na**
Illinois	10,959	22,007
Indiana	9,970	20,540
Michigan	11,032	21,886
Ohio	10,313	20,710
Wisconsin	10,068	21,113

(Continued on next page)

For footnotes and sources, see next page.

21 Median Family Income, by Region and State, 1969 and 1979—*Continued*

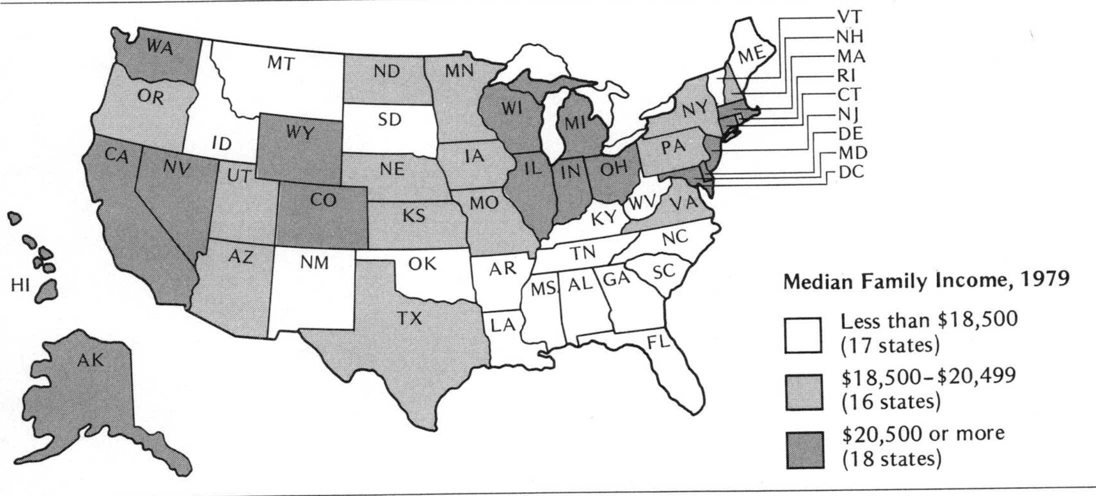

Region and State	Median Family Income 1969	1979
Plains	**8,985**	**na**
Iowa	9,018	20,243
Kansas	8,693	19,575
Minnesota	9,931	21,217
Missouri	8,914	18,746
Nebraska	8,564	19,110
North Dakota	7,838	18,239
South Dakota	7,494	16,431
Southwest	*	**na**
Arizona	9,187	19,150
New Mexico	7,849	17,151
Oklahoma	7,725	17,846
Texas	8,490	19,372
Rocky Mountains	*	**na**
Colorado	9,555	21,485
Idaho	8,381	17,278
Montana	8,512	18,839
Utah	9,320	20,035
Wyoming	8,943	22,497
Far West	**10,604**[a]	**na**
Alaska	12,443	28,266
California	10,732	21,479
Hawaii	11,554	23,066
Nevada	10,692	21,666
Oregon	9,489	19,837
Washington	10,407	21,635

* Census region for which data are available is not contiguous with the Office of Business Economics region that is shown here.

na Not available from source.

a Excludes Nevada.

Sources:

1. U. S. Bureau of the Census, *Census of Population, Characteristics of the Population, 1970,* Vol. 1 (Washington: GPO) 1973, table 178.

2. U. S. Bureau of the Census, *Population and Housing, Provisional Estimates of Social, Economic and Housing Characteristics, 1980,* (Washington: GPO) PHC 80-S1-1, March 1982, table P-4.

22 Income of Families with College-Age Members, by Enrollment Status and Race, 1979

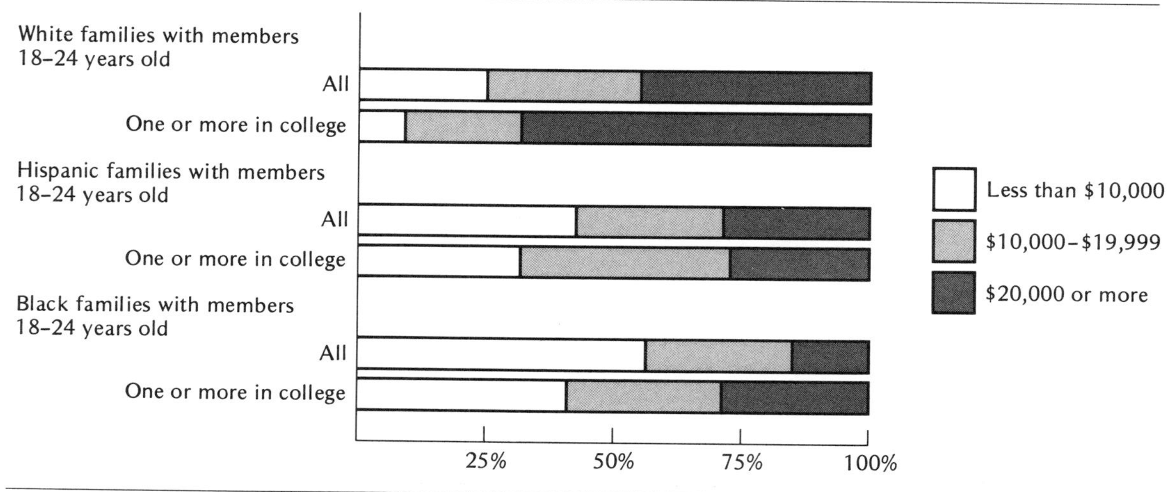

Race and Income Level	All	With No Members 18–24 Years Old Attending College Full-time	With One or More Members 18–24 Years Old Attending College Full-time
	Percentage of Families with Members 18–24 years Old[a]		
All Races			
All Income Levels	**100**	**100**	**100**
Less than $5,000	11	14	4
$5,000–$9,999	14	16	9
$10,000–$14,999	16	17	12
$15,000–$19,999	14	14	13
$20,000–$24,999	15	15	16
$25,000 and over	31	23	46
White			
All Income Levels	**100**	**100**	**100**
Less than $5,000	7	9	3
$5,000–$9,999	11	13	6
$10,000–$14,999	15	17	11
$15,000–$19,999	15	16	14
$20,000–$24,999	17	17	16
$25,000 and over	36	28	50
Black			
All Income Levels	**100**	**100**	**100**
Less than $5,000	30	34	16
$5,000–$9,999	27	27	25
$10,000–$14,999	18	19	18
$15,000–$19,999	10	9	13
$20,000–$24,999	8	7	14
$25,000 and over	7	5	14
Hispanic[b]			
All Income Levels	**100**	**100**	**100**
Less than $5,000	21	23	16
$5,000–$9,999	22	24	15
$10,000–$14,999	24	23	24
$15,000–$19,999	15	14	18
$20,000–$24,999	7	7	7
$25,000 and over	12	9	21

a Percentage of primary families as of October 1977 that reported income. Approximately 10 percent of the families in each of the three categories did not report their income level. Excluded are families whose only members 18 to 24 years old are the head, wife, or other members who are married, spouse present. Also excluded are families whose head is a member of the Armed Forces.

b Persons of Spanish origin may be of any race.

Source: U. S. Bureau of the Census, *Current Population Reports,* Series P-20 (Washington: GPO), No. 360, May 1982, table 12.

23 All Families and Families of First-time, Full-time Students, by Income Level, 1967, 1970, 1981

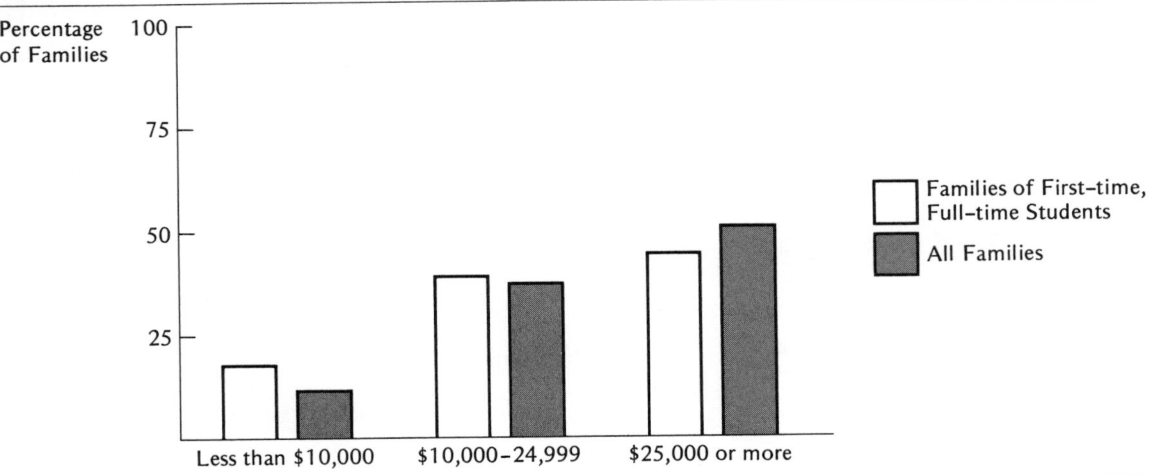

Annual Income Level[a]	All Families[b]	All Institutions	Two-Year Colleges	Four-Year Colleges	Universities
		Families of First-time, Full-time Students[c] (Percent)			
			1967		
Less than $4,000	18.9	4.7	5.9	4.9	3.0
$4,000–5,999	14.4	9.2	11.6	9.0	6.6
$6,000–7,999	17.3	13.3	16.1	12.8	11.0
$8,000–9,999	15.5	13.6	14.7	13.3	13.0
$10,000–14,999	22.6	21.4	19.8	21.5	23.1
$15,000–24,999	9.3	12.0	8.0	12.5	15.8
$25,000 and over	2.1	6.0	2.5	6.5	9.1
No idea	—	19.8	21.5	19.5	18.4
			1970		
Less than $4,000	13.9	5.9	9.2	5.0	2.6
$4,000–5,999	11.1	7.7	10.8	7.0	4.5
$6,000–7,999	12.3	10.7	13.3	10.4	7.5
$8,000–9,999	13.6	13.3	15.2	13.4	10.6
$10,000–14,999	26.8	31.0	29.5	32.1	31.6
$15,000–24,999	17.7	20.5	15.0	21.4	26.5
$25,000 and over	4.6	10.9	7.0	10.7	16.6
			1981		
Less than $4,000	d	3.3	4.5	3.2	1.7
$4,000–5,999	d	2.4	3.2	2.3	1.2
$6,000–7,999	d	2.7	3.3	2.8	1.5
$8,000–9,999	d	3.2	4.0	3.2	1.9
$10,000–14,999	13.6	11.8	14.0	11.8	8.1
$15,000–24,999	25.2	25.7	29.0	25.1	21.1
$25,000 and over	44.0	50.8	42.1	51.7	64.3

Note: Details may not add to totals because of rounding.

a Current dollars. Data for "all families" relate to total money income. **b** Census Bureau data.

c Data are from surveys in which each student queried was asked to estimate his family's income.

d Census no longer collects data using these income categories.

Sources:

1 U. S. Bureau of the Census, *Current Population Reports,* Series P-60 (Washington: GPO), No. 99, July 1975, table 2; No. 123, June 1980, table 1; No. 137, March 1983, table 14.

2 Robert J. Panos, Alexander W. Astin, and John A. Creager, *National Norms for Entering College Freshmen—Fall 1967* (Washington: American Council on Education (ACE), 1967, p. 33.

3 Office of Research, ACE, *National Norms for Entering College Freshmen—Fall 1970* (Washington: ACE), 1970, p. 38.

4 Alexander W. Astin, Margo R. King, and Gerald T. Richardson, *The American Freshman: National Norms for Fall 1978* (Los Angeles: Graduate School of Education, UCLA), 1978, p. 48; 1981 edition, p. 48.

24 Per Capita Personal Income, by Region and State, Selected Years, 1950–1981

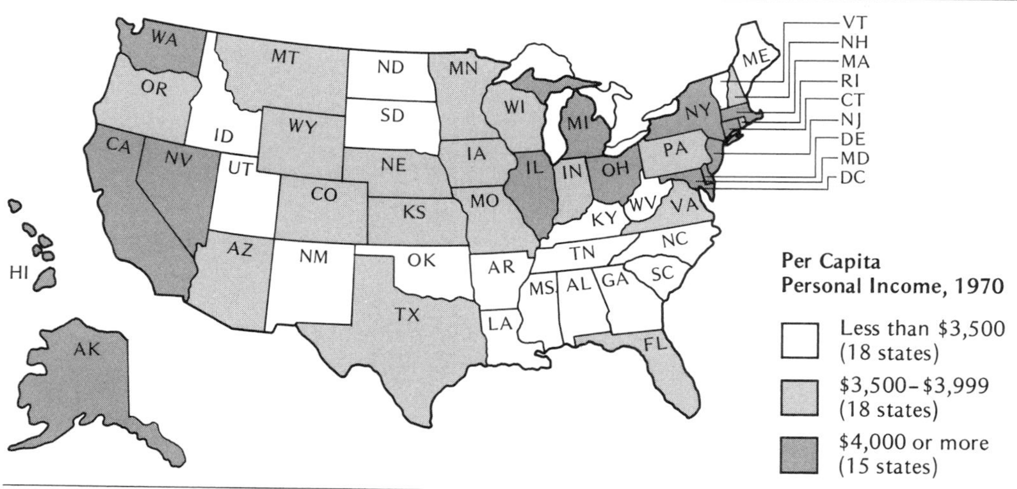

Region and State	1950	1960	1970	1979	1980	1981
	Per Capita Personal Income (in current dollars)					
U.S. Total	**1,496**	**2,222**	**3,966**	**7,320**	**8,004**	**8,813**
New England	**1,601**	**2,435**	**4,300**	**7,542**	**8,395**	**9,243**
Connecticut	1,875	2,838	4,917	8,687	9,695	10,709
Maine	1,185	1,862	3,302	6,055	6,673	7,360
Massachusetts	1,633	2,461	4,340	7,516	8,383	9,210
New Hampshire	1,323	2,135	3,737	7,014	7,769	8,579
Rhode Island	1,606	2,217	3,959	7,003	7,808	8,567
Vermont	1,121	1,847	3,468	6,102	6,638	7,403
Mideast	**1,756**	**2,573**	**4,471**	**7,678**	**8,525**	**9,388**
Delaware	2,131	2,785	4,524	7,361	8,169	8,914
D.C.	2,221	2,983	5,079	8,878	10,201	11,021
Maryland	1,602	2,341	4,309	7,633	8,568	9,355
New Jersey	1,834	2,727	4,701	8,303	9,242	10,202
New York	1,873	2,740	4,712	7,690	8,540	9,449
Pennsylvania	1,541	2,269	3,971	7,328	7,971	8,737
Southeast	**1,022**	**1,629**	**3,257**	**6,310**	**6,903**	**7,641**
Alabama	880	1,519	2,948	5,826	6,332	6,884
Arkansas	825	1,390	2,878	5,888	6,127	6,948
Florida	1,281	1,947	3,738	7,048	7,800	8,668
Georgia	1,034	1,651	3,354	6,214	6,779	7,493
Kentucky	981	1,586	3,112	6,102	6,463	7,143
Louisiana	1,120	1,668	3,090	6,378	7,229	8,114
Mississippi	755	1,222	2,626	5,276	5,707	6,324
North Carolina	1,037	1,590	3,252	6,081	6,604	7,323
South Carolina	893	1,397	2,990	5,668	6,178	6,796
Tennessee	994	1,576	3,119	6,120	6,578	7,250
Virginia	1,228	1,864	3,712	7,084	7,876	8,660
West Virginia	1,065	1,621	3,061	6,054	6,582	7,074
Great Lakes	**1,666**	**2,392**	**4,135**	**7,658**	**8,215**	**8,901**
Illinois	1,825	2,646	4,507	8,257	8,781	9,679
Indiana	1,512	2,178	3,772	7,133	7,539	8,158
Michigan	1,700	2,357	4,180	7,750	8,371	8,996
Ohio	1,620	2,345	4,020	7,376	8,011	8,642
Wisconsin	1,477	2,188	3,812	7,280	7,788	8,238

(Continued on next page)

For footnotes, see next page.

25 Per Capita Personal Income, by Region and State, Selected Years, 1950–1981—*Continued*

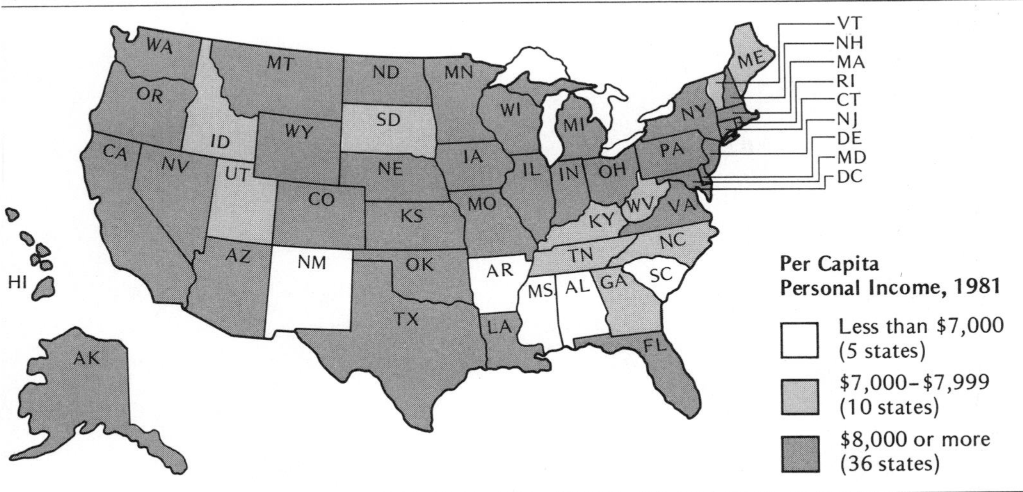

Region and State	1950	1960	1970	1979	1980	1981
	Per Capita Personal Income (in current dollars)					
Plains	**1,428**	**2,056**	**3,751**	**7,307**	**7,747**	**8,639**
Iowa	1,485	1,983	3,751	7,464	7,816	8,776
Kansas	1,443	2,160	3,853	7,919	8,377	9,083
Minnesota	1,410	2,075	3,859	7,388	8,078	8,905
Missouri	1,431	2,112	3,781	6,949	7,388	8,159
Nebraska	1,491	2,110	3,789	7,374	7,573	8,855
North Dakota	1,263	1,704	3,086	7,065	7,168	8,715
South Dakota	1,243	1,784	3,123	6,698	6,839	7,808
Southwest	**1,297**	**1,927**	**3,546**	**7,116**	**7,866**	**8,829**
Arizona	1,331	2,012	3,665	6,880	7,565	8,383
New Mexico	1,177	1,843	3,077	6,260	6,260	6,825
Oklahoma	1,143	1,876	3,387	6,964	7,711	8,635
Texas	1,349	1,936	3,606	7,272	8,051	9,090
Rocky Mountains	**1,457**	**2,099**	**3,590**	**6,970**	**7,669**	**8,499**
Colorado	1,487	2,252	3,855	7,558	8,370	9,395
Idaho	1,295	1,850	3,290	6,368	7,005	7,678
Montana	1,622	2,035	3,500	6,540	7,215	8,040
Utah	1,309	1,979	3,227	6,028	6,518	7,087
Wyoming	1,669	2,247	3,815	8,211	9,040	9,793
Far West	**1,801**	**2,618**	**4,374**	**8,170**	**8,978**	**9,834**
Alaska	2,385	2,809	4,644	9,136	10,393	11,307
California	1,852	2,706	4,493	8,305	9,157	10,056
Hawaii	1,387	2,368	4,623	7,791	8,658	9,328
Nevada	2,019	2,799	4,563	8,199	8,932	9,722
Oregon	1,620	2,220	3,719	7,198	7,738	8,259
Washington	1,674	2,360	4,053	8,007	8,756	9,574

Note: Prior to 1960, regional and U. S. totals exclude Alaska and Hawaii. 1979, 1980 and 1981 regional figures exclude Alaska and Hawaii.

Source: U. S. Department of Commerce, Bureau of Economic Analysis, *Survey of Current Business* (Washington: GPO), April 1969, p. 26; August 1976, p. 17; April 1983, p. 38.

26 State and Local Tax Capacity and Tax Effort, by State, 1979

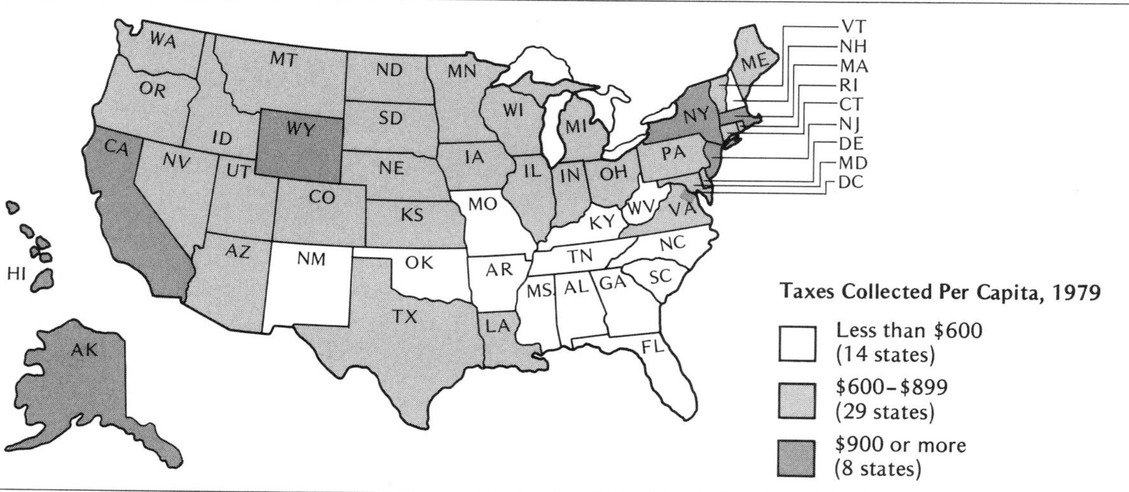

State	Tax Capacity[a] Per Capita	Tax Capacity[a] Index	Taxes Collected Per Capita	Tax Effort Index[b]
50 States & D. C.	**782**	**100**	**782**	**100**
New England				
Connecticut	879	112	877	100
Maine	645	82	648	101
Massachusetts	727	93	967	133
New Hampshire	799	102	583	73
Rhode Island	684	87	779	114
Vermont	714	91	753	106
Mideast				
Delaware	962	123	756	79
D.C.	919	118	1,099	120
Maryland	785	100	830	106
New Jersey	836	107	919	110
New York	744	95	1,208	162
Pennsylvania	766	98	719	94
Southeast				
Alabama	605	77	480	79
Arkansas	615	79	484	79
Florida	814	104	594	73
Georgia	666	85	595	89
Kentucky	681	87	554	81
Louisiana	815	104	617	76
Mississippi	542	69	520	96
North Carolina	651	83	573	88
South Carolina	605	77	528	87
Tennessee	645	83	538	83
Virginia	707	90	626	88
West Virginia	724	93	568	78
Great Lakes				
Illinois	877	112	845	96
Indiana	773	99	649	84
Michigan	816	104	869	106
Ohio	806	103	631	78
Wisconsin	750	96	862	115

(Continued on next page)

a The "tax capacity" of a state and its local governments is defined by the "representative tax system" as the amount of revenue the state and local governments **could raise** if all 50 systems applied to their respective tax bases tax rates equal to average tax rates of all fifty states. The index shows a state's "capacity" in relation to the national figure. For example, Mississippi's per capita capacity is only 70 percent of the national figure, whereas Nevada's is 151 percent of the national figure. For further explanation, see Source, next page.

b The "tax effort index" is a measure that compares the taxes collected with the "tax capacity." It is calculated by dividing the "taxes collected per capita" by the "tax capacity per capita."

27 State and Local Tax Capacity and Tax Effort, by State, 1979—*Continued*

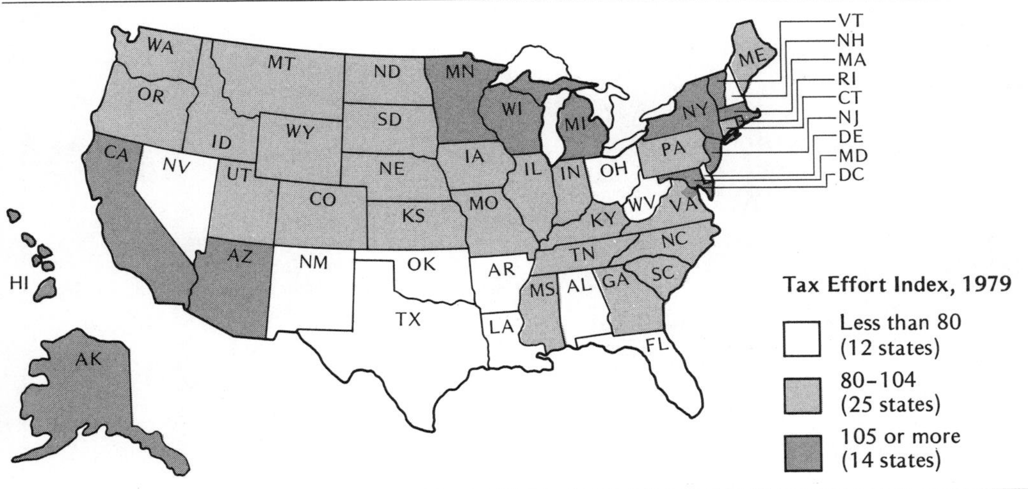

State	Tax Capacity[a]		Taxes Collected Per Capita	Tax Effort Index[b]
	Per Capita	Index		
Plains				
Iowa	807	103	738	91
Kansas	797	102	716	90
Minnesota	775	99	868	112
Missouri	734	94	597	81
Nebraska	770	98	761	99
North Dakota	735	94	662	90
South Dakota	678	87	605	89
Southwest				
Arizona	731	93	802	110
New Mexico	758	97	597	79
Oklahoma	804	103	576	72
Texas	884	113	604	68
Rocky Mountains				
Colorado	841	108	807	96
Idaho	688	88	623	91
Montana	792	101	753	95
Utah	698	89	643	92
Wyoming	1,210	155	979	81
Far West				
Alaska	1,129	144	1,201	106
California	869	111	1,401	120
Hawaii	839	107	963	115
Nevada	1,199	153	752	63
Oregon	795	102	759	95
Washington	776	99	758	98

For footnotes, see preceding page.

Source: Marilyn McCoy and D. Kent Halstead, Higher Education Financing in the Fifty States, Interstate Comparisons Fiscal Year 1979 (Colorado: NCHEMS), 1982, p. 15.

28 State Appropriations for Higher Education Operating Expenses, by Region and State, 1978–83

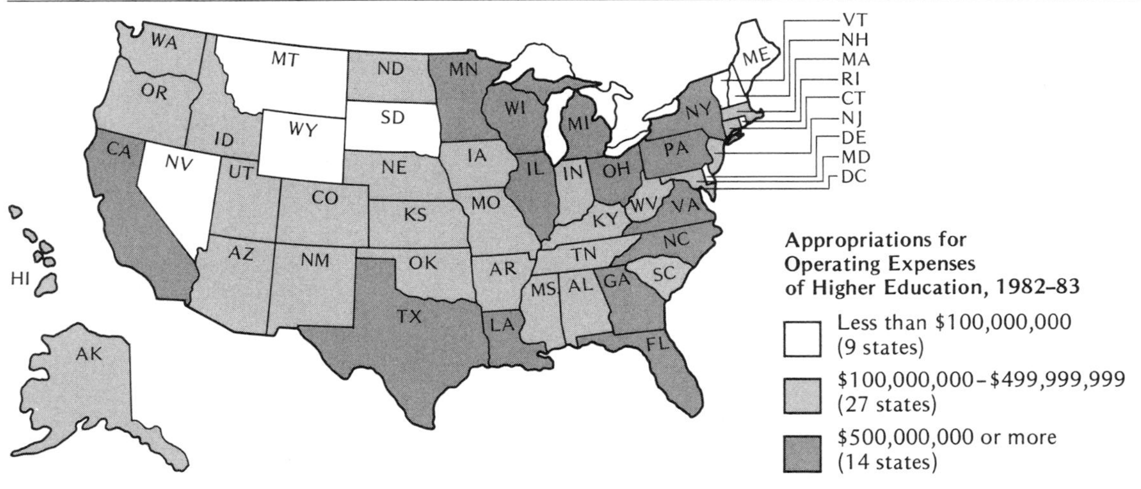

Region and State	Appropriations of State Tax Funds for Operating Expenses of Higher Education[a] (in thousands of dollars) 1977–78	1980–81	1982–83	Percent Change, 1980–81—1982–83 (for two years)
50 States	**15,350,496**	**20,931,931**	**24,249,393**	**16**
New England	**598,655**	**777,182**	**900,928**	**16**
Connecticut	190,757	209,802	252,608	20
Maine	45,911	62,628	71,915	15
Massachusetts	251,742	322,498	412,413	28
New Hampshire	27,519	32,919	35,246	7
Rhode Island	59,743	78,321	91,055	16
Vermont	22,983	30,459	37,691	24
Mideast	**2,623,699**	**3,252,146**	**3,888,584**	**20**
Delaware	44,190	63,811	76,900	21
Maryland	271,938	367,701	432,653	18
New Jersey	340,645	434,222	498,065	15
New York	1,298,754	1,644,361	2,010,001	22
Pennsylvania	668,172	780,166	870,965	12
Southeast	**3,321,286**	**4,742,469**	**5,558,100**	**17**
Alabama	310,974	427,499	407,082	6
Arkansas	126,155	187,567	198,090	6
Florida	489,609	718,509	905,796	26
Georgia	302,907	431,963	534,219	24
Kentucky	227,090	307,572	363,613	18
Louisiana	242,469	398,325	501,802	26
Mississippi	186,579	261,282	296,351	13
North Carolina	460,932	660,645	793,433	20
South Carolina	227,148	344,492	373,847	9
Tennessee	244,646	338,165	374,255	11
Virginia	366,586	509,731	616,475	21
West Virginia	136,191	169,819	193,137	14
Great Lakes	**2,703,584**	**3,471,591**	**3,775,993**	**9**
Illinois	740,190	989,934	1,029,282	4
Indiana	352,406	459,639	485,285	6
Michigan	660,404	757,770	865,000	14
Ohio	551,174	719,901	846,331	18
Wisconsin	399,410	511,067	550,095	8

(Continued on next page)

For footnotes and sources, see next page.

29 State Appropriations for Higher Education Operating Expenses, by Region and State, 1978–82—*Continued*

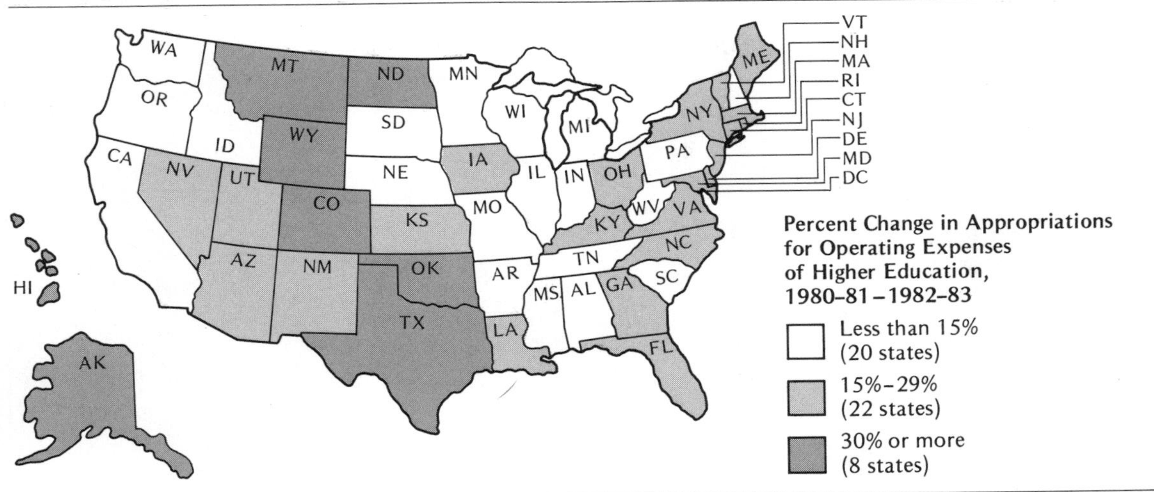

Region and State	Appropriations of State Tax Funds for Operating Expenses of Higher Education[a] (in thousands of dollars) 1977–78	1980–81	1982–83	Percent Change, 1980–81—1982–83 (for two years)
Plains	**1,308,307**	**1,716,318**	**1,923,797**	**12**
Iowa	245,552	318,883	381,112	20
Kansas	188,869	259,859	312,023	20
Minnesota	380,995	477,954	520,920	9
Missouri	259,359	353,252	358,090	1
Nebraska	131,199	166,155	189,610	14
North Dakota	61,240	75,660	108,539	43
South Dakota	41,093	53,739	53,503	0
Southwest	**1,527,378**	**2,159,823**	**2,942,029**	**55**
Arizona	207,961	280,446	322,525	15
New Mexico	95,756	143,316	184,084	28
Oklahoma	173,261	271,180	399,886	47
Texas	1,050,400	1,464,881	2,035,534	39
Rocky Mountains	**508,466**	**655,993**	**842,887**	**43**
Colorado	220,907	263,984	350,020	33
Idaho	75,279	94,146	104,019	10
Montana	52,251	67,348	95,273	42
Utah	117,146	160,856	196,376	22
Wyoming	42,883	70,504	97,199	38
Far West	**2,759,121**	**4,156,409**	**4,417,075**	**17**
Alaska	64,013	81,884	146,826	79
California	1,961,525	3,158,885	3,274,865	4
Hawaii	109,642	135,373	185,114	37
Nevada	45,457	62,107	71,929	16
Oregon	198,234	250,443	240,519	−4
Washington	380,250	467,717	497,822	6

a Includes appropriations for annual operating expenses for higher education, including funds appropriated to other agencies for ultimate allocation to institutions (for example, faculty fringe benefits), pre-allocated state taxes dedicated to any institutions of higher education, separate appropriations to medical centers and agricultural experiment stations, state scholarship programs, and statewide governing or coordinating boards of higher education. Excluded are sums that clearly originate from sources other than state taxes (for example, tuition and fees paid to the state and then appropriated to the institution); also excluded are appropriations for capital outlay. Variations in state practices make absolute comparability impossible; furthermore, the data are in preliminary form and subject to verification and change. For further details, see source.

Source: M. M. Chambers, *Appropriations of State Tax Funds for Operating Expenses of Higher Education* (Washington: National Association of State Universities and Land-Grant Colleges), *1979–80,* p. 6; *1982–83,* p. 6.

30 U. S. Gross National Product, 1946–1982

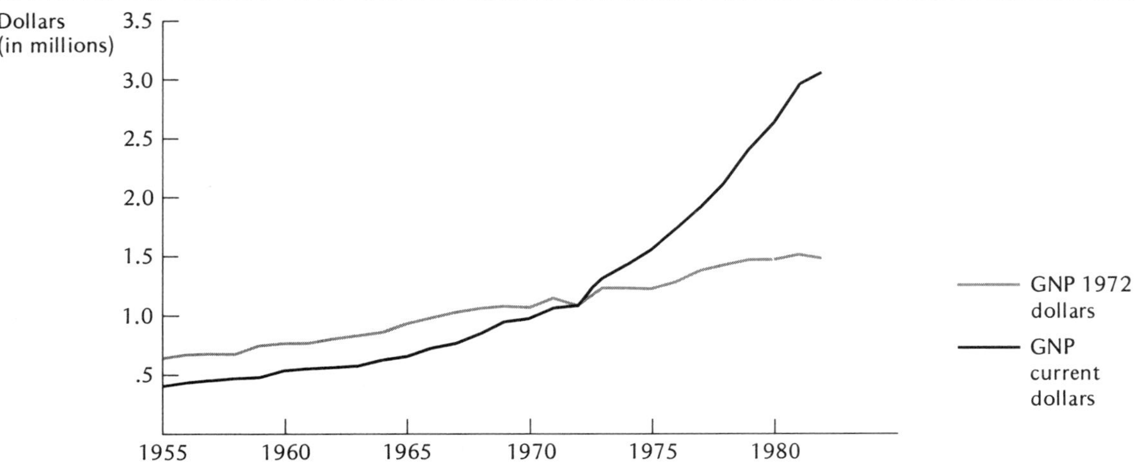

Year	GNP[a] (in billions of dollars) Current Dollars	1972 Dollars	Year	GNP[a] (in billions of dollars) Current Dollars	1972 Dollars
1946	209.8	478.3	1965	691.1	929.3
1947	233.1	470.3	1966	756.0	984.8
1948	259.5	489.8	1967	799.6	1,011.4
1949	258.3	492.2	1968	873.4	1,058.1
1950	286.5	534.8	1969	944.0	1,087.6
1951	330.8	579.4	1970	992.7	1,085.6
1952	348.0	600.8	1971	1,077.6	1,122.4
1953	366.8	623.6	1972	1,185.9	1,185.9
1954	366.8	616.1	1973	1,326.4	1,254.3
1955	400.0	657.5	1974	1,434.2	1,246.3
1956	421.7	671.6	1975	1,549.2	1,231.6
1957	444.0	683.8	1976	1,718.0	1,298.2
1958	449.7	680.9	1977	1,918.3	1,369.7
1959	487.9	721.7	1978	2,163.9	1,438.6
1960	506.5	737.1	1979	2,417.8	1,479.4
1961	524.6	756.6	1980	2,633.1	1,474.0
1962	565.0	800.3	1981	2,937.7	1,502.6
1963	596.7	832.5	1982	3,057.5	1,475.5
1964	637.7	876.4			

a "Gross National Product . . . represents the total national output of goods and services at current market prices. It measures this output in terms of the expenditures by which these goods are acquired. These expenditures are the sum of four major items: (1) personal consumption expenditures, (2) gross private domestic investment, (3) net exports of goods and services, and (4) government purchases of goods and services." *Economic Indicators, 1960 Supplement,* p. 4, prepared by the Joint Economic Committee Staff and the Office of Statistical Standards, Bureau of the Budget. These figures reflect the major 1980 benchmark revisions in the national income accounts. See Source 1.

b First quarter data at seasonally adjusted annual rate.

Sources:

1 Bureau of Economic Analysis, U. S. Department of Commerce, *Survey of Current Business,* Vol. 60, No. 12 (Washington: GPO), December 1980, p. 17.

2 Joint Economic Committee of the U. S. Congress, *Economic Indicators, April 1981* (Washington: GPO), pp. 1–2; *January 1983,* pp. 1–2.

31 Price Indexes, 1958–1982

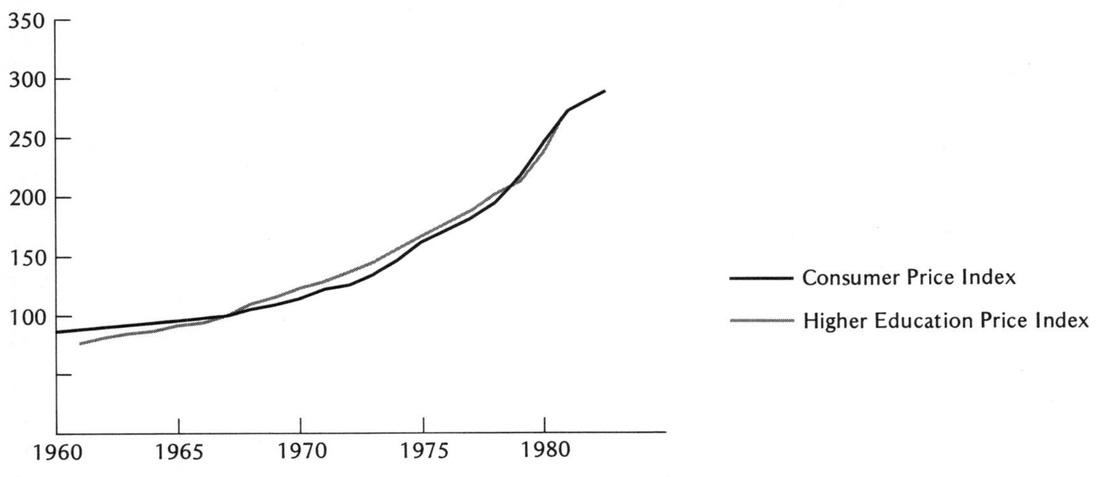

Year	Consumer Price Index	Wholesale Price Index	Producer Prices Total Finished Goods Index[a]	Higher Education Price Index[b]
1958	86.6	94.6	—	na
1959	87.3	94.8	—	na
1960	88.7	94.9	—	na
1961	89.6	94.5	—	77.7
1962	90.6	94.8	—	80.5
1963	91.7	94.5	—	83.6
1964	92.9	94.7	—	86.8
1965	94.5	96.6	—	90.5
1966	97.2	99.8	—	95.0
1967	100.0	100.0	—	100.0
1968	104.2	102.5	—	106.0
1969	109.8	106.5	—	113.2
1970	116.3	110.4	110.3	121.0
1971	121.3	114.0	113.7	128.6
1972	125.3	119.1	117.2	135.8
1973	133.1	134.7	127.9	143.0
1974	147.7	160.1	147.5	153.1
1975	161.2	174.9	163.4	166.2
1976	170.5	183.0	170.6	177.2
1977	181.5	194.2	181.7	188.7
1978	195.4	na	195.9	201.3
1979	217.4	na	217.7	216.9
1980	246.8	na	247.0	238.3
1981	272.4	na	269.8	na
1982	289.1	na	280.6[p]	na

na: Not available.

a The wholesale price index was discontinued in 1978 and replaced by "producer prices." The lead index in that series is the "total finished goods" index.

b Higher education price index for current operations. The index measures the effects of price change on a fixed group of services and goods purchased by colleges and universities through current fund educational and general expenditures excluding sponsored research. Index refers to fiscal year ending in the year indicated.

p Preliminary.

Sources:

1 *Economic Report of the President, 1976* (Washington: GPO), 1976, tables B-42, B-47.

2 D. Kent Halstead, *Higher Education Prices and Price Indexes* (Washington: GPO), 1975; *1979 Supplement,* table 1.

3 Joint Committee of the U. S. Congress, *Economic Indicators, April 1981* (Washington: GPO), pp. 22–23; *January 1983,* pp. 22–23.

4 D. Kent Halstead, "Higher Education Prices and Price Indexes: 1980 Update," *Business Officer,* Vol. 14, No. 4, October 1980, p. 18.

32 Civilian Labor Force, by Region and State, 1970, 1975, 1981

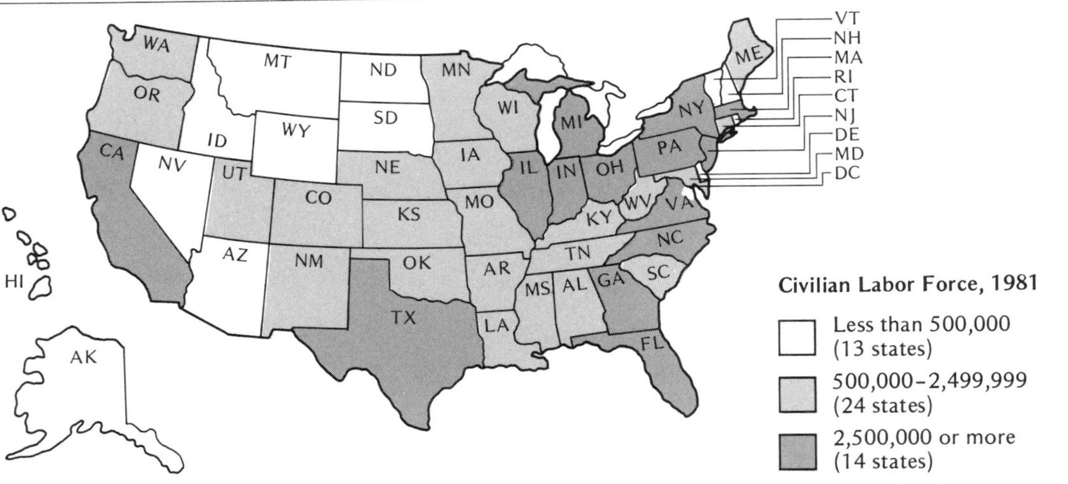

Region and State	Civilian Labor Force[a] (in thousands) 1970	1975	1981	Percent Change, 1975–1981
50 States & D. C.	**83,788.1**	**92,851.8**	**108,430.0**	**16.8**
New England	**5,120.6**	**5,648.1**	**6,227.0**	**11.1**
Connecticut	1,369.6	1,452.0	1,589.0	9.4
Maine	401.7	456.9	509.0	11.4
Massachusetts	2,463.0	2,724.0	2,961.0	8.7
New Hampshire	306.5	374.8	480.0	28.1
Rhode Island	393.3	429.8	478.0	11.2
Vermont	186.5	210.6	260.0	23.5
Mideast	**18,260.7**	**18,413.3**	**19,834.0**	**7.7**
Delaware	228.8	255.4	288.0	12.8
D. C.	1,230.6	338.0	312.0	7.7
Maryland	1,602.4	1,848.0	2,164.0	17.1
New Jersey	2,973.0	3,250.0	3,578.0	10.1
New York	7,407.0	7,653.0	8,016.0	17.8
Pennsylvania	4,818.9	5,069.0	5,476.0	8.0
Southeast	**17,179.1**	**20,059.6**	**24,163.0**	**20.5**
Alabama	1,325.4	1,439.0	1,665.0	15.7
Arkansas	724.6	854.2	1,029.0	20.5
Florida	2,642.0	3,424.0	4,513.0	31.8
Georgia	1,866.0	2,148.0	2,596.0	20.9
Kentucky	1,218.3	1,405.0	1,622.0	18.3
Louisiana	1,303.5	1,453.0	1,857.0	27.8
Mississippi	802.4	922.6	1,052.0	14.0
North Carolina	2,184.0	2,503.0	2,916.0	16.5
South Carolina	1,062.0	1,179.0	1,417.0	20.2
Tennessee	1,614.8	1,809.0	2,110.0	16.6
Virginia	1,815.0	2,256.0	2,600.0	15.2
West Virginia	621.1	666.8	786.0	17.9
Great Lakes	**16,713.8**	**18,131.0**	**19,951.0**	**10.5**
Illinois	4,719.0	5,010.0	5,577.0	11.3
Indiana	2,212.0	2,395.0	2,617.0	9.3
Michigan	3,580.8	3,901.0	4,301.0	10.3
Ohio	4,378.0	4,706.0	5,085.0	8.1
Wisconsin	1,824.0	2,119.0	2,371.0	11.9

(*Continued on next page*)

For footnotes, see next page.

33 Civilian Labor Force, by Region and State, 1970, 1975, 1981—*Continued*

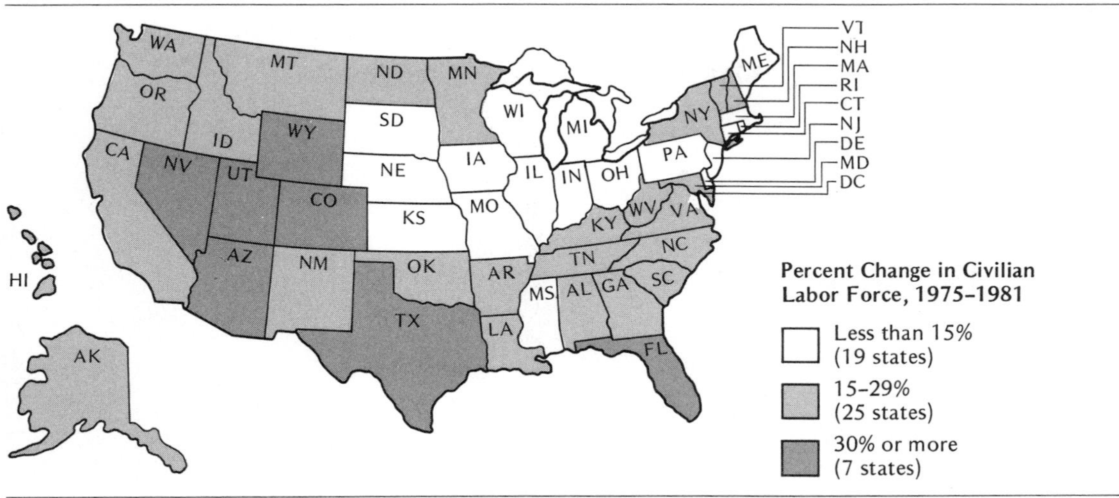

Region and State	Civilian Labor Force[a] (in thousands) 1970	1975	1981	Percent Change, 1975–1981
Plains	**6,805.7**	**7,486.8**	**8,481.0**	**13.3**
Iowa	1,200.5	1,290.0	1,418.0	9.9
Kansas	929.6	1,046.8	1,188.0	13.5
Minnesota	1,618.0	1,797.0	2,143.0	19.3
Missouri	1,921.0	2,075.0	2,317.0	11.7
Nebraska	631.7	703.7	773.0	9.8
North Dakota	238.6	266.5	309.0	15.9
South Dakota	266.3	307.8	333.0	8.2
Southwest	**6,598.6**	**7,851.9**	**10,337.0**	**31.6**
Arizona	648.1	927.6	1,265.0	36.4
New Mexico	355.6	444.3	575.0	29.4
Oklahoma	1,018.9	1,160.0	1,422.0	24.3
Texas	4,576.0	5,320.0	7,075.0	33.0
Rocky Mountains	**2,048.0**	**2,480.7**	**3,235.0**	**30.4**
Colorado	913.4	1,151.0	1,529.0	32.8
Idaho	302.6	346.2	428.0	23.6
Montana	278.0	322.6	382.0	18.4
Utah	416.0	495.0	646.0	30.5
Wyoming	138.0	165.9	250.0	50.7
Far West	**11,061.6**	**12,780.4**	**16,202.0**	**26.8**
Alaska	107.3	156.0	192.0	23.1
California	8,129.0	9,377.0	11,781.0	25.6
Hawaii	312.0	383.9	449.0	17.0
Nevada	218.2	289.5	463.0	59.9
Oregon	885.1	1,039.0	1,330.0	28.0
Washington	1,410.0	1,535.0	1,987.0	29.4

Note: National and regional totals may not agree with other labor force totals because of differences of sources and estimation techniques. Comparability of 1970 data with later figures is limited because of major estimating changes introduced in 1976.

a Annual averages of all civilians in the labor force ages 16 years and over.

Source: *Employment and Training Report of the President* (Washington: GPO), *1977,* table D-3; *1980,* table D-3; *1982,* table D-3.

34 U. S. Labor Force and Employment Status, Selected Years, 1950–1982

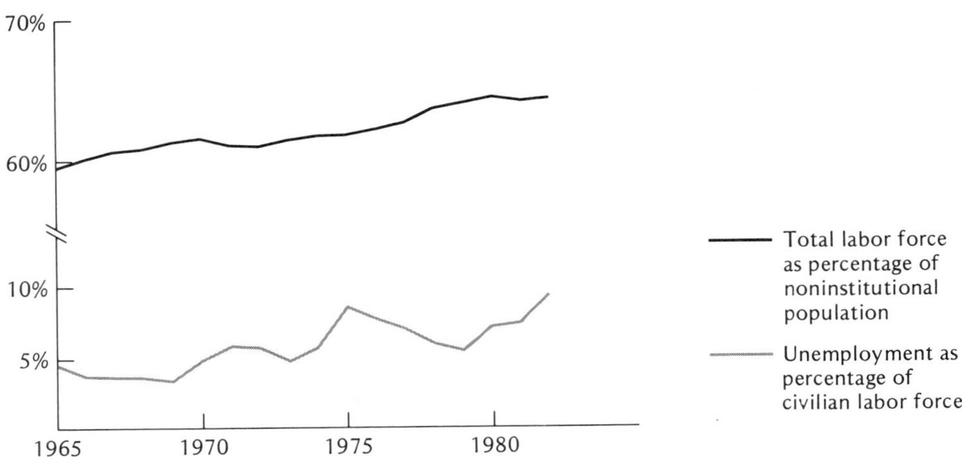

Year	Total Non-institutional Population	Total Labor Force: Number	Total Labor Force: Percentage of Population	Civilian Labor Force: Total	Civilian Labor Force: Employed	Unemployed: Number	Unemployed: Percentage of Civil Labor Force
1950	106,645	63,858	59.9	62,208	58,920	3,288	5.3
1955	112,732	68,072	60.4	65,023	62,171	2,852	4.4
1960	119,759	72,142	60.2	69,628	65,778	3,852	5.5
1965	129,236	77,178	59.7	74,455	71,088	3,366	4.5
1966	131,180	78,893	60.1	75,770	72,895	2,875	3.8
1967	133,319	80,793	60.6	77,347	74,372	2,975	3.8
1968	135,562	82,272	60.7	78,737	75,920	2,817	3.6
1969	137,841	84,239	61.1	80,733	77,902	2,831	3.5
1970	140,182	85,903	61.3	82,715	78,627	4,088	4.9
1971	142,596	86,929	61.0	84,113	79,120	4,993	5.9
1972	145,775	88,991	61.0	86,542	81,702	4,840	5.6
1973	148,263	91,040	61.4	88,714	84,409	4,304	4.9
1974	150,827	93,240	61.8	91,011	85,936	5,076	5.6
1975	153,449	94,793	61.8	92,613	84,783	7,830	8.5
1976	156,048	96,917	62.1	94,773	87,485	7,288	7.7
1977	158,559	99,534	62.8	97,401	90,546	6,855	7.0
1978	161,058	102,537	63.7	100,420	94,373	6,047	6.0
1979	163,620	104,996	64.2	102,908	96,945	5,963	5.8
1980	166,246	106,821	64.3	104,719	97,270	7,448	7.1
1981	171,775	110,315	64.2	108,670	100,397	8,273	7.6
1982	173,939	111,872	64.3	110,204	99,526	10,678	9.7

Note: All figures except percentages are in thousands.

Source: U. S. Bureau of Labor Statistics, *Monthly Labor Review,* Vol. 102, No. 9 (Washington: GPO), September 1979, p. 71; Vol. 104, No. 5, May 1981, p. 71; Vol. 106, No. 3, March 1983, pp. 56–57.

35 Total Labor Force, by Age Group, Sex, and Race, Selected Years, 1960–1990

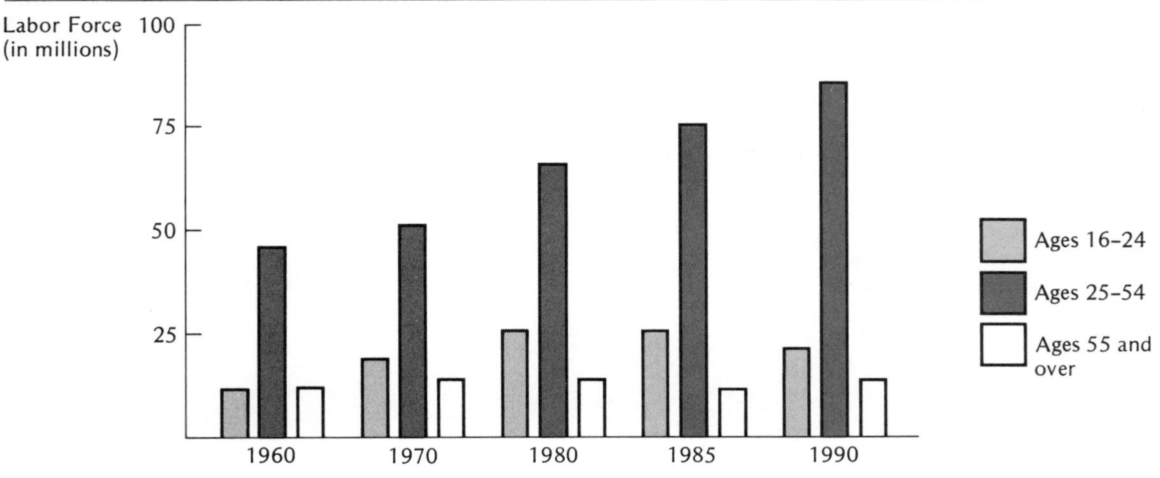

Age Group, Sex, and Race	Annual Average Labor Force[a] (in thousands)					
	1960	1970	1975	1980	1985[b]	1990[b]
	All Races					
Total U. S.	**72,104**	**85,903**	**94,798**	**106,821**	**117,115**	**124,505**
16–24	12,720	19,916	23,488	25,741	25,607	23,768
25–54	46,596	51,487	57,142	66,301	76,647	86,584
55 and over	12,788	14,500	14,168	14,777	14,861	14,153
Men, total	**48,933**	**54,343**	**57,712**	**62,088**	**65,472**	**67,752**
16–24	8,101	11,773	13,313	14,213	13,579	12,269
25–54	31,962	33,279	35,507	38,833	42,913	47,031
55 and over	8,870	9,291	8,892	9,042	8,980	8,452
Women, total	**23,171**	**31,560**	**37,086**	**44,733**	**51,643**	**56,753**
16–24	4,619	8,143	10,175	11,528	12,028	11,499
25–54	14,634	18,208	21,635	27,468	33,734	39,553
55 and over	3,918	5,209	5,276	5,735	5,881	5,701
	Black and Other					
Total	**7,894**	**9,526**	**10,691**	**13,026**	**15,101**	**16,940**
16–24	1,481	2,361	2,908	3,100	3,382	3,287
25–54	5,263	5,845	6,402	8,329	10,181	12,073
55 and over	1,150	1,320	1,381	1,429	1,538	1,580
Men, total	**4,814**	**5,507**	**6,358**	**6,955**	**7,741**	**8,449**
16–24	930	1,378	1,682	1,812	1,759	1,653
25–54	3,149	3,332	3,853	4,364	5,143	5,960
55 and over	735	797	823	784	839	836
Women, total	**3,080**	**4,019**	**4,333**	**6,071**	**7,360**	**8,491**
16–24	551	983	1,226	1,288	1,623	1,634
25–54	2,114	2,513	2,549	3,965	5,038	6,113
55 and over	415	523	558	645	699	744

a Total labor force. This figure is about 2 million greater than the civilian labor force. The difference is found principally among men in the 16–44 age groups.

b Intermediate growth level projections.

Source: *Employment and Training Report of the President* (Washington: GPO), *1976,* tables E-2 and E-4; *1977,* table E-2 and E-4; *1980,* table E-2; *1982,* table E-2.

36 Employed Persons, by Selected Industry and State, 1970 and 1980

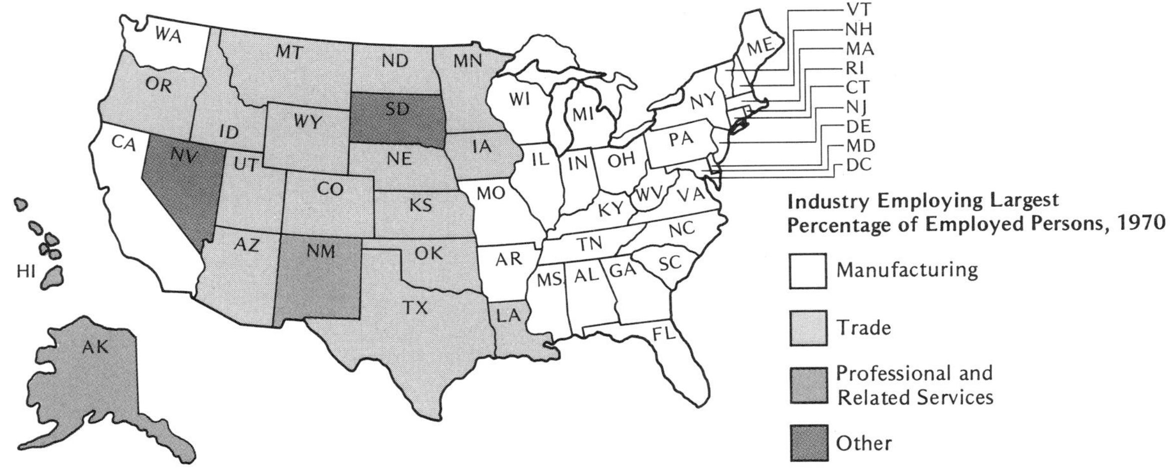

	Percentage of All Employed Persons in							
	Manufacturing[a]		Wholesale & Retail Trade		Professional & Related Services[b]		Public Administration[c]	
Region and State	**1970**	**1980**	**1970**	**1980**	**1970**	**1980**	**1970**	**1980**
50 States & D. C.	**26.1**	**22.3**	**20.0**	**16.2**	**17.6**	**20.3**	**5.5**	**5.4**
New England								
Connecticut	34.8	30.4	18.6	17.9	18.0	20.2	3.9	3.8
Maine	31.5	27.6	19.5	19.6	17.1	22.4	4.9	5.2
Massachusetts	29.2	26.2	20.2	19.5	20.9	24.3	5.1	5.1
New Hampshire	35.6	31.2	18.5	19.1	17.5	20.0	4.1	4.1
Rhode Island	35.0	32.3	19.0	19.2	17.9	21.5	6.2	5.3
Vermont	24.0	23.8	18.1	18.9	21.0	24.3	4.7	4.7
Mideast								
Delaware	29.6	23.8	19.1	22.8	17.3	19.9	4.4	5.5
D. C.	4.8	5.8	14.3	11.5	23.3	27.3	27.1	25.9
Maryland	19.4	14.1	19.1	19.1	19.0	22.3	13.5	14.6
New Jersey	32.2	24.9	19.1	28.4	15.8	19.8	5.1	5.4
New York	24.2	21.3	19.5	19.3	19.7	23.3	5.5	5.5
Pennsylvania	34.0	28.8	18.9	19.5	16.7	20.2	4.7	4.3
Southeast								
Alabama	28.7	25.6	19.0	19.1	15.3	19.1	5.8	6.4
Arkansas	26.1	25.3	19.2	20.4	16.0	18.3	3.8	4.0
Florida	14.1	12.5	23.5	23.6	16.8	18.8	5.6	5.4
Georgia	27.2	23.7	19.6	20.2	14.6	18.9	5.8	6.2
Kentucky	25.6	22.5	18.7	19.9	16.2	19.8	4.7	5.3
Louisiana	16.0	14.2	21.2	20.9	18.1	20.2	4.6	5.4
Mississippi	25.9	24.0	17.9	19.1	16.9	20.3	4.1	5.0
North Carolina	35.4	31.7	17.5	18.9	14.3	18.3	3.5	4.1
South Carolina	36.2	31.8	16.7	18.2	14.4	18.4	3.9	5.3
Tennessee	30.6	26.8	18.8	20.6	15.8	18.2	3.9	5.0
Virginia	22.4	18.5	18.0	19.0	16.9	20.9	11.4	10.8
West Virginia	23.4	18.8	19.1	19.1	17.5	19.1	4.1	5.4
Great Lakes								
Illinois	30.5	26.5	20.3	20.9	16.5	18.5	4.4	4.7
Indiana	35.7	30.6	19.1	20.6	15.6	19.7	3.7	3.3
Michigan	35.9	30.2	19.5	20.4	17.7	21.5	3.8	4.6
Ohio	35.9	29.6	19.3	20.9	16.2	20.1	4.2	4.0
Wisconsin	31.1	28.6	19.9	20.7	18.2	20.3	3.8	3.9

(Continued on next page)

For footnotes and sources, see next page.

37 Employed Persons, by Selected Industry and State, 1970 and 1980—*Continued*

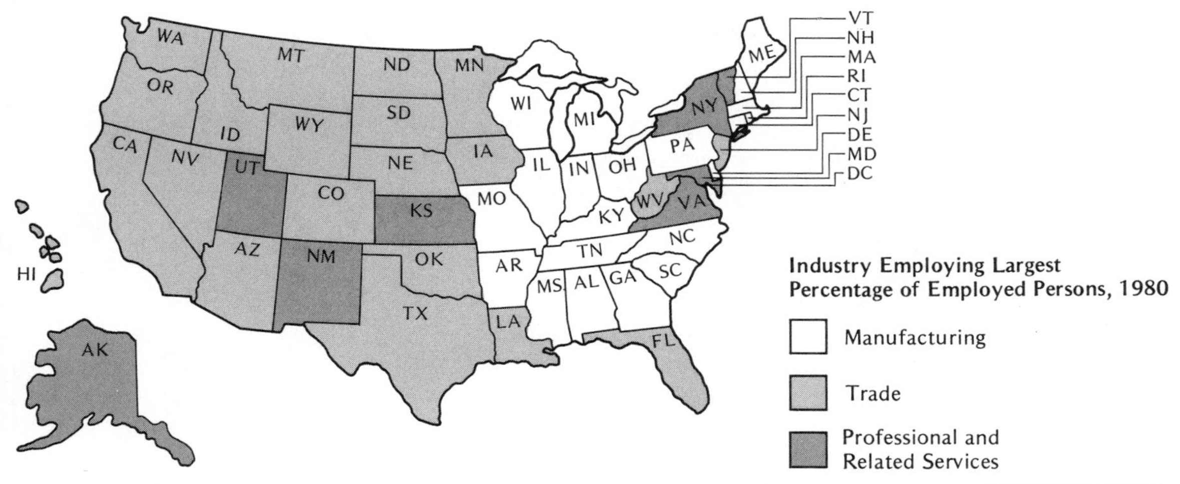

Region and State	Manufacturing[a] 1970	Manufacturing[a] 1980	Wholesale & Retail Trade 1970	Wholesale & Retail Trade 1980	Professional & Related Services[b] 1970	Professional & Related Services[b] 1980	Public Administration[c] 1970	Public Administration[c] 1980
Plains								
Iowa	20.0	19.9	21.5	22.3	18.8	21.3	3.6	3.7
Kansas	17.3	19.5	21.8	20.3	19.8	21.2	5.0	4.5
Minnesota	20.9	20.8	22.0	22.1	20.0	21.4	3.8	3.7
Missouri	24.3	21.1	21.5	21.0	17.4	20.7	5.2	4.9
Nebraska	13.7	13.1	22.3	21.7	18.7	21.4	4.4	4.1
North Dakota	4.7	6.2	23.1	23.7	21.9	22.8	5.4	5.2
South Dakota	7.4	9.8	21.6	21.9	20.7	21.5	5.2	6.3
Southwest								
Arizona	15.7	14.9	21.9	22.3	19.3	19.6	6.4	6.6
New Mexico	6.6	8.3	21.0	20.5	22.7	22.0	8.9	8.6
Oklahoma	15.6	16.0	21.7	21.1	18.8	20.2	7.8	6.4
Texas	18.7	17.4	22.2	21.2	16.9	18.7	5.5	4.6
Rocky Mountains								
Colorado	14.5	13.6	22.3	22.1	21.3	20.0	6.6	6.1
Idaho	14.7	13.3	22.7	21.0	16.5	18.1	5.1	6.3
Montana	9.6	7.4	22.3	22.9	19.9	22.3	5.9	6.2
Utah	14.6	15.5	21.6	20.9	20.0	21.2	12.6	8.4
Wyoming	6.5	5.6	20.3	19.4	19.4	18.3	6.3	5.8
Far West								
Alaska	7.0	6.6	18.9	17.2	20.4	23.0	16.4	15.7
California	21.6	20.1	20.9	21.2	18.7	19.9	6.5	5.2
Hawaii	10.9	7.8	21.4	23.7	17.2	17.8	11.4	10.0
Nevada	5.1	5.9	19.1	19.6	14.2	14.4	7.3	6.6
Oregon	21.4	20.0	22.1	22.6	19.7	21.0	4.9	4.7
Washington	21.7	19.9	21.5	21.8	19.0	20.2	5.6	5.1

Percentage of All Employed Persons in

a Durable goods and nondurable goods manufacturing combined.

b Includes hospitals, health services, elementary and secondary schools, colleges and universities, welfare and religious organizations, and "other."

c Includes workers involved in uniquely governmental activities, e.g., judicial and legislative employees.

Source: U. S. Bureau of the Census, *Population and Housing, Supplementary Report, Provisional Estimates of Social Economic and Housing Characteristics, 1980* (Washington: GPO), 1982, table P-3.

Note: The industries shown in this table account for approximately two-thirds of all employed persons in the U. S. Industries excluded from this table are agriculture, forestry, and fisheries; mining; construction; transportation, communication, and public utilities; finance, insurance, and real estate; business and repair services; personal, entertainment, and recreation services.

38 Estimated Employment in 1980 and Average Annual Openings in Selected Occupations, 1978–1990

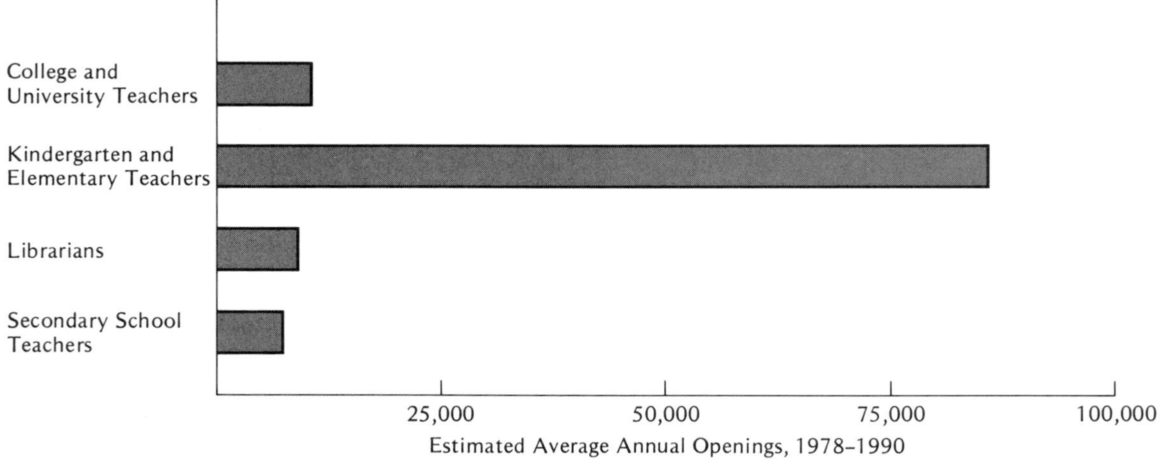

Occupation Group and Occupation[a]	Estimated Employment, 1980	Average Annual Openings 1978–90[b]
Office Occupations		
Accountants	900,000[e]	61,000
Computer programmers	228,000	9,200
Lawyers	425,000	37,000
Systems analysts	205,000	7,900
Urban planners	23,000	800
Education & Related Occupations		
College & university teachers	691,000[c]	11,000
Kindergarten & elem. school teachers	1,600,000	86,000
Librarians	135,000	8,000
Secondary school teachers	1,237,000	7,200
Scientific & Technical Occupations		
Astronomers	3,000	40
Biochemists	16,000	900
Chemists	113,000	6,100
Engineers	1,200,000[d]	46,500
Geologists	34,000	1,700
Life scientists	279,000	11,200
Mathematicians	40,000	1,000
Physicists	37,000	1,000
Statisticians	26,500	1,500
Health Occupations		
Dentists	126,000	5,500
Pharmacists	141,000	7,800
Physicians[d]	424,000	19,000
Registered nurses	1,105,000	85,000
Veterinarians	36,000	1,700
Social Science Occupations		
Economists	44,000	7,800
Historians	20,000	700
Political scientists	15,000	500
Psychologists	106,000	6,700
Sociologists	21,000	600

a The occupations listed are only a small fraction of those listed by the Department of Labor. See Source for the full list.

b Estimates of annual openings due to growth, deaths and retirements, and other causes of separation from the labor force; transfers out of occupations are not included.

c Excludes part-time junior instructors.

d Includes osteopathic physicians.

Source: U. S. Bureau of Labor Statistics, *Occupational Outlook Quarterly,* Vol. 24, No. 1 (Washington: GPO), Spring 1980, p. 6–20; Spring 1982, pp. 6–20.

39 Supply and Demand for Doctorates, 1976–1985

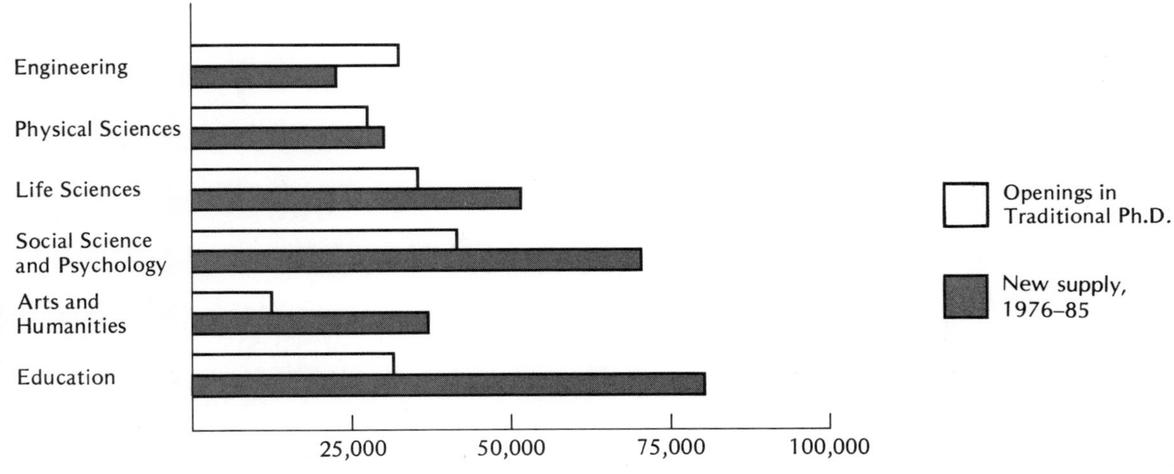

Estimated Openings for Traditional Ph.D. Employment,[a] 1976–1985

Field	Total	Created by: Growth[a]	Created by: Death & Retirement
All Fields	**192.8**	**138.1**	**54.7**
Engineering & natural science	100.8	72.5	28.3
Engineering	32.4	25.5	7.0
Physical science	27.4	17.9	9.5
Chemistry	14.7	9.4	5.2
Physics	3.7	1.5	2.2
Life science	35.4	25.6	9.8
Mathematics	5.6	3.5	2.0
Social science & psychology	41.5	31.2	10.3
Arts and humanities	12.4	7.2	5.1
Education	31.5	22.5	9.1
Business and commerce	2.9	2.1	.8
Other fields	3.6	2.6	1.1

Field	Projected New Supply of Ph.D.'s, 1976–1985[b]	Estimated Openings for Traditional Ph.D. Employment, 1976–1985	Difference between New Supply and Openings in Traditional Ph.D. Employment[c]: Number	Difference: Percentage of New Supply
All Fields	**323.0**	**192.8**	**130.2**	**40.3**
Engineering & natural science	114.7	100.8	13.8	12.1
Engineering	22.7	32.4	−9.7	−42.8
Physical sciences	30.7	27.4	3.3	10.8
Chemistry	16.6	14.7	1.8	11.2
Physics	7.6	3.7	3.9	51.2
Life science	51.7	35.4	16.2	31.4
Mathematics	9.6	5.6	4.0	41.6
Social science & psychology	70.5	41.5	29.0	41.2
Arts and humanities	37.0	12.4	24.6	66.6
Education	80.4	31.5	48.8	60.8
Business and commerce	8.0	2.9	5.1	63.6
Other fields	12.4	3.6	8.8	70.8

Note: Figures are in thousands, except for percentages.

a Openings resulting from growth are based on 1966–70 trends in the proportion of workers in each occupational field holding a doctorate. Job openings result from growth in the number of workers in each occupation and from the educational upgrading of jobs.

b Based on NCES projections.

c Does not take into account the 80,200 Ph.D.'s employed in 1976 in "nontraditional Ph.D. jobs." These individuals may try to change to "traditional Ph.D." jobs during the 1976–85 period and thus increase the competition for "traditional Ph.D." employment.

Source: Douglas Braddock, "The Oversupply of Ph.D.'s to Continue through 1985," *Monthly Labor Review,* Vol. 101, No. 10, October 1978, pp. 48–50.

40 Unemployment Rates, by Sex and Age Group, Selected Years, 1950–1982

	Annual Average Unemployment Rates for					
	Men			Women		
Year	All (16 Years & Over)	16–19 Years Old	20 Years & Over	All (16 Years & Over)	16–19 Years Old	20 Years & Over
1950	5.1	12.7	4.7	5.7	11.4	5.1
1955	4.2	11.6	3.8	4.9	10.2	4.4
1960	5.4	15.3	4.7	5.9	13.9	5.1
1961	6.4	17.2	5.7	7.2	16.3	6.3
1962	5.2	14.7	4.6	6.2	14.6	5.4
1963	5.2	17.2	4.5	6.5	17.2	5.4
1964	4.6	15.8	3.9	6.2	16.7	5.2
1965	4.0	14.1	3.2	5.5	15.7	4.5
1966	3.2	11.7	2.5	4.8	14.1	3.8
1967	3.1	12.3	2.3	5.2	13.5	4.2
1968	2.9	11.6	2.2	4.8	14.0	3.8
1969	2.8	11.4	2.1	4.7	13.3	3.7
1970	4.4	15.0	3.5	5.9	15.6	4.8
1971	5.3	16.6	4.4	6.9	17.2	5.7
1972	4.9	15.9	4.0	6.6	16.7	5.4
1973	4.1	13.9	3.2	6.0	15.2	4.8
1974	4.8	15.5	3.8	6.7	16.5	5.5
1975	7.9	20.1	6.7	9.3	19.7	8.0
1976	7.0	19.2	5.9	8.6	18.7	7.4
1977	6.2	17.3	5.2	8.2	18.3	7.0
1978	5.2	15.7	4.2	7.2	17.0	6.0
1979	5.1	15.8	4.1	6.8	16.4	5.7
1980	6.9	18.2	5.9	7.4	17.2	6.3
1981	7.4	20.1	6.3	7.9	19.0	6.8
1982	9.9	24.4	8.8	9.4	21.9	8.3

Sources:

1 *Economic Report of the President, 1977* (Washington: GPO), 1977, table B-28.

2 Department of Labor, *Monthly Labor Review* (Washington: GPO), September 1979, pp. 72, 75; May 1981, pp. 72, 75; March 1983, pp. 59–60.

41 Unemployment Rates, by Race and Kind of Workers, Selected Years, 1950–1982

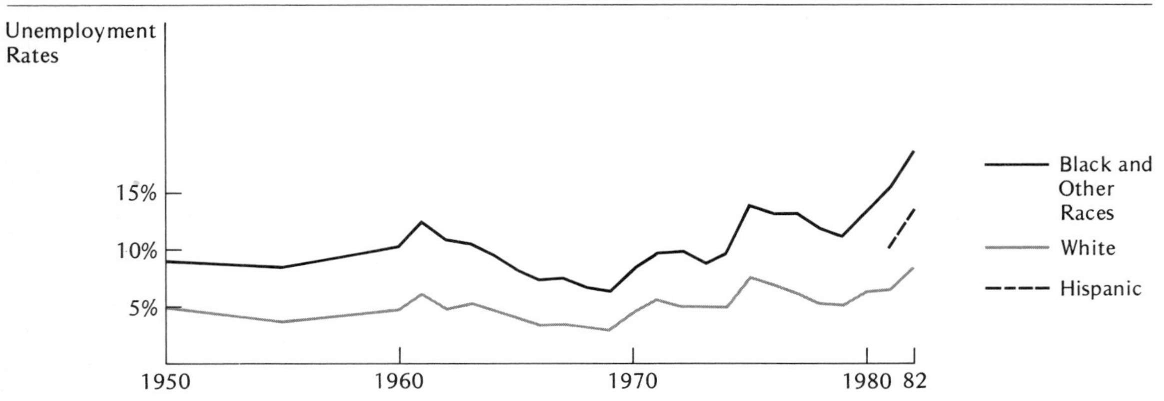

Year	All Workers	White	Black & Other Races	Hispanics	Blue-Collar Workers[a]	Labor Force Time Lost[b]
	Annual Average Unemployment Rates for (in percentage)					
1950	5.3	4.9	9.0	—	7.2	—
1955	4.4	3.9	8.7	—	5.8	4.8
1960	5.5	4.9	10.2	—	7.8	6.7
1961	6.7	6.0	12.4	—	9.2	8.0
1962	5.5	4.9	10.9	—	7.4	6.7
1963	5.7	5.0	10.8	—	7.3	6.4
1964	5.2	4.6	9.6	—	6.3	5.8
1965	4.5	4.1	8.1	—	5.3	5.0
1966	3.8	3.4	7.3	—	4.2	4.2
1967	3.8	3.4	7.4	—	4.4	4.2
1968	3.6	3.2	6.7	—	4.1	4.0
1969	3.5	3.1	6.4	—	3.9	3.9
1970	4.9	4.5	8.2	—	6.2	5.3
1971	5.9	5.4	9.9	—	7.4	6.4
1972	5.6	5.0	10.0	—	6.5	6.0
1973	4.9	4.3	8.9	—	5.3	5.2
1974	5.6	5.0	9.9	—	6.7	6.1
1975	8.5	7.8	13.9	—	11.7	9.1
1976	7.7	7.0	13.1	—	9.4	8.3
1977	7.0	6.2	13.1	—	8.1	7.6
1978	6.0	5.2	11.9	—	6.9	6.5
1979	5.8	5.1	11.3	—	6.9	6.3
1980	7.1	6.3	13.2	—	10.0	7.9
1981	7.6	6.7	15.6[c]	10.4	10.3	8.5
1982	9.7	8.6	18.9[c]	13.8	14.2	11.0

a Includes craft and kindred workers, operatives, and nonfarm laborers.

b Man-hours lost by the unemployed and persons on part-time for economic reasons as a percentage of potentially available labor force man-hours.

c These figures are for blacks only.

Sources:

1 *Economic Report of the President, 1977* (Washington: GPO), 1977, table B-29.

2 Department of Labor, *Monthly Labor Review* (Washington: GPO), September 1979, pp. 72, 74; May 1981, pp. 72, 74; February 1983, p. 62.

42 Education Expenditures, as a Percentage of the GNP, Selected Years, 1929–30—1980–81

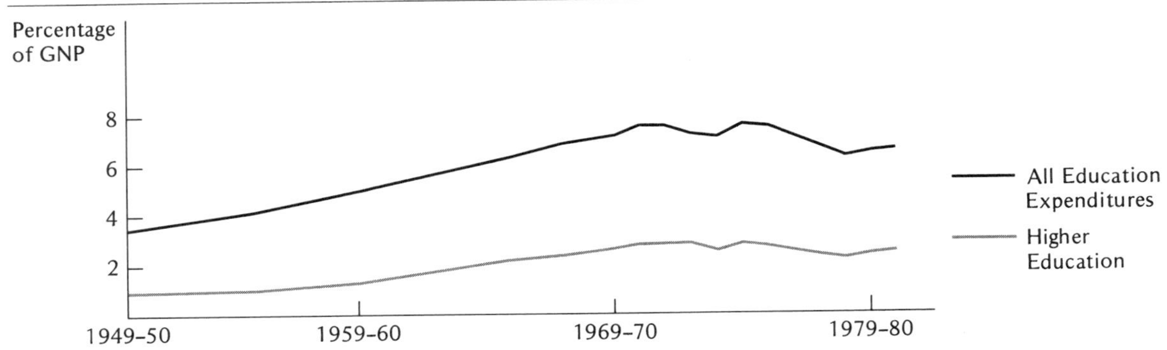

School Year	Education Expenditures[a] as Percentage of Gross National Product[b]			
	All Education[c]	Higher Education[d]		
		Total	Public	Private
1929–30	3.3	.6	.3	.4
1939–40	3.5	.8	.4	.4
1945–46	2.2	.5	.3	.3
1949–50	3.5	1.0	.5	.5
1955–56	4.1	1.0	.6	.4
1959–60	5.0	1.4	.8	.6
1965–66	6.3	2.1	1.2	.9
1967–68	6.9	2.4	1.5	.9
1969–70	7.3	2.6	1.6	.9
1970–71	7.5	2.7	1.7	.9
1971–72	7.5	2.7	1.8	.9
1972–73	7.2	2.6	1.7	.9
1973–74	7.2	2.5	1.7	.8
1974–75	7.6	2.7	1.8	.9
1975–76	7.5	2.6	1.8	.8
1976–77	7.1	2.5	1.7	.8
1977–78	6.7	2.4	1.6	.8
1978–79	6.4	2.3	1.5	.8
1979–80	6.5	2.4	1.6	.8
1980–81	6.6	2.5	1.6	.8

a Reported on school year basis. Includes current expenditures, interest, and capital outlay.

b Gross National Product adjusted to a school year basis. For figures prior to 1970–71, annual GNP figures were converted to the school year by averaging the two relevant adjacent calendar years. For 1970–71 and later, GNP figures are for the fiscal year and are taken from source 4. These adjustments result in figures that vary slightly from those found in USOE's *Digest of Education Statistics.*

c Includes elementary and secondary schools, higher educational institutions, residential schools for exceptional children, federal schools for Indians, federally operated elementary and secondary schools on posts, and subcollegiate departments of colleges.

d Includes auxiliary enterprises, hospitals, and independent operations.

Sources:

1 U. S. Department of Health, Education, and Welfare, *Education and Welfare Trends* (Washington: GPO), 1961, p. 53.

2 NCES, *Projections of Education Statistics* (Washington: GPO), *to 1978–79,* pp. 75–77; to 1982–83, pp. 77, 79; *to 1986–87,* pp. 80, 81, 84; *to 1988–89,* pp. 110, 112, 113; *to 1990–91,* p. 105.

3 *Economic Report of the President, 1976* (Washington: GPO), 1976, p. 171.

4 *The U. S. Budget in Brief, FY 1983* (Washington: GPO), p. 89.

43 Voluntary Support of Institutions of Higher Education, 1969–70—1981–82

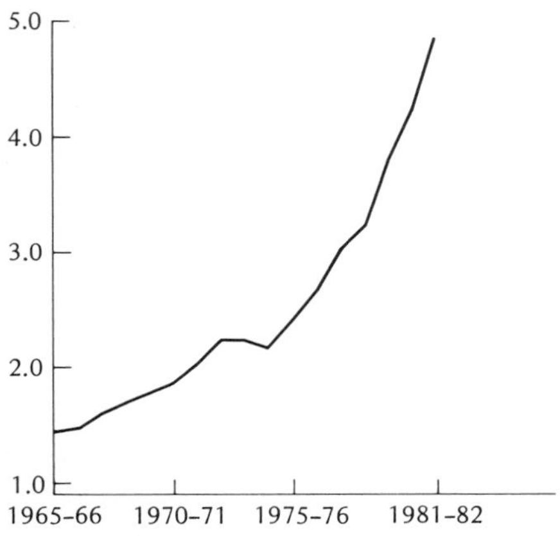

Voluntary Support (in millions of dollars)

Year	For All Institutions[a] Total Amount	For All Institutions[a] Percent Change	Per student Current Dollars	Per student Constant 1967 Dollars[b] Amount	Per student Constant 1967 Dollars[b] Percent Change
1969–70	1,780	na	222	196	na
1970–71	1,860	4.5	217	182	−7.1
1971–72	2,020	8.6	226	183	.5
1972–73	2,240	10.9	243	188	2.7
1973–74	2,240	0.0	233	166	−11.7
1974–75	2,160	−3.6	211	137	−17.5
1975–76	2,410	11.6	213	128	−6.6
1976–77	2,670	10.8	240	136	6.2
1977–78	3,040	13.9	269	143	5.1
1978–79	3,230	6.3	284	138	−3.5
1979–80	3,800	17.6	325	140	1.4
1980–81	4,230	11.3	350	135	−3.6
1981–82	4,860	14.9	393	140	3.7

Estimated Total Support[a]

	1971–72 Amount	1971–72 Percent-age	1975–76 Amount	1975–76 Percent-age	1981–82 Amount	1981–82 Percent-age
All Sources	**2,020**	**100.0**	**2,410**	**100.0**	**4,860**	**100.0**
Foundations	523	25.9	549	22.8	1,003	20.6
Non-alumni individuals	493	24.4	569	23.6	1,097	22.6
Alumni	481	23.8	588	24.4	1,240[c]	25.5
Business corporations	275	13.6	379	15.7	976[d]	20.1
Religious denominations	101	5.0	130	5.4	175	3.6
Other	147	7.3	195	8.1	369	7.6

na: Not applicable.

a Estimate for all institutions of higher education based on data from institutions responding to questionnaire; includes giving for current operations and capital purposes.

b Current dollar estimate converted by the Consumer Price Index (CPI, 100 = 1967) which, in turn, was converted to an academic year basis by averaging the CPI for the two calendar years that make up the academic year.

c Includes bequests from Edward Mallinckrodt, Jr., of $77 million to Harvard University and $38 million to Washington University for "other" capital purposes.

d Includes newsreel film library valued at $30.4 million from Hearst Corporation to University of California at Los Angeles.

Source: Council on Financial Aid to Education (CFAE), *Voluntary Support to Education* (New York: CFAE), 1971–72, p. 4; 1973–74, p. 5; 1975–76, pp. 4, 6; 1976–77, pp. 4–7; 1978–79, pp. 4, 6; 1979–80, pp. 4, 5; 1981–82, pp. 4, 5.

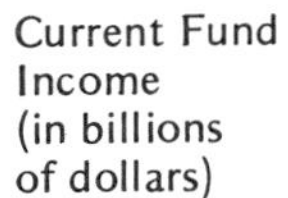

Current Fund Income of Institutions of Higher Education, Selected Years, 1909–10—1980–81

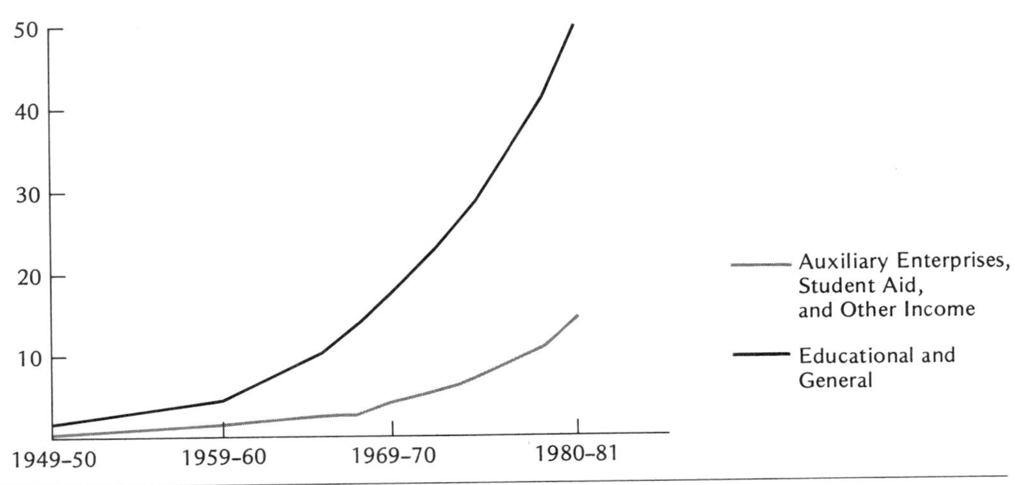

Kind of Income	Amount (in millions of dollars) 1909–10	1919–20	1929–30	1939–40	1949–50	1959–60
Total Current Fund Income	**82.0**	**199.9**	**554.5**	**715.2**	**2,374.6**	**5,785.5**
Total Educational & General	(73.0)	(172.9)	(483.1)	(571.3)	(1,833.8)	(4,688.4)
Student Tuition & Fees	19.4	42.3	144.1	200.9	394.6	1,157.5
Government	(26.0)	(74.5)	(171.5)	(214.5)	(1,077.6)	(2,563.2)
Federal	4.8	12.8	20.7	38.9	524.3[a]	1,037.0[a]
State	}21.2	}61.7	}150.8	151.2	491.6	1,374.5
Local				24.4	61.7	151.7
Endowment Earnings	12.7	26.5	68.6	71.3	96.3	206.6
Private Gifts and Grants	3.6	7.6	26.2	40.5	118.6	382.6
Other Educational & General	11.4	22.1	72.7	44.2	146.6	378.5
Auxiliary Enterprises	9.0	27.0	60.4	143.9	511.3	1,004.3
Student Aid Grants[b]	nr	nr	nr	nr	16.3	92.9
Other Current Income	nr	nr	11.0	nr	13.2	nr

Kind of Income	1965–66	1967–68	1969–70	1971–72	1973–74
Total Current Fund Income	**12,734.2**	**16,825.2**	**21,515.2**	**26,234.3**	**31,712.5**
Total Educational & General[c]	(10,285.3)	(13,845.6)	(17,254.7)	(21,136.9)	(25,607.2)
Student Tuition & Fees	2,669.7	3,380.3	4,419.8	5,594.1	6,500.1
Government[c]	(5,954.6)	(8,033.0)	(10,013.6)	(12,147.5)	(14,944.3)
Federal[c]	2,653.8	3,348.2	3,450.9	4,035.5	4,498.9
State	2,984.3	4,181.1	5,787.9	7,121.0	9,182.3
Local	316.5	503.7	774.8	991.0	1,263.1
Endowment Earnings	316.2	364.0	447.3	480.8	576.9
Private Gifts and Grants[d]	640.7	848.5	1,001.5	1,208.1	1,430.9
Other Educational & General	704.0	1,219.8	1,372.5	1,706.4	2,155.0
Auxiliary Enterprises	2,139.1	2,481.7	2,900.4	3,309.0	3,734.2
Student Aid Grants[b]	309.9	497.9	658.0	764.6	882.6
Other Current Income[e]	nr	nr	702.2	1,023.8	1,488.4

(Continued on next page)

Note: Data for 1909–10 include all states plus outlying parts; data for 1919–20 through 1949–50 include 48 states and D. C.; data for other years include 50 states and D. C. Because of rounding, details may not add to totals. Figures in parentheses are subtotals. Data for 1974–75 and later are *not* strictly comparable to previous data due to a major change in reporting categories and definitions.

nr: Not reported.

For footnotes and sources, see next page.

45 Current Fund Income of Institutions of Higher Education, Selected Years, 1909–10—1980–81—*Continued*

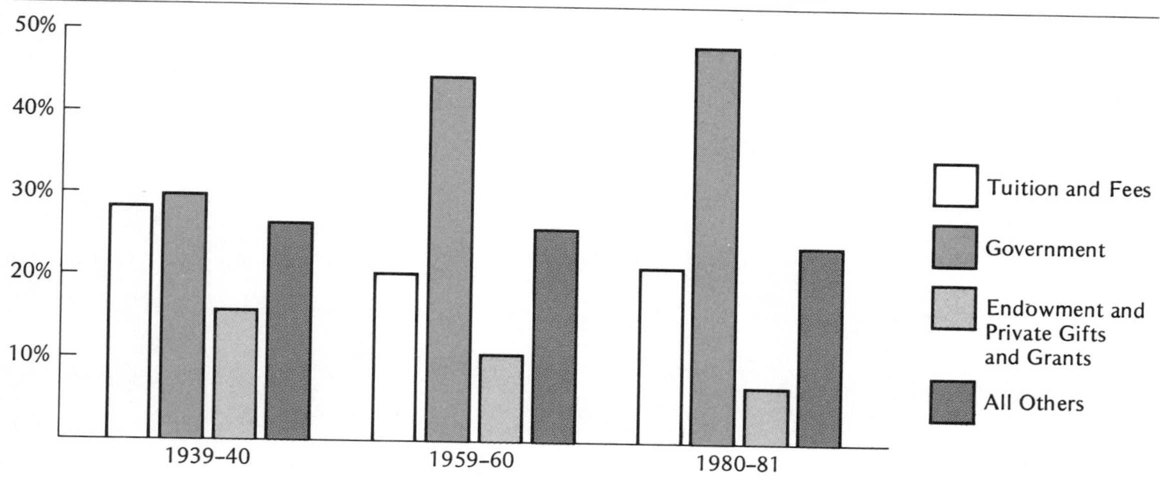

Kind of Income	Amount (in millions of dollars)			Percent Distribution		
	1974–75	**1978–79**	**1980–81**	**1974–75**	**1978–79**	**1980–81**
Total Current Fund Income	**35,686.9**	**51,837.8**	**65,584.8**	**100.0**	**100.0**	**100.0**
Student Tuition and Fees	7,232.9	10,704.2	13,773.3	20.3	20.6	21.0
Government[c]	(18,354.3)	(25,788.2)	(31,644.6)	(51.4)	(49.7)	(48.2)
Federal[c]	6,072.5	7,851.4	9,747.6	17.0	15.1	14.9
State	10,857.4	16,363.8	20,106.2	30.4	31.6	30.7
Local	1,424.4	1,573.0	1,790.7	4.0	3.0	2.7
Endowment Income	717.4	985.2	1,364.4	2.0	1.9	2.1
Private Gifts & Grants	1,745.0	2,489.4	3,176.6	4.9	4.8	4.8
Sales & Services of Educational Activities	554.9	1,037.1	1,409.7	1.6	2.0	2.1
Other	849.6	1,329.0	1,948.5	2.4	2.6	3.0
Auxiliary Enterprises	4,080.2	5,741.3	7,287.3	11.4	11.1	11.1
Sales & Services of Hospitals	2,152.1	3,763.5	4,980.3	6.0	7.3	7.6

a Includes tuition and fees for veterans.

b Includes federal, state, and local government and private grants specifically designated for student aid.

c Includes data for Federally Funded Research and Development Centers (FFRDC's). Beginning 1969–70 some NCES reports have included FFRDC data in "other current income" or "independent operations." In this table, in order to increase comparability with earlier years, estimates of revenue for FFRDC's have been included in those categories in which they were reported previously.

d From 1967–68 through 1973–74, includes nongovernment funds for "sponsored research" and "other sponsored programs."

e From 1969–70 through 1973–74, includes data for hospitals in which service to the community was paramount.

Sources:

1 NCES, *Digest of Educational Statistics* (Washington: GPO), 1971 edition, table 118; 1976 edition, tables 123, 126.

2 NCES, *Financial Statistics of Institutions of Higher Education, Current Funds Revenues and Expenditures* (Washington: GPO), 1965–66, p. 10; 1967–68, p. 12; 1969–70, pp. 14–15; 1971–72, pp. 16–17; 1973–74, p. 10; *Fiscal Year 1975,* p. 6; *Fiscal Year 1979,* p. 14.

3 NCES (Washington, 1983), unpublished data.

4 National Science Foundation (NSF), *Federal Support to Universities, Colleges, and Selected Nonprofit Institutions* (Washington: GPO), *Fiscal Year 1972,* p. 20; *Fiscal Year 1973,* p. 13; *Fiscal Year 1974,* p. 19.

5 NSF, *Federal Funds for Research, Development, and Other Scientific Activities, Fiscal Years 1974, 1975, and 1976, Detailed Statistical Tables, Appendixes, C & D* (Washington: GPO), 1975, table C-1.

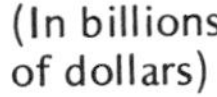

Current Fund Revenues of Public Institutions of Higher Education, Selected Years, 1965–66—1980–81

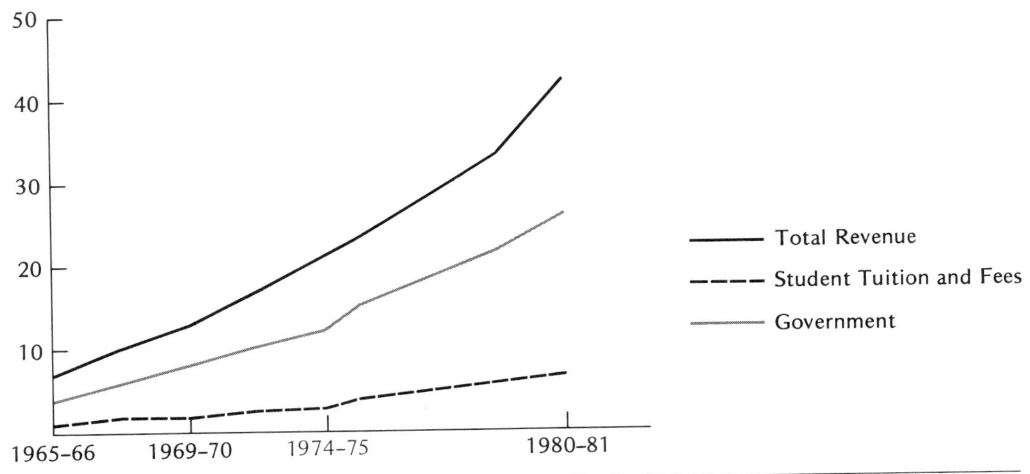

Kind of Revenues	Amount (in millions of dollars) 1965–66	1967–68	1969–70	1971–72	1973–74
Total Current Fund Revenues	**7,397.7**	**10,432.1**	**13,768.6**	**17,079.9**	**21,206.5**
Total Educational & General[a]	(6,047.3)	(8,645.1)	(11,254.6)	(14,015.4)	(17,474.3)
Student Tuition & Fees	854.5	1,205.0	1,735.0	2,332.5	2,734.7
Government[a]	(4,605.6)	(6,437.5)	(8,412.1)	(10,334.9)	(12,951.0)
Federal[a]	1,368.2	1,839.7	2,012.8	2,420.2	2,793.2
State	2,926.8	4,115.2	5,684.5	6,969.9	8,961.9
Local	310.6	482.6	714.8	944.8	1,195.9
Endowment Income	29.9	35.8	57.1	55.2	76.9
Private Gifts & Grants[b]	156.4	215.6	262.5	322.6	430.7
Other Educational & General	400.9	751.2	787.9	970.2	1,281.0
Auxiliary Enterprises	1,210.2	1,438.3	1,727.5	2,018.7	2,324.4
Student Aid Grants[c]	140.2	258.7	349.1	415.4	493.9
Other Current Revenues[d]	nr	nr	437.4	630.4	913.9

(Continued on next page)

Note: Data are for 50 states and D. C. Because of rounding, details may not add to totals. Figures in parentheses are subtotals. Data for 1974–75 and later are *not* strictly comparable to previous data. A major change in reporting categories and definitions was incorporated into the 1974–75 questionnaire to make it coincide with new standards of college and university financial reporting set forth in publications of the National Association of College and University Business Officers, NCES, and the American Institute of Certified Public Accountants.

nr: Not reported.

a Includes data for Federally Funded Research and Development Centers (FFRDC's). Beginning 1969–70 some NCES reports have included FFRDC data in "other current income" or "independent operations." In this table, in order to increase comparability with earlier years, estimates of revenue for FFRDC's have been included in those categories in which they were reported previously.

b From 1967–68 through 1973–74, includes nongovernmental funds for "sponsored research" and "other sponsored programs."

c Includes federal, state, and local government and private grants specifically designated for student aid.

d From 1969–70 through 1973–74, includes data for hospitals in which service to the community was paramount.

For sources, see next page.

47 Current Fund Revenues of Public Institutions of Higher Education, Selected Years, 1965–66—1980–81—*Continued*

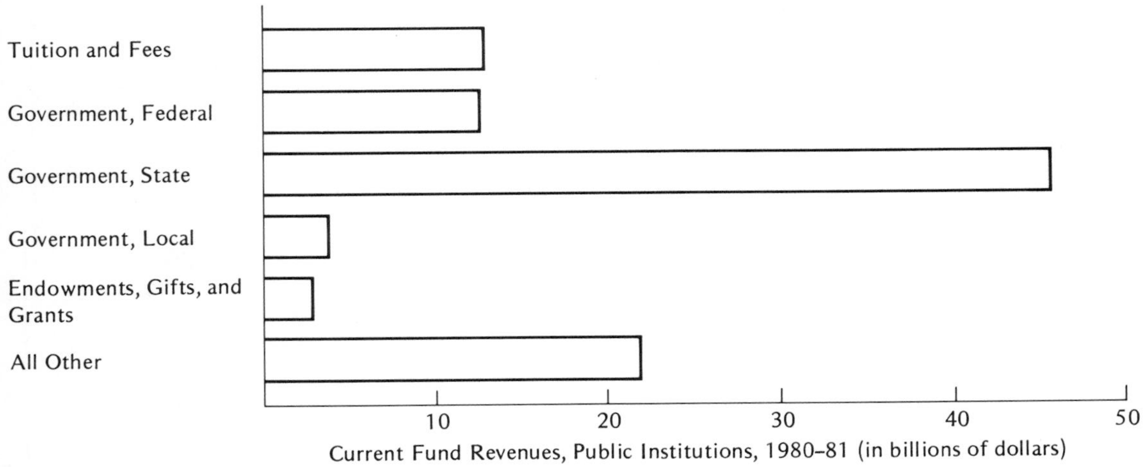

	Amount (in millions of dollars)			Percent Distribution		
Kind of Revenue	**1974–75**	**1978–79**	**1980–81**	**1974–75**	**1978–79**	**1980–81**
Total Current Fund Revenues	**24,004.9**	**34,527.5**	**43,195.6**	**100.0**	**100.0**	**100.0**
Student Tuition and Fees	3,078.5	4,380.6	5,570.4	12.8	12.7	12.9
Government[a]	(15,731.4)	(22,018.6)	(26,768.6)	(65.5)	(63.8)	(62.0)
Federal[a]	3,786.1	4,539.1	5,540.1	15.8	13.1	12.8
State	10,608.5	16,018.1	19,676.0	44.2	46.4	45.6
Local	1,336.8	1,461.4	1,622.9	5.6	4.2	3.8
Endowment Income	106.6	153.6	214.6	.4	.4	.4
Private Gifts & Grants	556.7	835.9	1,100.1	2.3	2.4	2.5
Sales & Services of Educational Activities	372.9	698.8	943.7	1.6	2.0	2.2
Other	488.2	683.3	1,016.1	2.0	2.0	2.4
Auxiliary Enterprises	2,548.5	3,627.9	4,614.6	10.6	10.5	10.7
Sales & Services of Hospitals	1,122.2	2,128.7	2,897.1	4.7	6.2	6.7

For footnotes, see preceding page.

Sources:

1 NCES, *Financial Statistics of Institutions of Higher Education, Current Funds Revenues and Expenditures* (Washington: GPO), *1965–66* p. 10; *1967–68,* p. 12; *1969–70,* pp. 14, 15; *1971–72,* pp. 16, 17; *1973–74,* p. 10; *Fiscal Year 1975,* p. 6; *Fiscal Year 1977,* p. 6; *Fiscal Year 1979,* p. 14.

2 NCES (Washington, 1983), unpublished data.

3 National Science Foundation (NSF), *Federal Support to Universities, Colleges, and Selected Nonprofit Institutions* (Washington: GPO), *Fiscal Year 1972,* p. 20; *Fiscal Year 1973,* p. 13; *Fiscal Year 1974,* p. 19.

4 NSF, *Federal Funds for Research, Development, and Other Scientific Activities, Fiscal Years 1974, 1975 and 1976, Detailed Statistical Tables, Appendixes C & D* (Washington: GPO), 1975, table C-1.

48 Current Fund Revenues of Private Institutions of Higher Education, Selected Years, 1965–66—1980–81

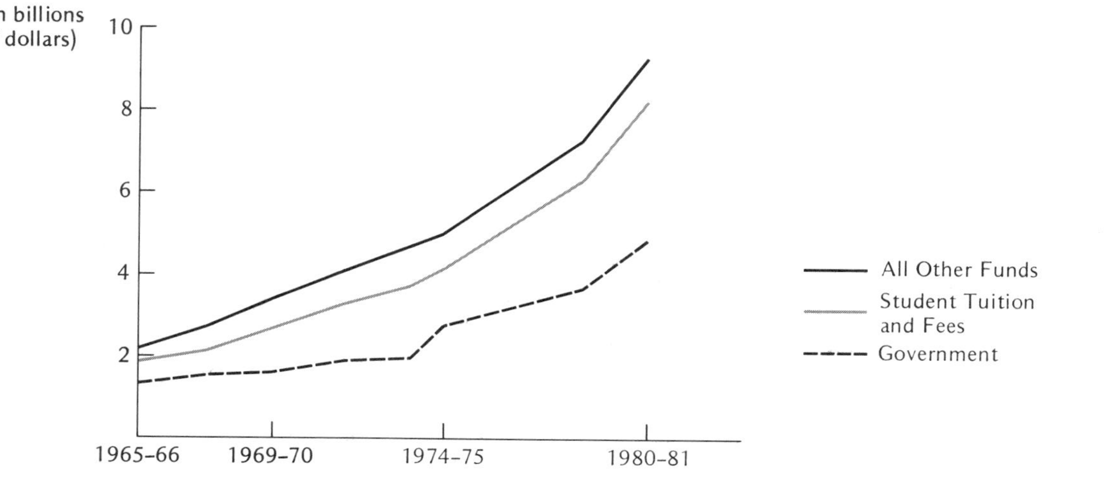

Kind of Revenues	Amount (in millions of dollars)				
	1965–66	1967–68	1969–70	1971–72	1973–74
Total Current Fund Revenues	**5,398.5**	**6,483.1**	**7,746.6**	**9,154.4**	**10,506.0**
Total Educational & General[a]	(4,292.9)	(5,200.5)	(6,000.0)	(7,121.6)	(8,133.0)
Student Tuition & Fees	1,825.1	2,175.3	2,684.8	3,261.6	3,765.4
Government[a]	(1,388.4)	(1,595.5)	(1,601.4)	(1,812.7)	(1,993.3)
Federal[a]	1,295.8	1,508.6	1,438.0	1,615.3	1,705.8
State	85.2	65.8	103.4	151.1	220.2
Local	7.4	21.1	60.0	46.3	67.3
Endowment Income	286.3	328.2	390.2	425.6	500.0
Private Gifts & Grants[b]	486.3	632.9	739.0	885.5	1,000.3
Other Educational & General	306.6	469.8	584.6	736.2	874.0
Auxiliary Enterprises	932.4	1,043.4	1,172.9	1,290.3	1,409.9
Student Aid Grants[c]	173.2	239.2	308.9	349.2	388.7
Other Current Revenues[d]	nr	nr	264.8	393.4	574.5

(Continued on next page)

For sources, see next page.

Note: Data are for 50 states and D. C. Because of rounding, details may not add to totals. Figures in parentheses are subtotals. Data for 1974–75 and later are *not* strictly comparable to previous data. A major change in reporting categories and definitions was incorporated into the 1974–75 questionnaire to make it coincide with new standards of college and university financial reporting set forth in publications of the National Association of College and University Business Officers, NCES, and the American Institute of Certified Public Accountants.

nr: Not reported.

a Includes data for Federally Funded Research and Development Centers (FFRDC's). Beginning 1969–70 some NCES reports have included FFRDC data in "other current income" or "independent operations." In this table, in order to increase comparability with earlier years, estimates of revenue for FFRDC's have been included in those categories in which they were reported previously.

b From 1967–68 through 1973–74, includes nongovernmental funds for "sponsored research" and "other sponsored programs."

c Includes federal, state, and local government and private grants specifically designated for student aid.

d From 1969–70 through 1973–74, includes data for hospitals in which service to the community was paramount.

49 Current Fund Revenues of Private Institutions of Higher Education, Selected Years, 1965–66—1980–81—*Continued*

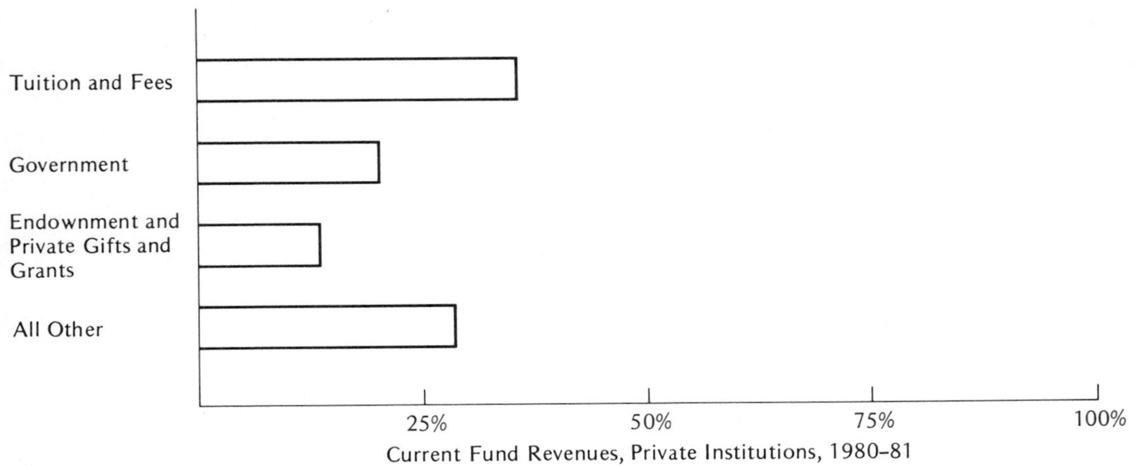

Current Fund Revenues, Private Institutions, 1980–81

Kind of Revenue	Amount (in millions of dollars)			Percent Distribution		
	1974–75	1978–79	1980–81	1974–75	1978–79	1980–81
Total Current Fund Revenues	**11,682.0**	**17,310.2**	**22,389.2**	**100.0**	**100.0**	**100.0**
Student Tuition and Fees	4,154.4	6,323.6	8,202.9	35.6	36.5	36.6
Government[b]	(2,622.9)	(3,769.5)	(4,805.5)	(22.5)	(21.8)	(21.5)
Federal[b]	2,286.4	3,312.2	4,207.5	19.6	19.1	18.8
State	248.9	345.7	430.3	2.1	2.0	1.9
Local	87.6	111.6	167.8	.7	.6	.7
Endowment Income	611.3	831.6	1,149.9	5.2	4.8	5.1
Private Gifts & Grants	1,188.3	1,653.5	2,076.6	10.2	9.6	9.3
Sales & Services of Educational Activities	182.0	338.4	466.0	1.6	2.0	2.1
Other	361.4	645.7	932.4	3.1	3.7	4.2
Auxiliary Enterprises	1,531.7	2,113.4	2,672.7	13.1	12.2	11.9
Sales & Services of Hospitals	1,029.9	1,634.7	2,083.2	8.8	9.4	9.3

For footnotes, see preceding page.

Sources:

1 NCES, *Financial Statistics of Institutions of Higher Education, Current Funds Revenues and Expenditures* (Washington, GPO), *1965–66,* p. 10; *1967–68,* p. 12; *1969–70,* pp. 14, 15; *1971–72,* pp. 16, 17; *1973–74,* p. 11; *Fiscal Year 1975,* p. 7; *Fiscal Year 1977,* p. 7; *Fiscal Year 1979,* p. 15.

2 NCES (Washington, 1983), unpublished data.

3 National Science Foundation (NSF), *Federal Support to Universities, Colleges, and Selected Nonprofit Institutions* (Washington: GPO), *Fiscal Year 1972,* p. 20; *Fiscal Year 1973,* p. 13; *Fiscal Year 1974,* p. 19.

4 NSF, *Federal Funds for Research, Development, and Other Scientific Activities, Fiscal Years 1974, 1975, and 1976, Detailed Statistical Tables, Apendixes C & D* (Washington: GPO), 1975, table C-1.

50 Current Fund Expenditures of Institutions of Higher Education, Selected Years, 1929–30—1980–81

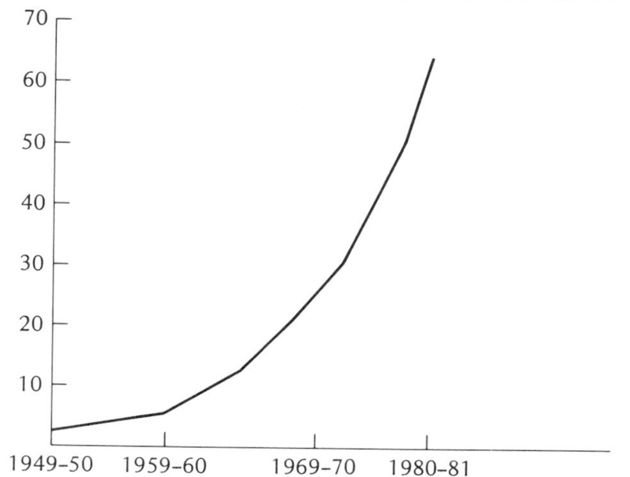

Kind of Expenditures	1929–30	1939–40	1949–50	1959–60	1965–66
	Amount (in millions of dollars)				
Total Current Fund Expenditures	**507.1**	**674.7**	**2,245.7**	**5,601.4**	**12,509.5**
Total Educational & General	(377.9)	(522.0)	(1,706.4)	(4,513.2)	(9,951.1)
Instruction & Depart'l Research	221.6	280.2	781.0	1,793.3	3,911.4[a]
Extension and Public Service	25.0	35.3	86.7	205.6	438.4
Libraries	9.7	19.5	56.1	135.4	346.2
Plant Operation & Maintenance	60.9	69.6	225.1	469.9	844.5
Sponsored Research	18.1	27.3	225.3	1,022.4	2,448.3
Related Activities	nr	27.2	119.1	294.3	558.2
Other Educational & General[b]	42.6	62.8	213.1	592.4	1,110.5
Auxiliary Enterprises	nr	124.2	476.4	916.1	1,887.7
Student Aid Expenditures	nr	nr	nr	172.1	425.5
Other Current Expenditures	129.2	28.5	62.8	nr	245.1[c]

Kind of Expenditures	1967–68	1969–70	1971–72	1973–74
Total Current Fund Expenditures	**16,480.8**	**21,043.1**	**25,559.6**	**30,713.6**
Total Educational & General[e]	(13,190.4)	(16,546.1)	(20,137.2)	(24,236.8)
Instruction & Depart'l Research[a]	5,653.5	7,653.1	9,503.3	11,574.1
Extension and Public Service	597.5	521.1	616.0	730.6
Libraries	493.3	652.6	764.5	939.0
Plant Operation & Maintenance	1,127.3	1,541.7	1,927.6	2,494.1
Sponsored Research[e]	2,699.0	2,901.5	3,201.9	3,459.8
Related Activities	640.7	648.1	779.7	838.2
Other Educational & General[b]	1,979.1	2,628.0	3,344.2	4,201.0
Auxiliary Enterprises	2,302.4	2,769.3	3,178.3	3,613.3
Student Aid Expenditures	712.4	984.6	1,241.4	1,396.5
Other Current Expenditures	275.5[c]	743.2[f]	1,002.8[f]	1,467.1[f]

(Continued on next page)

51 Current Fund Expenditures of Institutions of Higher Education, Selected Years, 1929–30—1980–81—*Continued*

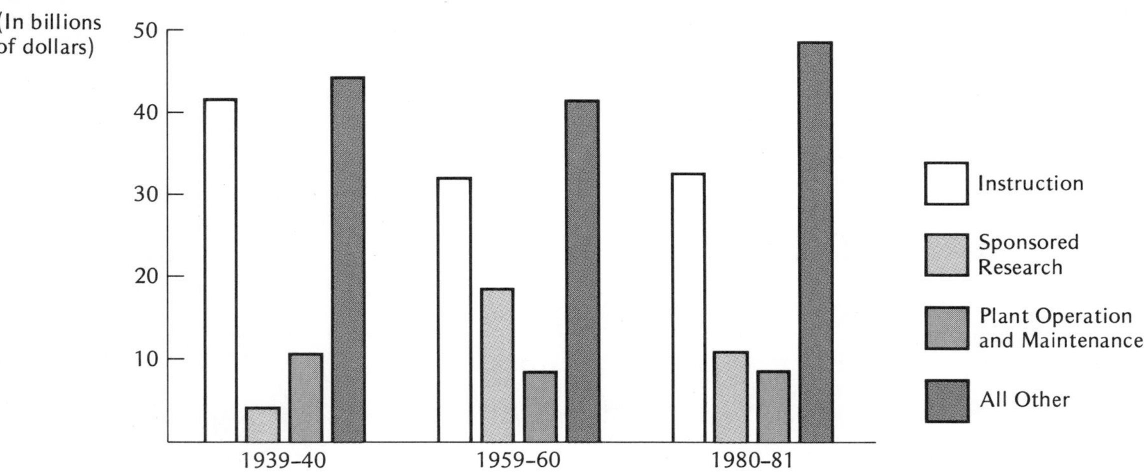

Kind of Expenditure	Amount (in millions of dollars) 1974–75	1978–79	1980–81	Percent Distribution 1974–75	1978–79	1980–81
Total Current Funds Expenditures and Mandatory Transfers	**35,057.6**	**50,721.0**	**64,052.9**	**100.0**	**100.0**	**100.0**
Educational & General Expenditures and Mandatory Transfers[d]	(27,183.7)	(38,895.7)	(48,827.2)	(77.5)	(76.7)	(76.2)
Instruction	11,797.8	16,662.8	20,733.2	33.6	32.9	32.4
Research[e]	4,217.7	5,454.9	6,915.6	12.0	10.8	10.8
Public Service	1,097.8	1,593.1	2,057.8	3.1	3.1	3.2
Academic Support	(2,255.7)	(3,471.0)	(4,273.2)	(6.4)	(6.8)	(6.7)
Libraries	1,001.9	1,426.6	1,759.8	2.9	2.8	2.7
Other Academic Support	1,253.8	2,044.4	2,513.5	3.6	4.0	3.9
Student Services	1,438.9	2,274.7	2,909.0	4.1	4.5	4.5
Institutional Support	3,056.5	4,557.3	5,772.5	8.7	9.0	9.0
Plant Operation and Maintenance	2,786.8	4,178.6	5,350.3	7.9	8.2	8.4
Ed. & Gen. Mandatory Transfers	532.5	703.3	815.5	1.5	1.4	1.3
Auxiliary Enterprises	4,073.6	5,750.0	7,288.1	11.6	11.3	11.4
Scholarships and Fellowships	1,449.5	1,944.6	2,504.5	4.1	3.8	3.9
Hospitals	2,350.8	4,130.8	5,433.1	6.7	8.1	8.5

Note: Data are for 50 states and D. C. Figures in parentheses are subtotals. Detail may not add to totals because of rounding. Data for 1974–75 and later are not strictly comparable to earlier figures. A major change in reporting categories and definitions was instituted with the 1974–75 questionnaire to make it coincide with new standards of college and university financial reporting set forth in publications of the National Association of College and University Business Officers, NCES, and the American Institute of Certified Public Accountants.

nr: Not reported.

a From 1965–66 through 1973–74, includes "other sponsored programs."

b Through 1973–74 includes "general administration" and "general expenditures."

c Current funds expended for physical plant not included elsewhere.

d Figures will not agree with some NCES reports that now include student aid expenditures in "education and general" expenditures and exclude FFRDC expenditures.

e Includes estimates of expenditures for Federally Funded Research and Development Centers (FFRDC's).

f Includes data for public service hospitals and other service programs that were shown prior to 1969–70 in "extension and public service" or "related activities."

Sources:

1 NCES, *Digest of Education Statistics, 1975 Edition* (Washington: GPO), 1976, p. 130; *1976 Edition,* p. 141.

2 NCES, *Financial Statistics of Institutions of Higher Education, Current Funds Revenues and Expenditures* (Washington: GPO), *1965–66,* pp. 40–53; *1967–68,* p. 80; *1969–70,* pp. 14, 15; *1971–72,* pp. 16, 17; *1973–74,* p. 10; *Fiscal Year 1975,* p. 6; *Fiscal Year 1979,* p. 14.

3 NCES (Washington, 1983), unpublished data.

4 NSF, *Federal Support of Universities, Colleges, and Selected Nonprofit Institutions* (Washington: GPO), *Fiscal Year 1972,* p. 20; *Fiscal Year 1973,* p. 13; *Fiscal Year 1974,* p. 19.

5 NSF, *Federal Funds for Research, Development, and Other Scientific Activities, Fiscal Years 1974, 1975, and 1976, Detailed Statistical Tables, Appendixes C & D* (Washington: GPO), 1975, table C-1.

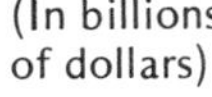

Current Fund Expenditures of Public Institutions of Higher Education, Selected Years, 1965–66—1980–81

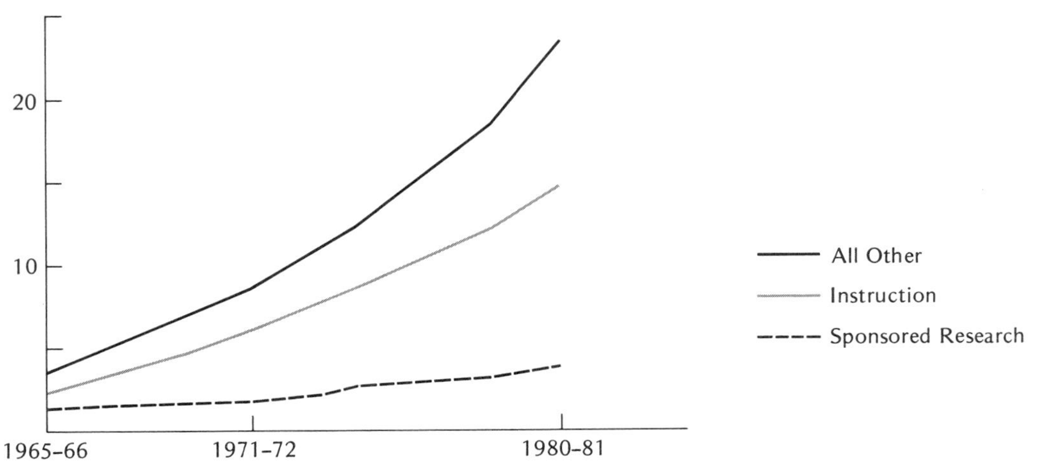

Kind of Expenditure	Amount (in millions of dollars) 1965–66	1967–68	1969–70	1971–72	1973–74
Total Current Fund Expenditures	**7,063.2**	**10,031.9**	**13,249.5**	**16,484.3**	**20,336.3**
Total Educational & General	(5,749.4)	(8,193.6)	(10,694.5)	(13,309.4)	(16,507.4)
Instruction & Depart'l Research[a]	2,355.9	3,435.4	4,731.6	5,978.4	7,374.1
Other Sponsored Programs	100.5	334.2	530.1	751.8	921.6
Extension & Public Service	392.5	488.0	476.1	559.6	662.3
Libraries	200.1	305.8	415.0	498.6	634.4
Plant Operation & Maintenance	498.2	698.8	1,000.1	1,284.1	1,717.1
Sponsored Research[e]	1,145.1	1,405.5	1,591.5	1,743.2	2,011.9
Related Activities	349.1	420.5	413.9	465.5	537.4
Other Educational & General[b]	717.0	1,105.4	1,536.2	2,028.2	2,648.5
Auxiliary Enterprises	1,041.7	1,337.2	1,624.4	1,912.1	2,207.9
Student Aid Expenditures	153.3	326.9	457.0	621.4	705.7
Other Current Expenditures	118.9[c]	174.1[c]	473.6[f]	641.3[f]	915.3[f]

(*Continued on next page*)

Note: Data are for 50 states and D. C. Figures in parentheses are subtotals. Details may not add to totals because of rounding. Data for 1974–75 and later are *not* strictly comparable to earlier figures. A major change in reporting categories and definitions was instituted with the 1974–75 questionnaire to make it coincide with new standards of college and university financial reporting set forth in publications of the National Association of College and University Business Officers, NCES, and the American Institute of Certified Public Accountants.

a From 1965–66 through 1973–74, includes "other sponsored programs."

b Through 1973–74 includes "general administration" and "general expenditures."

c Current funds expended for physical plant not included elsewhere.

d Figures will not agree with some NCES reports that now include student aid expenditures in "education and general" expenditures and exclude FFRDC expenditures.

e Includes estimates of expenditures for Federally Funded Research and Development Centers (FFRDC's).

f Includes data for public service hospitals and other service programs that were shown prior to 1969–70 in "extension and public service" or "related activities."

For sources, see next page.

53 Current Fund Expenditures of Public Institutions of Higher Education, Selected Years, 1965–66—1980–81—*Continued*

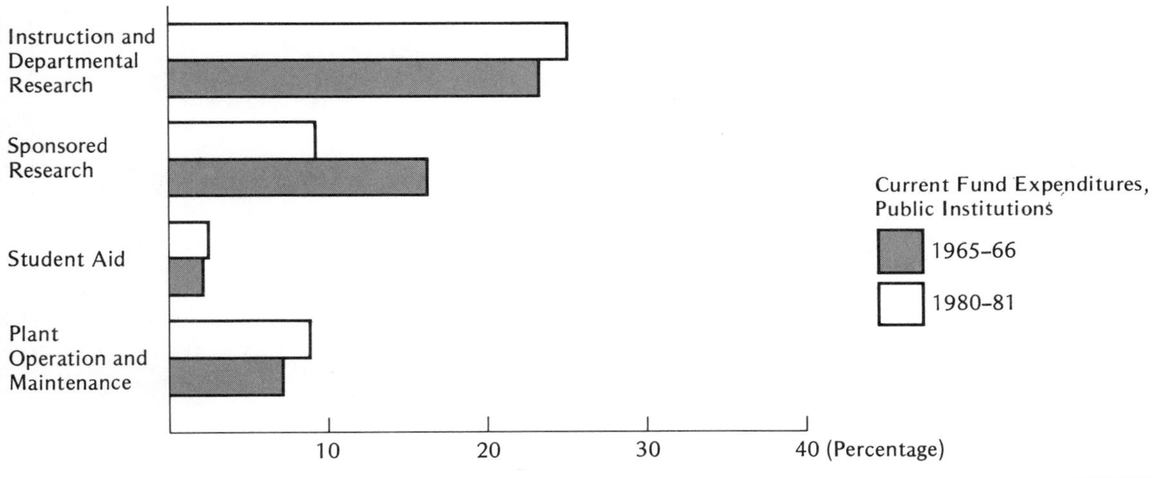

Kind of Expenditure	Amount (in millions of dollars) 1974–75	1978–79	1980–81	Percent Distribution 1974–75	1978–79	1980–81
Total Current Fund Expenditures and Mandatory Transfers	**23,490.0**	**33,732.9**	**42,279.8**	**100.0**	**100.0**	**100.0**
Educational & General Expenditures and Mandatory Transfers[d]	(18,865.5)	(26,691.3)	(33,178.8)	(80.3)	(79.1)	(78.5)
Instruction	8,573.7	12,065.3	14,849.8	36.5	35.8	35.1
Research[e]	2,534.2	3,005.9	3,884.1	10.8	8.9	9.2
Public Service	924.0	1,334.3	1,718.9	3.9	4.0	4.1
Academic Support	(1,611.6)	(2,498.9)	(3,029.3)	(6.9)	(7.4)	(7.2)
Libraries	679.9	953.0	1,187.1	2.9	2.8	2.8
Other Academic Support	931.7	1,545.9	1,842.2	4.0	4.6	4.4
Student Services	984.6	1,553.7	1.950.6	4.2	4.6	4.6
Institutional Support	1,916.6	2,845.8	3,563.2	8.2	8.4	8.4
Plant Operation and Maintenance	1,935.2	2,913.7	3,681.9	8.2	8.6	8.7
Ed. & Gen. Mandatory Transfers	385.6	473.7	501.1	1.6	1.4	1.2
Auxiliary Enterprises	2,536.5	3,657.9	4,658.1	10.8	10.8	11.0
Scholarships and Fellowships	718.8	861.6	1,064.9	3.1	2.6	2.5
Hospitals	1,369.0	2,522.2	3,378.0	5.8	7.6	8.0

For footnotes, see preceding page.

Sources:

1 NCES, *Digest of Education Statistics, 1975 Edition* (Washington: GPO), 1976, p. 130; *1976 Edition,* p. 141.

2 NCES, *Financial Statistics of Institutions of Higher Education, Current Funds Revenues and Expenditures* (Washington: GPO), *1965–66,* pp. 40–53; *1967–68,* p. 80; *1969–70,* pp. 14, 15; *1971–72,* pp. 16, 17; *1973–74,* p. 10; *Fiscal Year 1975,* p. 6; *Fiscal Year 1977,* p. 6; *Fiscal Year 1979,* p. 14.

3 NCES (Washington, 1983), unpublished data.

4 NSF, *Federal Support of Universities, Colleges, and Selected Nonprofit Institutions* (Washington: GPO), *Fiscal Year 1972,* p. 20; *Fiscal Year 1973,* p. 13; *Fiscal Year 1974,* p. 19.

5 NSF, *Federal Funds for Research, Development, and Other Scientific Activities, Fiscal Years 1974, 1975, and 1976, Detailed Statistical Tables, Appendixes C & D* (Washington: GPO), 1975, table C-1.

54 Current Fund Expenditures of Private Institutions of Higher Education, Selected Years, 1965–66—1980–81

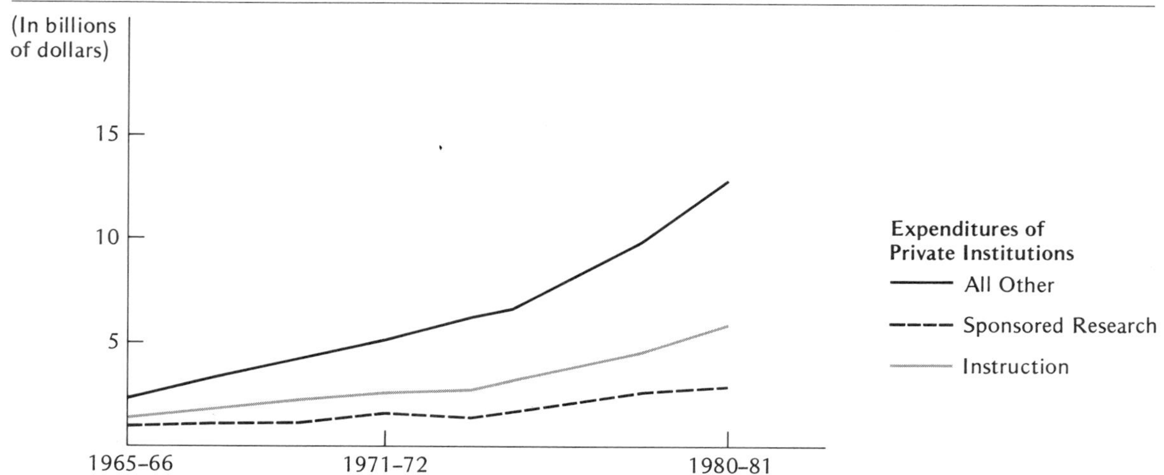

Kind of Expenditure	1965–66	1967–68	1969–70	1971–72	1973–74
	Amount (in millions of dollars)				
Total Current Fund Expenditures	**5,446.2**	**6,448.9**	**7,793.6**	**9,075.2**	**10,377.3**
Total Educational & General	(4,201.7)	(4,996.9)	(5,851.7)	(6,827.6)	(7,729.3)
Instruction & Depart'l Research[a]	1,400.2	1,703.8	2,152.2	2,464.8	2,845.0
Other Sponsored Programs	54.7	180.1	239.2	308.1	433.5
Extension & Public Service	45.9	109.6	45.1	56.3	68.3
Libraries	146.1	187.5	237.6	265.9	304.6
Plant Operation & Maintenance	355.3	428.5	541.6	643.5	776.9
Sponsored Research[e]	1,303.2	1,293.5	1,310.0	1,458.7	1,447.9
Related Activities	209.1	220.2	234.2	314.2	300.7
Other Educational & General[b]	687.1	873.7	1,091.8	1,316.0	1,552.4
Auxiliary Enterprises	846.1	965.2	1,144.9	1,266.1	1,405.4
Student Aid Expenditures	272.2	385.5	527.6	620.0	690.8
Other Current Expenditures	126.2[c]	101.4[c]	269.5[f]	361.5[f]	551.8[f]

(Continued on next page)

Note: Data are for 50 states and D. C. Figures in parentheses are subtotals. Details may not add to totals because of rounding. Data for 1974–75 and later are not strictly comparable to earlier figures. A major change in reporting categories and definitions was instituted with the 1974–75 questionnaire to make it coincide with new standards of college and university financial reporting set forth in publications of the National Association of College and University Business Officers, NCES, and the American Institute of Certified Public Accountants.

a From 1965–66 through 1973–74, includes "other sponsored programs."

b Through 1973–74 includes "general administration" and "general expenditures."

c Current funds expended for physical plant not included elsewhere.

d Figures will not agree with some NCES reports that now include student aid expenditures in "education and general" expenditures and exclude FFRDC expenditures.

e Includes estimates of expenditures for Federally Funded Research and Development Centers (FFRDC's).

f Includes data for public service hospitals and other service programs that were shown prior to 1969–70 in "extension and public service" or "related activities."

For sources, see next page.

55 Current Fund Expenditures of Private Institutions of Higher Education, Selected Years, 1965–66—1980–81—*Continued*

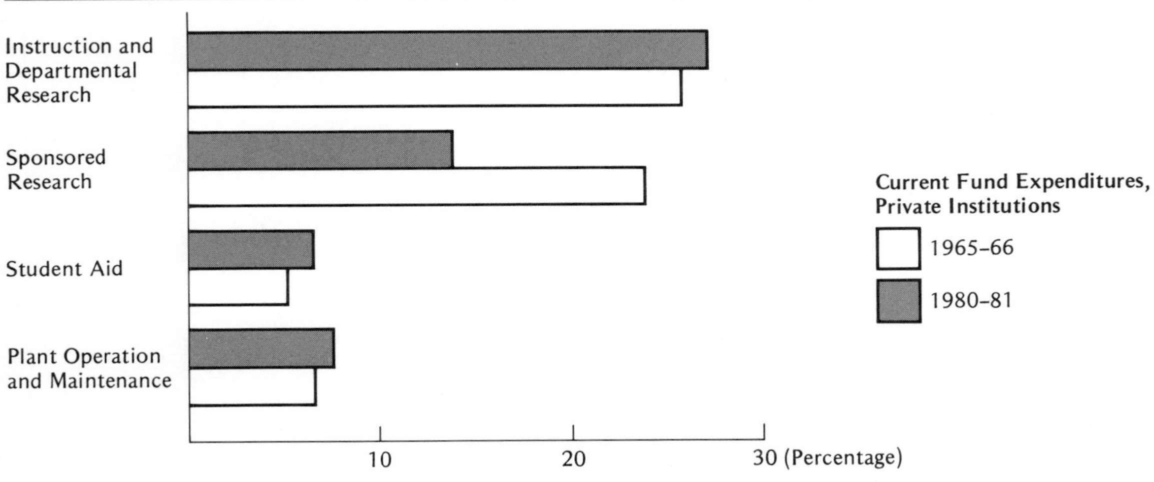

Kind of Expenditure	Amount (in millions of dollars) 1974–75	1978–79	1980–81	Percent Distribution 1974–75	1978–79	1980–81
Total Current Fund Experiments and Mandatory Transfers	**11,567.6**	**16,988.1**	**21,773.1**	**100.0**	**100.0**	**100.0**
Educational & General Expenditures and Mandatory Transfers[d]	(8,318.0)	(12,204.5)	(15,883.3)	(71.9)	(71.8)	(71.9)
Instruction	3,224.2	4,597.5	5,883.3	27.9	27.1	27.0
Research[e]	1,683.5	2,449.0	3,031.7	14.6	14.4	13.9
Public Service	173.8	258.8	338.8	1.5	1.5	1.6
Academic Support	(644.1)	(972.2)	(1,244.0)	(5.6)	(5.7)	(5.7)
Libraries	322.0	473.7	572.7	2.8	2.8	2.6
Other Academic Support	322.2	498.5	671.3	2.8	2.9	3.1
Student Services	454.2	721.0	958.4	3.9	4.2	4.4
Institutional Support	1,139.9	1,711.5	2,209.3	9.9	10.1	10.1
Plant Operation and Maintenance	851.5	1,264.9	1,668.4	7.4	7.4	7.7
Ed. & Gen. Mandatory Transfers	146.8	229.6	314.4	1.3	1.4	1.4
Auxiliary Enterprises	1,537.0	2,092.1	2,629.9	13.3	12.3	12.1
Scholarships and Fellowships	730.8	1,083.0	1,439.7	6.3	6.4	6.6
Hospitals	981.8	1,608.6	2,055.1	8.5	9.5	9.4

For footnotes, see preceding page.

Sources:

1 NCES, *Digest of Education Statistics, 1975 Edition* (Washington: GPO), 1976, p. 130; *1976 Edition,* p. 141.

2 NCES, *Financial Statistics of Institutions of Higher Education, Current Funds Revenues and Expenditures* (Washington: GPO), *1965–66,* pp. 40–53; *1967–68,* p. 80; *1969–70,* pp. 14, 15; *1971–72,* pp. 16, 17; *1973–74,* p. 11; *Fiscal Year 1975,* p. 7; *Fiscal Year 1977,* p. 7; *Fiscal Year 1979,* p. 15.

3 NCES (Washington, 1983), unpublished data.

4 NSF, *Federal Support of Universities, Colleges, and Selected Nonprofit Institutions* (Washington: GPO), *Fiscal Year 1972,* p. 20; *Fiscal Year 1973,* p. 13; *Fiscal Year 1974,* p. 19.

5 NSF, *Federal Funds for Research, Development, and Other Scientific Activities, Fiscal Years 1974, 1975, and 1976, Detailed Statistical Tables, Appendixes C & D* (Washington: GPO), 1975, table C-1.

56 Enrollment in All Levels of Education, Selected Years, 1960–1985

Students
(in millions)

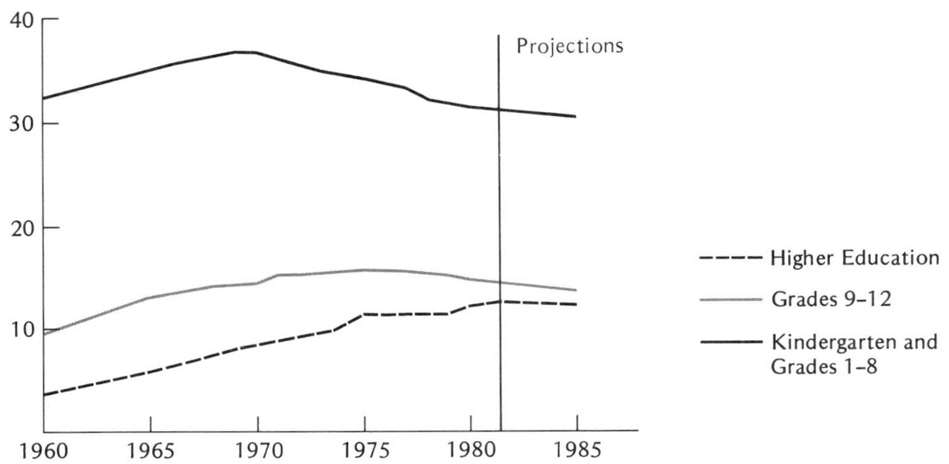

Year	Total	Elementary and Secondary Enrollment[a] (in thousands)			Higher Education Enrollment
		All Grades	Kindergarten & Grades 1–8	Grades 9–12	
1960	**45,970**	42,181	32,492	1,689	3,789
1965	**54,394**	48,473	35,463	13,010	5,921
1966	**55,629**	49,239	35,945	13,294	6,390
1967	**56,803**	49,891	36,241	13,650	6,912
1968	**58,257**	50,744	36,626	14,118	7,513
1969	**59,213**	51,119	36,797	14,322	8,094
1970	**58,890**	51,309	36,677	14,632	8,581
1971	**60,130**	51,181	36,065	15,116	8,949
1972	**59,959**	50,744	35,531	15,213	9,215
1973	**59,931**	50,329	34,953	15,377	9,602
1974	**60,277**	50,053	34,521	15,532	10,224
1975	**60,976**	49,791	34,187	15,604	11,185
1976	**60,496**	49,484	33,831	15,653	11,012
1977	**60,000**	48,716	33,133	15,583	11,284
1978	**58,895**	47,636	32,060	15,576	11,259
1979	**58,249**	46,679	31,585	15,094	11,570
1980	**58,192**	46,095	31,378	14,717	12,097
			Projections[b]		
1981	**57,631**	45,189	30,956	14,233	12,442
1985	**56,340**	44,166	30,551	13,615	12,174

a Enrollment in "regular" schools, public and private. Excludes independent nursery schools and kindergartens, residential schools for exceptional children, subcollegiate departments of institutions of higher education, federal schools for Indians, and other schools not in the regular school system. Data are for the fifty states and D. C.

b Intermediate alternative projections series. Projections are based largely on the assumptions that the enrollment rate of the six-year-old population in public schools will remain constant at the 1976 level and that retention rates in all other public school grades will remain constant at the average rate for the last five years. Estimates of the six-year-old population are consistent with the Census Bureau's Series II projections. Higher education data have been adjusted downward from published NCES figures.

Source: NCES, *Projections of Education Statistics* (Washington: GPO), 1971 edition, table 5; 1977 edition, tables 3, 5; 1980 edition, table 2; 1982 edition, table 4.

57 Enrollment, by Level of Study, Selected Years, 1899–1900—1990

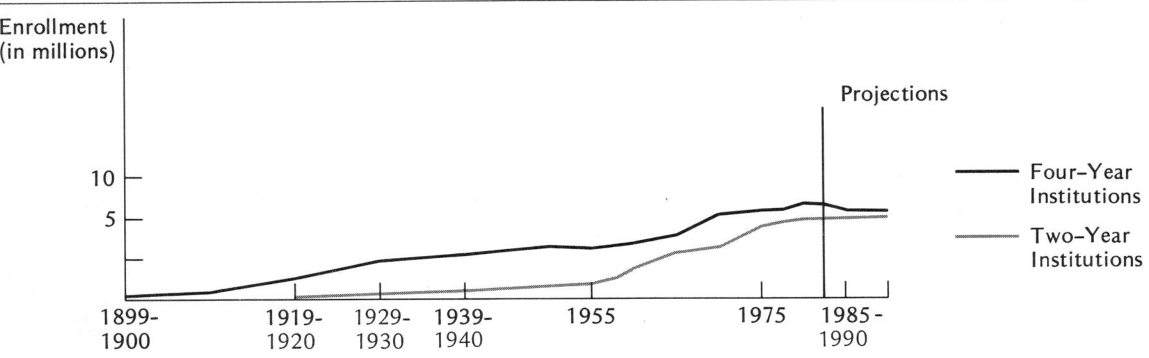

Year	Total	Undergraduate and First Professional: Total	Four-Year Institutions[b]	Two-Year Institutions[c]	Graduate
	Enrollment[a]				
1899–1900	**237,600**	231,800	231,800	—	5,800
1909–10	**355,200**	346,100	346,100	—	9,200
1919–20	**597,900**	582,300	547,200	8,100	15,600
1929–30	**1,100,000**	1,053,500	997,900	55,600	47,300
1939–40	**1,494,200**	1,388,500	1,238,500	150,000	105,700
1949–50	**2,659,000**	2,421,800	2,177,700	244,100	237,200
November 1955	**2,597,700**	2,347,700	2,051,700	296,000	250,000
1960	**3,582,700**	3,226,700	2,775,400	451,300	356,000
1965	**5,526,300**	4,829,300	3,987,900	841,400	697,000
1970[d]	**7,920,100**	6,889,200	5,259,200	1,630,000	1,031,000
1970[e]	**8,581,000**	7,550,000	5,327,000	2,223,000	1,031,000
1975	**11,185,000**	9,922,000	5,952,000	3,970,000	1,263,000
1976	**11,012,000**	9,679,000	5,796,000	3,883,000	1,333,000
1977	**11,286,000**	9,968,000	5,926,000	4,042,000	1,318,000
1978	**11,259,000**	9,947,000	5,919,000	4,028,000	1,319,000
1979	**11,570,000**	10,261,000	6,044,000	4,219,000	1,309,000
1980	**12,097,000**	10,754,000	6,228,000	4,526,000	1,343,000
			Projections		
1981	**12,442,000**	11,034,000	6,299,000	4,735,000	1,408,000
1982	**12,620,000**	11,189,000	6,358,000	4,831,000	1,431,000
1985	**12,174,000**	10,705,000	5,873,000	4,832,000	1,469,000
1990	**12,101,000**	10,664,000	5,664,000	5,000,000	1,437,000

a Data through 1970[d] are degree-credit enrollments; for 1970[e] and later, degree-credit and non-degree-credit. Data for 1899–1900 through November 1955 are for the contiguous states; for fall 1960 and later, for fifty states and D. C. Beginning with 1972 enrollment data are distributed between two- and four-year institutions so that enrollments at two-year branches of four-year institutions are counted with other two-year institutions instead of in the parent institution's category.

b Undergraduate enrollment for four-year institutions has been estimated by subtracting two-year institutions from total estimated undergraduate enrollment.

c For November 1955 and earlier, data are for "junior colleges."

d Degree-credit enrollment. Data below this line of the table show total (degree-credit and non-degree-credit) enrollment.

e Data on this line and those below show total (degree-credit and non-degree-credit) enrollment.

Sources:

1 USOE, Statistics of Higher Education, 1957–58, *Faculty, Students, and Degrees,* chap. 4, sec. 1, Biennial Survey of Education (Washington: GPO), 1962, pp. 7, 11.

2 NCES, *Projections of Education Statistics* (Washington: GPO), 1971 edition, pp. 24, 26, 31; 1974 edition, pp. 23, 26, 31; 1977 edition, pp. 20, 22, 24, 28; 1980 edition, tables 7B, 8, 10; 1982 edition, tables 9B, 10, 12.

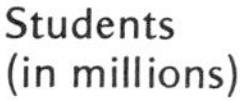

Opening Fall Enrollment of All Students in All Institutions, by Sex, Selected Years, 1950–1982

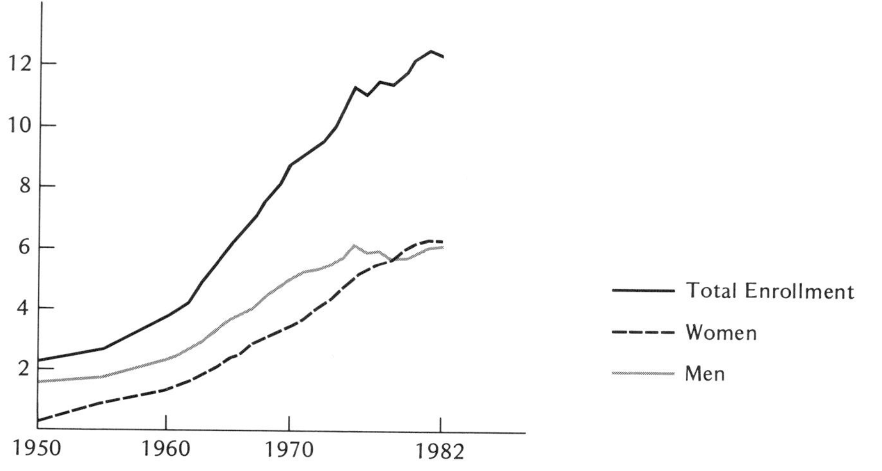

Opening Fall Enrollment in All Institutions in the U. S. & Outlaying Parts[a]

	Number			Percent Distribution		Indexes (1965 = 100)		
Year	**Total**	**Men**	**Women**	**Men**	**Women**	**Total**	**Men**	**Women**
1950	**2,296,592**	1,569,322	727,270	68	32	**38**	43	31
1955	**2,678,623**	1,747,429	931,194	65	35	**45**	48	40
1960	**3,610,007**	2,270,640	1,339,367	63	37	**60**	62	58
1961	**3,891,230**	2,423,987	1,467,243	62	38	**65**	66	63
1962	**4,206,672**	2,603,072	1,603,600	62	38	**70**	71	69
1963	**4,800,332**	2,972,344	1,827,988	62	38	**80**	81	79
1964	**5,320,294**	3,268,188	2,052,106	61	39	**89**	89	89
1965	**5,967,411**	3,652,675	2,314,736	61	39	**100**	100	100
1966	**6,438,477**	3,880,557	2,557,920	60	40	**108**	106	111
1967	**6,963,687**	4,158,557	2,805,130	60	40	**117**	114	121
1968	**7,571,636**	4,505,833	3,065,803	60	40	**127**	123	132
1969	**8,066,233**	4,775,622	3,290,611	59	41	**135**	131	142
1970	**8,649,368**	5,076,023	3,573,345	59	41	**145**	139	154
1971	**9,025,031**	5,242,740	3,782,291	58	42	**151**	144	163
1972	**9,297,787**	5,275,902	4,021,885	57	43	**156**	144	174
1973	**9,694,297**	5,414,164	4,280,133	56	44	**162**	148	185
1974	**10,321,539**	5,667,053	4,654,486	55	45	**173**	155	201
1975	**11,290,719**	6,198,623	5,092,096	55	45	**189**	170	220
1976	**11,121,426**	5,860,215	5,261,211	53	47	**186**	160	227
1977	**11,415,020**	5,846,098	5,568,922	51	49	**191**	160	241
1978	**11,391,950**	5,697,834	5,694,116	50	50	**191**	156	246
1979	**11,707,126**	5,740,551	5,966,575	49	51	**196**	157	258
1980	**12,096,895**	5,874,374	6,222,521	49	51	**203**	161	269
1981	**12,371,672**	5,975,056	6,396,616	48	52	**207**	164	276
1982[p]	**12,358,216**	5,984,211	6,374,005	48	52	**207**	164	275

a Data are for the fifty states, D. C., Canal Zone, Guam, Puerto Rico, the Virgin Islands, and Trust Territories of the Pacific. Data prior to 1963 show enrollment of degree-credit students only. Figures for all other years are for degree-credit *and* non-degree-credit students. Beginning in 1976, NCES has gathered data on total enrollments only, making no differentiation between degree-credit and non-degree-credit students.

p Preliminary.

For sources, see next page.

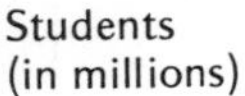

Opening Fall Enrollment of All Students in All Institutions, by Control of Institution, Selected Years, 1950–1982

Opening Fall Enrollment in All Institutions in the U. S. & Outlying Parts[a]

Year	Number			Percent Distribution		Indexes (1965 = 100)		
	Total	Public	Private	Public	Private	Total	Public	Private
1950	**2,296,592**	1,154,456	1,142,136	50	50	**38**	29	58
1955	**2,678,623**	1,498,510	1,180,113	56	44	**45**	37	60
1960	**3,610,007**	2,135,690	1,474,317	59	41	**60**	53	75
1961	**3,891,230**	2,351,719	1,539,511	60	40	**65**	59	78
1962	**4,206,672**	2,596,904	1,609,768	62	38	**70**	65	82
1963	**4,800,332**	3,090,578	1,709,754	64	36	**80**	77	87
1964	**5,320,294**	3,494,489	1,825,805	66	34	**89**	87	93
1965	**5,967,411**	3,999,940	1,967,471	67	33	**100**	100	100
1966	**6,438,477**	4,381,086	2,057,391	68	32	**108**	110	105
1967	**6,963,687**	4,850,330	2,113,357	70	30	**117**	121	107
1968	**7,571,636**	5,469,472	2,102,164	72	28	**127**	137	107
1969	**8,066,233**	5,939,513	2,126,720	74	26	**135**	148	108
1970	**8,649,368**	6,476,058	2,173,310	75	25	**145**	162	110
1971	**9,025,031**	6,854,685	2,170,346	76	24	**151**	171	110
1972	**9,297,787**	7,122,875	2,174,912	77	23	**156**	178	111
1973	**9,694,297**	7,478,407	2,215,890	77	23	**162**	187	113
1974	**10,321,539**	8,049,595	2,271,944	78	22	**173**	201	115
1975	**11,290,719**	8,896,021	2,394,698	79	21	**189**	222	122
1976	**11,121,426**	8,712,634	2,408,792	78	22	**186**	218	122
1977	**11,415,020**	8,907,591	2,507,429	78	22	**191**	223	127
1978	**11,391,950**	8,843,201	2,548,749	78	22	**191**	221	130
1979	**11,707,126**	9,096,404	2,610,722	78	22	**196**	227	133
1980	**12,096,895**	9,457,394	2,639,501	78	22	**203**	236	134
1981	**12,371,672**	9,647,032	2,724,640	78	22	**207**	241	138
1982[p]	**12,358,216**	9,674,538	2,683,678	78	22	**207**	242	136

For footnotes, see preceding page.

Sources:

1 *Opening (Fall) Enrollment in Higher Education, 1960: Analytic Report* (Washington: GPO), 1961, p. 10.

2 USOE, *Opening (Fall) Enrollment in Higher Education, 1962: Institutional Data* (Washington: GPO), 1962, p. 3.

3 NCES, *Fall Enrollment in Higher Education* (Washington: GPO), *1971,* p. 13; *1977,* p. 27; *1979,* pp. 12, 13.

4 NCES, "Fall Enrollment in Colleges and Universities, 1981, Preliminary Estimates," *NCES Early Release,* November 30, 1981, tables A and B; January 1983, tables A and B.

Opening Fall Enrollment of All Students in All Institutions, by Region and State, Selected Years, 1965–1981

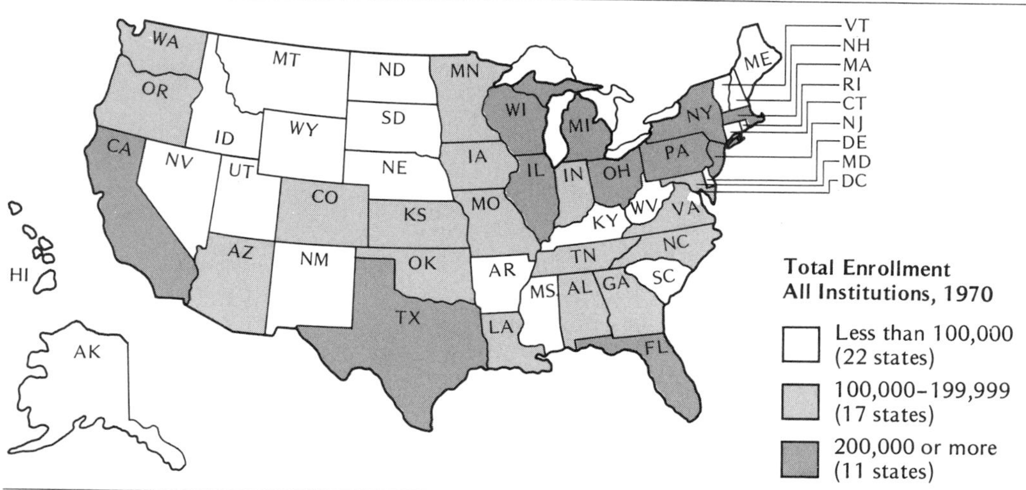

Region and State	Opening Fall Enrollment of All Students[a] in All Institutions				
	1965	1970	1975	1980	1981
U.S. & Outlying Parts	**5,967,411**	**8,649,368**	**11,290,719**	**12,234,644**	**12,517,753**
50 States & D. C.	**5,920,411**	**8,580,887**	**11,184,859**	**12,096,895**	**12,371,672**
New England	**386,574**	**560,150**	**708,023**	**765,602**	**771,645**
Connecticut	84,048	124,700	148,491	159,632	162,367
Maine	22,999	34,134	40,443	43,264	44,012
Massachusetts	211,251	303,809	384,485	418,415	417,830
New Hampshire	20,480	29,400	41,030	46,794	48,524
Rhode Island	33,741	45,898	64,479	66,869	68,339
Vermont	14,055	22,209	29,095	30,628	30,573
Mideast	**1,176,323**	**1,685,669**	**2,094,862**	**2,166,703**	**2,206,089**
Delaware	13,167	25,260	32,389	32,939	32,061
D. C.	60,865	77,158	84,190	86,675	88,553
Maryland	98,594	149,607	205,570	225,526	229,936
New Jersey	129,684	216,121	297,114	321,610	322,797
New York	586,462	806,479	1,005,063	992,237	1,014,863
Pennsylvania	287,551	411,044	470,536	507,716	517,879
Southeast	**949,405**	**1,402,911**	**2,016,061**	**2,230,522**	**2,281,883**
Alabama	67,151	103,936	164,700	164,306	166,375
Arkansas	43,026	52,039	65,547	77,607	76,032
Florida	141,591	235,525	344,267	411,891	426,570
Georgia	82,347	126,511	173,585	184,159	191,384
Kentucky	76,440	98,591	125,253	143,066	144,154
Louisiana	89,050	120,728	153,213	160,058	174,656
Mississippi	55,790	73,967	99,962	102,364	105,974
North Carolina	110,977	171,925	251,786	287,537	295,771
South Carolina	43,946	69,518	133,023	132,476	132,394
Tennessee	99,989	135,103	181,435	204,581	200,183
Virginia	91,696	151,915	244,671	280,504	286,015
West Virginia	47,402	63,153	78,619	81,973	82,375
Great Lakes	**1,125,951**	**1,615,865**	**1,971,067**	**2,169,860**	**2,221,203**
Illinois	305,107	452,146	584,089	644,245	659,623
Indiana	142,113	192,668	213,820	247,253	251,826
Michigan	270,918	392,726	496,405	520,131	513,033
Ohio	278,506	376,267	436,052	489,145	521,396
Wisconsin	129,307	202,058	240,701	269,086	275,325

(Continued on next page)

a Degree-credit and non-degree-credit combined.

61 Opening Fall Enrollment of All Students in All Institutions, by Region and State, Selected Years, 1965–1981—*Continued*

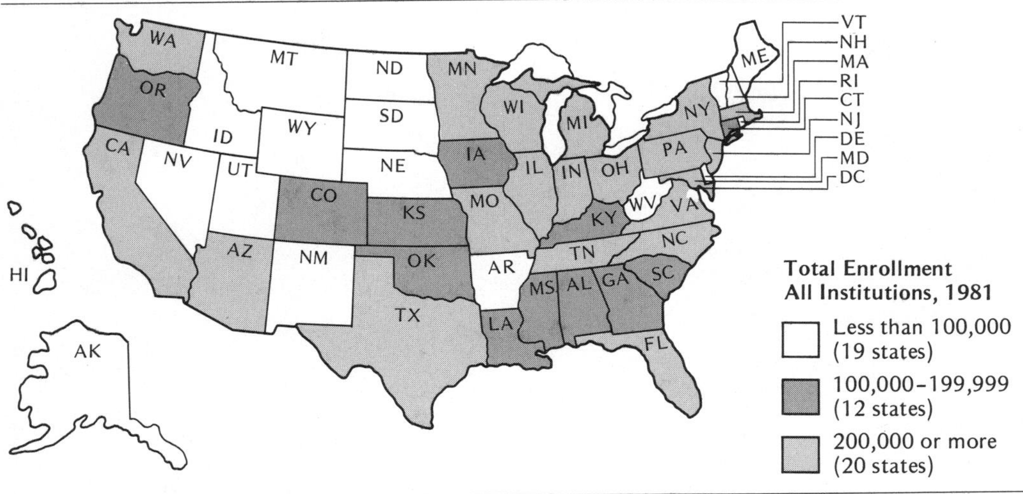

Region and State	Opening Fall Enrollment of All Students[a] in All Institutions				
	1965	1970	1975	1980	1981
Plains	**517,875**	**685,154**	**785,090**	**874,484**	**899,911**
Iowa	86,588	108,902	121,678	140,449	143,105
Kansas	81,574	102,485	120,833	136,605	138,453
Minnesota	118,533	160,788	184,756	206,691	210,713
Missouri	135,652	183,930	223,115	234,421	243,672
Nebraska	49,805	66,915	74,705	89,488	93,507
North Dakota	22,470	31,495	29,743	34,069	35,446
South Dakota	23,253	30,639	30,260	32,761	35,015
Southwest	**486,746**	**706,460**	**996,489**	**1,122,685**	**1,144,704**
Arizona	72,503	109,619	173,542	202,716	205,169
New Mexico	30,388	44,461	51,944	58,283	60,413
Oklahoma	89,326	110,155	146,613	160,295	162,825
Texas	294,529	442,225	624,390	701,391	716,297
Rocky Mountains	**184,419**	**284,931**	**325,133**	**356,245**	**364,977**
Colorado	74,285	123,395	149,814	162,916	167,977
Idaho	20,788	34,567	39,075	43,018	42,758
Montana	20,308	30,062	30,843	35,177	35,959
Utah	58,323	81,687	87,323	93,987	97,048
Wyoming	10,715	15,220	18,078	21,147	21,235
Far West	**1,079,946**	**1,622,668**	**2,251,237**	**2,360,986**	**2,427,172**
Alaska	4,734	9,471	13,998	21,296	24,754
California	866,746	1,257,245	1,787,932	1,790,993	1,885,757
Hawaii	19,247	36,562	46,671	47,181	48,121
Nevada	8,039	13,669	30,187	40,455	39,936
Oregon	71,601	122,177	145,281	157,458	149,924
Washington	109,579	183,544	227,168	303,603	278,680
U. S. Service Schools	**13,625**	**17,079**	**36,897**	**49,808**	**54,088**
Outlying Parts	**46,547**	**68,481**	**105,860**	**137,749**	**146,081**

For footnotes, see preceding page.

Sources:

1 USOE, *Opening Fall Enrollment in Higher Education, 1965* (Washington: GPO), 1966, p. 10.

2 NCES, *Fall Enrollment in Higher Education, 1970 Supplementary Information, Summary Data* (Washington: GPO), 1971, p. 16.

3 NCES, *Fall Enrollment in Higher Education, 1975, Summary Report* (Washington: GPO), 1977, p. 32.

4 NCES, "1978 Fall Enrollment in Higher Education—Final Count," *NCES Announcement,* July 5, 1979, tables 1, 5.

5 NCES, "Fall Enrollment in Higher Education, 1979" (Washington: GPO), 1980, table 9.

6 NCES, "Fall Enrollment in Higher Education," 1981 prepublication data.

62 Percent Change in Opening Fall Enrollment of All Students, by Region and State, Selected Years, 1965–1981

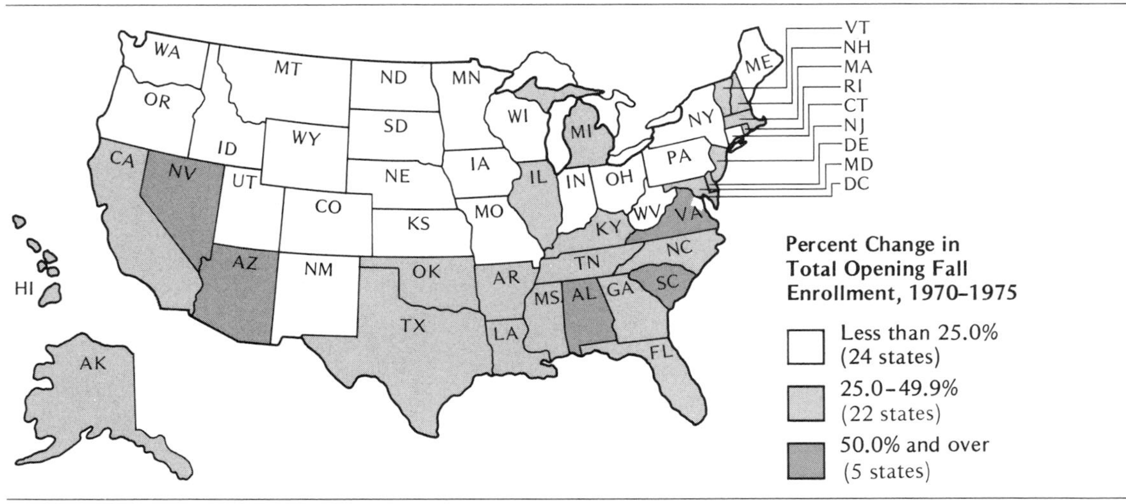

Region and State	Percent Change in Opening Fall Enrollment of All Students at All Institutions 1965–70	1970–75	1975–81	1980–81
U. S. & Outlying Parts	**44.9**	**30.5**	**8.4**	**2.3**
50 States & D. C.	**44.9**	**30.3**	**8.2**	**2.3**
New England	**44.9**	**26.4**	**8.1**	**0.8**
Connecticut	48.4	19.1	7.5	1.7
Maine	48.4	18.5	7.0	1.7
Massachusetts	43.8	26.6	8.8	−0.1
New Hampshire	43.6	39.6	14.1	3.7
Rhode Island	36.0	40.5	3.7	2.2
Vermont	58.0	31.0	5.3	−0.2
Mideast	**43.3**	**24.3**	**3.4**	**1.8**
Delaware	91.8	28.2	1.7	−2.7
D. C.	26.8	9.1	3.0	2.2
Maryland	51.7	37.4	9.7	2.0
New Jersey	66.7	37.5	8.2	0.4
New York	37.5	24.6	−1.3	2.3
Pennsylvania	42.9	14.5	7.9	2.0
Southeast	**47.8**	**43.7**	**10.6**	**2.3**
Alabama	54.8	58.5	−0.2	1.3
Arkansas	20.9	26.0	18.4	−2.0
Florida	66.3	46.2	19.6	3.6
Georgia	53.6	37.2	6.1	3.9
Kentucky	29.0	27.0	14.2	0.8
Louisiana	35.6	26.9	4.5	9.1
Mississippi	32.6	35.1	2.4	3.5
North Carolina	54.9	46.5	14.2	2.9
South Carolina	58.2	91.4	−0.4	−0.1
Tennessee	35.1	34.3	12.8	−2.1
Virginia	65.7	61.1	14.7	2.0
West Virginia	33.2	24.5	4.3	0.5
Great Lakes	**43.5**	**22.0**	**10.1**	**2.4**
Illinois	48.2	29.2	10.3	2.4
Indiana	35.6	11.0	15.6	1.8
Michigan	45.0	26.4	4.8	−1.4
Ohio	35.1	15.9	12.2	6.6
Wisconsin	56.3	19.1	11.8	2.3

(Continued on next page)

63 Percent Change in Opening Fall Enrollment of All Students, by Region and State, Selected Years, 1965–1981—*Continued*

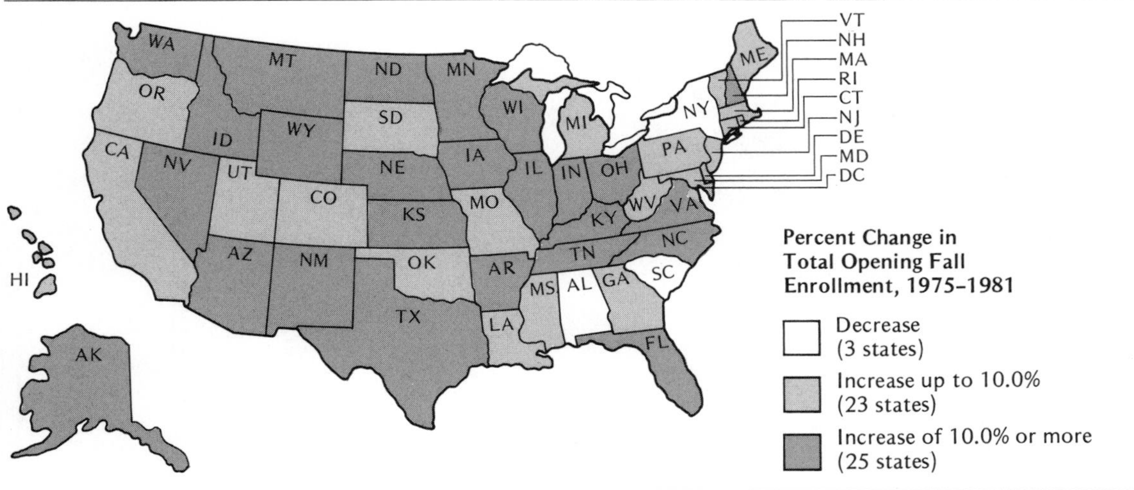

Region and State	Percent Change in Opening Fall Enrollment of All Students at All Institutions 1965–70	1970–75	1975–81	1980–81
Plains	**32.3**	**14.6**	**11.4**	**2.9**
Iowa	25.8	11.7	15.4	1.9
Kansas	25.6	17.9	13.1	1.4
Minnesota	35.6	14.9	11.9	2.0
Missouri	35.6	21.3	5.1	4.0
Nebraska	34.4	11.6	19.8	4.5
North Dakota	40.2	−5.6	14.5	4.0
South Dakota	31.8	−1.2	8.3	6.9
Southwest	**45.1**	**41.1**	**12.7**	**2.0**
Arizona	51.2	58.3	16.8	1.2
New Mexico	46.3	16.8	12.2	3.7
Oklahoma	23.3	33.1	9.3	1.6
Texas	50.1	41.2	12.3	2.1
Rocky Mountains	**54.5**	**14.1**	**9.6**	**2.5**
Colorado	66.1	21.4	8.7	3.1
Idaho	66.3	13.0	10.1	−0.6
Montana	48.0	2.6	14.1	2.2
Utah	40.1	6.9	7.6	3.3
Wyoming	42.0	18.8	17.0	0.4
Far West	**50.3**	**38.7**	**4.9**	**2.8**
Alaska	100.1	47.8	52.1	16.2
California	45.1	42.2	0.2	5.3
Hawaii	90.0	27.6	1.1	2.0
Nevada	70.0	120.8	34.0	−1.3
Oregon	70.6	18.9	8.4	−4.8
Washington	67.5	23.8	33.6	−8.2
U. S. Service Schools	**25.4**	**116.0**	**35.0**	**8.6**
Outlying Parts	**47.1**	**54.6**	**30.1**	**6.1**

Source: Calculated from data on the preceding pages.

64 Total Enrollment, by Control of Institution and by Region and State, 1967 and 1981

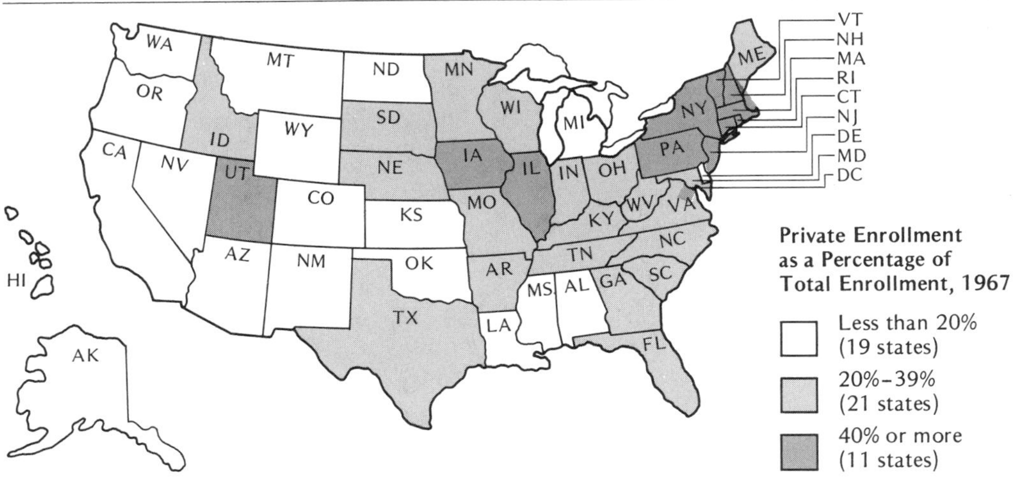

Region and State	Public Enrollment	1967 Private Enrollment: Number	1967 Private Enrollment: As Percentage of Total Enrollment	Public Enrollment	1981 Private Enrollment: Number	1981 Private Enrollment: As Percentage of Total Enrollment
U. S. & Outlying Parts	**4,850,330**	**2,113,357**	**30**	**9,709,219**	**2,808,534**	**22**
50 States & D. C.	**4,816,028**	**2,095,720**	**30**	**9,647,032**	**2,724,640**	**22**
New England	**183,060**	**270,002**	**60**	**389,435**	**382,210**	**50**
Connecticut	48,615	47,181	49	99,578	62,789	39
Maine	17,299	8,220	32	32,375	11,637	26
Massachusetts	75,903	176,735	70	178,383	239,447	57
New Hampshire	13,810	11,983	46	25,531	22,993	47
Rhode Island	19,521	17,388	47	35,308	33,031	48
Vermont	7,912	8,495	52	18,260	12,313	40
Mideast	**662,705**	**710,775**	**52**	**1,354,093**	**851,996**	**39**
Delaware	12,781	2,392	16	28,151	3,910	12
D. C.	2,371	62,733	96	14,115	74,438	84
Maryland	82,547	32,963	29	197,492	32,444	14
New Jersey	90,421	62,127	41	248,482	74,315	23
New York	326,961	350,290	52	572,443	442,420	44
Pennsylvania	147,624	200,270	58	293,410	224,469	43
Southeast	**854,765**	**289,329**	**25**	**1,883,474**	**398,409**	**18**
Alabama	71,348	17,227	19	145,166	21,209	13
Arkansas	37,221	11,284	23	64,567	11,465	15
Florida	138,506	41,341	23	345,503	81,067	19
Georgia	74,231	24,245	25	146,271	45,113	24
Kentucky	66,086	24,125	27	115,508	28,646	20
Louisiana	84,807	19,364	19	150,773	23,883	14
Mississippi	56,732	7,984	12	94,995	10,979	10
North Carolina	87,372	47,607	35	236,349	59,422	20
South Carolina	32,402	19,410	37	108,952	23,442	18
Tennessee	75,591	36,992	33	152,873	47,310	24
Virginia	89,446	28,085	24	251,077	34,938	12
West Virginia	41,023	11,665	22	71,440	10,935	13
Great Lakes	**923,531**	**371,129**	**29**	**1,768,784**	**452,419**	**20**
Illinois	205,605	137,687	40	504,225	155,398	24
Indiana	111,341	52,052	32	193,107	58,719	23
Michigan	266,225	51,241	16	445,804	67,229	13
Ohio	218,229	95,727	30	384,633	136,763	26
Wisconsin	122,131	34,422	22	241,015	34,310	13

(*Continued on next page*)

Note: Figures show total (degree-credit plus non-degree-credit) enrollment. — No enrollment: zero percent.

65 Total Enrollment, by Control of Institution and by Region and State, 1967 and 1981—*Continued*

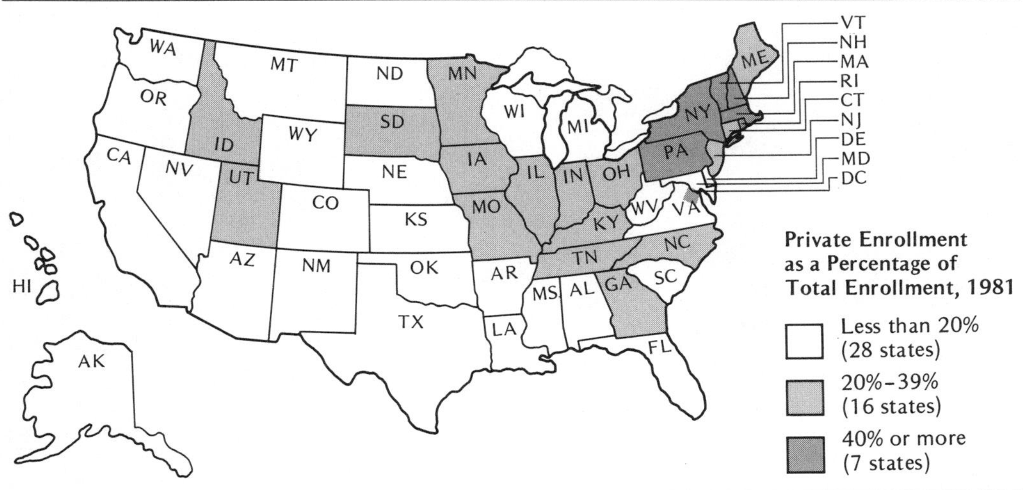

Region and State	Public Enrollment	1967 Private Enrollment: Number	1967 Private Enrollment: As Percentage of Total Enrollment	Public Enrollment	1981 Private Enrollment: Number	1981 Private Enrollment: As Percentage of Total Enrollment
Plains	**431,817**	**156,783**	**27**	**698,309**	**201,602**	**22**
Iowa	58,441	40,631	41	99,860	43,245	30
Kansas	73,796	15,273	17	124,218	14,235	10
Minnesota	109,510	28,729	21	165,429	45,284	22
Missouri	101,962	51,319	33	172,931	70,741	29
Nebraska	41,753	13,202	24	76,755	16,752	18
North Dakota	25,590	911	3		32,8[illegible]99	7
South Dakota	20,765	6,718	24	26,269	8,746	25
Southwest	**469,466**	**91,683**	**16**	**1,018,322**	**126,382**	**11**
Arizona	77,366	1,183	2	195,602	9,567	5
New Mexico	30,992	2,775	8	57,280	3,133	5
Oklahoma	82,952	17,400	17	139,701	23,124	14
Texas	278,156	70,325	20	625,739	90,558	13
Rocky Mountains	**172,920**	**57,719**	**25**	**298,377**	**66,600**	**18**
Colorado	79,325	13,984	15	149,694	18,283	11
Idaho	20,511	5,861	22	33,858	8,900	21
Montana	20,663	2,512	11	31,867	4,092	11
Utah	40,411	35,362	47	61,749	35,299	36
Wyoming	12,010	—	—	21,209	26	—
Far West	**1,103,185**	**148,300**	**12**	**2,182,150**	**245,022**	**10**
Alaska	5,180	656	11	23,858	896	4
California	863,139	111,287	11	1,691,223	194,534	10
Hawaii	25,584	2,263	8	45,085	3,036	6
Nevada	8,575	—	—	39,740	196	1
Oregon	76,832	13,473	15	132,507	17,417	12
Washington	123,875	20,621	14	249,737	28,943	10
U. S. Service Schools	**14,579**	**—**	**—**	**54,088**	**—**	**—**
Outlying Parts	**34,302**	**17,637**	**34**	**62,187**	**83,894**	**57**

For footnotes, see preceding page.

Sources:

1 USOE, *Opening Fall Enrollment in Higher Education* (Washington: GPO), *1967,* pp. 15, 22, 28.

2 NCES (Washington, 1983), unpublished data.

66 Percentage of "In-state" Students, by Control of Institution and by State, 1972 and 1975

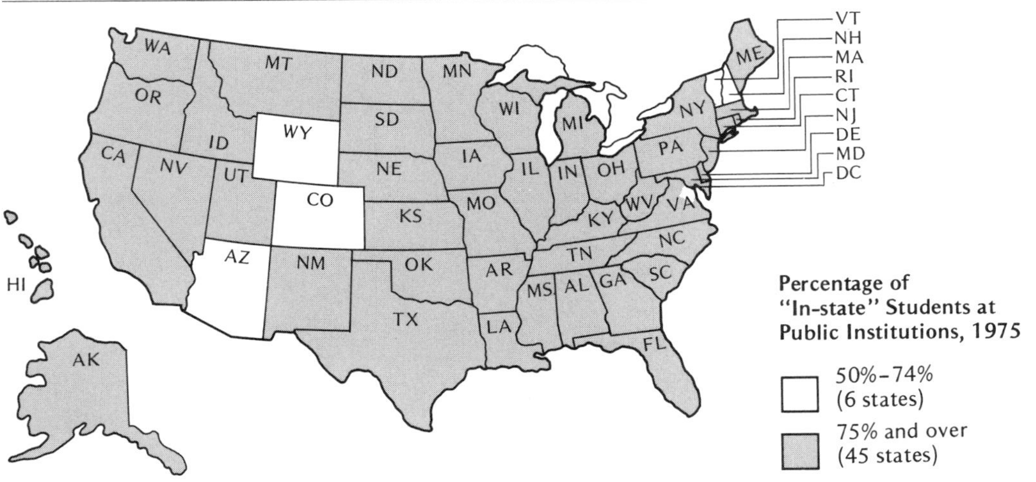

	Percentage of "In-state" Students[a] at					
	All Institutions		Public Institutions		Private Institutions	
Region and State	**1972**	**1975**	**1972**	**1975**	**1972**	**1975**
50 States & D. C.	**84**	**83**	**91**	**88**	**63**	**64**
New England	**na**	**na**	**na**	**na**	**na**	**na**
Connecticut	83	81	94	90	66	66
Maine	71	73	88	83	29	39
Massachusetts	68	74	93	93	53	59
New Hampshire	46	53	66	67	25	33
Rhode Island	64	70	80	85	45	55
Vermont	46	51	68	70	19	23
Mideast	**na**	**na**	**na**	**na**	**na**	**na**
Delaware	56	72	57	76	45	50
D. C.	31	28	88	68	18	20
Maryland	82	81	86	84	65	63
New Jersey	90	90	96	96	78	73
New York	89	89	97	97	76	77
Pennsylvania	82	84	93	94	70	69
Southeast	**na**	**na**	**na**	**na**	**na**	**na**
Alabama	87	83	90	86	68	65
Arkansas	86	83	90	87	66	61
Florida	85	83	92	89	58	49
Georgia	81	79	86	84	58	54
Kentucky	80	82	85	87	59	56
Louisiana	88	84	93	88	63	59
Mississippi	90	89	91	90	81	78
North Carolina	76	81	87	88	53	54
South Carolina	82	86	89	90	67	68
Tennessee	76	79	88	89	41	45
Virginia	79	77	84	79	57	56
West Virginia	73	77	78	81	47	52
Great Lakes	**na**	**na**	**na**	**na**	**na**	**na**
Illinois	89	88	96	93	74	72
Indiana	76	77	86	85	52	53
Michigan	90	87	93	89	74	76
Ohio	84	86	91	92	65	65
Wisconsin	84	87	89	90	60	63

(*Continued on next page*)

Note: No state has less than 50% "in-state" students.

na: Not available. The total number of students from within a region who are attending institutions within the region is not available. Institutions provided data on the basis of "in-state" or "out-of-state" residence only; the "home state" of "out-of-state" students was not provided; hence, regional data are not available.

— No enrollment.

67 Percentage of "In-state" Students, by Control of Institution and by State, 1972 and 1975—*Continued*

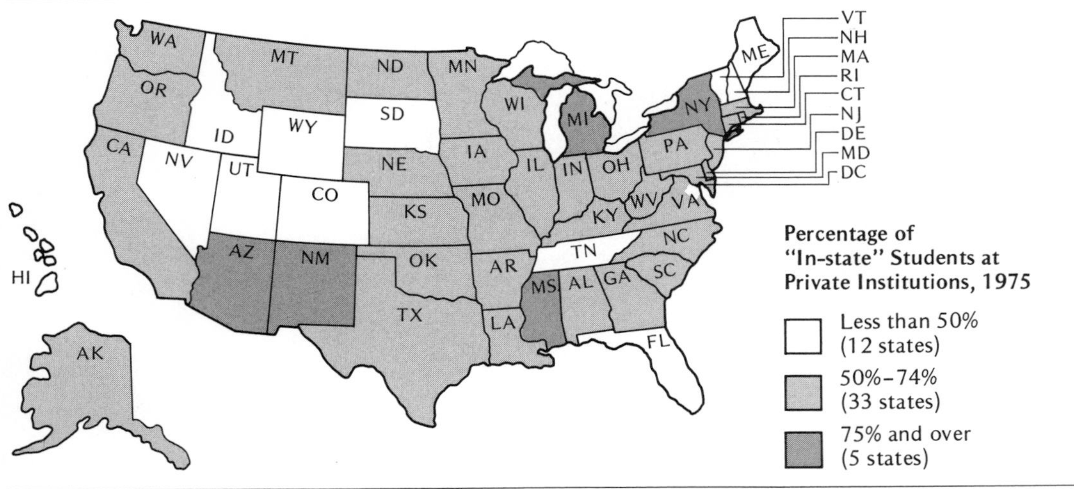

Region and State	All Institutions 1972	All Institutions 1975	Public Institutions 1972	Public Institutions 1975	Private Institutions 1972	Private Institutions 1975
	Percentage of "In-state" Students[a] at					
Plains	**na**	**na**	**na**	**na**	**na**	**na**
Iowa	75	77	84	85	59	59
Kansas	82	82	86	85	54	58
Minnesota	84	83	90	87	61	65
Missouri	80	82	89	89	57	63
Nebraska	81	80	89	85	52	54
North Dakota	83	81	84	82	69	62
South Dakota	77	75	85	87	54	48
Southwest	**na**	**na**	**na**	**na**	**na**	**na**
Arizona	82	70	84	69	46	79
New Mexico	85	77	86	77	76	77
Oklahoma	87	81	91	83	64	67
Texas	90	88	93	90	75	72
Rocky Mountains	**na**	**na**	**na**	**na**	**na**	**na**
Colorado	70	71	76	74	31	42
Idaho	75	68	85	76	42	37
Montana	83	80	85	82	67	60
Utah	64	66	82	82	37	38
Wyoming	79	71	79	71	—	—
Far West	**na**	**na**	**na**	**na**	**na**	**na**
Alaska	90	94	89	96	92	60
California	94	86	97	88	74	72
Hawaii	86	75	89	78	52	42
Nevada	81	80	82	81	29	16
Oregon	81	79	87	83	45	50
Washington	88	87	91	90	65	68

a Caution is urged in making comparisons between the two years inasmuch as definitions and survey instruments differed.

In 1972, institutions were asked to provide the numbers of students in three categories: in-state, out-of-state, and foreign. "Out-of-state" students were not further categorized by state. "In-state" students were to be those whose "home state" was the one in which the institution that they were attending was located. Each responding institution used its own definition for "home state."

In 1975, institutions provided the numbers of students by specific "home state," i.e., so many students from Alabama, so many from Alaska, etc. "Home state" in the 1975 survey was defined as the state in which the student completed his secondary education.

Sources:

1 Policy Analysis Service, American Council on Education, from data tapes from the NCES survey, "Residence and Migration of Students, Fall 1972."

2 NCES, *Migration of College Students* (Washington: GPO), 1978, tables 2, 3, 4.

68 Minority Enrollment, by Region and State, Fall 1972, 1976, and 1980

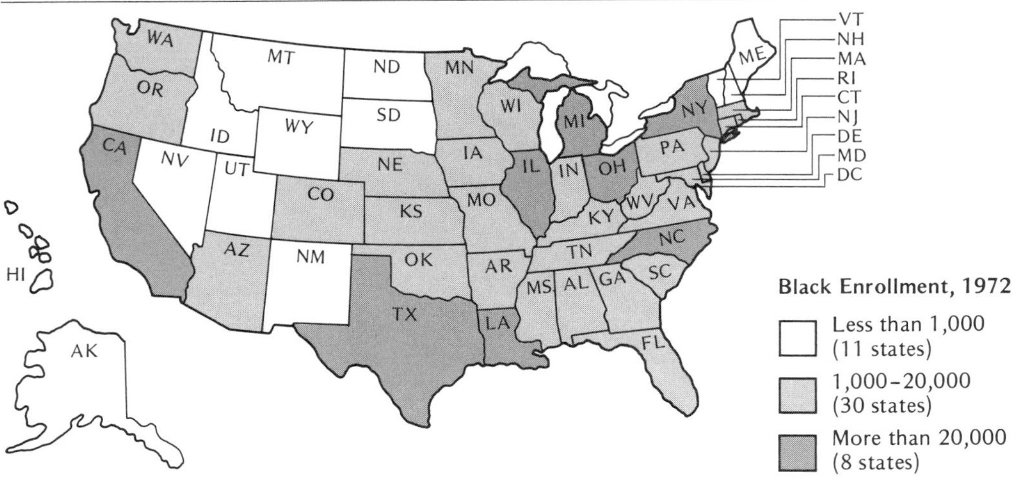

Full-time Minority Enrollment[a]

Region and State	1972 All Minorities	1972 Negro	1978 All Minorities	1978 Black	1980 All Minorities	1980 Black
All States & D. C.	**736,642**	**494,660**	**1,046,985**	**653,537**	**1,131,010**	**680,208**
New England	**21,976**	**14,835**	**29,472**	**17,146**	**30,338**	**17,136**
Connecticut	4,989	3,549	6,419	4,012	7,008	4,195
Maine	517	245	419	148	447	150
Massachusetts	13,047	9,084	18,875	10,593	18,584	10,318
New Hampshire	791	535	1,028	585	1,170	705
Rhode Island	2,051	1,021	2,172	1,495	2,572	1,472
Vermont	581	401	559	313	557	296
Mideast	**139,431**	**102,972**	**210,405**	**142,518**	**230,066**	**150,303**
Delaware	1,951	1,844	2,519	2,347	2,673	2,367
D. C.	16,011	14,979	15,295	13,601	16,678	14,478
Maryland	17,785	15,004	22,351	19,714	24,262	19,951
New Jersey	17,165	13,224	27,661	18,269	31,131	19,167
New York	69,011	43,310	115,476	66,743	124,595	70,145
Pennsylvania	17,508	14,611	27,103	21,844	30,727	24,195
Southeast	**195,675**	**181,279**	**282,443**	**252,994**	**299,773**	**263,426**
Alabama	19,349	18,501	29,185	28,303	30,198	28,898
Arkansas	7,821	7,502	9,424	8,609	10,279	9,367
Florida	21,718	16,210	41,824	26,240	44,481	25,731
Georgia	17,719	16,799	26,256	24,989	27,492	25,744
Kentucky	5,486	4,648	7,616	6,585	8,387	7,234
Louisiana	30,744	29,031	28,243	26,185	29,586	27,079
Mississippi	17,740	17,124	24,029	23,600	24,615	24,127
North Carolina	20,724	29,128	42,672	39,945	44,178	40,829
South Carolina	10,236	10,082	20,642	19,969	23,517	22,590
Tennessee	14,924	14,230	23,907	22,755	24,812	23,441
Virginia	26,746	15,788	25,967	23,542	29,470	26,056
West Virginia	2,468	2,236	2,678	2,272	2,758	2,330
Great Lakes	**111,853**	**92,049**	**137,305**	**107,963**	**149,263**	**112,556**
Illinois	42,692	35,143	55,233	42,269	58,194	41,013
Indiana	9,077	6,505	10,039	7,543	12,959	9,688
Michigan	28,764	24,330	33,132	26,630	34,815	27,537
Ohio	25,226	22,317	30,870	26,728	33,621	28,775
Wisconsin	6,094	3,754	8,031	4,793	9,674	5,543

Sources:

1 DHEW, Office for Civil Rights, *Racial and Ethnic Enrollment Data from Institutions of Higher Education, Fall 1972* (Washington: OCR), pp. 89–101.

2 DHEW, OCR, *Racial, Ethnic, and Sex Enrollment Data from Institutions of Higher Education* (Washington: GPO), *Fall 1976,* pp. 410–428; *Fall 1978,* pp. 250–262.

3 ED, OCR, *Racial, Ethnic and Sex Enrollment Data, Fall 1980,* unpublished data tabulations.

69 Minority Enrollment, by Region and State, Fall 1972, 1976, and 1980—*Continued*

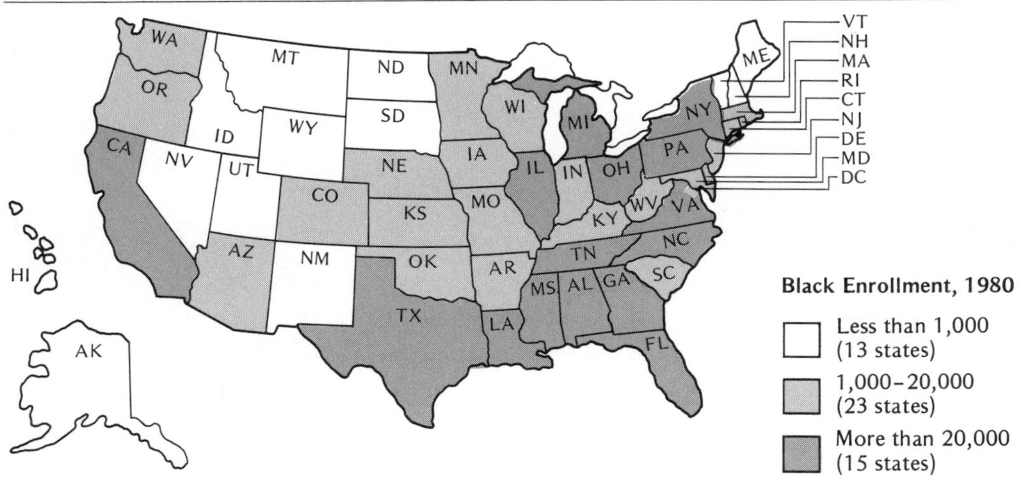

	Full-time Minority Enrollment[a]					
	1972		1978		1980	
Region and State	All Minorities	Negro	All Minorities	Black	All Minorities	Black
Plains	**26,189**	**17,339**	**32,818**	**20,680**	**35,539**	**21,561**
Iowa	3,606	2,757	3,732	2,324	4,501	2,661
Kansas	5,829	2,864	6,586	3,751	7,010	3,900
Minnesota	3,976	2,065	4,248	1,813	4,678	1,713
Missouri	9,615	8,191	13,376	10,871	14,242	11,276
Nebraska	1,809	1,161	2,450	1,456	2,782	1,573
North Dakota	680	108	1,091	151	936	145
South Dakota	674	193	1,335	314	1,390	293
Southwest	**91,073**	**36,025**	**116,966**	**43,844**	**129,596**	**48,447**
Arizona	11,573	2,266	11,158	2,253	12,645	2,622
New Mexico	8,027	738	11,340	883	12,118	960
Oklahoma	10,396	4,969	10,946	5,883	12,285	6,264
Texas	61,077	28,052	83,522	34,825	92,548	38,601
Rocky Mountains	**12,574**	**2,658**	**16,079**	**3,804**	**17,755**	**3,780**
Colorado	7,880	1,862	10,827	3,015	11,031	2,934
Idaho	807	196	887	156	1,340	199
Montana	938	132	809	86	1,274	94
Utah	2,521	360	3,011	381	3,545	424
Wyoming	428	108	545	166	565	129
Far West	**137,871**	**47,503**	**221,497**	**64,588**	**238,680**	**62,999**
Alaska	b	b	1,314	241	884	148
California	122,581	41,832	180,451	58,130	194,565	56,238
Hawaii	b	b	20,861	325	20,233	304
Nevada	579	261	1,171	580	1,681	907
Oregon	4,389	1,400	5,149	1,138	5,627	1,078
Washington	10,322	4,010	12,551	4,174	15,690	4,324
U. S. Service Schools	**b**	**b**	**b**	**b**	**b**	**b**

a Figures for 1972 are full-time undergraduate, graduate, and professional enrollments from surveys conducted by the Office for Civil Rights (OCR) of the Department of Health, Education, and Welfare (DHEW). Institutions in the forty-eight contiguous states receiving or expecting to receive some form of federal financial aid or assistance were asked to report. Institutions were asked to report full-time students enrolled in degree-credit programs and in vocational-technical programs (1) for which a high school diploma is a prerequisite, (2) that are normally terminal, and (3) that result in certificate, diploma, or similar award.

b No data reported.

70 Minorities as a Percentage of Total Enrollment, by Region and State, Fall 1972, 1978, and 1980

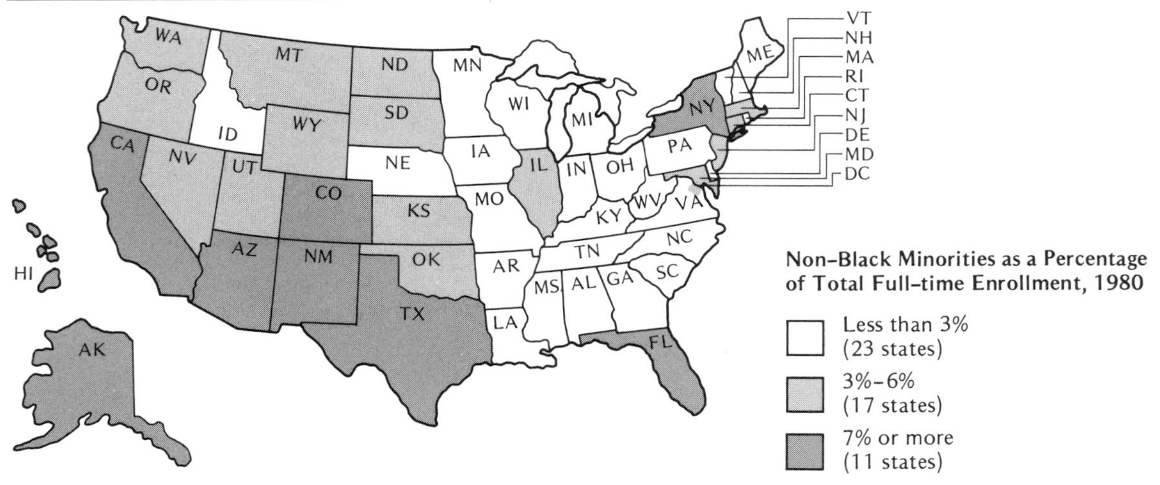

	Minorities as a Percentage of Total Full-Time Enrollment								
	1972[a]			1978[b]			1980[b]		
Region and State	**Total**	**Non-Negro**	**Negro**	**Total**	**Non-Black**	**Black**	**Total**	**Non-Black**	**Black**
All States & D. C.	**12**	**4**	**8**	**16**	**6**	**10**	**16**	**6**	**10**
New England	**5**	**2**	**4**	**6**	**2**	**4**	**6**	**3**	**4**
Connecticut	6	2	5	8	3	5	8	3	5
Maine	2	1	1	1	*	1	1	1	1
Massachusetts	6	2	4	7	3	4	7	3	4
New Hampshire	3	1	2	3	1	2	3	1	2
Rhode Island	7	3	3	5	1	4	6	3	4
Vermont	3	1	2	2	1	1	2	1	1
Mideast	**12**	**3**	**9**	**17**	**6**	**11**	**17**	**6**	**11**
Delaware	11	1	11	13	1	12	12	1	11
D. C.	34	2	32	33	3	30	34	4	29
Maryland	14	2	11	21	3	18	22	4	18
New Jersey	13	3	10	17	6	11	18	7	11
New York	13	5	8	19	8	11	20	9	11
Pennsylvania	6	1	5	8	1	7	9	2	7
Southeast	**17**	**1**	**15**	**21**	**3**	**18**	**21**	**2**	**18**
Alabama	22	1	21	26	1	25	25	1	24
Arkansas	15	1	14	18	2	16	18	2	16
Florida	13	3	10	20	7	13	20	8	11
Georgia	17	1	16	22	1	21	22	1	20
Kentucky	7	1	6	9	2	7	9	1	7
Louisiana	25	1	24	26	2	24	25	2	23
Mississippi	26	1	25	33	1	32	32	1	32
North Carolina	19	1	18	23	2	21	22	2	21
South Carolina	17	*	16	23	1	22	25	1	24
Tennessee	13	1	13	18	1	17	18	1	17
Virginia	15	1	14	17	1	16	18	2	16
West Virginia	5	*	4	6	1	5	6	1	5
Great Lakes	**9**	**2**	**8**	**12**	**3**	**9**	**12**	**3**	**9**
Illinois	13	2	11	17	4	13	18	5	12
Indiana	6	2	4	7	2	5	8	2	6
Michigan	10	2	9	12	2	10	12	3	10
Ohio	9	1	8	11	2	9	11	2	9
Wisconsin	4	2	2	5	2	3	5	2	3

* Less than .50 percent.

a Percentages are calculated from Office of Civil Rights (OCR) data. See page 68 for sources.

b Percentages are calculated from NCES data.

c No data gathered.

71 Minorities as a Percentage of Total Enrollment, by Region and State, Fall 1972, 1978, and 1980—*Continued*

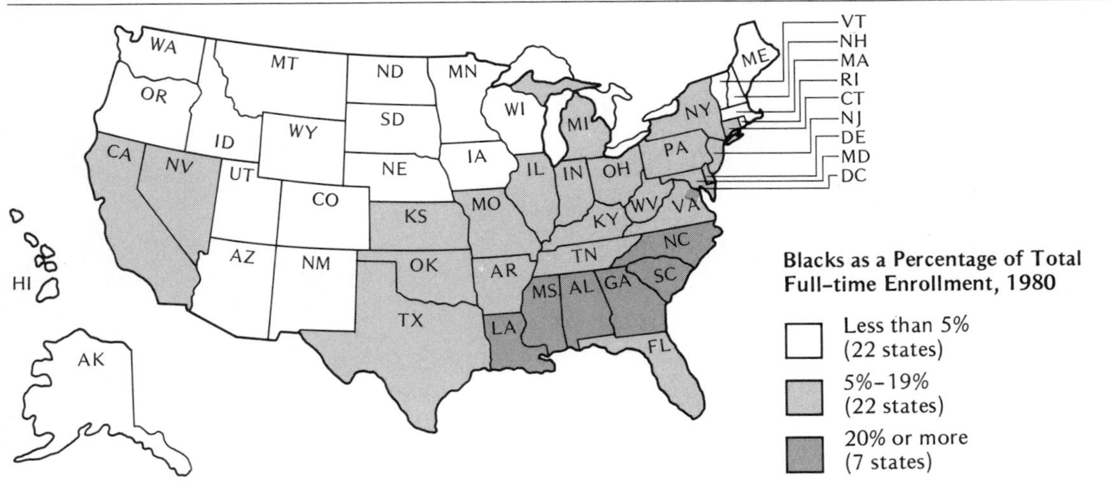

Minorities as a Percentage of Total Full-Time Enrollment

Region and State	1972[a] Total	1972[a] Non-Negro	1972[a] Negro	1978[b] Total	1978[b] Non-Black	1978[b] Black	1980[b] Total	1980[b] Non-Black	1980[b] Black
Plains	**5**	**2**	**3**	**6**	**2**	**4**	**6**	**2**	**4**
Iowa	3	1	2	4	2	2	4	2	2
Kansas	7	4	3	8	3	5	8	4	5
Minnesota	3	2	2	3	2	1	3	2	1
Missouri	7	1	6	10	2	8	10	2	8
Nebraska	4	1	2	5	2	3	5	2	3
North Dakota	3	2	*	4	3	1	3	3	1
South Dakota	3	2	1	5	4	1	5	4	1
Southwest	**17**	**10**	**7**	**19**	**12**	**7**	**20**	**13**	**8**
Arizona	13	11	3	13	10	3	14	11	3
New Mexico	24	21	2	32	29	3	33	31	3
Oklahoma	11	6	5	11	5	6	12	6	6
Texas	18	10	8	21	12	9	22	13	9
Rocky Mountains	**7**	**5**	**1**	**7**	**5**	**2**	**7**	**6**	**2**
Colorado	11	8	3	11	8	3	10	8	3
Idaho	4	3	1	3	2	1	5	4	1
Montana	4	4	1	3	3	*	5	5	*
Utah	4	4	1	5	4	1	5	5	1
Wyoming	4	3	1	5	4	1	5	4	1
Far West	**16**	**10**	**5**	**22**	**15**	**7**	**23**	**17**	**6**
Alaska	c	c	c	21	17	4	16	13	3
California	19	12	6	25	17	8	26	19	8
Hawaii	c	c	c	71	70	1	70	68	1
Nevada	7	4	3	11	6	5	12	6	7
Oregon	6	4	2	6	5	1	6	5	1
Washington	8	5	3	9	6	3	10	7	3

For footnotes, see preceding page.

Sources:

1 DHEW, Office for Civil Rights (OCR), *Racial and Ethnic Enrollment Data from Institutions of Higher Education* (Washington: OCR), *Fall 1972,* pp. 89–101.

2 DHEW, OCR, *Racial, Ethnic, and Sex Enrollment Data from Institutions of Higher Education* (Washington: GPO); *Fall 1976,* pp. 410–428; *Fall 1978,* pp. 250–262.

3 NCES, *Digest of Education Statistics, 1982* (Washington: GPO), 1982, p. 84.

72 Opening Fall Enrollment of All Students in Four-Year Institutions, by Sex, Selected Years, 1950–1982

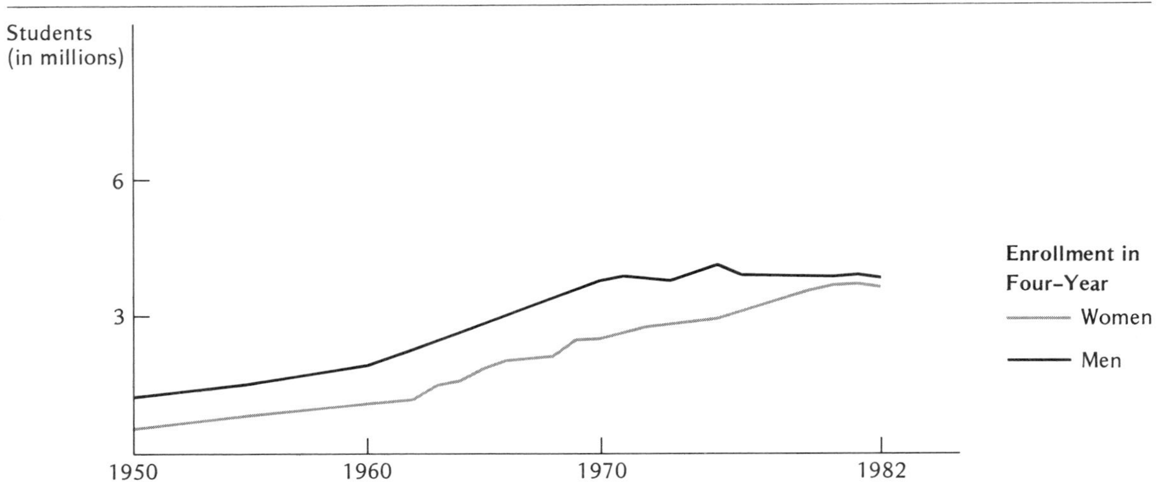

Opening Fall Enrollment in Four-Year Institutions in the U.S. & Outlying Parts[a]

	Number			Percent Distribution		Indexes (1965 = 100)		
Year	**Total**	**Men**	**Women**	**Men**	**Women**	**Total**	**Men**	**Women**
1950	**2,079,020**	1,429,349	649,671	69	31	**43**	49	35
1955	**2,369,647**	1,550,474	819,173	65	35	**49**	53	44
1960	**3,156,390**	1,987,348	1,169,042	63	37	**66**	68	62
1961	**3,370,227**	2,102,219	1,268,008	62	38	**70**	72	68
1962	**3,614,344**	2,235,936	1,378,408	62	38	**75**	77	74
1963	**3,952,760**	2,437,861	1,514,899	62	38	**83**	84	81
1964	**4,328,861**	2,648,434	1,680,427	61	39	**90**	91	90
1965	**4,790,559**	2,917,314	1,873,245	61	39	**100**	100	100
1966	**5,107,621**	3,069,370	2,038,251	60	40	**107**	105	109
1967	**5,445,608**	3,241,292	2,204,316	60	40	**114**	111	118
1968	**5,775,210**	3,413,732	2,361,478	59	41	**121**	117	126
1969	**6,085,083**	3,582,992	2,502,091	59	41	**127**	123	134
1970	**6,422,154**	3,757,222	2,664,932	59	41	**134**	129	142
1971	**6,533,611**	3,791,169	2,742,442	58	42	**136**	130	146
1972[b]	**6,626,853**	3,779,645	2,847,208	57	43	**138**	130	152
1972[b]	**6,525,973**	3,725,393	2,800,580	57	43	**136**	128	150
1973	**6,660,536**	3,751,703	2,908,833	56	44	**139**	129	155
1974	**6,892,897**	3,824,202	3,068,695	55	45	**144**	131	164
1975	**7,288,749**	4,018,105	3,270,644	55	45	**152**	138	175
1976	**7,204,813**	3,865,863	3,338,950	54	46	**150**	133	178
1977	**7,336,036**	3,865,857	3,470,179	53	47	**153**	133	185
1978	**7,327,118**	3,797,072	3,530,046	52	48	**153**	130	188
1979	**7,457,099**	3,804,577	3,652,522	51	49	**156**	130	195
1980	**7,577,763**	3,831,299	3,746,464	51	49	**158**	131	200
1981[c]	**7,655,461**	3,850,591	3,804,870	50	50	**160**	132	203
1981[c]	**7,631,267**	3,852,056	3,779,211	50	50	**159**	132	202
1982[p]	**7,542,312**	3,821,366	3,720,946	51	49	**157**	131	198

a Prior to 1963 enrollment figures were degree-credit only. Data for all other years are for both degree-credit and non-degree credit. As of 1976, NCES gathered data on total enrollments only and not separately for degree-credit and non-credit students.

b From 1972 to 1981, the NCES method of aggregating data was based on type of institution. It aggregated data from two-year branches of four-year institutions with other two-year institutions. Earlier, branch enrollments were aggregated with the parent institution's category.

c In 1981, NCES developed a new method for classifying institutions. Figures prior to 1981 and data on the upper 1981 line show totals using the traditional method; figures on the lower 1981 line and following lines are aggregated by the new method. For further information on the new classification method see NCES Bulletin April 7, 1981.

p Preliminary.

73 Opening Fall Enrollment of All Students in Four-Year Institutions, by Control of Institution, Selected Years, 1950–1982

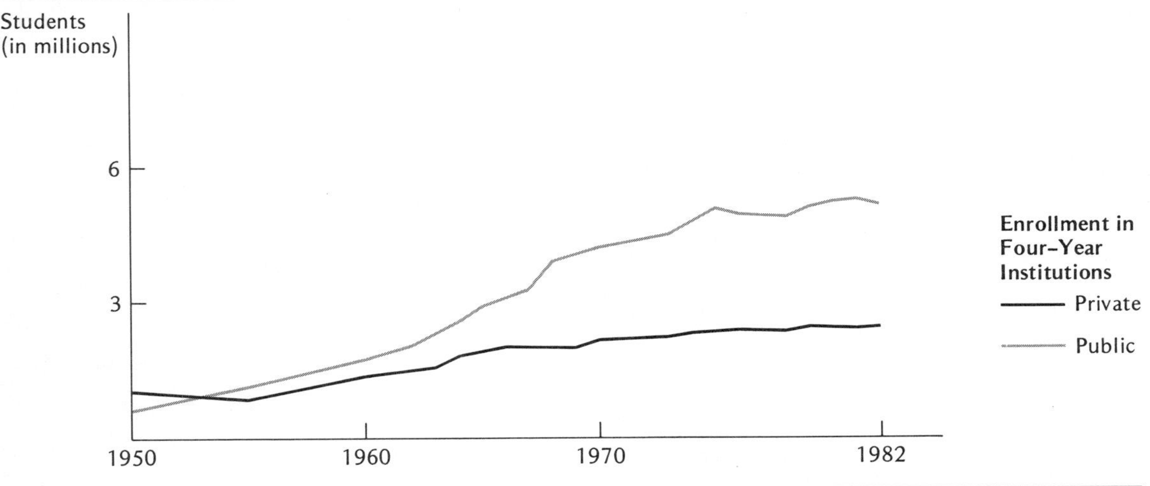

Opening Fall Enrollment in Four-Year Institutions in the U.S. & Outlying Parts[a]

	Number			Percent Distribution		Indexes (1965 = 100)		
Year	**Total**	**Public**	**Private**	**Public**	**Private**	**Total**	**Public**	**Private**
1950	**2,079,020**	986,413	1,092,607	47	53	**43**	33	60
1955	**2,369,647**	1,232,619	1,137,028	52	48	**49**	42	62
1960	**3,156,390**	1,742,137	1,414,253	55	45	**66**	59	77
1961	**3,370,227**	1,893,423	1,476,804	56	44	**70**	64	81
1962	**3,614,344**	2,075,917	1,538,427	57	43	**75**	70	84
1963	**3,952,760**	2,353,512	1,599,248	60	40	**83**	80	87
1964	**4,328,861**	2,618,495	1,710,366	60	40	**90**	89	93
1965	**4,790,559**	2,956,562	1,833,997	62	38	**100**	100	100
1966	**5,107,621**	3,189,304	1,918,317	62	38	**107**	108	105
1967	**5,445,608**	3,475,660	1,969,948	64	36	**114**	118	107
1968	**5,775,210**	3,821,808	1,953,402	66	34	**121**	129	107
1969	**6,085,083**	4,091,603	1,993,480	67	33	**127**	138	109
1970	**6,422,154**	4,374,086	2,048,068	68	32	**134**	148	112
1971	**6,533,611**	4,488,073	2,045,538	69	31	**136**	152	112
1972[b]	**6,626,853**	4,569,342	2,057,511	69	31	**138**	155	112
1972[b]	**6,525,973**	4,475,961	2,050,012	69	31	**136**	151	112
1973	**6,660,536**	4,577,423	2,083,113	69	31	**139**	155	114
1974	**6,892,897**	4,750,724	2,142,173	69	31	**144**	161	117
1975	**7,288,749**	5,045,024	2,243,725	69	31	**152**	171	122
1976	**7,204,813**	4,946,727	2,258,086	69	31	**150**	167	123
1977	**7,336,036**	4,994,623	2,341,413	68	32	**153**	169	128
1978	**7,327,118**	4,960,378	2,366,740	68	32	**153**	168	129
1979	**7,457,099**	5,026,942	2,430,157	67	33	**156**	170	133
1980	**7,577,763**	5,132,761	2,445,802	68	32	**158**	174	133
1981[c]	**7,655,461**	5,166,324	2,489,137	67	33	**160**	175	135
1981[c]	**7,631,267**	5,182,977	2,448,290	68	32	**159**	175	133
1982[p]	**7,542,312**	5,140,880	2,401,432	68	32	**157**	174	131

For footnotes, see preceding page.

Sources:

1 USOE, *Opening (Fall) Enrollment in Higher Education, 1960: Analytic Report* (Washington: GPO), 1961, p. 10.

2 USOE, *Opening Fall Enrollment in Higher Education* (Washington: GPO), *1962,* p. 3; *1963,* p. 6; *1964,* p. 5; *1965,* p. 7; *1966,* p. 8; *1967,* p. 10; *1968,* p. 6.

3 NCES, *Fall Enrollment in Higher Education* (Washington: GPO), *1971,* p. 3; *1972,* pp. 3, 738; *1975,* p. 3; *1977,* p. 2; *1979,* pp. 12, 13.

4 NCES, "Fall Enrollment in Colleges and Universities, 1981, Preliminary Estimates," *NCES Early Release,* October 31, 1981, table B; November 30, 1981, table B; 1982 Preliminary Estimates, January 1983, table B.

74 Opening Fall Enrollment of All Students in Two-Year Institutions, by Sex, Selected Years, 1950–1982

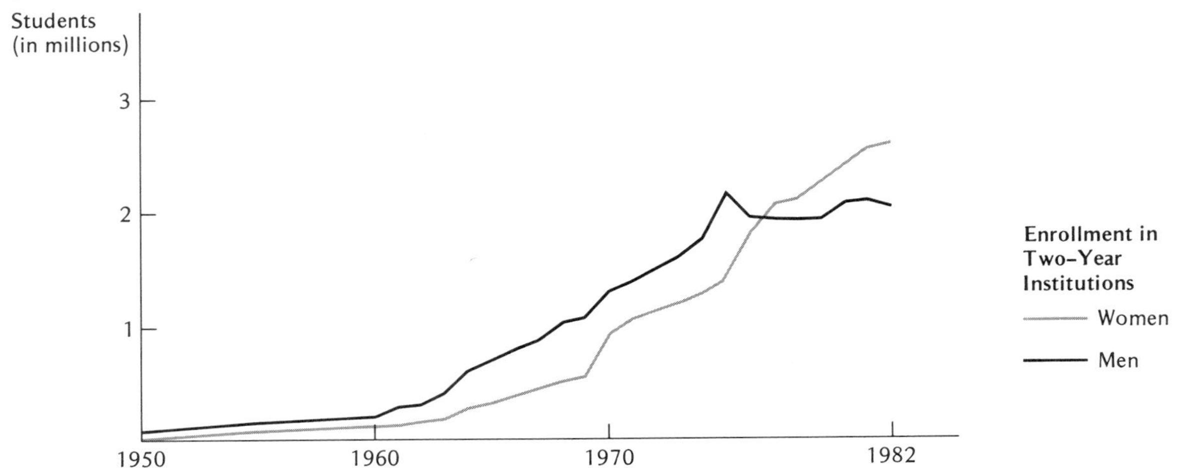

Opening Fall Enrollment in Two-Year Institutions in the U.S. & Outlying Parts[a]

Year	Number: Total	Number: Men	Number: Women	Percent Distribution: Men	Percent Distribution: Women	Indexes (1965 = 100): Total	Indexes (1965 = 100): Men	Indexes (1965 = 100): Women
1950	**217,572**	139,973	77,599	64	36	**18**	19	18
1955	**308,976**	196,955	112,021	64	36	**26**	27	25
1960	**453,617**	283,292	170,325	62	38	**39**	39	39
1961	**521,003**	321,768	199,235	62	38	**44**	44	45
1962	**592,328**	367,136	225,192	62	38	**50**	50	51
1963	**771,637**	478,645	292,992	62	38	**66**	65	66
1964	**991,433**	619,754	371,679	63	37	**84**	84	84
1965	**1,176,852**	735,361	441,491	62	38	**100**	100	100
1966	**1,330,856**	811,187	519,669	61	39	**113**	110	118
1967	**1,518,079**	917,265	600,814	60	40	**129**	125	136
1968	**1,796,426**	1,092,101	704,325	61	39	**153**	149	160
1969	**1,981,150**	1,192,630	788,520	60	40	**168**	162	179
1970	**2,227,214**	1,318,810	908,413	59	41	**189**	179	206
1971	**2,491,420**	1,451,571	1,039,849	58	42	**212**	197	236
1972[b]	**2,670,934**	1,496,257	1,174,677	56	44	**227**	203	266
1972[b]	**2,771,814**	1,550,509	1,221,305	56	44	**236**	211	277
1973	**3,033,761**	1,662,461	1,371,300	55	45	**258**	226	311
1974	**3,428,642**	1,842,851	1,585,791	54	46	**291**	251	359
1975	**4,001,970**	2,180,518	1,821,452	54	46	**340**	297	413
1976	**3,916,613**	1,994,352	1,922,261	51	49	**333**	271	435
1977	**4,078,984**	1,980,241	2,098,743	49	51	**347**	269	475
1978	**4,064,832**	1,900,762	2,164,070	47	53	**345**	258	490
1979	**4,250,027**	1,935,974	2,314,053	46	54	**361**	263	524
1980	**4,519,132**	2,043,075	2,476,057	45	55	**384**	278	561
1981[c]	**4,716,211**	2,124,465	2,591,746	45	55	**401**	289	561
1981[c]	**4,630,108**	2,054,820	2,575,288	44	56	**393**	279	583
1982[p]	**4,701,869**	2,092,115	2,609,754	45	56	**400**	285	591

a Prior to 1963 enrollment figures were degree-credit only. Data for all other years are for both degree-credit and non-degree credit. As of 1976, NCES gathered data on total enrollments only and not separately for degree-credit and non-credit students.

b From 1972 to 1981, the NCES method of aggregating data was based on type of institution. It aggregated data from two-year branches of four-year institutions with other two-year institutions. Earlier, branch enrollments were aggregated with the parent institution's category.

c In 1981, NCES developed a new method for classifying institutions. Figures prior to 1981 and data on the upper 1981 line show totals using the traditional method; figures on the lower 1981 line and following lines are aggregated by the new method. For further information on the new classification method see NCES Bulletin April 7, 1981.

p preliminary.

For sources, see next page.

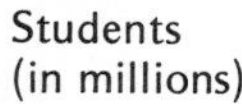

Opening Fall Enrollment of All Students in Two-Year Institutions, by Control of Institution, Selected Years, 1950–1982

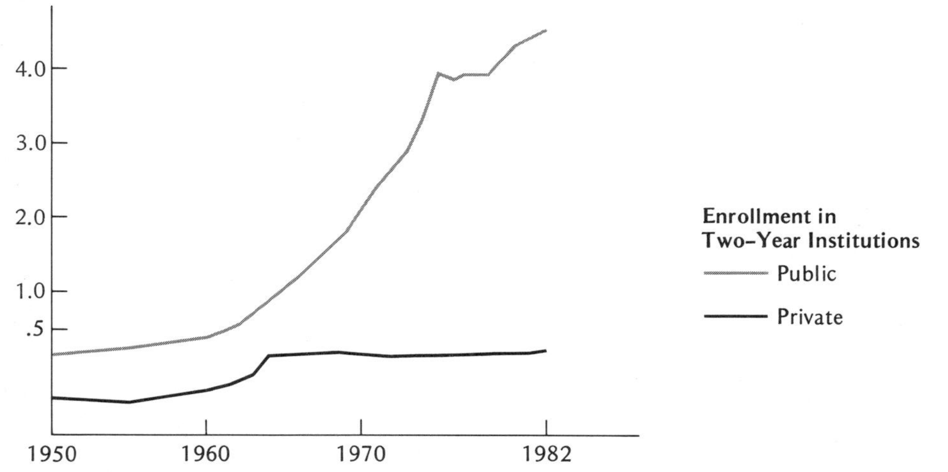

Opening Fall Enrollment in Two-Year Institutions in the U.S. & Outlying Parts[a]

Year	Number			Percent Distribution		Indexes (1965 = 100)		
	Total	Public	Private	Public	Private	Total	Public	Private
1950	**217,572**	168,043	49,529	77	23	**18**	16	37
1955	**308,976**	265,891	43,085	86	14	**26**	25	32
1960	**453,617**	393,553	60,064	87	13	**39**	38	45
1961	**521,003**	458,396	62,707	88	12	**44**	44	47
1962	**592,328**	520,987	71,341	88	12	**50**	50	53
1963	**771,637**	691,678	79,959	90	10	**66**	66	60
1964	**991,433**	875,994	115,439	88	12	**84**	84	86
1965	**1,176,852**	1,043,378	133,474	89	11	**100**	100	100
1966	**1,330,856**	1,191,782	139,074	90	10	**113**	114	104
1967	**1,518,079**	1,374,670	143,409	91	9	**129**	132	107
1968	**1,796,426**	1,647,664	148,762	92	8	**153**	158	111
1969	**1,981,150**	1,847,910	133,240	93	7	**168**	177	100
1970	**2,227,214**	2,101,972	125,242	94	6	**189**	201	110
1971	**2,491,420**	2,366,612	124,808	95	5	**212**	227	110
1972[b]	**2,670,934**	2,553,533	117,401	96	4	**227**	245	103
1972[b]	**2,771,814**	2,646,914	124,900	95	5	**236**	254	110
1973	**3,033,761**	2,900,984	132,777	96	4	**258**	278	117
1974	**3,428,642**	3,298,871	129,771	96	4	**291**	316	114
1975	**4,001,970**	3,850,997	150,973	96	4	**340**	369	133
1976	**3,916,613**	3,765,907	150,706	96	4	**333**	361	133
1977	**4,078,984**	3,912,968	166,016	96	4	**347**	375	124
1978	**4,064,832**	3,882,823	182,009	96	4	**345**	372	136
1979	**4,250,027**	4,069,462	180,565	96	4	**361**	390	135
1980	**4,519,132**	4,324,633	194,499	96	4	**384**	414	145
1981[c]	**4,716,211**	4,480,708	235,503	95	5	**401**	429	176
1981[c]	**4,630,108**	4,432,157	197,951	96	4	**393**	425	148
1982[p]	**4,701,869**	4,494,202	207,667	96	4	**400**	431	156

For footnotes, see preceding page.

Sources:

1 USOE, *Opening (Fall) Enrollment in Higher Education, 1960: Analytic Report* (Washington: GPO), 1961, p. 10.

2 USOE, *Opening Fall Enrollment in Higher Education* (Washington: GPO), *1962,* p. 3; *1963,* p. 6; *1964,* p. 5; *1965,* p. 7; *1966,* p. 8; *1967,* p. 10; *1968,* p. 6.

3 NCES, *Fall Enrollment in Higher Education* (Washington: GPO), *1971,* p. 3; *1972,* pp. 4, 738; *1975,* p. 3; *1977,* p. 2; *1979,* pp. 12, 13.

4 NCES, "Fall Enrollment in Colleges and Universities, 1980, Preliminary Estimates," *NCES Early Release,* October 31, 1980, table B; November 31, 1981, table B; 1982 Preliminary Estimates, January 1983, table B.

76 Enrollment of All Students in All Institutions, by Attendance Status, 1962–1982

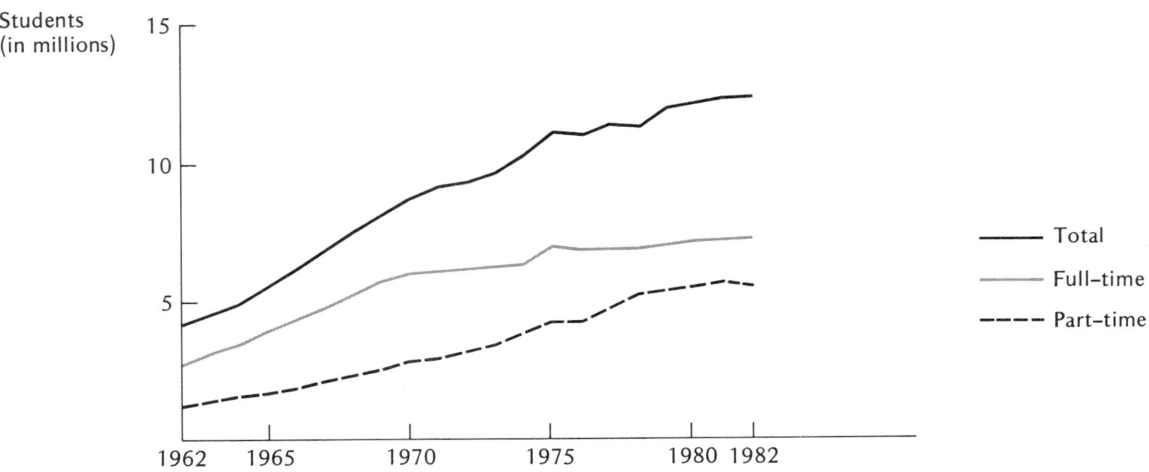

Year	Number of Students			Percentage	
	Total	**Full-time**	**Part-time**	**Full-time**	**Part-time**
1962[a]	**4,206,672**	2,921,552	1,285,120	69	31
1963[a]	**4,528,516**	3,089,614	1,438,902	68	32
1964[a]	**4,987,867**	3,441,814	1,546,053	69	31
1965[a]	**5,570,271**	3,937,255	1,633,016	71	29
1966	**6,438,477**	4,469,771	1,968,706	69	31
1967	**6,963,687**	4,826,991	2,136,696	69	31
1968	**7,571,636**	5,250,480	2,321,156	69	31
1969	**8,066,233**	5,541,621	2,524,612	69	31
1970	**8,649,368**	5,865,475	2,783,893	68	32
1971	**9,025,031**	6,132,154	2,892,877	68	32
1972	**9,297,787**	6,131,407	3,166,380	66	34
1973	**9,694,297**	6,256,685	3,437,612	65	35
1974	**10,321,539**	6,442,469	3,879,070	62	38
1975	**11,290,719**	6,922,895	4,367,823	61	39
1976	**11,121,426**	6,803,089	4,318,337	61	39
1977	**11,415,020**	6,895,809	4,519,211	60	40
1978	**11,391,950**	6,770,611	4,621,339	59	41
1979	**11,707,126**	6,901,426	4,805,700	59	41
1980	**12,096,895**	7,097,958	4,998,937	59	41
1981	**12,371,672**	7,181,250	5,190,422	58	42
1982[p]	**12,358,216**	7,203,027	5,155,189	58	42

For sources, see next page.

Note: Data show opening fall enrollment of all students (degree-credit and non-degree-credit) in institutions of higher education for aggregate U.S. (50 states, D.C., and outlying parts) unless footnoted otherwise.

a Degree-credit enrollment only.

p Preliminary.

77 Enrollment in All Institutions, by Control of Institution and by Attendance Status, 1962–1982

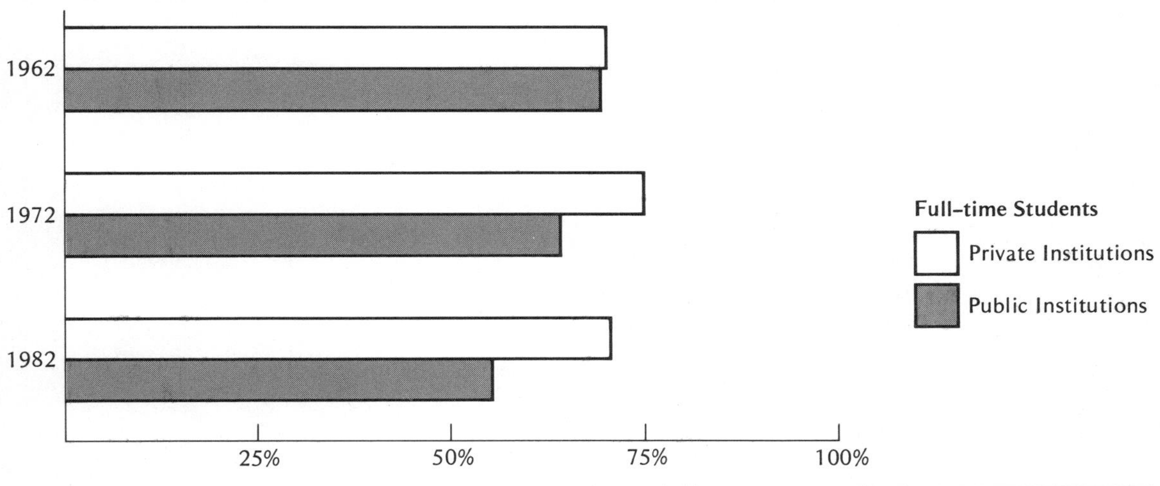

Year	Public Institutions: Number of Students: Full-time	Public: Number of Students: Part-time	Public: Percentage: Full-time	Public: Percentage: Part-time	Private Institutions: Number of Students: Full-time	Private: Number of Students: Part-time	Private: Percentage: Full-time	Private: Percentage: Part-time
1962[a]	1,792,553	804,351	69	31	1,128,999	480,769	70	30
1963[a]	1,933,327	939,496	67	33	1,156,287	499,406	70	30
1964[a]	2,188,183	1,017,600	68	32	1,253,631	528,453	70	30
1965[a]	2,554,622	1,099,956	70	30	1,382,633	533,060	72	28
1966	2,967,259	1,413,827	68	32	1,502,512	554,879	73	27
1967	3,281,231	1,569,099	68	32	1,545,760	567,597	73	27
1968	3,684,022	1,785,450	67	33	1,566,458	535,706	75	25
1969	3,948,086	1,991,427	66	34	1,593,535	533,185	75	25
1970	4,249,228	2,226,830	66	34	1,616,247	557,063	74	26
1971	4,503,458	2,351,227	66	34	1,628,696	541,650	75	25
1972	4,504,362	2,618,513	63	37	1,627,045	547,867	75	25
1973	4,624,471	2,853,936	62	38	1,632,214	583,676	74	26
1974	4,781,196	3,268,399	59	41	1,661,273	610,671	73	27
1975	5,178,704	3,717,317	58	42	1,744,192	650,506	73	27
1976	5,040,169	3,672,465	58	42	1,762,920	645,872	73	27
1977	5,069,071	3,838,520	57	43	1,826,738	680,691	73	27
1978	4,917,443	3,925,758	56	44	1,853,168	695,581	73	27
1979	5,006,777	4,089,627	55	45	1,894,649	716,073	73	27
1980	5,187,686	4,269,708	55	45	1,910,272	729,229	72	28
1981	5,246,505	4,400,527	54	46	1,934,745	789,895	71	29
1982[p]	5,287,970	4,386,568	55	45	1,915,057	768,621	71	29

For footnotes, see preceding page.

Sources:

1 NCES, *Opening Fall Enrollment in Higher Education* (Washington: GPO), *1965,* p. 6; *1966,* p. 9; *1967,* p. 3; *1968,* p. 6; *1969,* p. 153; *1970,* p. 241; *1972,* pp. 4, 6; *1975,* pp. 11, 22; *1977,* pp. 4, 23; *1979,* pp. 11, 12.

2 NCES, *Fall Enrollment in Higher Education (Analytic Report), 1974* (Washington: GPO), 1976, p. 13.

3 NCES, "Fall Enrollment in Colleges and Universities, 1981 Preliminary Estimates," *NCES Early Release,* November 30, 1981, tables A, C, D; 1982 Preliminary Estimates, January 1983, tables A, C, D.

78 Enrollment of Men in All Institutions, by Attendance Status, 1962–1982

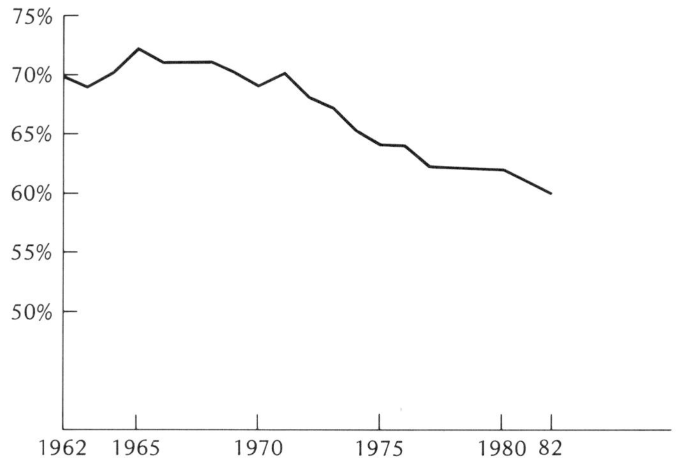

Year	Number of Students			Percentage	
	Total	Full-time	Part-time	Full-time	Part-time
1962[a]	**2,603,072**	1,821,513	781,559	70	30
1963[a]	**2,789,527**	1,913,977	875,550	69	31
1964[a]	**3,051,761**	2,121,319	930,442	70	30
1965[a]	**3,396,573**	2,433,962	962,612	72	28
1966	**3,880,557**	2,748,410	1,132,147	71	29
1967	**4,158,557**	2,940,988	1,217,569	71	29
1968	**4,505,833**	3,188,039	1,317,794	71	29
1969	**4,775,622**	3,356,159	1,419,463	70	30
1970	**5,076,023**	3,527,415	1,548,608	69	31
1971	**5,242,740**	3,654,937	1,587,803	70	30
1972	**5,275,902**	3,583,728	1,692,174	68	32
1973	**5,414,164**	3,610,200	1,803,964	67	33
1974	**5,667,053**	3,679,735	1,987,318	65	35
1975	**6,198,623**	3,965,160	2,233,463	64	36
1976	**5,860,215**	3,742,049	2,118,166	64	36
1977	**5,846,098**	3,695,761	2,150,337	63	37
1978	**5,697,834**	3,571,715	2,126,119	63	37
1979	**5,740,551**	3,588,195	2,152,356	63	37
1980	**5,874,374**	3,689,244	2,185,130	63	37
1981	**5,975,056**	3,712,837	2,262,219	62	38
1982[p]	**5,984,211**	3,731,521	2,252,690	62	38

For sources, see next page.

Note: Data show opening fall enrollment of all students (degree-credit and non-degree-credit) in institutions of higher education for aggregate U.S. (50 states, D.C., and outlying parts) unless footnoted otherwise.

a Degree-credit enrollment only.

p Preliminary.

79 Enrollment of Women in All Institutions, by Attendance Status, 1962–1982

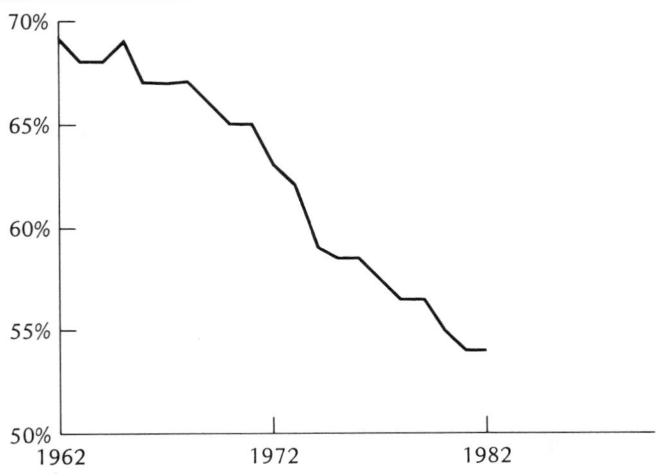

Year	Number of Women: Total	Number of Women: Full-time	Number of Women: Part-time	Percentage: Full-time	Percentage: Part-time
1962[a]	**1,603,600**	1,100,039	503,561	69	31
1963[a]	**1,738,989**	1,175,637	563,352	68	32
1964[a]	**1,936,106**	1,320,495	615,611	68	32
1965[a]	**2,173,697**	1,503,293	670,404	69	31
1966	**2,551,920**	1,721,361	836,559	67	33
1967	**2,805,130**	1,886,003	919,127	67	33
1968	**3,065,803**	2,062,441	1,003,362	67	33
1969	**3,290,611**	2,185,462	1,105,149	66	34
1970	**3,573,345**	2,338,060	1,235,285	65	35
1971	**3,782,291**	2,477,217	1,305,074	65	35
1972	**4,021,885**	2,547,679	1,474,206	63	37
1973	**4,280,133**	2,646,485	1,633,648	62	38
1974	**4,654,486**	2,762,734	1,891,752	59	41
1975	**5,092,096**	2,957,736	2,134,360	58	42
1976	**5,261,211**	3,061,040	2,200,171	58	42
1977	**5,568,922**	3,200,048	2,368,874	57	43
1978	**5,694,116**	3,198,896	2,495,220	56	44
1979	**5,966,575**	3,313,231	2,653,344	56	44
1980	**6,222,521**	3,408,714	2,813,807	55	45
1981	**6,396,616**	3,468,413	2,928,203	54	46
1982[p]	**6,374,005**	3,471,506	2,902,499	54	46

For footnotes, see preceding page.

Sources:

1 NCES, *Opening Fall Enrollment in Higher Education* (Washington: GPO), *1965,* p. 6; *1966,* p. 9; *1967,* p. 3; *1968,* p. 6; *1969,* p. 153; *1970,* p. 241; *1972,* pp. 4, 6; *1975,* pp. 11, 22; *1977,* pp. 4, 23; *1979,* p. 13.

2 NCES, *Fall Enrollment in Higher Education (Analytic Report), 1974* (Washington: GPO), 1976, p. 13.

3 NCES, "Fall Enrollment in Colleges and Universities, 1981, Preliminary Estimates," *NCES Early Release,* November 30, 1981, table A; January 1983 edition, table A.

80 Enrollment of All Students in Four-Year Institutions, by Attendance Status, 1963–1982

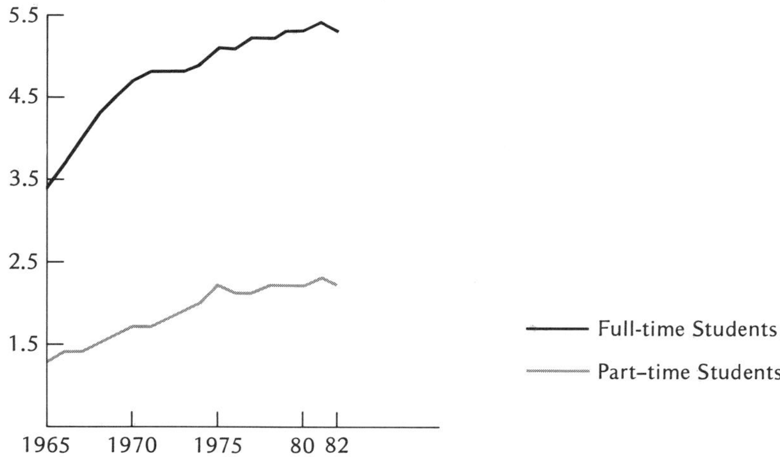

Year	Number of Students at Four-Year Institutions			Percentage	
	Total	Full-time	Part-time	Full-time	Part-time
1963[a]	**3,900,710**	2,760,721	1,139,989	71	29
1964[a]	**4,274,591**	3,043,761	1,230,830	71	29
1965[a]	**4,725,027**	3,439,582	1,285,445	73	27
1966	**5,107,621**	3,729,891	1,377,730	73	27
1967	**5,445,608**	4,003,630	1,441,978	74	26
1968	**5,775,210**	4,271,884	1,503,326	74	26
1969	**6,085,083**	4,481,318	1,603,765	74	26
1970	**6,422,154**	4,696,575	1,725,579	73	27
1971	**6,533,611**	4,836,908	1,696,703	74	26
1972[b]	**6,626,853**	4,840,057	1,786,796	73	27
1972[b]	**6,525,973**	4,778,607	1,747,366	73	27
1973	**6,660,536**	4,807,017	1,853,519	72	28
1974	**6,892,897**	4,912,902	1,979,995	71	29
1975	**7,288,749**	5,134,275	2,154,474	70	30
1976	**7,204,813**	5,110,148	2,094,665	71	29
1977	**7,336,036**	5,209,664	2,126,372	71	29
1978	**7,327,118**	5,180,673	2,146,445	71	29
1979	**7,457,099**	5,281,319	2,175,780	71	29
1980	**7,577,763**	5,349,601	2,228,162	71	29
1981[c]	**7,578,283**	5,372,204	2,206,079	71	29
1981[c]	**7,631,267**	5,379,020	2,252,247	70	30
1982[p]	**7,542,312**	5,339,343	2,202,969	71	29

For sources, see next page.

Note: Unless otherwise footnoted, data show opening fall enrollment of all students (degree-credit and non-degree-credit) in four-year institutions of higher education in the fifty states, D. C., Canal Zone, Guam, Puerto Rico, the Virgin Islands, and the Trust Territories of the Pacific.

a Degree-credit only.

b From 1972 to 1981, NCES aggregated data from two-year branches of four-year institutions with other two-year institutions. Earlier, branch enrollments were aggregated with the parent institution's category.

c In 1981, NCES developed a new method for classifying institutions. Figures prior to 1981 and data on the upper 1981 line show totals using the traditional method; figures on the lower 1981 line and following lines are aggregated by the new method. For further information on the new classification method see NCES Bulletin April 7, 1981.

p Preliminary.

81 Enrollment of All Students in Four-Year Institutions, by Control of Institution and by Attendance Status, 1963–1982

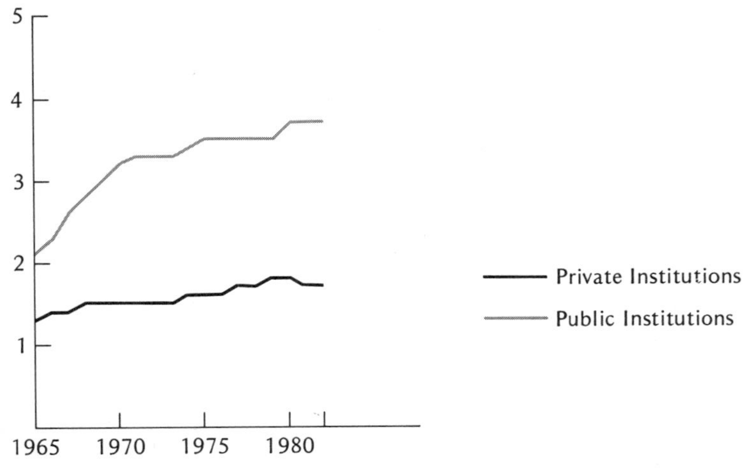

Year	Public Four-Year Institutions				Private Four-Year Institutions			
	Number of Students		Percentage		Number of Students		Percentage	
	Full-time	Part-time	Full-time	Part-time	Full-time	Part-time	Full-time	Part-time
1963[a]	1,664,296	655,225	72	28	1,096,425	484,764	69	31
1964[a]	1,864,338	719,467	72	28	1,179,423	511,363	70	30
1965[a]	2,144,295	770,365	74	26	1,295,287	515,080	72	28
1966	2,344,150	845,154	74	26	1,385,741	532,576	72	28
1967	2,575,706	899,954	74	26	1,427,924	542,024	72	28
1968	2,826,744	995,064	74	26	1,445,140	508,262	74	26
1969	2,995,587	1,096,016	73	27	1,485,731	507,749	75	25
1970	3,181,329	1,192,757	73	27	1,515,246	532,822	74	26
1971	3,308,430	1,179,643	74	26	1,528,478	517,060	75	25
1972[b]	3,306,006	1,263,336	72	28	1,534,051	523,460	75	25
1972[b]	3,250,947	1,225,914	73	27	1,528,560	521,452	75	25
1973	3,277,095	1,300,328	72	28	1,529,922	553,191	73	27
1974	3,350,411	1,400,313	71	29	1,562,491	579,682	73	27
1975	3,503,152	1,541,872	69	31	1,631,123	612,602	73	27
1976	3,466,189	1,480,538	70	30	1,643,959	614,127	73	27
1977	3,515,123	1,479,500	70	30	1,694,541	646,872	72	28
1978	3,479,327	1,490,051	70	30	1,710,346	656,394	72	28
1979	3,528,633	1,498,309	70	30	1,752,686	677,471	72	28
1980	3,595,355	1,537,406	70	30	1,754,246	690,756	72	28
1981[c]	3,622,988	1,516,493	70	30	1,749,216	698,586	71	29
1981[c]	3,642,574	1,540,403	70	30	1,736,446	711,844	71	29
1982[p]	3,626,407	1,514,473	71	29	1,712,936	688,496	71	29

For footnotes, see preceding page.

Sources:

1 NCES, *Opening Fall Enrollment in Higher Education* (Washington: GPO), *1965,* p. 6; *1966,* p. 9; *1967,* p. 3; *1968,* p. 6; *1969,* p. 153; *1970,* p. 241; *1972,* pp. 4, 6; *1975,* pp. 11, 22; *1977,* pp. 4, 23; *1979,* pp. 11, 12.

2 NCES, *Fall Enrollment in Higher Education (Analytic Report), 1974* (Washington: GPO), 1976, p. 13.

3 NCES, "Fall Enrollment in Colleges and Universities, 1980, Preliminary Estimates," *NCES Early Release,* November 30, 1981, tables A, C, D; 1982 Preliminary Estimates, January 1983, tables A, C, D.

82 Enrollment of Men in Four-Year Institutions, by Attendance Status, 1963–1982

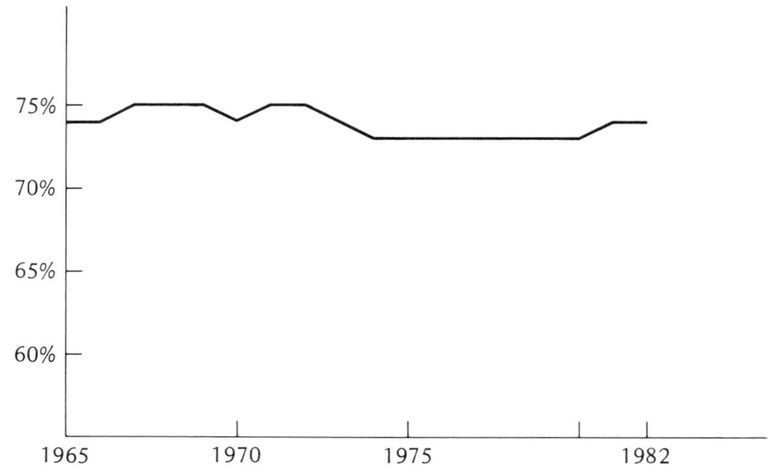

Year	Number of Men at Four-Year Institutions			Percentage	
	Total	**Full-time**	**Part-time**	**Full-time**	**Part-time**
1963[a]	**2,401,230**	1,708,354	692,876	71	29
1964[a]	**2,611,191**	1,870,670	740,521	72	28
1965[a]	**2,873,042**	2,111,933	761,109	74	26
1966	**3,069,370**	2,281,219	788,151	74	26
1967	**3,241,292**	2,418,630	822,662	75	25
1968	**3,413,732**	2,562,803	850,929	75	25
1969	**3,582,992**	2,680,827	902,165	75	25
1970	**3,757,222**	2,795,167	962,055	74	26
1971	**3,791,169**	2,858,919	932,250	75	25
1972[b]	**3,779,645**	2,820,560	959,085	75	25
1972[b]	**3,725,393**	2,785,400	939,993	75	25
1973	**3,751,703**	2,765,024	986,679	74	26
1974	**3,824,202**	2,796,337	1,027,864	73	27
1975	**4,018,105**	2,916,385	1,101,720	73	27
1976	**3,865,863**	2,825,936	1,039,927	73	27
1977	**3,865,857**	2,829,920	1,035,927	73	27
1978	**3,797,072**	2,772,161	1,024,911	73	27
1979	**3,804,577**	2,789,505	1,015,072	73	27
1980	**3,831,299**	2,812,797	1,018,502	73	27
1981[c]	**3,805,727**	2,801,430	1,004,297	74	26
1981[c]	**3,852,056**	2,823,381	1,028,675	74	27
1982[p]	**3,821,366**	2,808,911	1,012,455	74	26

For sources, see next page.

Note: Unless otherwise footnoted, data show opening fall enrollment of all students (degree-credit and non-degree-credit) in four-year institutions of higher education in the fifty states, D. C., Canal Zone, Guam, Puerto Rico, the Virgin Islands, and the Trust Territories of the Pacific.

a Degree-credit only.

b From 1972 to 1981, NCES aggregated data from two-year branches of four-year institutions with other two-year institutions. Earlier, branch enrollments were aggregated with the parent institution's category.

c In 1981, NCES developed a new method for classifying institutions. Figures prior to 1981 and data on the upper 1981 line show totals using the traditional method; figures on the lower 1981 line and following lines are aggregated by the new method. For further information on the new classification method see NCES Bulletin April 7, 1981.

p Preliminary.

83 Enrollment of Women in Four-Year Institutions, by Attendance Status, 1963–1982

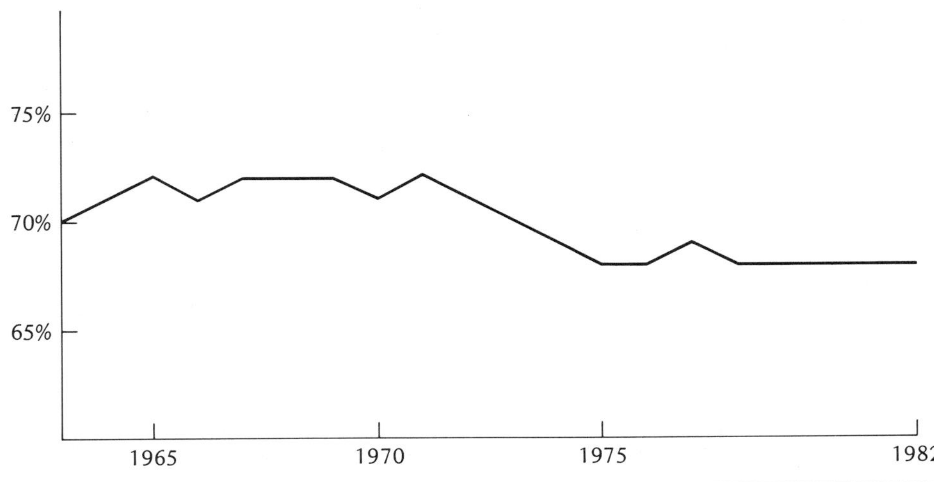

Year	Number of Women at Four-Year Institutions: Total	Full-time	Part-time	Percentage: Full-time	Part-time
1963[a]	**1,499,480**	1,052,367	447,113	70	30
1964[a]	**1,663,400**	1,172,091	490,309	71	29
1965[a]	**1,851,985**	1,327,649	524,336	72	28
1966	**2,038,251**	1,448,672	589,579	71	29
1967	**2,204,316**	1,585,000	619,316	72	28
1968	**2,361,478**	1,709,081	652,397	72	28
1969	**2,502,091**	1,800,491	701,600	72	28
1970	**2,664,932**	1,901,408	763,524	71	29
1971	**2,742,442**	1,977,989	764,453	72	28
1972[b]	**2,847,208**	2,019,497	827,711	71	29
1972[b]	**2,800,580**	1,993,207	807,373	71	29
1973	**2,908,833**	2,041,993	866,840	70	30
1974	**3,068,695**	2,116,564	952,131	69	31
1975	**3,270,644**	2,217,890	1,052,754	68	32
1976	**3,338,950**	2,284,212	1,054,738	68	32
1977	**3,470,179**	2,379,744	1,090,435	69	31
1978	**3,530,046**	2,408,512	1,121,534	68	32
1979	**3,652,522**	2,491,814	1,160,708	68	32
1980	**3,746,464**	2,536,804	1,209,660	68	32
1981[c]	**3,772,556**	2,570,774	1,201,782	68	32
1981[c]	**3,779,211**	2,555,639	1,223,572	68	32
1982[p]	**3,720,946**	2,530,432	1,190,514	68	32

For footnotes, see preceding page.

Sources:

1 NCES, *Opening Fall Enrollment in Higher Education* (Washington: GPO), *1965,* p. 6; *1966,* p. 9; *1967,* p. 3; *1968,* p. 6; *1969,* p. 153; *1970,* p. 241; *1972,* pp. 4, 6; *1975,* pp. 11, 22; *1977,* pp. 4, 23.

2 NCES, *Fall Enrollment in Higher Education (Analytic Report)*, 1974 (Washington: GPO), 1976, p. 13.

3 NCES, "Fall Enrollment in Colleges and Universities, 1981, Preliminary Estimates," *NCES Early Release,* November 30, 1981, table E; 1982 Preliminary Estimates, January 1982, table E.

84 Enrollment of All Students in Two-Year Institutions, by Attendance Status, 1963–1982

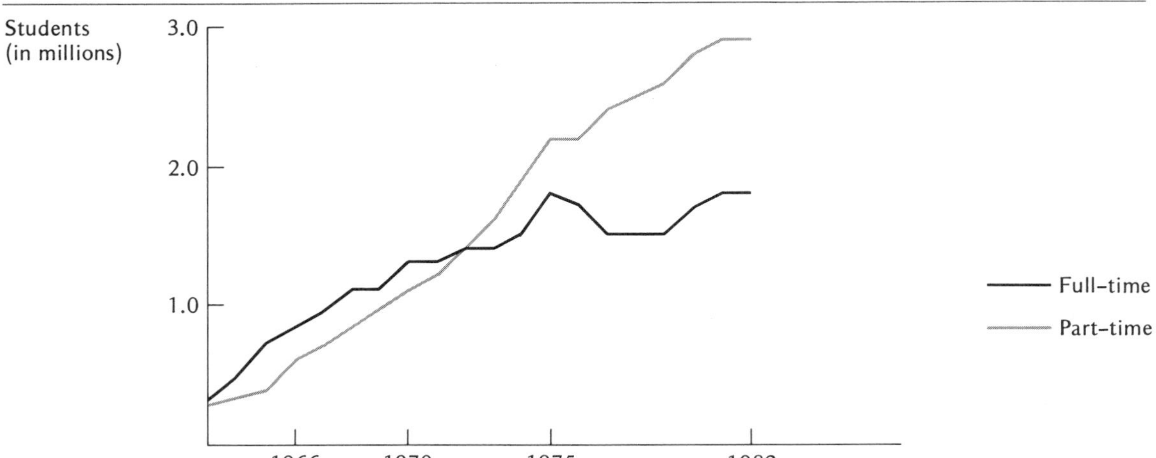

Year	Number of Students at Two-Year Institutions			Percentage	
	Total	Full-time	Part-time	Full-time	Part-time
1963[a]	**627,806**	328,893	298,913	52	48
1964[a]	**713,276**	398,053	315,223	56	44
1965[a]	**845,244**	497,673	347,571	59	41
1966	**1,330,856**	739,880	590,976	56	44
1967	**1,518,079**	823,361	694,718	54	46
1968	**1,796,426**	978,596	817,830	54	46
1969	**1,981,150**	1,060,303	920,847	54	46
1970	**2,227,214**	1,168,900	1,058,314	52	48
1971	**2,491,420**	1,295,246	1,196,174	52	48
1972[b]	**2,670,934**	1,291,350	1,379,584	48	52
1972[b]	**2,771,814**	1,352,800	1,419,014	49	51
1973	**3,033,761**	1,449,668	1,584,093	48	52
1974	**3,428,642**	1,529,567	1,899,075	45	55
1975	**4,001,970**	1,788,621	2,213,349	45	55
1976	**3,916,613**	1,692,941	2,223,672	43	57
1977	**4,078,984**	1,686,145	2,392,839	41	59
1978	**4,064,832**	1,589,938	2,474,894	39	61
1979	**4,250,027**	1,620,107	2,629,920	38	62
1980	**4,519,132**	1,748,357	2,770,775	39	61
1981[c]	**4,744,186**	1,837,621	2,906,565	39	61
1981[c]	**4,630,108**	1,748,292	2,881,816	38	62
1982[p]	**4,701,869**	1,804,954	2,896,915	38	62

For sources, see next page.

Notes: Unless otherwise footnoted, data show opening fall enrollment of all students (degree-credit and non-degree-credit) in two-year institutions of higher education in the fifty states, D. C., Canal Zone, Guam, Puerto Rico, the Virgin Islands, and the Trust Territories of the Pacific.

As of April 1981, NCES adopted a new definition of two-year institutions. They are now defined as any institution in which less than 25 percent of the degrees awarded are at the baccalaureate level.

a Degree-credit only.

b From 1972 to 1981, NCES aggregated data from two-year branches of four-year institutions with other two-year institutions. Earlier, branch enrollments were aggregated with the parent institution's category.

c In 1981, NCES developed a new method for classifying institutions. Figures prior to 1981 and data on the upper 1981 line show totals using the traditional method; figures on the lower 1981 line and following lines are aggregated by the new method. For further information on the new classification method see NCES Bulletin April 7, 1981.

p Preliminary.

85 Enrollment of All Students in Two-Year Institutions, by Control of Institution and by Attendance Status, 1963–1982

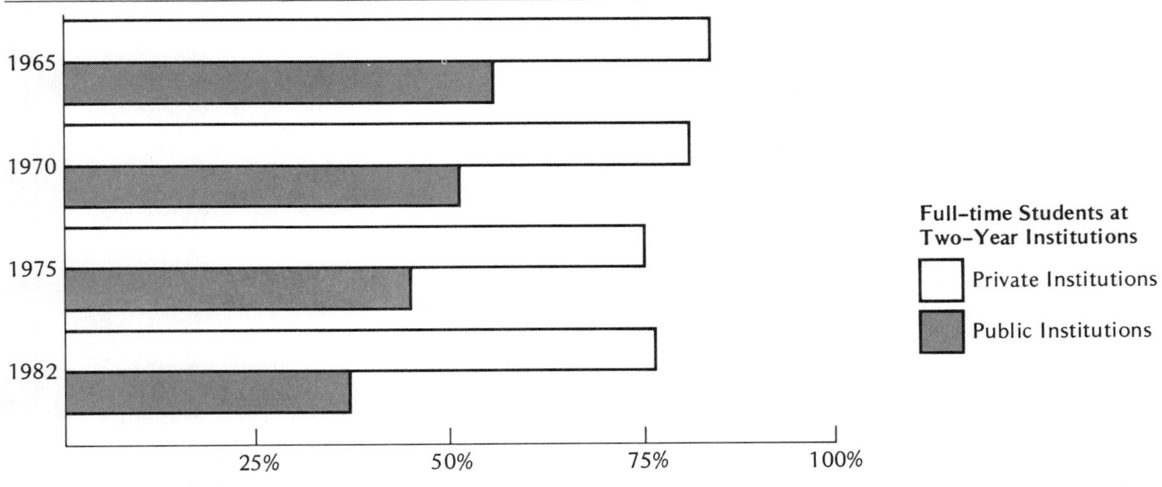

	Public Two-Year Institutions				Private Two-Year Institutions			
	Number of Students		Percentage		Number of Students		Percentage	
Year	Full-time	Part-time	Full-time	Part-time	Full-time	Part-time	Full-time	Part-time
1963[a]	269,031	284,271	49	51	59,862	14,642	80	20
1964[a]	323,845	298,133	52	48	74,208	17,090	81	19
1965[a]	410,327	329,591	55	45	87,346	17,980	83	17
1966	623,109	568,673	52	48	116,771	22,303	84	16
1967	705,525	669,145	51	49	117,836	25,573	82	18
1968	857,278	790,386	52	48	121,318	27,444	82	18
1969	952,499	895,411	52	48	107,804	25,436	81	19
1970	1,067,899	1,034,073	51	49	101,001	24,241	81	19
1971	1,195,028	1,171,584	50	50	100,218	24,590	80	20
1972[b]	1,198,356	1,355,177	47	53	92,994	24,407	79	21
1972[b]	1,254,315	1,392,599	47	53	98,485	26,415	79	21
1973	1,347,376	1,553,608	46	54	102,292	30,485	77	23
1974	1,430,785	1,868,086	43	57	98,782	30,989	76	24
1975	1,675,552	2,175,445	44	56	113,069	37,904	75	25
1976	1,573,980	2,191,927	42	58	118,961	31,745	79	21
1977	1,553,948	2,359,020	40	60	132,197	33,819	80	20
1978	1,447,116	2,435,707	37	63	142,822	39,187	78	22
1979	1,478,144	2,591,318	36	64	141,963	38,602	79	21
1980	1,592,331	2,732,302	37	63	156,026	38,473	80	20
1981[c]	1,663,216	2,863,178	37	63	174,405	43,387	80	20
1981[c]	1,595,799	2,836,358	36	64	152,493	45,458	77	23
1982[p]	1,645,869	2,848,333	37	63	159,085	48,582	77	23

For footnotes, see preceding page.

Sources:

1 NCES, *Opening Fall Enrollment in Higher Education* (Washington: GPO), *1965,* p. 6; *1966,* p. 9; *1967,* p. 3; *1968,* p. 6; *1969,* p. 153; *1970,* p. 241; *1972,* pp. 4, 6; *1975,* pp. 11, 22; *1977,* pp. 4, 23; *1979,* p. 12.

2 NCES, *Fall Enrollment in Higher Education* (*Analytic Report*), *1974* (Washington: GPO), 1976, p. 13.

3 NCES, "Fall Enrollment in Colleges and Universities, 1980, Preliminary Estimates," *NCES Early Release,* November 31, 1981, tables C, D; 1982 Preliminary Estimates, January 1983, tables C, D.

86 Enrollment of Men in Two-Year Institutions, by Attendance Status, 1963–1982

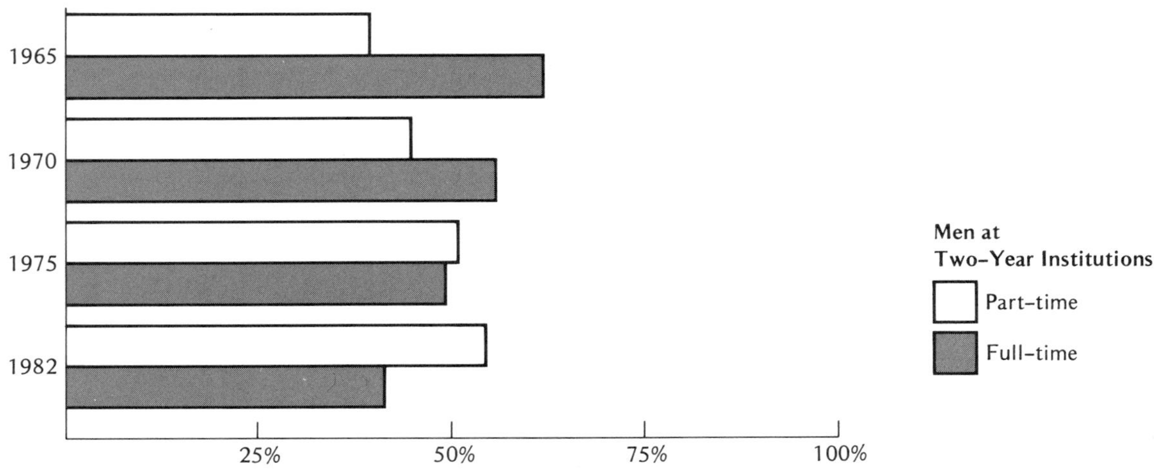

Year	Number of Men at Two-Year Institutions			Percentage	
	Total	**Full-time**	**Part-time**	**Full-time**	**Part-time**
1963[a]	**388,297**	205,623	182,674	53	47
1964[a]	**440,570**	250,649	189,921	57	43
1965[a]	**523,532**	322,029	201,503	62	38
1966	**811,187**	467,191	343,996	58	42
1967	**917,265**	522,358	394,907	57	43
1968	**1,092,101**	625,236	466,865	57	43
1969	**1,192,630**	675,332	517,298	57	43
1970	**1,318,801**	732,248	586,553	56	44
1971	**1,451,571**	796,018	655,553	55	45
1972[b]	**1,496,257**	763,168	733,089	51	49
1972[b]	**1,550,509**	798,328	752,181	51	49
1973	**1,662,461**	845,176	817,285	51	49
1974	**1,842,851**	883,397	959,454	48	52
1975	**2,180,518**	1,048,775	1,131,743	48	52
1976	**1,994,352**	916,113	1,078,239	46	54
1977	**1,980,241**	865,841	1,114,400	44	56
1978	**1,900,762**	799,554	1,101,208	42	58
1979	**1,935,974**	798,690	1,137,284	41	59
1980	**2,043,075**	876,447	1,166,628	43	57
1981[c]	**2,136,422**	918,935	1,217,487	43	57
1981[c]	**2,054,820**	854,114	1,200,706	42	58
1982[p]	**2,092,115**	883,544	1,208,571	42	58

For sources, see next page.

Notes: Data show opening fall enrollment of all students (degree-credit and non-degree-credit) in two-year institutions of higher education in the U. S., and outlying parts.

As of April 1981, NCES adopted a new definition of two-year institutions. They are now defined as any institution in which less than 25 percent of the degrees awarded are at the baccalaureate level.

a Degree-credit only.

b From 1972 to 1981, NCES aggregated data from two-year branches of four-year institutions with other two-year institutions. Earlier, branch enrollments were aggregated with the parent institution's category.

c In 1981, NCES developed a new method for classifying institutions. Figures prior to 1981 and data on the upper 1981 line show totals using the traditional method; figures on the lower 1981 line and following lines are aggregated by the new method. For further information on the new classification method see NCES Bulletin April 7, 1981.

p Preliminary.

87 Enrollment of Women in Two-Year Institutions, by Attendance Status, 1963–1982

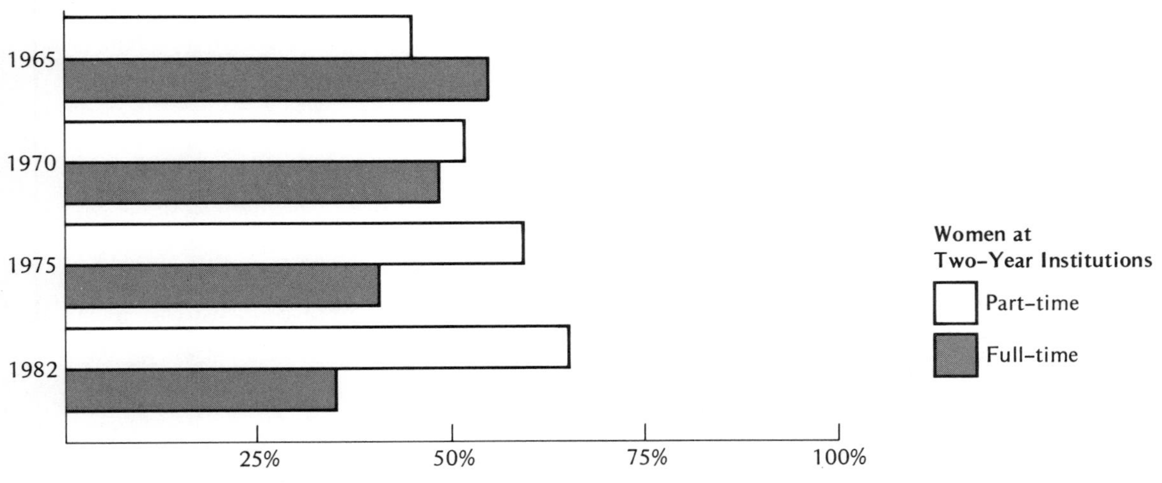

Year	Number of Women at Two-Year Institutions			Percentage	
	Total	Full-time	Part-time	Full-time	Part-time
1963[a]	**239,509**	123,270	116,239	51	49
1964[a]	**272,706**	147,404	125,302	54	46
1965[a]	**321,712**	175,644	146,068	55	45
1966	**519,669**	272,689	246,980	52	48
1967	**600,814**	301,003	299,811	50	50
1968	**704,325**	353,360	350,965	50	50
1969	**788,520**	384,971	403,549	49	51
1970	**908,413**	436,652	471,761	48	52
1971	**1,039,849**	499,228	540,621	48	52
1972[b]	**1,174,677**	528,182	646,495	45	55
1972[b]	**1,221,305**	554,472	666,833	45	55
1973	**1,371,300**	604,492	766,808	44	56
1974	**1,585,791**	646,170	939,621	41	49
1975	**1,821,452**	739,846	1,081,606	41	59
1976	**1,922,261**	776,828	1,145,433	40	60
1977	**2,098,743**	820,304	1,278,439	39	61
1978	**2,164,070**	790,384	1,373,686	37	63
1979	**2,314,053**	821,417	1,492,636	35	65
1980	**2,476,057**	871,910	1,604,147	35	65
1981[c]	**2,607,764**	918,686	1,689,078	35	65
1981[c]	**2,575,288**	894,178	1,681,110	35	65
1982[p]	**2,609,754**	921,410	1,688,344	35	65

For footnotes, see preceding page.

Sources:

1 NCES, *Opening Fall Enrollment in Higher Education* (Washington: GPO), *1965,* p. 6; *1966,* p. 9; *1967,* p. 3; *1968,* p. 6; *1969,* p. 153; *1970,* p. 241; *1972,* pp. 4, 6; *1975,* pp. 11, 22; *1977,* pp. 4, 23; *1979,* p. 13.

2 NCES, *Fall Enrollment in Higher Education* (*Analytic Report*), *1974* (Washington: GPO), 1976, p. 13.

88 Enrollment of First-time Students in All Institutions, by Sex, Selected Years, 1950–1981

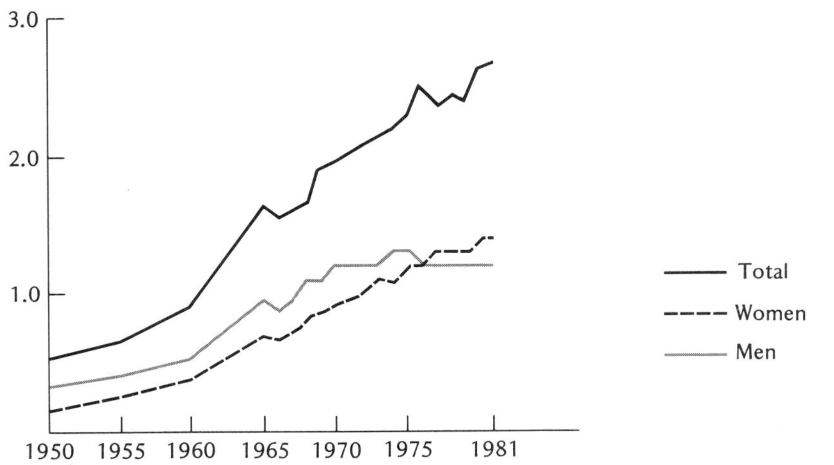

	First-time Students in All Institutions in the U. S. and Outlying Parts[a]				
	Number			Percent Distribution	
Year	Total	Men	Women	Men	Women
1950	**516,836**	319,733	197,103	62	38
1955	**675,060**	418,363	256,697	62	38
1960	**929,823**	542,774	387,049	58	42
1965[e]	**1,642,000**	947,000	695,000	58	42
1966	**1,565,564**	894,916	670,648	57	43
1967	**1,652,317**	936,406	715,911	57	43
1968	**1,907,938**	1,089,412	818,526	57	43
1969	**1,983,992**	1,126,189	857,803	57	43
1970	**2,080,244**	1,159,393	920,851	56	44
1971	**2,135,947**	1,178,399	957,548	55	45
1972	**2,171,268**	1,166,197	1,005,071	54	46
1973	**2,248,100**	1,192,464	1,055,636	53	47
1974	**2,392,869**	1,255,985	1,136,884	52	48
1975	**2,543,552**	1,340,621	1,202,931	53	47
1976	**2,377,242**	1,183,745	1,193,497	50	50
1977	**2,431,600**	1,172,147	1,259,453	48	52
1978	**2,422,398**	1,155,747	1,266,651	48	52
1979	**2,538,119**	1,194,534	1,343,585	47	53
1980	**2,625,138**	1,233,446	1,391,692	47	53
1981	**2,636,231**	1,233,157	1,403,074	47	53

For sources, see next page.

a Data are opening fall enrollments of first-time students for the fifty states and D. C., Canal Zone, Puerto Rico, the Pacific Islands, and the Virgin Islands. Data prior to 1965 are degree-credit enrollments only. For 1965 and later, they are total (degree-credit and non-degree-credit) enrollments.

e Estimates.

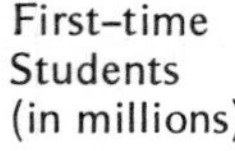

89 Enrollment of First-time Students in All Institutions, by Control of Institution, Selected Years, 1950–1980

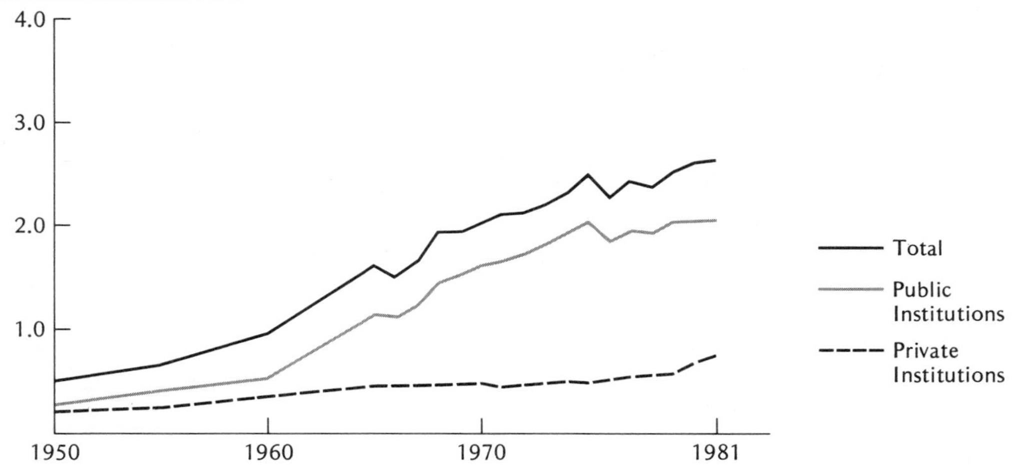

First-time Students in All Institutions in the U. S. and Outlying Parts[a]

Year	Number			Percent Distribution	
	Total	Public	Private	Public	Private
1950	**516,836**	286,131	230,705	55	45
1955	**675,060**	404,303	270,757	60	40
1960	**929,823**	581,890	347,933	63	37
1965[e]	**1,642,000**	1,166,000	476,000	71	29
1966	**1,565,564**	1,111,032	454,532	71	29
1967	**1,652,317**	1,212,846	439,471	73	27
1968	**1,907,938**	1,452,193	455,745	76	24
1969	**1,983,992**	1,522,978	461,014	77	23
1970	**2,080,244**	1,618,301	461,943	78	22
1971	**2,135,947**	1,684,983	450,964	79	21
1972	**2,171,268**	1,725,934	445,334	79	21
1973	**2,248,100**	1,800,931	447,169	80	20
1974	**2,393,869**	1,935,838	457,031	81	19
1975	**2,543,552**	2,067,860	475,692	81	19
1976	**2,377,242**	1,880,968	496,274	79	21
1977	**2,431,600**	1,936,019	495,581	80	20
1978	**2,422,398**	1,922,057	500,341	79	21
1979	**2,538,119**	2,027,672	510,447	80	20
1980	**2,625,138**	2,092,759	532,379	80	20
1981	**2,636,231**	2,086,873	549,358	79	21

For footnotes, see preceding page.

Sources:

1 USOE, *Opening (Fall) Enrollment in Higher Education, 1960 Analytic Report* (Washington: GPO), 1961, p. 11.

2 USOE, *Opening Fall Enrollment in Higher Education* (Washington: GPO), *1965,* p. 7; *1967,* p. 6; *1968,* p. 26.

3 NCES, *Fall Enrollment in Higher Education* (Washington: GPO), *1969, Supplementary Data,* p. 17; *1970, Supplementary Information, Summary Data,* p. 15; *1971,* pp. 390, 391; *1972,* pp. 20, 21; *1973,* pp. 209, 214, 219; *1974,* pp. 5, 194, 199, 204; *1975,* pp. 30, 31; *1977,* p. 23; *1979,* pp. 12, 13.

4 NCES, *Fall Enrollment in Colleges and Universities, 1980* (Washington: GPO), 1982, p. 12.

First-time Enrollment in All Institutions, by Region and State, Selected Years, 1970–1981

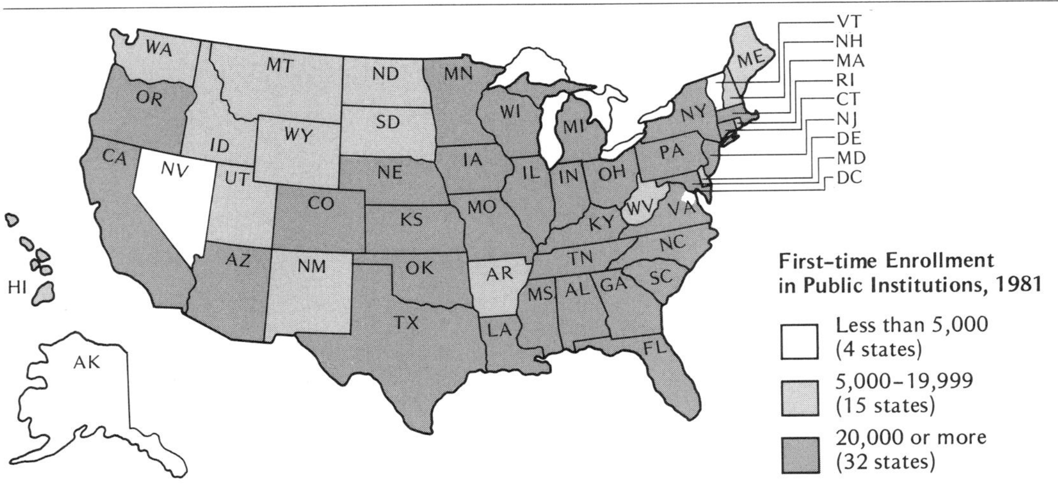

Region and State	1970 All Institutions	1975 All Institutions	1981 All Institutions	1981 Public	1981 Private
U. S. & Outlying Parts	**2,080,244**	**2,543,552**	**2,636,231**	**2,086,873**	**549,358**
50 States & D. C.	**2,063,397**	**2,515,155**	**2,595,421**	**2,072,443**	**522,978**
New England	**141,467**	**161,185**	**173,566**	**94,704**	**78,862**
Connecticut	31,089	33,768	38,739	26,300	12,439
Maine	9,956	9,802	10,233	6,912	3,321
Massachusetts	76,130	86,956	88,867	42,706	46,161
New Hampshire	7,573	11,190	11,099	5,202	5,897
Rhode Island	10,746	12,224	18,526	10,382	8,144
Vermont	5,973	7,245	6,102	3,202	2,900
Mideast	**372,318**	**438,312**	**424,853**	**286,108**	**138,745**
Delaware	8,755	7,876	7,206	6,286	920
D. C.	10,400	10,425	11,920	4,678	7,242
Maryland	33,638	43,007	45,795	41,394	4,401
New Jersey	56,867	65,378	65,044	54,061	10,983
New York	172,121	203,025	185,748	114,530	71,218
Pennsylvania	90,537	108,601	109,140	65,159	43,981
Southeast	**364,344**	**467,111**	**477,177**	**380,072**	**97,105**
Alabama	25,479	38,152	36,595	31,504	5,091
Arkansas	13,475	16,896	18,269	14,936	3,333
Florida	56,949	64,515	88,316	72,515	15,801
Georgia	27,608	37,625	37,250	26,253	10,997
Kentucky	21,265	28,662	28,975	21,332	7,643
Louisiana	27,188	35,278	34,457	30,003	4,454
Mississippi	22,940	35,585	29,812	27,588	2,224
North Carolina	57,200	74,951	70,094	55,405	14,689
South Carolina	23,753	38,624	32,072	25,010	7,062
Tennessee	29,148	38,184	42,072	29,077	12,995
Virginia	43,407	39,343	41,960	32,405	9,555
West Virginia	15,932	19,296	17,305	14,044	3,261
Great Lakes	**388,834**	**471,239**	**513,769**	**417,429**	**96,340**
Illinois	114,834	136,596	158,812	135,415	23,397
Indiana	43,341	49,461	59,709	45,757	13,952
Michigan	90,815	113,335	106,447	91,023	15,424
Ohio	88,426	101,550	118,714	82,196	36,518
Wisconsin	51,418	70,297	70,087	63,038	7,049

Enrollment of First-time Students[a]

(*Continued on next page*)

— No data reported. For sources, see next page.

a Figures show degree-credit and non-degree-credit enrollment data. The 1970 questionnaire requested data on "first-time students" who had not previously attended any institution of higher education. The 1975 and 1978 questionnaries asked for data on "first-time students (entering freshmen)."

91 First-time Enrollment in All Institutions, by Region and State, Selected Years, 1970–1981—*Continued*

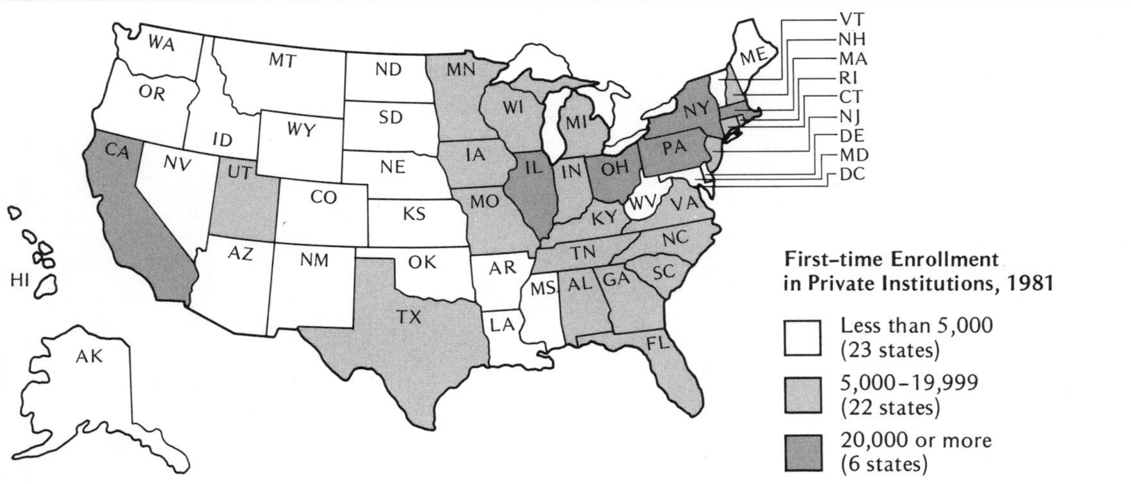

	Enrollment of First-time Students[a]				
	1970	1975	1981		
Region and State	All Institutions	All Institutions	All Institutions	Public	Private
Plains	**165,807**	**175,090**	**206,558**	**164,830**	**41,728**
Iowa	29,292	32,022	39,146	29,785	9,361
Kansas	26,067	28,743	28,441	24,971	3,470
Minnesota	36,672	36,384	42,508	32,280	10,228
Missouri	41,335	42,888	52,983	42,107	10,876
Nebraska	15,348	18,386	25,570	21,419	4,151
North Dakota	9,358	9,313	9,556	8,825	731
South Dakota	7,735	7,354	8,354	5,443	2,911
Southwest	**164,800**	**224,312**	**280,451**	**257,194**	**23,257**
Arizona	25,895	45,655	75,596	73,844	1,752
New Mexico	9,441	8,821	9,660	9,258	402
Oklahoma	27,445	30,640	34,485	29,512	4,973
Texas	102,019	139,126	160,710	144,580	16,130
Rocky Mountains	**69,265**	**76,757**	**72,225**	**58,535**	**13,690**
Colorado	28,933	33,343	28,731	25,718	3,013
Idaho	11,628	11,118	10,905	6,822	4,083
Montana	7,250	7,394	7,610	6,337	1,273
Utah	16,612	20,109	19,793	14,484	5,309
Wyoming	4,842	4,793	5,186	5,174	12
Far West	**392,247**	**484,045**	**442,149**	**408,898**	**33,251**
Alaska	2,157	2,885	1,331	1,125	206
California	284,796	349,152	365,348	341,870	23,478
Hawaii	10,867	9,402	8,872	8,056	816
Nevada	3,440	9,795	4,101	4,088	13
Oregon	37,702	46,994	37,451	34,068	3,383
Washington	53,285	65,817	25,046	19,691	5,355
U. S. Service Schools	**4,315**	**17,104**	**4,673**	**4,673**	**—**
Outlying Parts	**16,847**	**28,397**	**40,810**	**14,430**	**26,380**

For footnote, see preceding page.

Sources:

1 NCES, *Fall Enrollment in Higher Education, 1970, Supplementary Information, Summary Data* (Washington: GPO), 1971, p. 61.

2 NCES, *Fall Enrollment in Higher Education, 1975, Summary Data* (Washington: GPO), 1977, pp. 167, 172, 177.

3 NCES, "1978 Fall Enrollment in Higher Education—Final Count," *NCES Announcement,* July 5, 1979, table 1.

4 NCES (Washington, 1983), unpublished data.

92 Percent Change in First-time Enrollment, by Region and State, 1970–1981

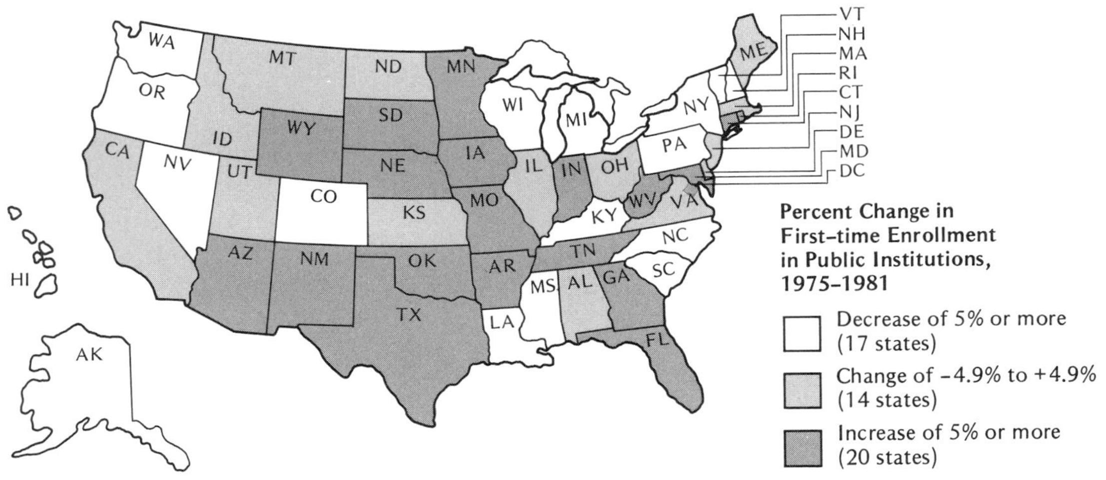

Region and State	1970–1981 All Institutions	1975–1981 All Institutions	1975–1981 Public	1975–1981 Private
U. S. & Outlying Parts	**26.7**	**3.6**	**0.9**	**15.5**
50 States & D. C.	**25.8**	**3.2**	**0.8**	**13.7**
New England	**22.7**	**7.7**	**6.5**	**9.2**
Connecticut	24.6	14.7	9.6	27.2
Maine	−2.8	4.4	1.4	11.3
Massachusetts	16.7	2.2	0.5	3.9
New Hampshire	46.6	−0.8	−18.3	22.3
Rhode Island	72.4	51.6	99.7	15.9
Vermont	2.2	−15.8	−21.2	−8.8
Mideast	**14.1**	**−3.1**	**−9.2**	**12.6**
Delaware	−17.7	−8.5	0.8	−43.9
D. C.	14.6	14.3	26.3	7.8
Maryland	36.1	6.5	6.7	4.1
New Jersey	14.4	−0.5	0.3	−4.1
New York	7.9	−8.5	−18.2	13.0
Pennsylvania	20.6	0.5	−10.0	21.5
Southeast	**31.0**	**2.2**	**−1.4**	**18.8**
Alabama	43.6	−4.1	−2.5	−12.9
Arkansas	35.6	8.1	6.4	16.6
Florida	55.1	36.9	34.8	47.5
Georgia	34.9	−1.0	11.7	39.3
Kentucky	36.3	1.1	−9.4	49.3
Louisiana	26.7	−2.3	−5.6	27.3
Mississippi	30.0	−16.2	−17.3	0.3
North Carolina	22.5	−6.5	−9.9	8.9
South Carolina	35.0	−17.0	−19.1	−8.2
Tennessee	44.3	−10.2	7.3	17.4
Virginia	−3.3	6.7	2.9	21.5
West Virginia	8.6	−10.3	11.1	−6.8
Great Lakes	**32.1**	**9.0**	**6.2**	**23.4**
Illinois	38.3	16.3	18.9	3.1
Indiana	37.8	20.7	26.6	4.7
Michigan	17.2	−6.7	−8.8	14.1
Ohio	34.3	16.9	3.5	64.9
Wisconsin	36.3	−0.3	−1.4	10.2

(Continued on next page)

— Not calculated. No data reported for one or both years.

For source, see next page.

93 Percent Change in First-time Enrollment, by Region and State, 1970–1981—*Continued*

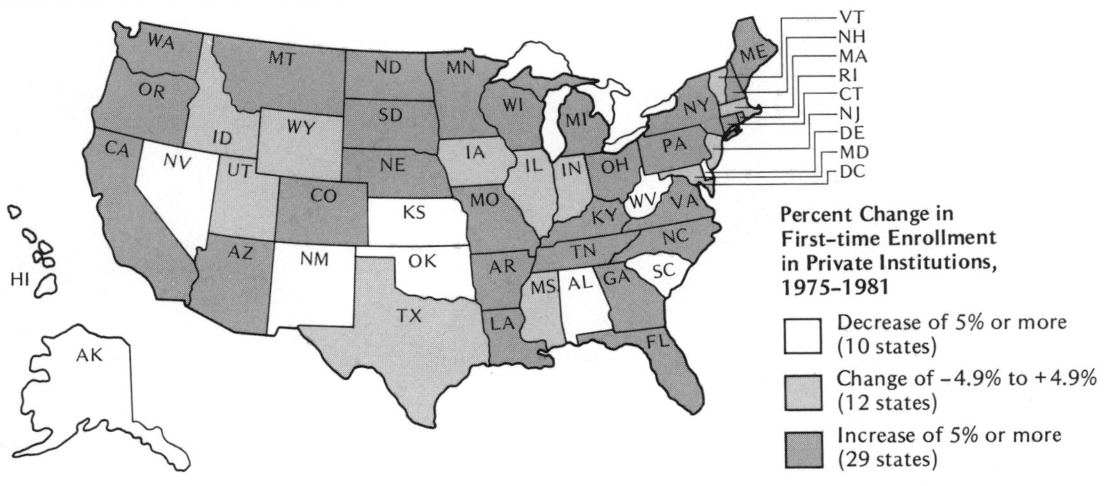

	Percent Change in First-time Enrollment			
	1970–81	**1975–81**		
Region and State	**All Institutions**	**All Institutions**	**Public**	**Private**
Plains	**24.6**	**18.0**	**21.9**	**7.2**
Iowa	33.6	22.3	33.2	−3.1
Kansas	9.1	−1.1	0.7	−12.1
Minnesota	15.9	16.8	19.3	9.6
Missouri	28.2	23.5	27.4	10.6
Nebraska	66.6	39.1	41.0	30.1
North Dakota	2.1	2.6	0.4	39.0
South Dakota	8.0	13.6	10.7	19.5
Southwest	**70.2**	**25.0**	**28.0**	**−0.2**
Arizona	191.9	65.6	66.4	37.1
New Mexico	2.3	9.5	17.9	−58.4
Oklahoma	25.7	12.6	16.3	−5.7
Texas	57.5	15.5	17.2	2.2
Rocky Mountains	**4.3**	**−5.9**	**−9.3**	**11.8**
Colorado	−0.7	−13.8	−17.8	−17.7
Idaho	−6.2	−1.9	−3.1	0.1
Montana	5.0	2.9	−4.0	60.3
Utah	19.2	−1.6	−2.0	0.5
Wyoming	7.1	8.2	8.0	—
Far West	**12.7**	**−8.7**	**−9.9**	**10.6**
Alaska	−38.3	−53.9	−56.7	−27.5
California	28.3	4.6	4.4	8.9
Hawaii	18.4	−5.6	−5.4	−7.6
Nevada	19.2	−58.1	−58.1	−61.8
Oregon	−0.7	−20.3	−22.5	12.0
Washington	−53.0	−61.9	−68.0	24.9
U. S. Service Schools	**8.3**	**−72.7**	**72.7**	**—**
Outlying Parts	**142.2**	**43.7**	**14.4**	**67.1**

For symbol explanation, see preceding page.

Source: Calculated from data on the two preceding pages.

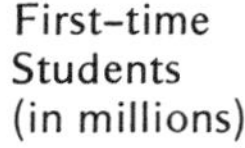

Enrollment of First-Time Students in Four-Year Institutions, by Sex, Selected Years, 1950–1981

First-time Students in Four-Year Institutions in the U. S. and Outlying Parts[a]

Year	Number			Percent Distribution	
	Total	**Men**	**Women**	**Men**	**Women**
1950	**410,325**	254,413	155,912	62	38
1955	**534,800**	332,024	202,776	62	38
1960	**714,440**	413,497	300,943	58	42
1965[e]	**1,082,000**	609,000	473,000	56	44
1966	**1,018,592**	570,438	448,154	56	44
1968	**1,115,900**	612,941	502,959	55	45
1970	**1,166,391**	630,970	535,421	54	46
1971	**1,138,418**	608,190	530,228	53	47
1972[b]	**1,108,175**	582,736	525,439	53	47
1972[b]	**1,073,427**	563,848	509,579	53	47
1973	**1,091,143**	568,567	522,576	52	48
1974	**1,147,158**	593,726	553,432	52	48
1975	**1,182,945**	607,518	575,427	51	49
1976	**1,146,781**	577,838	568,942	50	50
1977	**1,163,004**	575,273	587,731	49	51
1978	**1,163,685**	572,368	591,317	49	51
1979	**1,197,571**	584,152	613,419	49	51
1980	**1,209,451**	588,146	621,305	49	51
1981	**1,201,264**	581,312	619,952	48	52

For sources, see next page.

a Data are opening fall enrollments of first-time students for the fifty states and D. C., Canal Zone, Puerto Rico, the Pacific Islands, and the Virgin Islands. Data prior to 1965 are degree-credit enrollments only. For 1965 and later, they are total (degree-credit and non-degree-credit) enrollments.

b In 1972, NCES developed a new, or "current," method of aggregating enrollment data by type of institution (four-year and two-year). Under it, enrollments at two-year branches of four-year institutions are aggregated with other two-year institutions. (Under the former, or "traditional," method, branch enrollments were aggregated in the parent institution's category.) The figures prior to 1972 and the top line for 1972 show totals according to the "traditional" method; those on the lower line for 1972 and subsequent years show data aggregated by the "current" method.

e Estimates.

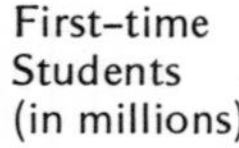

Enrollment of First-Time Students in Four-Year Institutions, by Control of Institution, Selected Years, 1950–1981

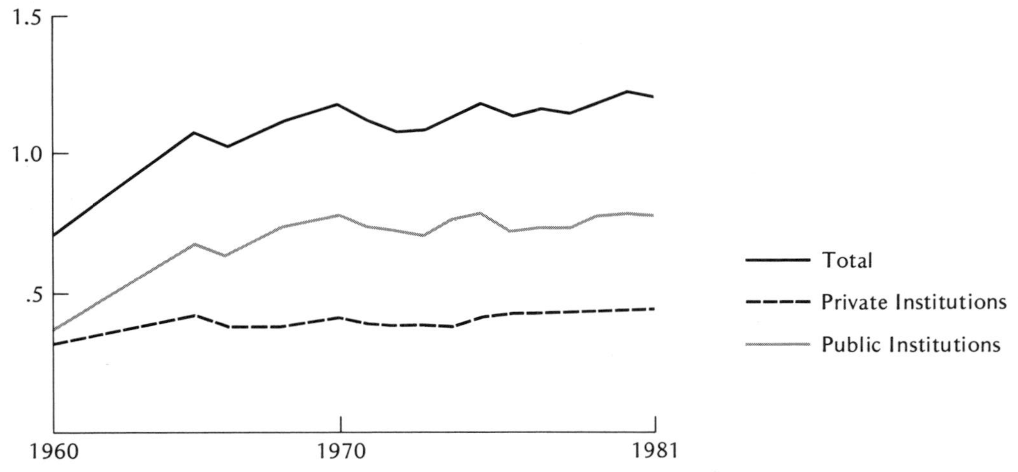

Year	Total	Public	Private	Public	Private
	First-time Students in Four-Year Institutions in the U. S. and Outlying Parts[a]				
	Number			**Percent Distribution**	
Year	**Total**	**Public**	**Private**	**Public**	**Private**
1950	**410,325**	204,073	206,252	50	50
1955	**534,800**	286,724	248,076	54	46
1960	**714,440**	399,307	315,133	56	44
1965[e]	**1,082,000**	672,000	410,000	62	38
1966	**1,018,592**	631,967	386,625	62	38
1968	**1,115,900**	733,532	382,368	66	34
1970	**1,166,391**	764,466	401,925	66	34
1971	**1,138,418**	747,520	390,898	66	34
1972[b]	**1,108,175**	718,841	389,334	65	35
1972[b]	**1,073,427**	687,755	385,672	64	36
1973	**1,091,143**	706,203	384,940	65	35
1974	**1,147,158**	753,456	393,702	66	34
1975	**1,182,945**	779,737	403,208	66	34
1976	**1,146,781**	722,186	424,595	63	37
1977	**1,163,004**	745,340	417,664	64	36
1978	**1,163,685**	744,544	419,141	64	36
1979	**1,197,571**	767,896	429,675	64	36
1980	**1,209,451**	773,847	435,604	64	36
1981	**1,201,264**	761,821	439,437	63	37

For footnotes, see preceding page.

Sources:

1 USOE, *Opening (Fall) Enrollment in Higher Education, 1960 Analytic Report* (Washington: GPO), 1961, p. 11.

2 USOE, *Opening Fall Enrollment in Higher Education* (Washington: GPO), *1965,* p. 7.

3 NCES, *Fall Enrollment in Higher Education* (Washington: GPO), *1970, Supplementary Information, Summary Data,* p. 15; *1971,* pp. 390, 391; *1972,* pp. 20, 21; *1973,* pp. 209, 214, 219; *1974,* pp. 5, 194, 199, 204; *1975,* pp. 30, 31; *1977,* p. 23; *1979,* p. 12.

4 NCES, "Fall Enrollment in Colleges and Universities, 1980, Preliminary Estimates," *NCES Early Release,* October 31, 1980, table B.

5 NCES (Washington, 1983), unpublished data.

96 Enrollment of First-Time Students in Two-Year Institutions, by Sex, Selected Years, 1950–1981

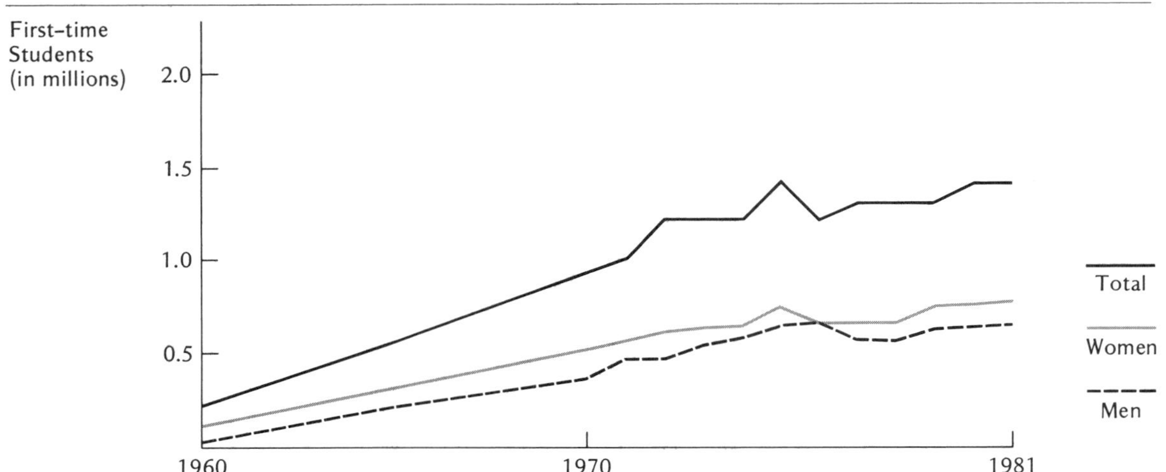

First-time Students in Two-Year Institutions in the U. S. and Outlying Parts[a]

Year	Number: Total	Number: Men	Number: Women	Percent Distribution: Men	Percent Distribution: Women
1950	**106,511**	65,320	41,191	61	39
1955	**140,260**	86,339	53,921	62	38
1960	**215,383**	129,277	83,106	60	40
1965[e]	**560,000**	338,000	222,000	60	40
1970	**913,853**	528,423	385,430	58	42
1971	**997,529**	570,209	427,320	57	43
1972[b]	**1,063,093**	583,461	479.632	55	45
1972[b]	**1,097,841**	602,349	495,492	55	45
1973	**1,156,957**	623,897	533,060	54	46
1974	**1,245,711**	662,259	583,452	53	47
1975	**1,360,607**	733,103	627,504	54	46
1976	**1,230,461**	605,907	624,554	49	51
1977	**1,268,596**	596,874	671,722	47	53
1978	**1,258,713**	583,379	675,334	46	54
1979	**1,340,548**	610,382	730,166	46	54
1980	**1,404,312**	640,735	763,577	46	54
1981	**1,422,157**	646,756	775,401	45	55

For sources, see next page.

a Data are opening fall enrollments of first-time students for the fifty states and D. C., Canal Zone, Puerto Rico, the Pacific Islands, and the Virgin Islands. Data prior to 1965 are degree-credit enrollments only. For 1965 and later, they are total (degree-credit and non-degree-credit) enrollments.

b From 1972 to 1981, the NCES method of aggregating data was based on type of institution. It aggregated data from two-year branches of four-year institutions with other two-year institutions. Earlier, branch enrollments were aggregated with the parent institution's category.

e Estimates.

97 Enrollment of First-Time Students in Two-Year Institutions, by Control of Institution, Selected Years, 1950–1981

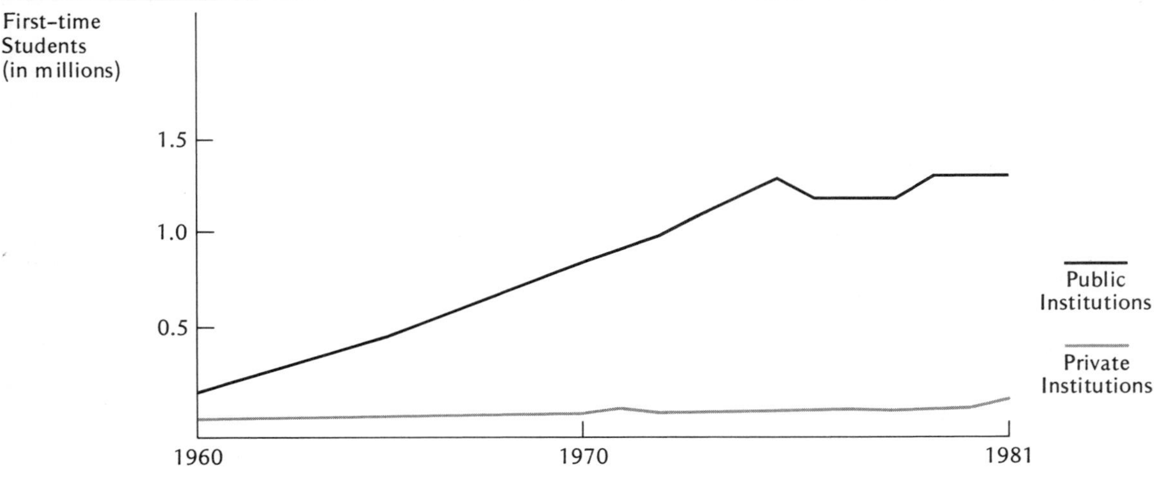

	First-time Students in Two-Year Institutions in the U. S. and Outlying Parts[a]				
	Number			Percent Distribution	
Year	Total	Public	Private	Public	Private
1950	**106,511**	82,058	24,453	77	23
1955	**140,260**	117,579	22,681	84	16
1960	**215,383**	182,583	32,800	85	15
1965[e]	**560,000**	494,000	66,000	88	12
1970	**913,853**	853,835	60,018	93	7
1971	**997,529**	937,463	60,066	94	6
1972[b]	**1,063,093**	1,007,093	56,000	95	5
1972[b]	**1,097,841**	1,038,179	59,662	95	5
1973	**1,156,957**	1,094,728	62,229	95	5
1974	**1,245,711**	1,182,382	63,329	95	5
1975	**1,360,607**	1,288,123	72,484	95	5
1976	**1,230,461**	1,158,782	71,679	94	6
1977	**1,268,596**	1,190,679	77,917	94	6
1978	**1,258,713**	1,177,513	81,200	94	6
1979	**1,340,548**	1,259,776	80,772	94	6
1980	**1,415,687**	1,318,912	96,775	93	7
1981	**1,434,967**	1,325,046	109,921	92	8

For footnotes, see preceding page.

Sources:

1 USOE, *Opening (Fall) Enrollment in Higher Education, 1960 Analytic Report* (Washington: GPO), 1961, p. 11.

2 USOE, *Opening Fall Enrollment in Higher Education* (Washington: GPO), *1965,* p. 7.

3 NCES, *Fall Enrollment in Higher Education* (Washington: GPO), *1970, Supplementary Information, Summary Data,* p. 15; *1971,* pp. 390, 391; *1972,* pp. 20, 21; *1973,* pp. 209, 214, 219; *1974,* pp. 5, 194, 199, 204; *1975,* pp. 30, 31; *1977,* p. 23; *1979,* p. 12.

4 NCES, "Fall Enrollment in Colleges and Universities, 1980, Preliminary Estimates," *NCES Early Release,* October 31, 1980, Table B.

5 NCES (Washington, 1983), unpublished data.

98 Graduate Enrollment, by Sex, Selected Years, 1929–30—1988

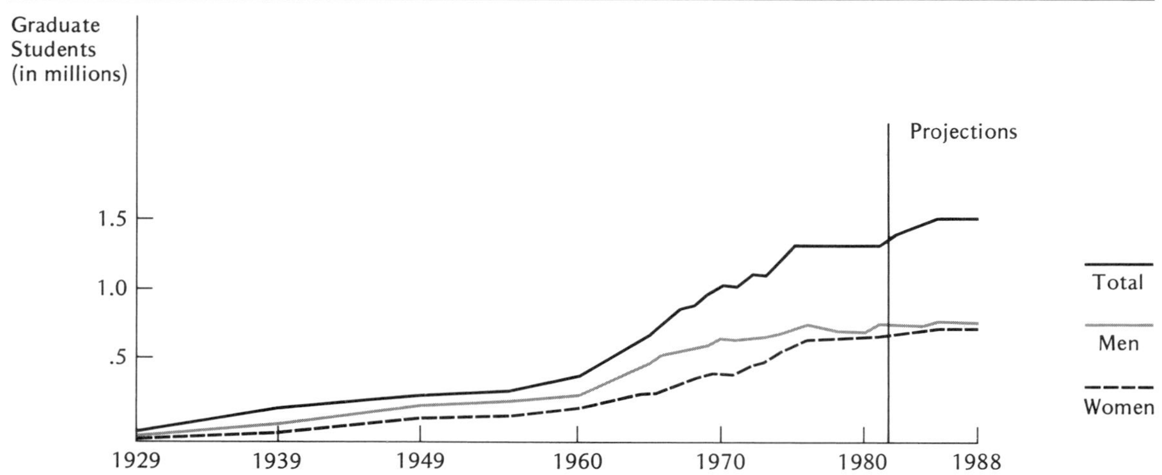

Year	Graduate Enrollment[a]: Number: Total	Number: Men	Number: Women	Percent Distribution: Men	Percent Distribution: Women
1929–30	**47,255**	29,070	18,185	62	38
1939–40	**105,748**	67,417	38,331	64	36
1949–50	**237,572**	172,310	65,262	73	27
1955	**250,771**	177,163	73,608	71	29
1960[e]	**356,000**	253,000	103,000	71	29
1965[e]	**697,000**	465,000	232,000	67	33
1966[e]	**768,000**	503,000	265,000	65	35
1967[e]	**849,000**	547,000	302,000	64	36
1968[e]	**885,000**	558,000	327,000	63	37
1969	**955,000**	590,000	366,000	62	38
1970	**1,031,000**	632,000	399,000	61	39
1971	**1,012,000**	615,000	397,000	61	39
1972	**1,066,000**	627,000	439,000	59	41
1973	**1,123,000**	647,000	476,000	58	42
1974	**1,190,000**	663,000	527,000	56	44
1975	**1,263,000**	700,000	563,000	55	45
1976	**1,333,000**	714,000	619,000	54	46
1977	**1,318,000**	700,000	617,000	53	47
1978	**1,319,000**	688,000	632,000	52	48
1979	**1,309,000**	669,000	640,000	51	49
1980	**1,343,000**	673,000	670,000	50	50
1981[e]	**1,342,555**[c]	673,849	668,706	50	50
Projections[b]					
1982	**1,431,000**	731,000	700,000	51	49
1985	**1,469,000**	741,000	728,000	50	50
1988	**1,470,000**	737,000	733,000	50	50

a Data for 1929–30 and 1939–40 are for forty-eight states and D. C. Data for all other years are for fifty states and D. C. Data through 1960 are resident graduate enrollments; those for 1965 and later are resident and extension enrollments. Data through 1949–50 are for the regular academic year; those for 1955 are as of November 1955; those for 1960 and later are opening fall enrollments. In 1976 the questionnaire definition of graduate student was changed from students holding a bachelor's or first professional degree and "taking work at the graduate level which is creditable toward a master's or doctor's degree" to students holding a bachelor's or first professional degree and "working toward a master's or doctor's degree." At the same time, unclassified students were to be reported at either the undergraduate or postbaccalaureate level. Those reported at the postbaccalaureate level were added to the graduate student total to produce the graduate enrollment figures shown in the source.

b NCES intermediate alternative projections.

c This figure includes unclassified (postbaccalaureate) students.

e Estimates.

For sources, see next page.

99 Graduate Enrollment, by Control of Institution, Selected Years, 1929–30—1988

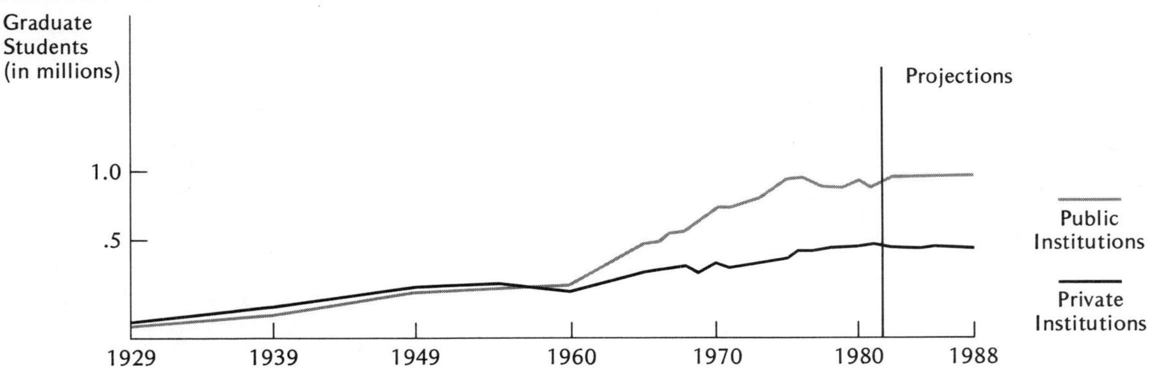

Year	Graduate Enrollment[a]				
	Number			Percent Distribution	
	Total	**Public**	**Private**	**Public**	**Private**
1929–30	**47,255**	20,198	27,057	43	57
1939–40	**105,748**	44,562	61,186	42	58
1949–50	**237,572**	108,296	129,276	46	54
1955	**250,771**	122,977	127,794	49	51
1960[e]	**356,000**	187,000	169,000	53	47
1965[e]	**697,000**	440,000	257,000	63	37
1966[e]	**768,000**	489,000	279,000	64	36
1967[e]	**849,000**	550,000	299,000	65	35
1968[e]	**885,000**	584,000	301,000	66	34
1969	**955,000**	666,000	289,000	70	30
1970	**1,031,000**	724,000	307,000	70	30
1971	**1,012,000**	712,000	300,000	70	30
1972	**1,066,000**	757,000	309,000	71	29
1973	**1,123,000**	799,000	324,000	71	29
1974	**1,190,000**	852,000	338,000	72	28
1975	**1,263,000**	906,000	357,000	72	28
1976	**1,333,000**	932,000	401,000	70	30
1977	**1,318,000**	900,000	416,000	68	32
1978	**1,319,000**	894,000	425,000	68	32
1979	**1,309,000**	884,000	425,000	68	32
1980	**1,343,000**	901,000	442,000	67	33
1981[e]	**1,342,555**[c]	886,930	455,625	67	33
	Projections[b]				
1982	**1,431,000**	965,000	466,000	68	32
1985	**1,469,000**	990,000	479,000	67	34
1988	**1,470,000**	990,000	480,000	67	34

For footnotes, see preceding page.

Sources:

1 USOE, *Statistics of Higher Education* (Washington: GPO), *1947–48,* pp. 72–77; *1949–50,* pp. 56, 61; *1955–56,* pp. 124, 135.

2 NCES, *Projections of Education Statistics* (Washington: GPO), *to 1979–80,* p. 34; *to 1986–87,* table 9; *to 1988–89,* pp. 27–29, *to 1990–91,* pp. 52–54.

3 NCES (Washington, 1983), unpublished data.

Enrollment for Advanced Degrees, by Region and State, Selected Years, 1960–1981

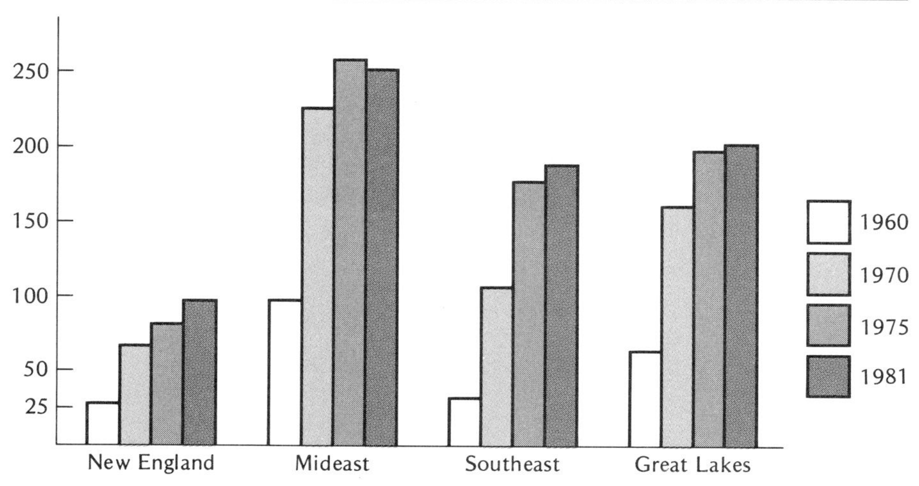

Region and State	Enrollment for Advanced Degrees 1960	1965	1970	1975	1981
U. S. & Outlying Parts	**314,349**	**535,332**	**816,207**	**1,053,769**	**1,107,121**
50 States & D. C.	**313,961**	**534,295**	**813,551**	**1,049,510**	**1,101,272**
New England	**28,269**	**48,573**	**67,893**	**83,210**	**90,538**
Connecticut	7,173	12,239	19,831	24,925	25,462
Maine	167	965	1,075	2,033	1,591
Massachusetts	18,852	30,277	40,053	46,167	51,346
New Hampshire	638	1,686	1,356	2,361	3,875
Rhode Island	1,236	2,983	4,671	5,896	5,973
Vermont	203	423	907	1,828	2,291
Mideast	**97,626**	**156,459**	**226,959**	**258,674**	**251,757**
Delaware	1,047	1,501	2,078	1,780	2,055
D. C.	7,560	13,933	16,564	18,218	21,141
Maryland	5,335	10,621	16,369	25,370	22,247
New Jersey	8,608	17,129	26,122	31,636	31,093
New York	54,446	79,553	115,445	131,698	119,718
Pennsylvania	20,630	33,722	50,381	49,972	55,503
Southeast	**31,414**	**55,343**	**106,520**	**176,148**	**187,563**
Alabama	2,474	3,702	7,640	14,938	13,676
Arkansas	1,230	2,018	2,817	4,133	5,823
Florida	3,856	7,788	14,698	23,562	28,378
Georgia	2,637	5,020	11,961	22,283	22,233
Kentucky	2,908	3,496	7,354	15,559	13,992
Louisiana	3,961	7,496	11,826	15,320	23,765
Mississippi	1,205	2,394	4,486	9,481	7,390
North Carolina	4,385	7,687	11,538	16,941	18,444
South Carolina	1,788	1,698	4,016	12,131	9,104
Tennessee	3,983	6,615	10,716	16,993	13,772
Virginia	2,048	4,634	15,129	15,958	20,554
West Virginia	939	2,795	4,339	8,849	10,432
Great Lakes	**64,423**	**107,945**	**160,583**	**197,983**	**201,200**
Illinois	16,798	28,053	44,039	56,356	59,603
Indiana	9,117	17,431	26,995	29,832	27,142
Michigan	18,888	28,143	36,607	45,967	44,838
Ohio	13,687	23,150	35,440	44,729	49,943
Wisconsin	5,933	11,168	17,502	21,099	19,674

Sources:

1 USOE, *Enrollment for Advanced Degrees, Fall 1960* (Washington: GPO), 163, p. 28.

2 USOE, *Summary Report, Students Enrolled for Master's and Higher Degrees, Fall 1965* (Washington: USOE), 1967, table 4.

3 NCES, *Students Enrolled for Advanced Degrees* (Washington: GPO), *Fall 1970, Summary Data,* p. 11; *Fall 1975, Summary Data,* p. 23.

4 NCES, *Fall Enrollment in Higher Education, 1979* (Washington: GPO), 1980, pp. 24, 25.

5 NCES (Washington, 1983), unpublished data.

101 Enrollment for Advanced Degrees, by Region and State, Selected Years, 1960–1981—*Continued*

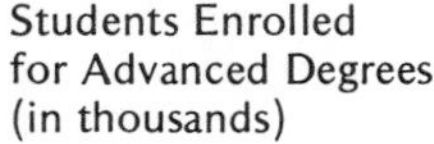

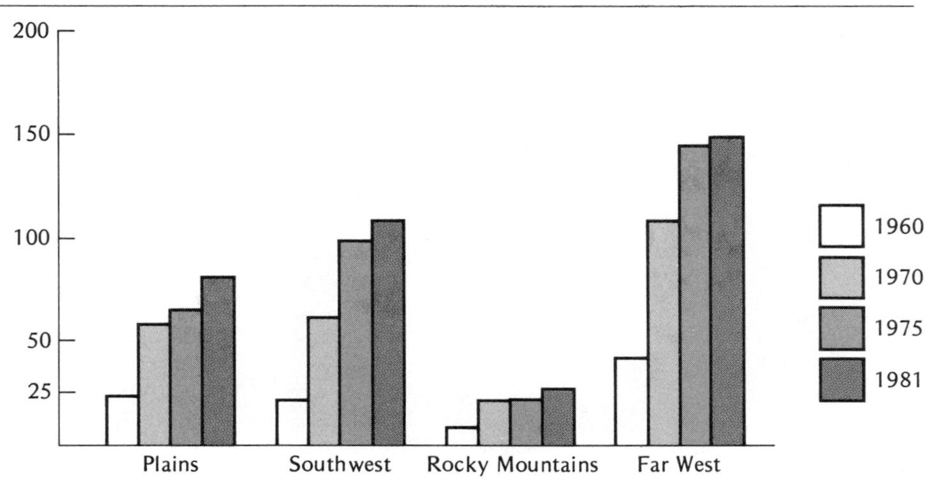

Region and State	Enrollment for Advanced Degrees 1960	1965	1970	1975	1981
Plains	**22,098**	**41,205**	**57,524**	**64,801**	**80,648**
Iowa	4,120	6,705	9,362	9,080	13,540
Kansas	3,867	7,058	8,588	12,467	14,772
Minnesota	5,620	9,761	12,302	12,370	16,327
Missouri	5,771	12,095	18,865	21,318	24,105
Nebraska	1,672	3,522	4,985	6,341	8,168
North Dakota	579	1,180	1,683	1,871	1,696
South Dakota	469	884	1,739	1,354	2,040
Southwest	**20,215**	**37,746**	**61,857**	**99,348**	**109,326**
Arizona	3,116	5,306	10,485	16,949	17,263
New Mexico	2,003	2,911	4,562	5,427	6,731
Oklahoma	3,720	7,689	9,637	15,140	15,090
Texas	11,376	21,840	37,173	62,832	70,242
Rocky Mountains	**7,004**	**14,683**	**20,995**	**22,737**	**26,881**
Colorado	3,499	8,267	9,934	12,252	13,776
Idaho	363	769	1,416	2,351	3,306
Montana	538	918	1,698	1,674	1,720
Utah	2,272	3,970	6,908	5,438	6,897
Wyoming	332	759	1,039	1,022	1,182
Far West	**42,446**	**71,411**	**109,074**	**145,070**	**150,200**
Alaska	64	102	377	508	930
California	35,549	58,766	85,682	117,010	120,398
Hawaii	237	1,345	2,960	3,492	3,622
Nevada	100	374	1,581	1,988	1,497
Oregon	2,091	3,899	7,676	9,601	9,267
Washington	4,405	6,925	10,798	12,471	14,486
U. S. Service Schools	**466**	**930**	**2,146**	**1,539**	**3,159**
Outlying Parts	**388**	**1,037**	**2,656**	**4,259**	**5,849**

Note: Data for 1960–1975 come from the "Enrollment for Advanced Degrees" survey conducted by USOE and NCES. Included in that survey are students who were enrolled in the fall term for a doctorate (Ph.D., Ed.D., and so forth) or a second level degree (generally a master's except for first professional). In 1964 the scope of the survey was expanded to include all master's degrees, including those in fields such as library science and social work administration, even though such degrees are usually considered first professional degrees. Excluded were those students taking graduate work but not enrolled for an advanced degree.

Data for 1979 come from the opening fall enrollment survey of that year and show graduate student enrollment. Graduate students are defined as students "who hold the bachelor's or first-professional degree, or equivalent, and are working toward a master's or doctor's degree."

102 Enrollment for Advanced Degrees, by Field of Study, Selected Years, 1960–1976

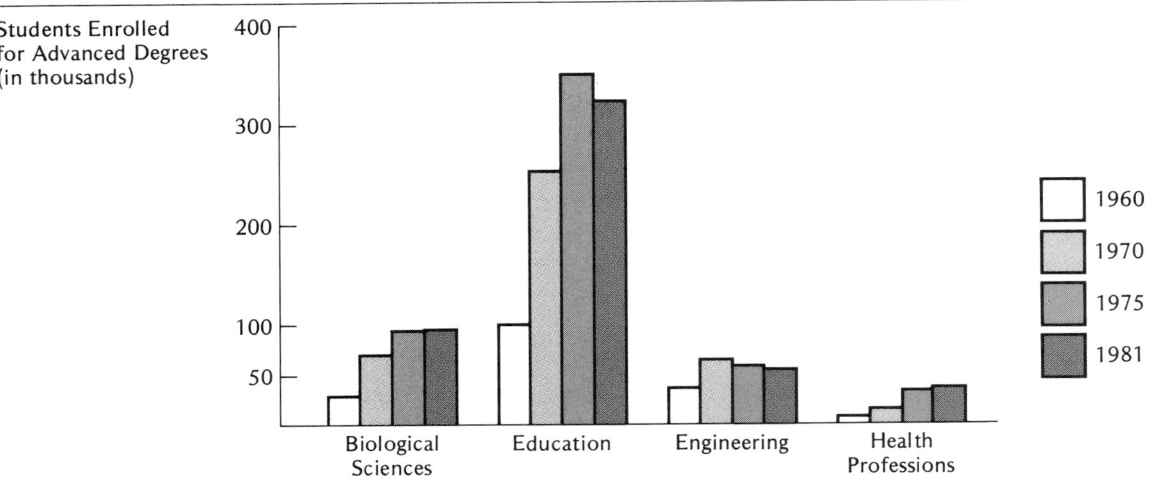

Field of Study	Enrollment for Advanced Degrees 1960	1965	1970	1975	1976
All Fields	**314,349**	**535,332**	**816,207**	**1,053,769**	**1,030,007**
Biological Sciences	**29,864**	**49,142**	**70,492**	**92,062**	**92,435**
Agriculture	3,852	5,405	7,166	10,726	11,262
Anatomy & histology	460	839	1,036	1,178	1,182
Bacteriology, microbiology[a]	1,878	2,935	3,686	4,129	4,015
Biochemistry	1,749	2,933	3,367	3,509	3,655
Biology, general	2,972	6,389	10,712	15,632	15,864
Biophysics	204	555	745	653	652
Botany	1,180	1,795	1,748	1,926	2,008
Entomology	783	1,172	1,408	1,424	1,475
Genetics	391	727	859	1,029	1,043
Forestry	560	1,021	1,485	1,861	1,853
Pharmacology	461	832	1,096	1,486	1,397
Physiology	802	1,564	1,973	2,019	1,993
Plant pathology	454	649	682	693	765
Psychology	10,677	15,551	25,342	35,318	35,363
Zoology	2,305	3,504	3,771	3,566	3,299
Other biological sciences	1,136	3,271	5,416	6,913	6,609
Education	**94,993**	**150,300**	**254,473**	**350,316**	**325,684**
Engineering[b]	**36,636**	**57,516**	**64,788**	**59,402**	**57,330**
Aeronautical	1,680	3,029	2,880	1,782	1,574
Chemical	3,043	4,232	4,621	4,114	4,295
Civil	3,925	6,356	7,684	9,117	8,803
Electrical	11,982	17,654	16,836	14,377	13,490
Mechanical	6,090	8,789	8,161	7,227	6,807
Other engineering fields	10,940	18,095	24,606	22,785	22,361
Health Professions	**5,842**	**8,909**	**14,242**	**35,463**	**38,101**
Humanities	**37,185**	**70,057**	**104,474**	**124,602**	**121,513**
Architecture	585	1,085	2,240	10,231	10,128
English & journalism	13,463	25,991	35,957	38,336	35,415
Fine & applied arts	9,255	17,792	28,748	36,195	35,598
Foreign language & lit.	6,310	14,299	20,451	17,256	16,303
Philosophy	2,258	3,862	4,851	4,576	4,295
Religion[c]	5,314	7,028	12,227	18,008	19,774

(Continued on next page)

Note: Included are students in the fifty states, D. C., and outlying areas who were enrolled in the fall term for a doctorate (Ph.D., Ed.D., etc.) or a second level degree (generally a master's, except first professional). In 1964 the scope of the survey was expanded to include all master's degrees in such fields as library science, social work, and administration, etc., even though the master's in those fields is usually considered a first professional degree.

Excluded are those students taking graduate work but not enrolled for an advanced degree.

For additional footnotes, see next page.

103 Enrollment for Advanced Degrees, by Field of Study, Selected Years, 1960–1976—*Continued*

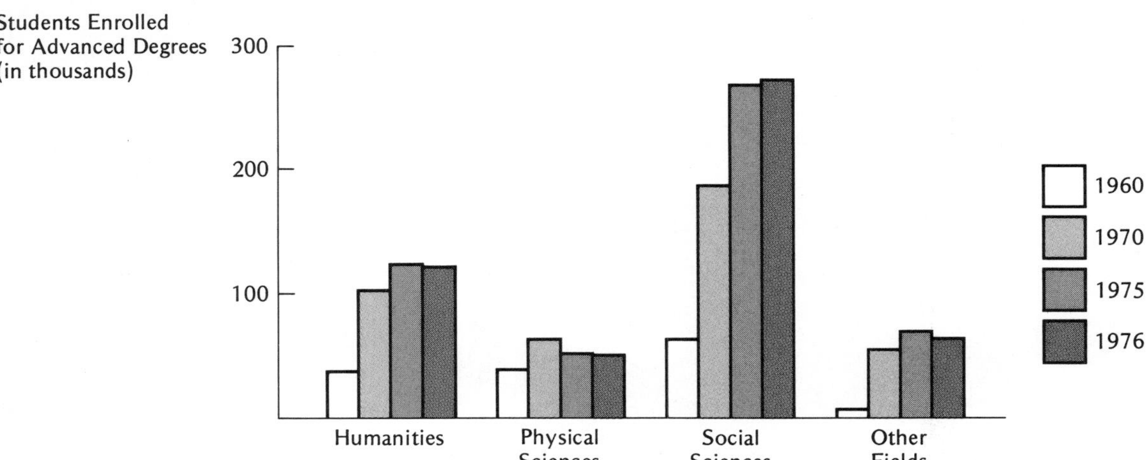

Field of Study	Enrollment for Advanced Degrees 1960	1965	1970	1975	1976
Physical Sciences	**37,477**	**56,704**	**62,785**	**51,665**	**51,073**
Astronomy	272	630	709	683	697
Chemistry	11,169	16,193	17,168	14,832	15,145
Earth sciences other than geology	359	1,006	2,593	2,037	1,963
Geology	2,557	2,923	3,666	4,747	5,173
Mathematical subjects	11,770	20,198	22,672	16,168	14,926
Meteorology	373	643	687	864	906
Physics	9,675	13,681	13,479	9,173	9,018
Other physical sciences	1,302	1,430	1,811	3,161	3,245
Social Sciences	**63,700**	**120,694**	**188,006**	**270,129**	**276,318**
American civilization & culture	na	661	1,319	1,545	1,515
Anthropology	1,006	2,323	4,691	6,062	5,944
Area or regional studies	669	1,412	2,262	2,756	2,697
Business & commerce	25,342	50,920	87,487	143,162	148,258
Economics	5,076	8,600	11,507	10,074	9,892
Economics, agricultural	1,081	1,613	1,781	2,087	2,091
Geography	1,041	1,972	3,334	3,412	3,299
History	9,170	16,443	22,322	17,895	15,944
Industrial relations	na	659	915	1,791	1,718
International relations	715	2,582	1,985	2,092	1,946
Political science	4,245	8,014	11,528	11,475	10,189
Public administration	1,535	3,536	5,400	15,199	19,827
Sociology	3,277	6,190	10,323	10,416	9,674
Social work & administration	6,700	9,929	14,271	22,215	21,772
Other social sciences	3,843	5,840	8,881	19,948	21,552
Other Fields	**8,652**	**22,010**	**56,947**	**70,130**	**67,553**
Home economics	1,580	2,358	4,611	7,664	8,085
Law	1,651	2,465	2,533	3,604	3,586
Library science	1,360	8,597	12,416	14,731	13,307
Computer sci. & systems analysis	na	816	7,936	10,856	11,852
Miscellaneous & combined fields	4,061	7,774	29,451	33,275	30,723

See note on preceding page.

na Field of study not separately identified.

a Includes virology, mycology, and parasitology.

b All totals are taken from USOE sources. For 1960 and 1965, totals are smaller than the sum of the fields because data for individual fields came from separate surveys conducted by USOE and the American Society for Engineering Education.

c Sum of theology and religious studies; does not include enrollment for professional degrees in theology.

Sources:

1 USOE, *Enrollment for Advanced Degrees, Fall 1960* (Washington: GPO), 1963, pp. 47–49.

2 USOE, *Summary Report, Students Enrolled for Master's and Higher Degrees, Fall 1965* (Washington: USOE), 1967, table 3.

3 NCES, *Students Enrolled for Advanced Degrees* (Washington: GPO), *Fall 1970, Summary Data*, pp. 14–17; *Fall 1975, Summary Data*, pp. 26–31; *Fall 1976*, table 6.

104 Elementary and Secondary School Enrollment, by Control of School, Selected Years, 1899–1900—1985

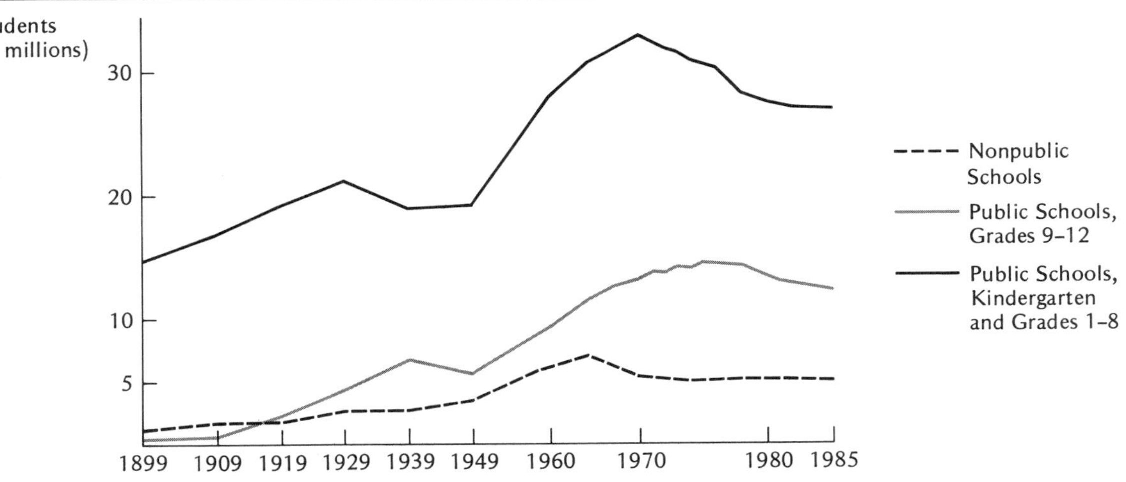

Elementary and Secondary Regular Day School Enrollment (in thousands)

Year	All Schools	Public Schools: All Grades	Public Schools: Kindergarten & Grades 1–8	Public Schools: Grades 9–12	Nonpublic Schools: All Grades	Nonpublic Schools: Kindergarten & Grades 1–8	Nonpublic Schools: Grades 9–12
1899–1900	**16,855**	15,503	14,984	519	1,352	1,241	111
1909–10	**19,490**	17,814	16,899	915	1,676	1,558	117
1919–20	**23,279**	21,579	19,379	2,200	1,699	1,486	214
1929–30	**28,329**	25,678	21,279	4,399	2,651	2,310	341
1939–40	**28,045**	25,434	18,832	6,601	2,611	2,153	458
1949–50	**28,492**	25,111	19,387	5,725	3,380	2,708	672
1960	**42,181**	36,281	27,692	8,589	5,900	4,800	1,100[a]
1965	**48,473**	42,173	30,563	11,610	6,300	4,900[a]	1,400[a]
1970	**51,272**	45,909	32,577	13,332	5,363	4,052	1,311
1971	**51,281**	46,081	32,265	13,816	5,200[e]	3,900	1,300
1972	**50,744**	45,744	31,831	13,913	5,000	3,700	1,300
1973	**50,430**	45,429	31,353	14,077	5,000[e]	3,700	1,300
1974	**50,053**	45,053	30,921	14,132	5,000[e]	3,700	1,300
1975	**49,791**	44,791	30,487	14,304	5,000[e]	3,700	1,300
1976	**49,484**	44,317	30,006	14,311	5,167[e]	3,825	1,342
1977	**48,716**	43,577	29,336	14,240	5,140	3,797	1,343
1978	**47,636**	42,550	28,328	14,223	5,085	3,732	1,353
1979[e]	**46,679**	41,579	27,855	13,694	5,100[e]	3,700	1,400
1980	**46,095[p]**	40,995	27,678	13,317	5,100[e]	3,700	1,400
Projections[b]							
1981	**45,189**	40,189	27,356	12,833	5,000	3,600	1,400
1985	**44,166**	39,166	26,951	12,215	5,000	3,600	1,400

Note: Nonpublic data; totals for 1949–50 and later are estimated. Public school grade breakdown for Fall 1955–Fall 1961 are estimated. Data for 1899–1950 are for the continental U. S. and show total school year enrollments. They therefore contain duplications, e.g., students who, during the school year, move from one state to another or from public to private school systems. Data for 1955 and later are fall enrollments for the fifty states and D. C. Excluded from all data are pupils enrolled in residential schools for exceptional children, subcollegiate departments of institutions of higher education, and federal schools. Details may not add to totals because of rounding.

a Reported data from USOE surveys.

b Projections are based on the assumptions that the enrollment rate of the six-year-old population in public schools will remain constant at the 1976 level and that retention rates in all other public school grades will remain constant at the average rate for the last five years. Estimates of the six-year-old population are consistent with the Census Bureau's Series II projections.

e Estimates.

p Preliminary, private figures rounded to the nearest 100,000.

Sources:

1 USOE, *Statistical Summary of Education, 1957–58* (Washington: GPO), 1962, p. 5.

2 NCES, *Projections of Education Statistics* (Washington: GPO), *1986–87,* table 3; *1988–89,* table 4; *1990–91,* table 6.

105 Estimated Retention Rates, Fifth Grade through College Entrance, Selected Years, 1924–32—1970–80

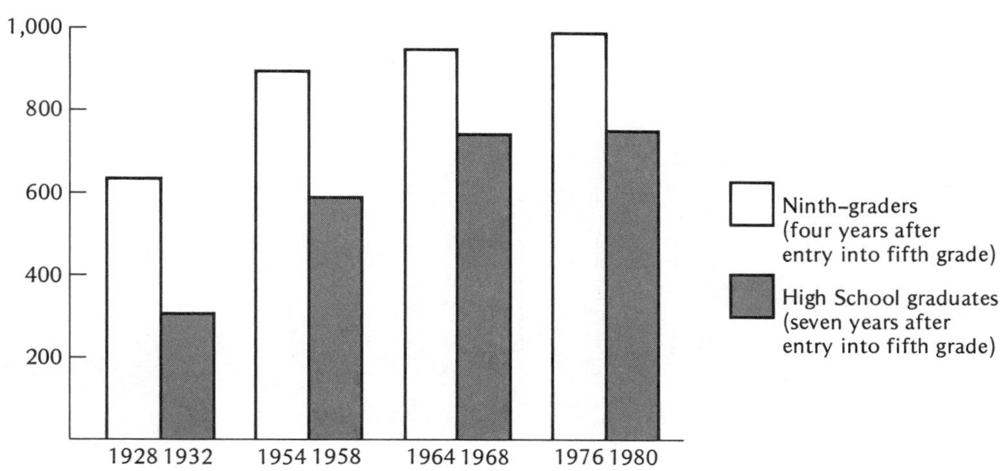

Year of Entrance into Fifth Grade	Retention per 1,000 Students Who Entered Fifth Grade[a] Ninth Grade	High School Graduates	Year of High School Graduation	First-Time College Students[b]
1924	612	302	1932	118
1928	736	378	1936	137
1930	770	417	1938	148
1934	803	467	1942	129
1938	796	419	1946	na
1940	781	481	1948	na
1942	807	505	1950	205
1944	848	522	1952	234
1946	872	553	1954	283
1948	863	581	1956	301
1950	886	582	1958	308
1952	904	621	1960	328
1954	915	642	1962	343
1956	930	676	1964	362
1958	946	732	1966	384
1960	952	749	1968	452
1962	959	750	1970	461
1964	975	748	1972	433
1965	980	749	1973	433
1966	985	744	1974	448
1967	984	743	1975	452
1968	983	749	1976	435
1969	984	744	1977	na
1970	979	746	1978	439
1972	994	744	1980	463

Note: Beginning with the class in the fifth grade in 1958, data are based on fall enrollment and exclude ungraded pupils. The net effect of these changes is to increase high school graduation and college entrance rates slightly.

na Data not available.

a Based on data from public schools adjusted to include estimates for nonpublic schools.

b Rates include full-time and part-time students enrolled in programs creditable toward a bachelor's degree.

Source: NCES, *Digest of Education Statistics* (Washington: GPO), 1974 edition, table 13; 1976 edition, table 10; 1980 edition, table 10; 1982 edition, table 9.

106 Number of Institutions of Higher Education, by Highest Level of Offering, Selected Years, 1950–1982

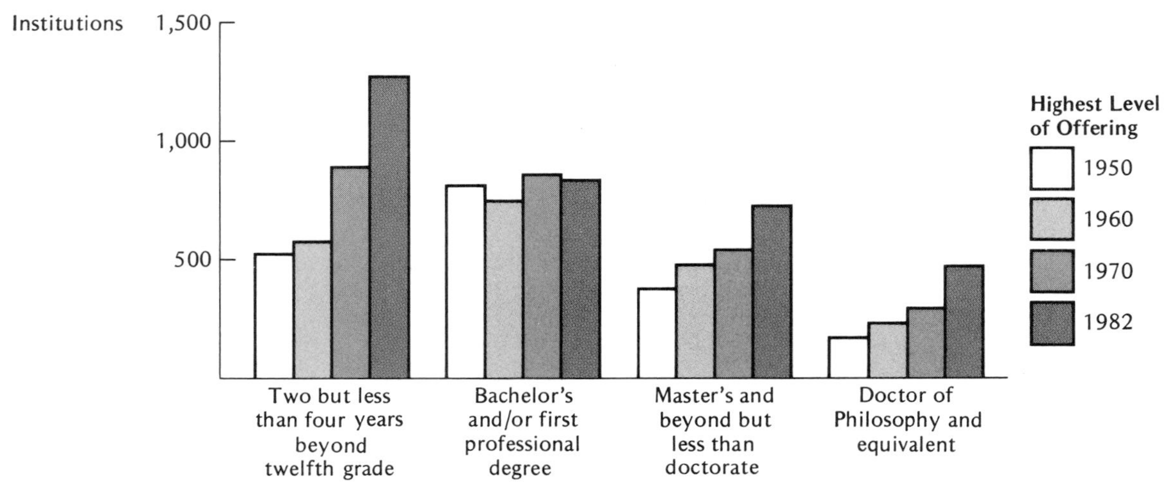

		Number of Institutions[a] Offering as Highest Level				
Year	All Institutions	I Two but Less than Four Years beyond the Twelfth Grade	II Bachelor's and/or First Professional Degree	III Master's and beyond, but Less than Doctorate[b]	IV Doctor of Philosophy and Equivalent	Other[c]
1950–51	**1,859**	527	800	360	155	17
1952–53	**1,851**	517	768	390	163	13
1954–55	**1,855**	510	732	415	180	18
1955–56	**1,886**	525	714	426	191	30
1956–57	**1,937**	548	723	442	193	31
1958–59	**2,011**	585	718	462	205	41
1960–61	**2,040**	593	741	455	219	32
Fall 1962	**2,100**	628	766	458	223	25
Fall 1963	**2,139**	644	792	455	223	25
Fall 1964	**2,168**	656	801	464	224	23
Fall 1965	**2,207**	664	823	472	227	21
Fall 1966	**2,252**	685	828	483	235	21
Fall 1967	**2,489**	866	828	511	263	21
Fall 1968	**2,537**	867	833	509	278	12
Fall 1969	**2,551**	903	835	517	296	d
Fall 1970	**2,573**	897	850	528	298	d
Fall 1971	**2,626**	943	828	543	312	d
Fall 1972	**2,686**	970	843	546	327	d
Fall 1973	**2,738**	1,008	847	547	336	d
Fall 1974	**3,038**	1,152	903	599	384	e
Fall 1975	**3,055**	1,141	872	637	405	e
Fall 1976	**3,075**	1,147	862	656	410	e
Fall 1977	**3,130**	1,172	857	623	423	55
Fall 1978	**3,173**	1,211	858	630	431	43
Fall 1982	**3,273**	1,281	827	709	456	d

a Institutions in U. S. and outlying parts listed in directories of the U. S. Office of Education and the National Center for Education Statistics.

b Data prior to 1968 are for "master's and/or second professional degree."

c Includes non-degree-granting institutions and institutions with accelerated programs.

d Not separately identified in source; included in other categories.

e Institutions classified as "non-degree-granting" have been included in categories II and III depending on whether they provide undergraduate level study. Most such institutions are rabbinical seminaries.

Sources:

1 USOE, *Education Directory, Higher Education* (Washington: GPO), various editions through 1976–77.

2 NCES computer tapes from HEGIS, "Institutional Characteristics," 1977–78, 1978–79, 1982–83.

107 Percent Distribution of Institutions of Higher Education, by Highest Level of Offering, Selected Years, 1950–1982

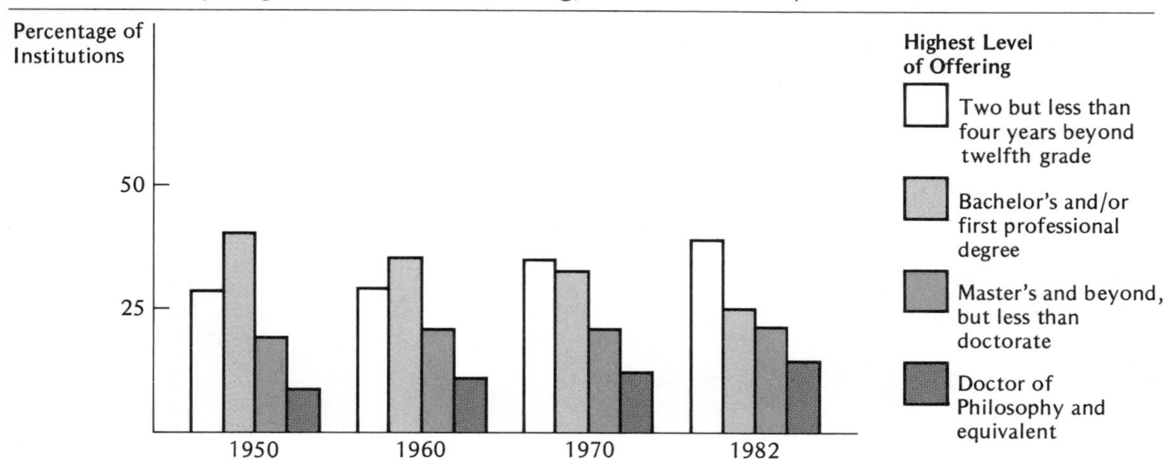

Year	All Institutions	I Two but Less than Four Years beyond the Twelfth Grade	II Bachelor's and/or First Professional Degree	III Master's and beyond, but Less than Doctorate	IV Doctor of Philosophy and Equivalent	Graduate Study (Columns III & IV)
		Percentage[a] of Institutions Offering as Highest Level				
1950–51	**100**	28	43	19	8	**27**
1952–53	**100**	28	41	21	9	**30**
1954–55	**100**	27	39	22	10	**32**
1955–56	**100**	28	38	23	10	**33**
1956–57	**100**	28	37	23	10	**33**
1958–59	**100**	29	36	23	10	**33**
1960–61	**100**	29	36	22	11	**33**
Fall 1962	**100**	30	36	22	11	**33**
Fall 1963	**100**	30	37	21	10	**31**
Fall 1964	**100**	30	37	21	10	**31**
Fall 1965	**100**	30	37	21	10	**31**
Fall 1966	**100**	30	37	21	10	**31**
Fall 1967	**100**	35	33	21	11	**31**
Fall 1968	**100**	34	33	20	11	**31**
Fall 1969	**100**	35	33	20	12	**32**
Fall 1970	**100**	35	33	21	12	**32**
Fall 1971	**100**	36	32	21	12	**33**
Fall 1972	**100**	36	31	20	12	**33**
Fall 1973	**100**	36	31	20	12	**32**
Fall 1974	**100**	38	30	20	13	**32**
Fall 1975	**100**	37	29	21	13	**33**
Fall 1976	**100**	37	28	21	13	**35**
Fall 1977	**100**	37	27	20	14	**33**
Fall 1978	**100**	38	27	20	14	**33**
Fall 1982	**100**	39	25	22	14	**36**

a Columns I–IV do not necessarily total 100% because of rounding and because the category "other" has been omitted.

Source: Calculated from data on the preceding page.

108 Institutions of Higher Education, by Highest Level of Offering and by Region and State, Fall 1982

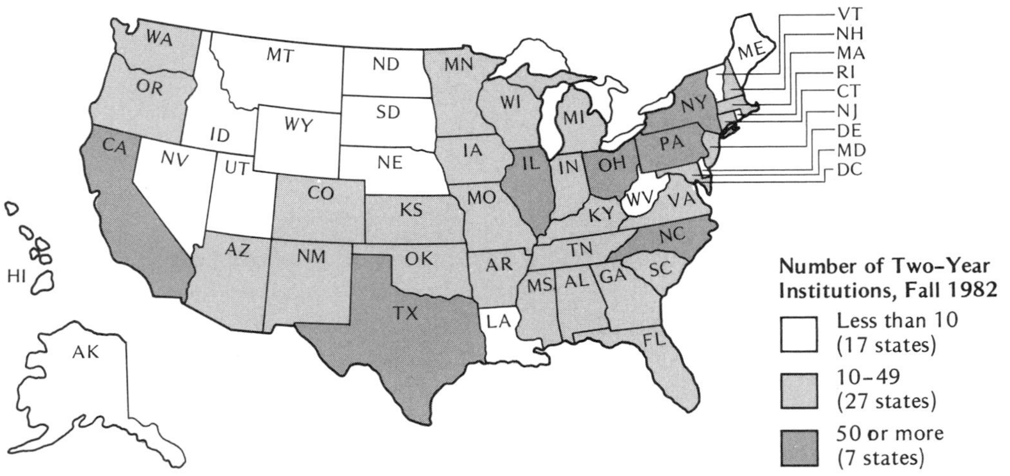

Region and State	All Institutions	Two but Less than Four Years	Four or More Years of Study: All	Bachelor's & First Professional	Graduate Study: All	Graduate Study: Doctorate
		Number of Institutions[a] Offering as Highest Level				
U. S. & Outlying Parts	**3,273**	**1,281**	**1,992**	**827**	**1,165**	**456**
50 States & D. C.	**3,231**	**1,266**	**1,965**	**810**	**1,155**	**452**
New England	**252**	**82**	**170**	**66**	**104**	**32**
Connecticut	47	21	26	7	19	6
Maine	29	8	21	17	4	1
Massachusetts	116	36	80	26	54	18
New Hampshire	26	12	14	6	8	2
Rhode Island	13	2	11	4	7	3
Vermont	21	3	18	6	12	2
Mideast	**631**	**202**	**429**	**136**	**293**	**107**
Delaware	10	4	6	3	3	1
D. C.	18	—	18	3	15	8
Maryland	55	22	33	6	27	10
New Jersey	60	20	40	13	27	13
New York	292	86	206[b]	59	147[b]	51
Pennsylvania	196	70	126	52	74	24
Southeast	**746**	**336**	**410**	**201**	**209**	**78**
Alabama	59	28	31	12	19	5
Arkansas	34	15	19	8	11	2
Florida	81	37	44	22	22	9
Georgia	78	32	46	21	25	8
Kentucky	56	27	29	13	16	6
Louisiana	32	7	25	6	19	9
Mississippi	42	22	20	7	13	6
North Carolina	127	77	50	30	20	8
South Carolina	60	28	32	17	15	5
Tennessee	80	29	51	31	20	11
Virginia	69	26	43	21	22	8
West Virginia	28	8	20	13	7	1
Great Lakes	**523**	**200**	**323**	**142**	**181**	**70**
Illinois	159	62	97	34	63	26
Indiana	74	25	49	19	30	9
Michigan	92	35	57	29	28	10
Ohio	135	57	78[b]	41	37	20
Wisconsin	63	21	42	19	23	5

— No data.

For source and footnotes, see next page.

109 Institutions of Higher Education, by Highest Level of Offering and by Region and State, Fall 1982—*Continued*

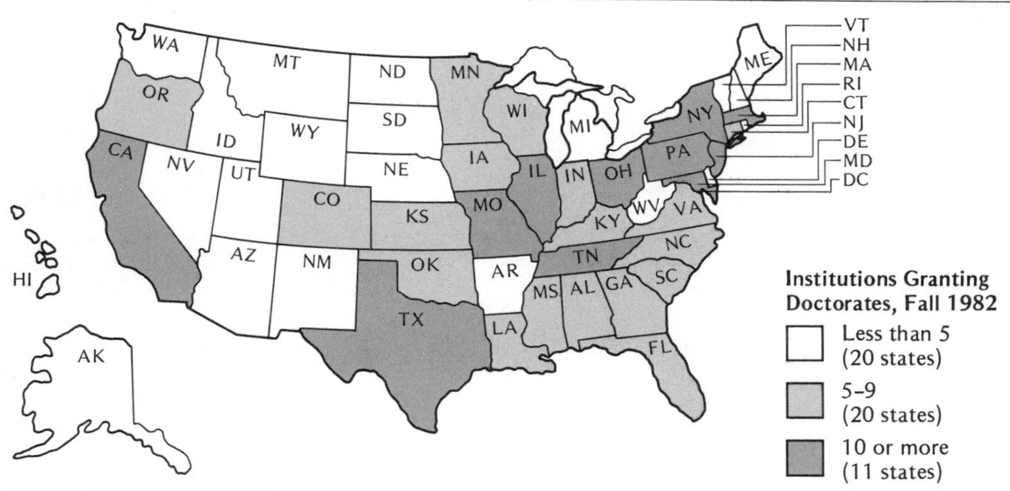

Region and State	All Institutions	Two but Less than Four Years	Four or More Years of Study: All	Bachelor's & First Professional	Graduate Study: All	Graduate Study: Doctorate
	Number of Institutions[a] Offering as Highest Level					
Plains	**331**	**112**	**219**	**132**	**87**	**40**
Iowa	60	23	37	25	12	5
Kansas	52	24	28	19	9	5
Minnesota	65	24	41	25	16	5
Missouri	89	22	67	35	32	15
Nebraska	28	8	20	12	8	4
North Dakota	17	7	10	7	3	2
South Dakota	20	4	16	9	7	4
Southwest	**249**	**111**	**138**	**52**	**86**	**41**
Arizona	28	17	11	5	6	3
New Mexico	20	10	10	3	7	3
Oklahoma	45	19	26	12	14	6
Texas	156	65	91	32	59	29
Rocky Mountains	**90**	**40**	**50**	**15**	**35**	**17**
Colorado	44	17	27	9	18	9
Idaho	9	3	6	1	5	2
Montana	16	6	10	4	6	2
Utah	13	7	6	1	5	3
Wyoming	8	7	1	—	1	1
Far West	**399**	**182**	**217**	**61**	**156**	**64**
Alaska	15	9	6	2	4	1
California	269	119	150	37	113	50
Hawaii	13	6	7	5	2	1
Nevada	7	4	3	1	2	2
Oregon	45	16	29	10	19	6
Washington	50	28	22	6	16	4
U. S. Service Schools	**10**	**1**	**9**	**5**	**4**	**3**
Outlying Parts	**42**	**15**	**27**	**17**	**10**	**4**

a Institutions reported in the institutional characteristics portion of HEGIS.

b Includes non-degree-granting institutions, most of which are rabbinical seminaries.

Source: NCES computer tapes from HEGIS, "Institutional Characteristics," 1982–83, with special analysis by ACE's Division of Policy Analysis and Research.

Institutions of Higher Education, by Control, Selected Years, 1950–1981

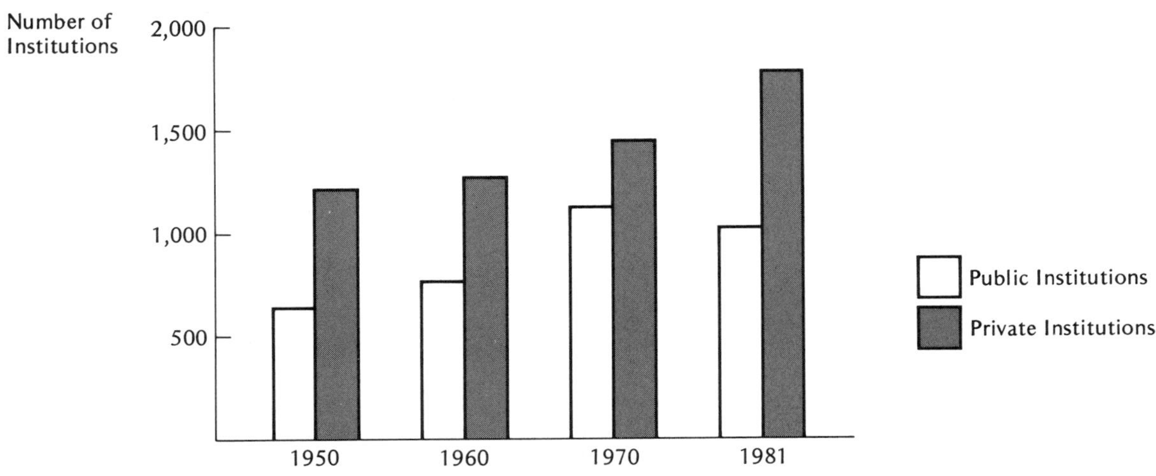

Year	Institutions of Higher Education[a] Number[b] Total	Public	Private	Percent Distribution Public	Private
1950–51	**1,859**	638	1,221	34	66
1954–55	**1,855**	652	1,203	35	65
1960–61	**2,040**	721	1,319	35	65
Fall 1965	**2,207**	790	1,417	36	64
Fall 1967	**2,489**	1,000	1,489	41	59
Fall 1969	**2,551**	1,079	1,472	42	58
Fall 1970	**2,573**	1,101	1,472	43	57
Fall 1971	**2,626**	1,152	1,474	44	56
Fall 1972	**2,686**	1,193	1,493	44	56
Fall 1973	**2,738**	1,210	1,528	44	56
Fall 1974	**3,038**	1,453	1,585	48	52
Fall 1975	**3,055**	1,454	1,601	48	52
Fall 1976	**3,075**	1,467	1,608	48	52
Fall 1977	**3,130**	1,486	1,644	47	53
Fall 1978	**3,173**	1,488	1,685	47	53
Fall 1979	**3,190**	1,488	1,702	47	53
Fall 1980	**3,270**	1,510	1,760	46	54
Fall 1981	**3,295**	1,512	1,783	46	54

a Institutions are those in the U. S. and outlying parts included in the annual directories of higher education issued by the U. S. Office of Education and the National Center for Education Statistics (NCES).

Prior to 1967–68, an institution was listed in the *Education Directory, Part 3* if it (1) offered at least a two-year program of college-level studies in residence; (2) submitted the necessary information for a listing; and (3) met certain accreditation criteria. The latter required that an institution either (*a*) be accredited or approved by a nationally recognized accrediting agency, by a state department of education, or by a state university; or (*b*) have its credits accepted as if coming from an accredited institution by no fewer than three accredited institutions.

The 1967 list included, in addition, those institutions that attained a preaccredited status with designated nationally recognized accrediting agencies. In 1968 the directory included all institutions that applied for a listing.

Directories published from 1968 through 1977–78 used the 1967 criteria.

The 1978–79 directory included institutions that (1) are legally authorized to offer and are offering at least a one-year program of college-level studies leading toward a degree; (2) have submitted required information; and (3) have met certain accreditation criteria. Those criteria require an institution either (*a*) to be accredited or hold preaccredited status at the college level by a nationally recognized accrediting agency; or (*b*), if public or nonprofit, to have its credits accepted as though coming from an accredited institution by no fewer than three accredited institutions.

b Caution must be used in making year-to-year comparisons. Part of the yearly increase may be due to how branch campuses are tallied. For example, in the 1973–74 directory, the University of Alaska was counted as one institution although it was composed of five two-year units and one four-year unit in addition to the main campus. In the 1974–75 directory, the seven units were counted separately.

Source: USOE and NCES, *Education Directory, Higher Education* (Washington: GPO), various annual editions through 1981–82.

Percent Distribution of Institutions, by Size and Region, 1950, 1960, 1970, 1980

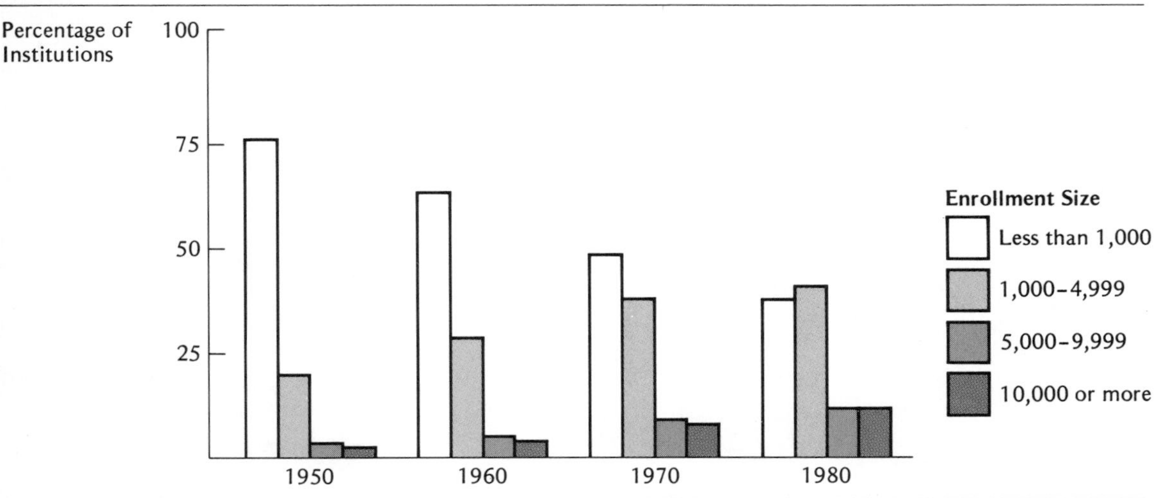

Percentage of Institutions[a] with Enrollment of

Region	Less than 1,000				1,000–4,999			
	1950	1960	1970	1980	1950	1960	1970	1980
All Institutions	**76**	**63**	**47**	**36**	**18**	**28**	**37**	**40**
New England	79	67	50	37	16	26	40	43
Mideast	74	63	44	40	19	28	38	37
Southeast	79	69	52	37	18	26	36	45
Great Lakes	77	62	48	33	17	27	36	43
Plains	84	74	60	46	12	21	28	39
Southwest	70	57	36	24	24	33	43	48
Rocky Mountains	69	54	34	29	23	35	43	41
Far West	66	48	32	33	27	38	35	26

Region	5,000–9,999				10,000 and over			
	1950	1960	1970	1980	1950	1960	1970	1980
All Institutions	**3**	**5**	**9**	**12**	**2**	**4**	**7**	**12**
New England	3	5	6	13	1	2	4	7
Mideast	3	4	11	12	4	5	7	11
Southeast	3	4	7	10	*	2	5	8
Great Lakes	3	6	8	11	3	5	8	14
Plains	2	3	7	8	1	2	5	7
Southwest	5	6	12	13	1	4	9	15
Rocky Mountains	8	6	15	15	—	6	8	14
Far West	4	9	15	15	2	5	18	26

Note: The growth in the number and autonomy of branch campuses complicates this kind of analysis. A university reported as one institution in 1950 may have been reported as a main campus and three branch campuses in 1960, and accordingly it would be counted as four institutions. Thus some of the change indicates a difference in reporting rather than an actual growth in the number of institutions. Such discrepancies make the percentages shown here general trend indicators, not precise measures.

— No institution in this enrollment category.

a Data are from USOE and NCES reports of opening fall enrollment for the years indicated. Included are two-year and four-year institutions. The total number of institutions for each year is as follows: 1950, 1,885; 1960, 1,973; 1970, 2,820; 1980, 3,231.

Sources:

1 USOE, *1950 Fall Enrollment in Higher Educational Institutions* (Washington: Federal Security Agency), 1950.

2 USOE, *Opening Fall Enrollment in Higher Education, 1960: Institutional Data* (Washington: GPO), 1960.

3 USOE, *Opening Fall Enrollment in Higher Education, 1970: Report on Preliminary Survey* (Washington: GPO, 1970), table 5.

4 NCES computer tapes containing data from HEGIS, 1980–81.

Institutions, by Type of Calendar and by Region and State, 1982–83

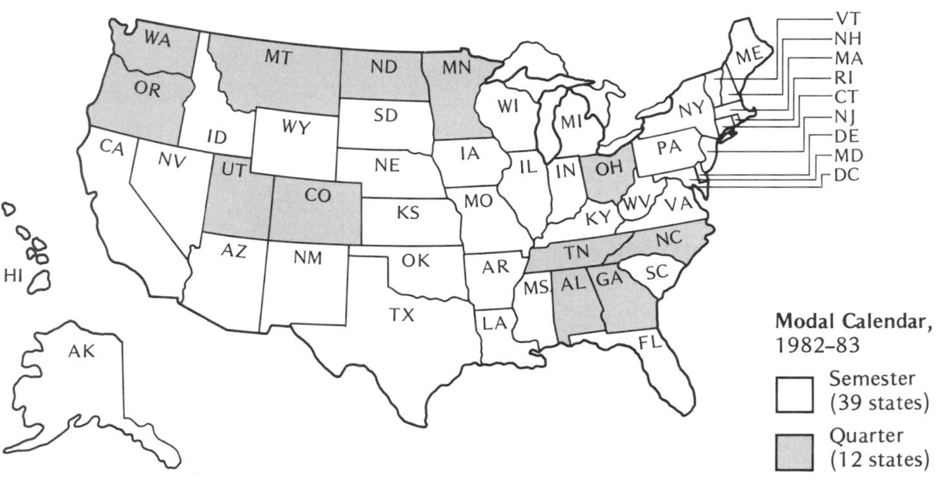

Region and State	All Institutions Reporting	Number of Institutions Using				
		Semester	Quarter	Trimester	4–1–4	Other
U. S. & Outlying Parts	**3,271**	**1,929**	**789**	**123**	**253**	**177**
50 States & D. C.	**3,229**	**1,897**	**786**	**117**	**253**	**176**
New England	**252**	**184**	**16**	**12**	**22**	**18**
Connecticut	47	35	5	4	1	2
Maine	29	23	—	1	3	2
Massachusetts	116	86	7	3	12	8
New Hampshire	26	13	3	3	3	4
Rhode Island	13	10	1	1	1	—
Vermont	21	17	—	—	2	2
Mideast	**631**	**446**	**34**	**22**	**57**	**72**
Delware	10	6	3	—	1	—
D. C.	18	13	1	2	—	2
Maryland	55	44	2	2	6	1
New Jersey	60	46	1	1	7	5
New York	292	228	16	9	20	19
Pennsylvania	196	109	11	8	23	45
Southeast	**746**	**385**	**283**	**16**	**39**	**22**
Alabama	59	20	35	1	2	1
Arkansas	34	28	4	0	2	—
Florida	81	50	12	10	6	3
Georgia	78	13	63	1	1	—
Kentucky	56	37	8	2	6	3
Louisiana	32	29	2	—	1	—
Mississippi	42	38	2	—	—	2
North Carolina	127	52	70	1	4	—
South Carolina	60	32	21	—	4	2
Tennessee	80	34	38	1	5	2
Virginia	69	28	27	—	6	8
West Virginia	28	24	1	—	2	1
Great Lakes	**522**	**264**	**172**	**28**	**33**	**25**
Illinois	159	87	46	10	10	6
Indiana	74	33	26	1	10	4
Michigan	92	58	20	10	2	2
Ohio	134	42	73	4	5	10
Wisconsin	63	44	7	3	6	3

(Continued on next page)

For footnotes and source, see next page.

113 Institutions, by Type of Calendar and by Region and State, 1981–83—*Continued*

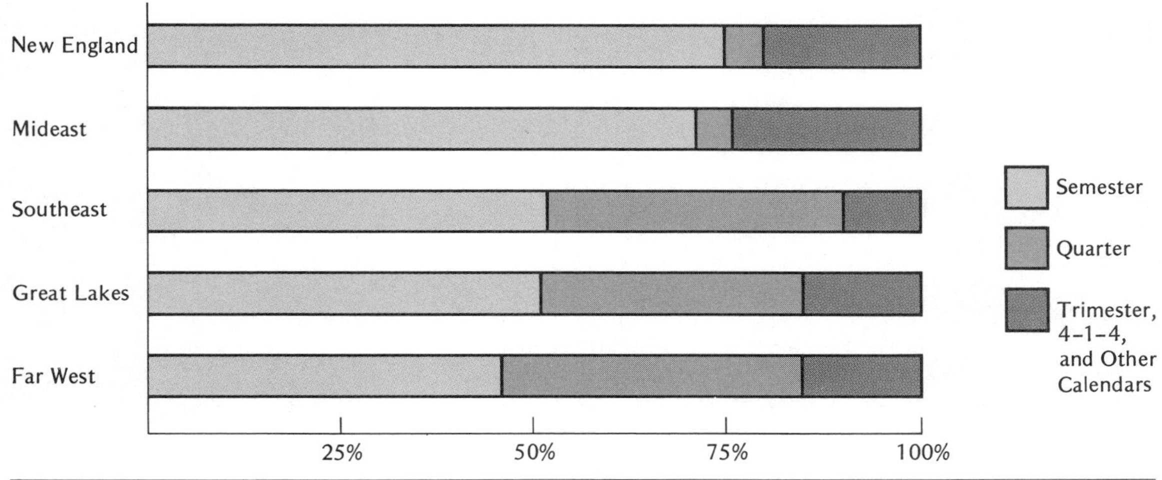

Region and State	All Institutions Reporting	Number of Institutions Using				
		Semester	Quarter	Trimester	4–1–4	Other
Plains	**331**	**176**	**69**	**8**	**61**	**17**
Iowa	60	31	13	—	10	6
Kansas	52	38	—	—	14	—
Minnesota	65	11	39	2	12	1
Missouri	89	60	5	6	11	7
Nebraska	28	19	2	—	5	2
North Dakota	17	7	8	—	1	1
South Dakota	20	10	2	—	8	—
Southwest	**249**	**215**	**11**	**6**	**10**	**7**
Arizona	28	23	—	1	3	1
New Mexico	20	19	—	1	—	—
Oklahoma	45	38	1	3	1	2
Texas	156	135	10	1	6	4
Rocky Mountains	**90**	**41**	**43**	**2**	**1**	**3**
Colorado	44	20	21	2	—	1
Idaho	9	7	1	—	1	—
Montana	16	6	10	—	—	—
Utah	13	—	11	—	—	2
Wyoming	8	8	—	—	—	—
Far West	**399**	**182**	**154**	**22**	**30**	**11**
Alaska	15	11	—	3	1	—
California	269	145	75	18	23	8
Hawaii	13	11	—	1	1	—
Nevada	7	5	1	—	1	—
Oregon	45	5	37	—	—	3
Washington	50	5	41	—	4	—
U. S. Service Schools	**10**	**4**	**4**	**1**	**—**	**1**
Outlying Parts	**42**	**32**	**3**	**6**	**—**	**1**

Definitions based on a nine-month college year beginning in late August or September:

Semester—College year divided into two parts, each of about seventeen weeks of classes, running from September to June. Semester hours are used for credits.

Quarter—College year divided into three equal parts of about twelve weeks each, with a great variation about the starting and ending times. Quarter hours are used for credits (three quarter hours equal two semester hours).

Trimester—College year divided into three equal parts of about sixteen weeks each.

4–1–4—College year divided into two equal terms of about sixteen weeks each plus a four-week term between the two.

Other—Calendars that are not defined by any of the four types above.

Source: Computer tapes of NCES HEGIS, "Institutional Characteristics," 1982–83, with special analysis by ACE's Division of Policy Analysis and Research.

114 Instructional Faculty, by Employment Status, Selected Years, 1959–1988

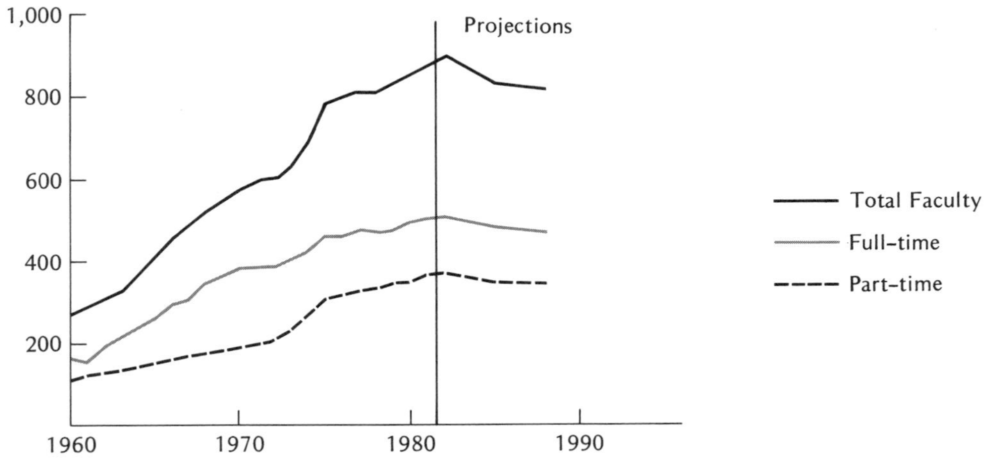

Staff for Instruction in Resident Courses (in thousands)

		Instructor and Above			Junior Instructor		
Year	**Total**	**Total**	**Full-time**	**Part-time**	**Total**	**Full-time**	**Part-time**
1959	**282**	**243**	162	81	**39**	8[e]	31[e]
1960[e]	**276**	**236**	154	82	**40**	8	32
1961	**292**	**248**	162	86	**44**	9	35
1963	**331**	**281**	184	97	**50**	10	40
1965[e]	**412**	**340**	248	92	**72**	14	58
1966	**445**	**362**	278	84	**83**	16	67
1967	**484**	**390**	299	91	**94**	13	81
1968[e]	**523**	**428**	332	96	**95**	15	80
1969[e]	**546**	**450**	350	100	**97**	15	82
1970	**573**	**474**	369	104	**101**	14	87
1971[e]	**590**	**492**	379	113	**97**	10	88
1972	**590**	**500**	380	120	**90**	6	84
1973[e]	**634**	**527**	389	138	**107**	13	94
1974[e]	**695**	**567**	406	161	**128**	17	111
1975[e]	**781**	**628**	440	188	**153**	22	131
1976	**793**	**633**	434	199	**160**	28	132
1977[e]	**812**	**650**	447	203	**162**	29	134
1978[e]	**809**	**647**	445	202	**162**	29	134
1979[e]	**823**	**657**	451	206	**166**	28	138
1980[e]	**846**	**678**	466	212	**168**	30	138
				Projections[p]			
1981	**877**	**704**	480	224	**173**	30	143
1982	**888**	**713**	485	228	**175**	30	145
1985	**824**	**663**	453	210	**161**	28	133
1988	**806**	**652**	442	210	**154**	27	127

Note: All data are for 50 states and D. C.

e Estimates.

p NCES intermediate alternative projections.

Sources:

1 USOE, *Faculty and Other Professional Staff in Institutions of Higher Education, First Term 1959–60* (Washington: GPO), 1963, pp. 16, 18.

2 NCES, *Projections of Education Statistics* (Washington: GPO), 1971 edition, table 31; 1977 edition, table 22; 1980 edition, table 33; 1982 edition, table 22.

115 Faculty and Enrollment, Selected Years, 1959–1988

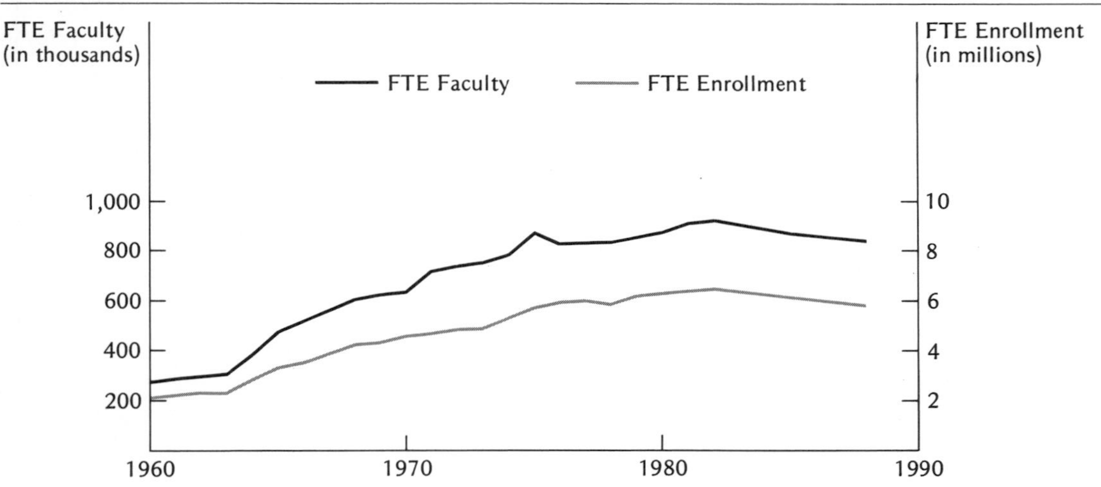

Year	Instructional Staff[a] (in thousands) Total	Full-time	Part-time	Full-time Equivalent (FTE)	Full-time Equivalent (FTE)[b] Enrollment (in thousands)	Ratio of FTE Staff to FTE Enrollment
1959	**282**	170[e]	112[e]	209[e]	2,777	1:13.3
1960[e]	**276**	162	114	202	2,954	1:14.6
1961	**292**	171	121	214	3,200	1:15.0
1963	**331**	194	137	242	3,696	1:15.3
1965[e]	**412**	262	150	316	4,671	1:14.8
1966	**445**	294	151	351	5,070	1:14.4
1967	**484**	312	172	378	5,480	1:14.5
1968[e]	**523**	347	176	412	5,954	1:14.5
1969[e]	**546**	365	182	430	6,319	1:14.7
1970	**573**	383	191	451	6,737	1:14.9
1971	**590**	389	201	458	7,149	1:15.6
1972	**590**	386	204	455	7,254	1:15.9
1973[e]	**634**	402	232	481	7,453	1:15.5
1974	**695**	423	272	516	7,805	1:15.1
1975[e]	**781**	462	319	574	8,481	1:14.8
1976	**793**	462	331	584	8,313	1:14.2
1977[e]	**812**	476	337	599	8,415	1:14.0
1978[e]	**809**	474	336	597	8,335	1:14.0
1979[e]	**823**	479	344	605	8,487	1:14.0
1980[e]	**846**	496	350	624	8,749	1:14.0
				Projections[p]		
1981[e]	**877**	510	367	644	9,108	1:14.1
1982	**888**	515	373	651	9,221	1:14.2
1985	**824**	481	343	606	8,620	1:14.2
1988	**806**	469	337	592	8,462	1:14.3

Note: All data are for the 50 states and D. C.

a Instructor and above plus junior instructional staff for instruction in resident courses.

b Estimated full-time equivalent enrollment of degree-credit and non-degree-credit students.

e Estimates.

p NCES intermediate alternative projections.

Sources:

1 USOE, *Faculty and Other Professional Staff in Institutions of Higher Education, First Term 1959–60* (Washington: GPO), 1963, pp. 16, 18.

2 NCES, *Projections of Education Statistics* (Washington: GPO), 1970 edition, table 12; 1971 edition, tables 12, 31, 32; 1977 edition, tables 8, 22, 23; 1980 edition, tables 12, 33, 34; 1982 edition, tables 14, 22, 23.

116 Full-Time Faculty and the Percentage with Tenure by Sex and by Region and State, Fall 1981

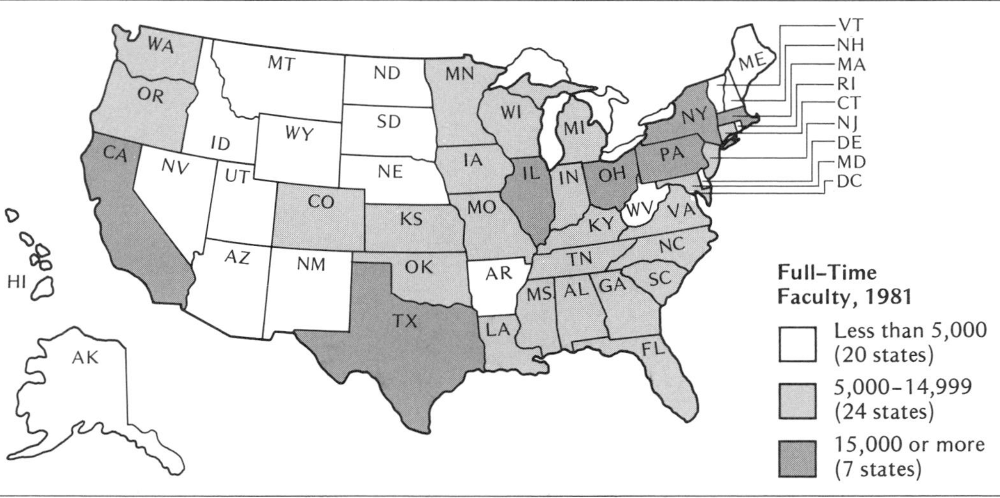

Region and State	All Full-Time Faculty			Percentage with Tenure	
	Both Sexes	Men	Women	Men	Women
U. S. & Outlying Parts	**406,671**	**296,690**	**109,981**	**64**	**44**
50 States & D. C.	**401,581**	**294,023**	**107,558**	**65**	**45**
New England	**28,372**	**20,985**	**7,387**	**64**	**42**
Connecticut	5,659	4,262	1,397	71	49
Maine	1,866	1,399	467	57	28
Massachusetts	15,098	11,042	4,056	62	40
New Hampshire	1,881	1,410	471	59	34
Rhode Island	2,418	1,799	619	70	56
Vermont	1,450	1,073	377	57	32
Mideast	**77,914**	**56,495**	**21,419**	**68**	**48**
Delaware	1,273	882	391	57	27
D. C.	3,455	2,391	1,064	55	31
Maryland	6,983	4,728	2,255	66	45
New Jersey	9,448	6,708	2,740	73	56
New York	36,310	26,244	10,066	67	48
Pennsylvania	20,445	15,542	4,903	70	49
Southeast	**86,573**	**60,427**	**26,146**	**57**	**37**
Alabama	6,563	4,340	2,223	61	49
Arkansas	3,235	2,326	909	62	41
Florida	12,567	9,043	3,524	66	54
Georgia	8,162	5,691	2,471	60	37
Kentucky	5,738	4,082	1,656	65	42
Louisiana	6,687	4,626	2,061	62	42
Mississippi	5,028	3,207	1,821	37	17
North Carolina	12,253	8,360	3,893	47	28
South Carolina	5,414	3,777	1,637	51	25
Tennessee	7,673	5,529	2,144	61	41
Virginia	10,269	7,343	2,926	53	31
West Virginia	2,984	2,103	881	63	43
Great Lakes	**70,332**	**52,472**	**17,860**	**67**	**45**
Illinois	20,603	15,132	5,471	71	55
Indiana	9,178	6,881	2,297	66	39
Michigan	14,741	11,137	3,604	72	51
Ohio	15,872	11,878	3,994	64	41
Wisconsin	9,938	7,444	2,494	57	28

(Continued on next page)

For footnotes, see next page.

117 Full-Time Faculty and the Percentage with Tenure by Sex and by Region and State, Fall 1981—*Continued*

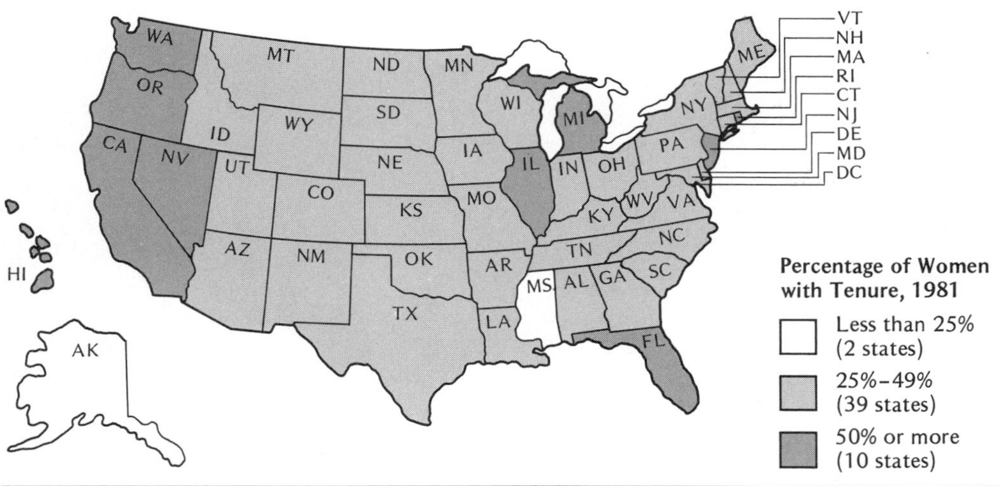

Region and State	All Full-Time Faculty: Both Sexes	Men	Women	Percentage with Tenure: Men	Women
Plains	**32,783**	**24,516**	**8,267**	**60**	**35**
Iowa	6,257	4,680	1,577	54	29
Kansas	5,203	3,870	1,333	63	38
Minnesota	7,028	5,354	1,674	62	38
Missouri	7,878	5,802	2,076	61	37
Nebraska	3,550	2,657	893	57	30
North Dakota	1,483	1,100	383	57	32
South Dakota	1,384	1,053	331	60	33
Southwest	**35,738**	**26,112**	**9,626**	**56**	**36**
Arizona	4,712	3,591	1,121	55	36
New Mexico	2,277	1,775	502	60	36
Oklahoma	5,424	3,936	1,488	53	35
Texas	23,325	16,810	6,515	57	37
Rocky Mountains	**13,359**	**10,605**	**2,754**	**62**	**41**
Colorado	5,820	4,555	1,265	63	44
Idaho	1,585	1,272	313	50	37
Montana	1,473	1,194	279	65	35
Utah	3,419	2,762	657	67	37
Wyoming	1,062	822	240	53	45
Far West	**55,733**	**41,694**	**14,039**	**77**	**63**
Alaska	612	411	201	24	10
California	40,069	29,916	10,153	79	67
Hawaii	1,854	1,360	494	69	51
Nevada	795	599	196	69	54
Oregon	5,187	3,886	1,301	69	50
Washington	7,216	5,522	1,694	78	61
U. S. Service Schools	**777**	**717**	**60**	**62**	**18**
Outlying Parts	**5,090**	**2,667**	**2,423**	**50**	**46**
American Samoa	56	33	23	79	78
Canal Zone	0	0	0	—	—
Guam	48	31	17	—	—
Puerto Rico	4,895	2,546	2,349	50	46
Trust Terr. of Pacific	25	15	10	—	—
Virgin Islands	66	42	24	31	42

Source: NCES HEGIS, computer tapes, with special analysis by ACE's Division of Policy Analysis and Research.

118 Faculty by Highest Degree Held and by Type and Control of Institution, Selected Years, 1950–1972

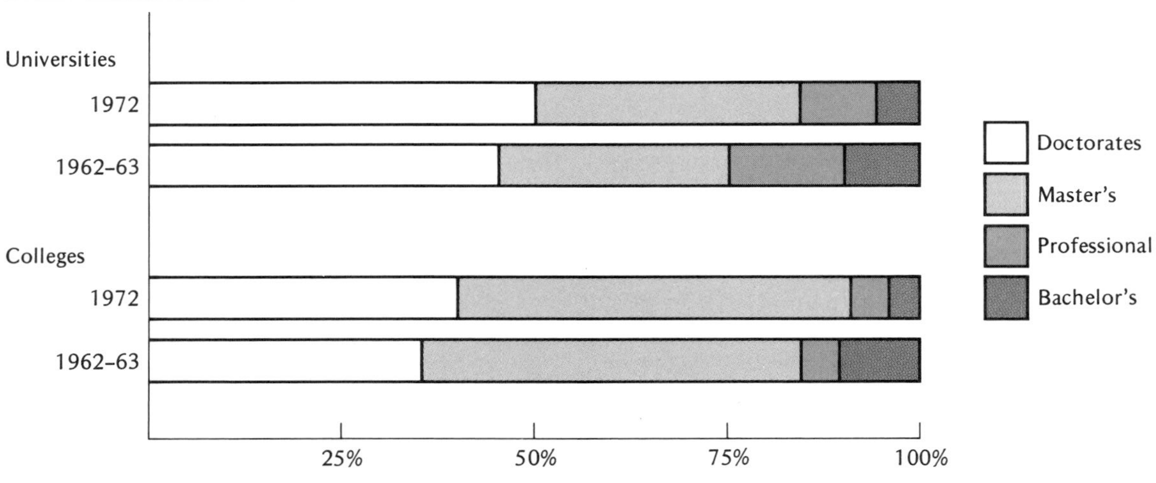

Highest Degree Held	Percentage of Faculty					
	1950–51[a]	1954–55[a]	1958–59[a]	1962–63[a]	1966[b]	1972
Public and Private Universities						
All Faculty	100	100	100	100	100	100
Doctorates	37	40	41	45	54	50
Master's	41	38	32	30	28	34
Professional	4	8	13	15	11	9
Bachelor's	19	14	13	11	7	7
Public Universities						
All Faculty	100	100	100	100	100	—
Doctorates	36	41	42	45	54	—
Master's	44	39	35	32	31	—
Professional	3	7	11	13	7	—
Bachelor's	17	14	13	10	8	—
Private Universities						
All Faculty	100	100	100	100	100	—
Doctorates	37	40	41	44	55	—
Master's	38	37	28	27	22	—
Professional	5	9	17	17	18	—
Bachelor's	21	15	14	12	5	—
Public and Private Colleges						
All Faculty	100	100	100	100	100	100
Doctorates	27	32	33	35	38	40
Master's	54	52	50	49	52	51
Professional	2	4	5	5	2	5
Bachelor's	17	13	12	11	7	4

a Data are for 781 institutions for which figures for the four years were available as published in *American Universities and Colleges,* 6th, 7th, 8th, and 9th eds. (Washington: American Council on Education, 1952, 1956, 1960, 1964). Full- and part-time faculty are included in most cases. Adjustments were made to exclude faculty at schools of medicine, dentistry, and veterinary science.

b Data are from USOE study (Source 2) that included 297,747 full-time senior teaching and research staff at 1,582 four-year institutions. This study used "bachelor's degree or lower" while Source 1 used "bachelor's" only.

Sources:

1 Allan M. Cartter, "A New Look at the Supply of College Teachers," *Educational Record,* Summer 1965, Vol. 46, No. 3, pp. 267–277. Used by permission.

2 National Center for Educational Statistics, USOE, *Numbers and Characteristics of Employees in Institutions of Higher Education, Fall 1966* (Washington: GPO), 1969.

3 Alan E. Bayer, *Teaching Faculty in Academe,* 1972–73 (Washington: American Council on Education), 1973, p. 26.

119 Women, as a Percentage of Instructional Faculty, by Rank, 1962–63, 1972–73, and 1979–80

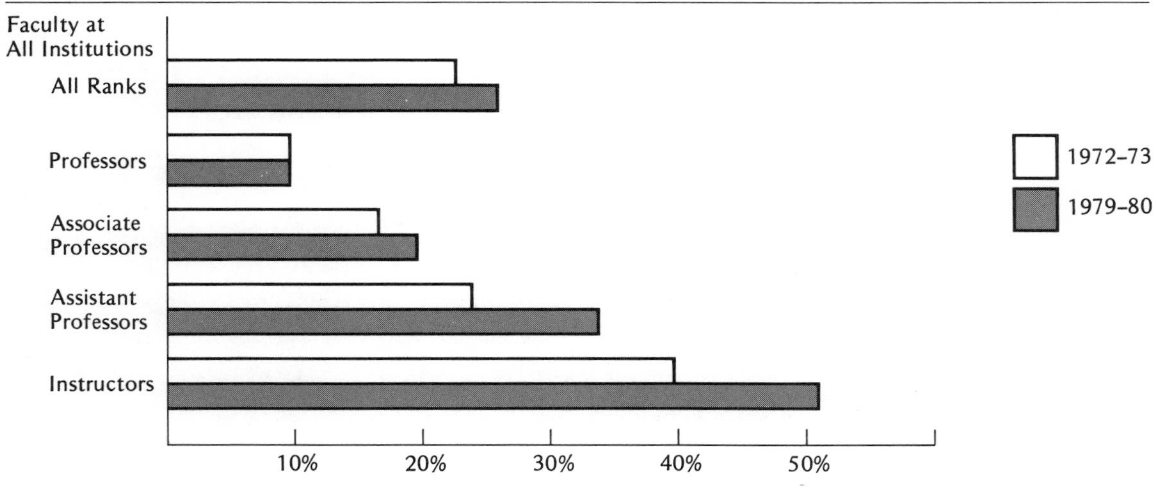

Type of Institution and Year	Women as a Percentage of Full-time Instructional Faculty[a] with Rank of				
	All Ranks	Professors	Associate Professors	Assistant Professors	Instructors
Four-Year Institutions					
1962–63[b]	19.0	8.7	16.1	22.5	30.9
1972–73[c]	20.6	9.4	15.8	23.1	43.5
All Institutions					
1972–73	22.3	9.8	16.3	23.8	39.9
1979–80	25.9	9.8	19.4	33.9	51.8
All Public Institutions					
1972–73	22.7	10.0	15.8	23.7	39.2
1979–80	26.4	9.7	19.1	33.8	52.1
Public Universities					
1972–73	17.1	6.7	12.3	20.0	44.4
1979–80	20.0	6.4	16.2	31.1	55.7
Public "Other Four-Year"					
1972–73	23.2	12.7	17.4	24.7	44.0
1979–80	26.4	11.8	18.9	34.5	52.7
Public Two-Year					
1972–73	32.3	21.2	24.3	31.3	35.1
1979–80	34.7	23.5	29.4	38.6	47.7
All Private Institutions					
1972–73	21.2	9.5	17.2	24.1	42.5
1979–80	24.8	10.1	20.3	34.2	51.0
Private Universities					
1972–73	14.5	5.4	12.9	19.0	41.0
1979–80	18.2	6.0	16.6	30.0	48.6
Private "Other Four-Year"					
1972–73	23.6	12.3	19.1	25.7	41.5
1979–80	27.4	12.7	21.6	35.4	51.0
Private Two-Year					
1972–73	45.4	31.5	34.3	41.3	53.8
1979–80	48.6	29.6	42.7	52.9	57.4

Note: Unless footnoted otherwise, data for 1972–73 are for the fifty states and D. C.; all other data are for aggregate U. S. Data for 1972–73 and 1979–80 are preliminary.

a Full-time instructional faculty on nine- or ten-month contracts.

b Figures are based on a 10 percent sample of faculty within four-year institutions except separately organized professional schools.

c Data are for aggregate U. S.

Sources:

1 NCES, letter from Assistant Commissioner for Educational Statistics, February 16, 1973.

2 NCES, "Women faculty still lag in salary and tenure for the 1979–80 academic year," *NCES Early Release,* undated, NCES 80–342, table 7.

120 Selected Faculty Characteristics, by Sex and by Type of Institution, 1973

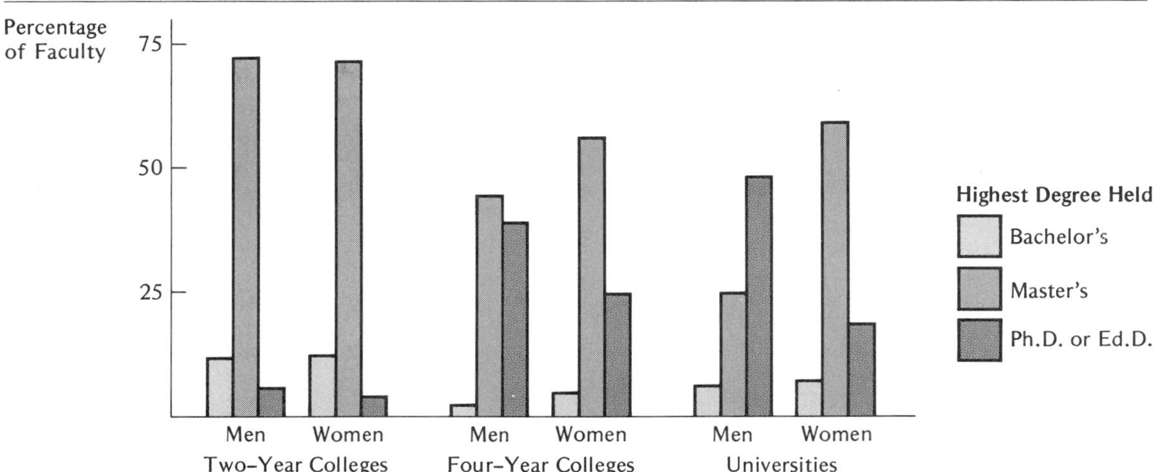

Characteristic	All Institutions		Two-Year Colleges		Four-Year Colleges		Universities	
	Men	Women	Men	Women	Men	Women	Men	Women
Age								
Over 60	7.6	8.4	4.8	5.9	7.0	8.6	9.2	9.6
51–60	20.4	21.0	20.0	18.9	18.5	19.6	22.1	24.1
41–50	30.8	28.8	36.0	34.3	29.4	28.6	30.0	25.6
36–40	16.3	13.2	16.7	11.4	16.7	14.7	15.7	12.6
31–35	15.7	13.5	14.2	13.2	17.3	12.7	15.0	14.7
30 or less	6.0	11.3	6.1	13.3	7.1	10.6	4.9	10.8
Father's Educational Attainment								
Eighth grade or less	29.8	25.1	35.6	29.6	31.4	26.9	26.3	20.2
Some high school	14.0	13.9	16.8	15.8	13.9	13.5	12.9	13.2
Completed high school	19.0	17.8	21.0	16.1	18.2	18.5	18.8	18.0
Some college	12.1	14.3	11.0	17.7	12.0	11.4	12.6	15.7
College graduate	9.8	10.9	7.5	9.4	8.8	10.1	11.4	12.9
Some graduate school	4.7	5.2	2.7	2.9	5.1	5.2	5.1	6.8
Advanced degree	10.7	12.7	5.4	8.6	10.6	14.4	12.8	13.2
Highest Degree Held								
Bachelor's or less	5.8	7.5	10.9	13.2	3.3	5.0	6.0	6.7
Master's	40.8	61.6	73.6	73.2	44.3	56.8	25.0	59.9
LL.B., J.D., other professional (except medical)	5.4	3.7	2.9	3.8	5.1	3.6	6.6	3.8
Medical	1.2	0.5	0.3	0.2	0.1	0.1	2.5	1.1
Ph.D. or Ed.D.	36.9	18.2	6.2	4.8	38.2	24.6	47.6	19.1
Other doctorate	1.6	1.2	1.1	0.9	1.8	1.6	1.7	1.0
No answer	8.3	7.4	4.9	4.0	7.1	8.2	10.6	8.5

Column heading: Percent Distribution[a] in

(*Continued on next page*)

a Based on 42,345 responding regular faculty from both academic departments and professional schools. For sampling design and weighting procedure see source, pp. 2–10.

b Includes social work, law, journalism, and library science.

c Includes home economics, industrial arts, and vocational-technical.

For source, see next page.

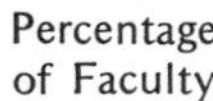

121 Selected Faculty Characteristics, by Sex and by Type of Institution, 1973—*Continued*

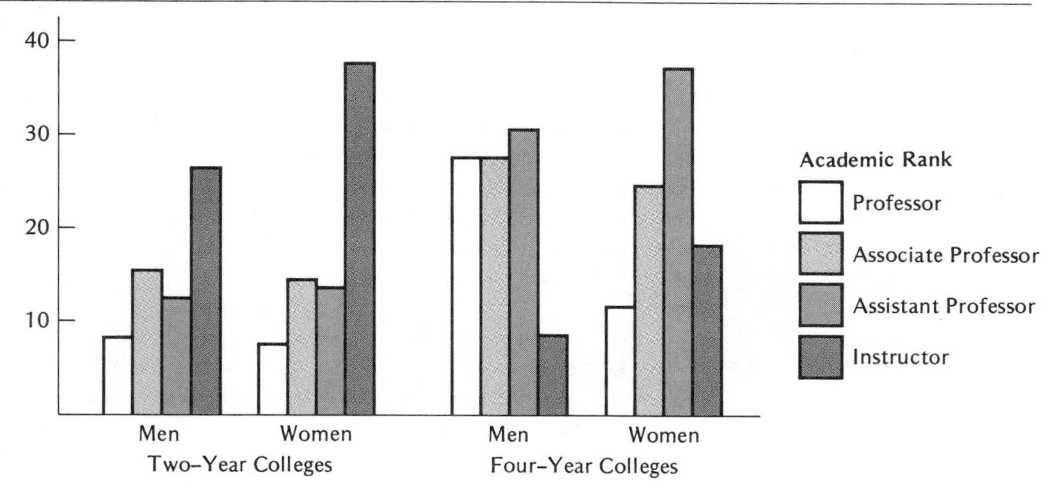

	Percent Distribution[a] in							
	All Institutions		Two-Year Colleges		Four-Year Colleges		Universities	
Characteristic	**Men**	**Women**	**Men**	**Women**	**Men**	**Women**	**Men**	**Women**
Present Rank								
Professor	30.3	11.0	8.2	7.4	27.8	11.9	40.9	12.3
Associate professor	25.1	21.0	15.8	14.6	27.8	24.9	26.4	20.4
Assistant professor	23.8	31.2	12.5	13.9	30.8	37.1	22.3	35.1
Instructor	10.4	24.3	26.2	37.8	8.6	18.4	5.9	22.8
Lecturer	2.2	4.0	0.4	0.4	2.4	4.3	2.7	5.8
No ranks designated	6.8	6.4	34.4	25.0	1.6	1.6	0.5	0.4
Other	1.4	2.1	2.5	1.0	1.0	1.8	1.4	3.2
Major Field of Highest Degree								
Business	4.7	1.9	5.5	3.5	5.5	2.0	3.7	0.9
Education (incl. phys. and health ed.)	12.6	23.4	18.8	22.9	13.9	24.8	9.1	21.9
Biological sciences (incl. agriculture)	7.4	4.3	5.4	4.1	5.1	4.2	10.1	4.7
Physical sciences (incl. math, statistics and computer sciences)	13.3	4.3	13.0	6.2	14.6	4.4	12.3	3.0
Engineering (incl. design and architecture)	7.8	0.4	5.3	0.0	5.8	0.3	10.5	0.8
Social sciences (incl. psych. and geog.)	13.3	8.6	9.2	10.5	14.1	8.7	14.2	7.4
Fine Arts	8.3	9.2	8.2	5.9	9.8	11.6	7.0	8.4
Humanities	16.8	20.6	16.2	22.3	20.5	23.9	14.0	15.7
Health sciences	3.2	10.2	0.6	10.1	0.5	5.1	6.6	16.4
Other professions[b]	3.7	4.9	1.0	2.6	3.3	5.1	5.1	6.2
All other fields[c]	2.1	5.4	4.3	3.8	1.5	3.6	1.7	8.4
None, no postgrad. degree (incl. no answer)	6.7	6.6	12.5	8.1	5.3	6.3	5.7	6.2

For footnotes, see preceding page.

Source: Alan E. Bayer, *Teaching Faculty in Academe: 1972–73,* A.C.E. Research Reports, Vol. 8, No. 2 (Washington: American Council on Education), 1973.

122 Average Faculty Salary, by Rank and by Type of Institution, Selected Years, 1970–71—1982–83

Category I

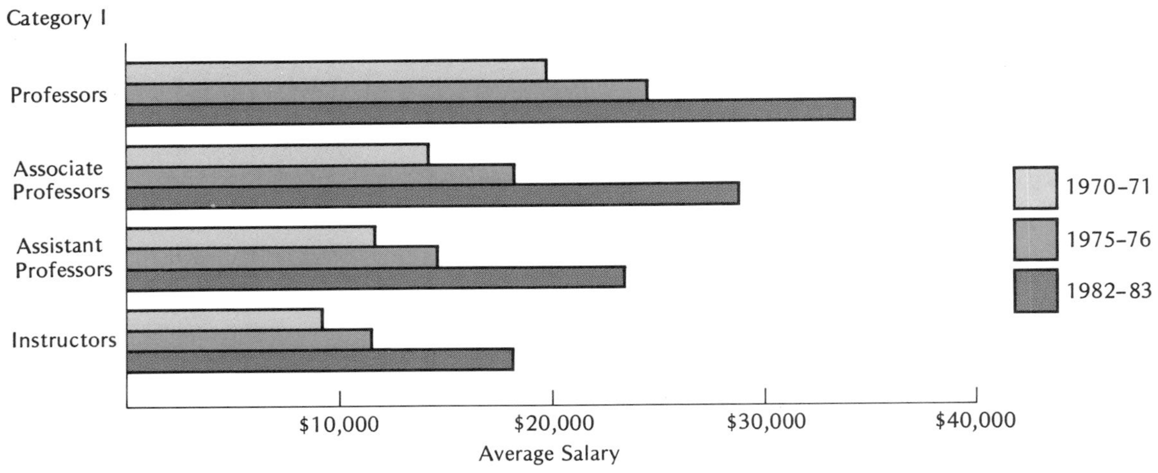

Category[b]	Average Salary[a] All Institutions 1970–71	1975–76	1982–83	Public Institutions 1970–71	1975–76	1982–83
			Professor			
I	19,600	24,590	39,380	19,150	24,150	38,180
IIA	17,090	22,010	33,480	17,420	22,500	33,490
IIB	14,760	19,270	29,320	15,250	21,460	30,770
IIC[c]	na	na	32,380	na	na	37,970
III	16,920	22,130	30,080	17,100	22,280	30,480
			Associate Professor			
I	14,380	18,060	28,700	14,350	18,010	28,310
IIA	13,570	17,340	26,720	13,830	17,680	26,770
IIB	11,880	15,300	23,580	12,590	17,340	25,530
IIC[c]	na	na	26,280	na	na	29,530
III	13,980	17,680	25,560	14,120	17,840	25,840
			Assistant Professor			
I	11,760	14,670	23,440	11,760	14,690	23,170
IIA	11,240	14,320	21,910	11,440	14,570	22,040
IIB	10,210	12,930	19,650	10,810	14,350	21,550
IIC[c]	na	na	21,960	na	na	24,620
III	11,660	15,080	21,490	11,760	15,180	21,840
			Instructor			
I	9,020	11,540	18,060	8,970	11,510	17,550
IIA	9,100	11,730	17,580	9,220	11,950	17,660
IIB	8,590	10,820	16,720	8,910	11,740	21,550
IIC[c]	na	na	17,170	na	na	19,070
III	9,670	12,210	18,880	9,760	12,390	18,880

(*Continued on next page*)

For sources, see next page.

a Calculated on a standard academic year basis. Fringe benefits not included.

b Institutional categories are as follows:
I —Doctoral-level institutions
IIA—Comprehensive institutions
IIB—General baccalaureate institutions
IIC—Specialized institutions
III —Two-year institutions

c As a result of reclassification of institutions in 1982, this category has been added. Data for years prior to 1982 are unavailable.

na Not available.

123 Average Faculty Salary, by Rank and by Type of Institution, Selected Years, 1970–71—1982–83—*Continued*

Category IIB

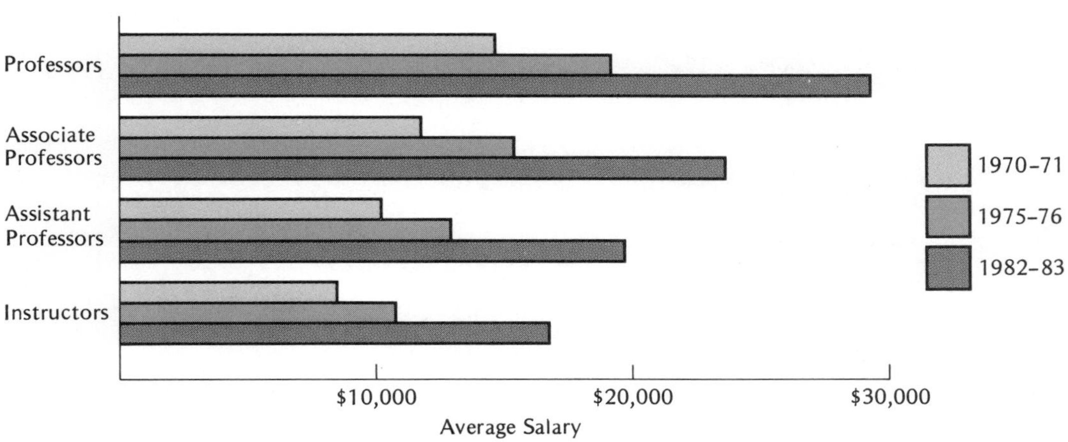

Category[b]	Average Salary[a]					
	Private Independent Institutions			Church-related Institutions		
	1970–71	1975–76	1982–83	1970–71	1975–76	1982–83
Professor						
I	21,080	26,540	43,950	18,100	22,220	38,710
IIA	17,120	21,010	33,750	15,430	19,490	32,890
IIB	15,700	20,430	32,410	14,280	17,640	26,130
IIC[c]	na	na	33,260	na	na	23,330
III	12,620	15,000	22,690	12,140	13,660	19,750
Associate Professor						
I	14,640	18,550	30,440	13,930	17,230	29,290
IIA	13,390	16,700	26,800	12,410	15,650	26,080
IIB	12,130	15,570	24,370	11,520	14,160	21,710
IIC[c]	na	na	25,880	na	na	20,180
III	11,340	12,930	20,640	10,600	12,550	18,720
Assistant Professor						
I	11,840	14,740	24,530	11,390	14,150	23,690
IIA	11,040	13,800	21,590	10,390	13,130	21,380
IIB	10,270	13,020	19,900	9,890	12,100	18,220
IIC[c]	na	na	21,400	na	na	17,690
III	9,780	11,840	17,130	9,290	10,670	16,920
Instructor						
I	9,290	11,750	19,970	9,030	11,600	19,880
IIA	9,070	11,360	17,230	8,520	10,690	17,350
IIB	8,790	10,900	16,940	8,360	10,180	15,580
IIC[c]	na	na	17,120	na	na	14,740
III	8,470	8,630	13,500	8,200	9,700	13,540

For footnotes, see preceding page.

Sources:

1 "At the Brink," *AAUP Bulletin,* American Association of University Professors, Summer Issue, June 1971, p. 240. Used by permission.

2 "Nearly Keeping Up," *AAUP Bulletin,* Summer Issue, August 1976, pp. 208, 209. Used by permission.

3 American Association of University Professors (AAUP), *Annual Report on the Economic Status of the Profession, 1982–83* (Washington: AAUP), 1983.

124 Average Faculty Compensation (Salary and Benefits), by Rank, Selected Years, 1965–66—1982–83

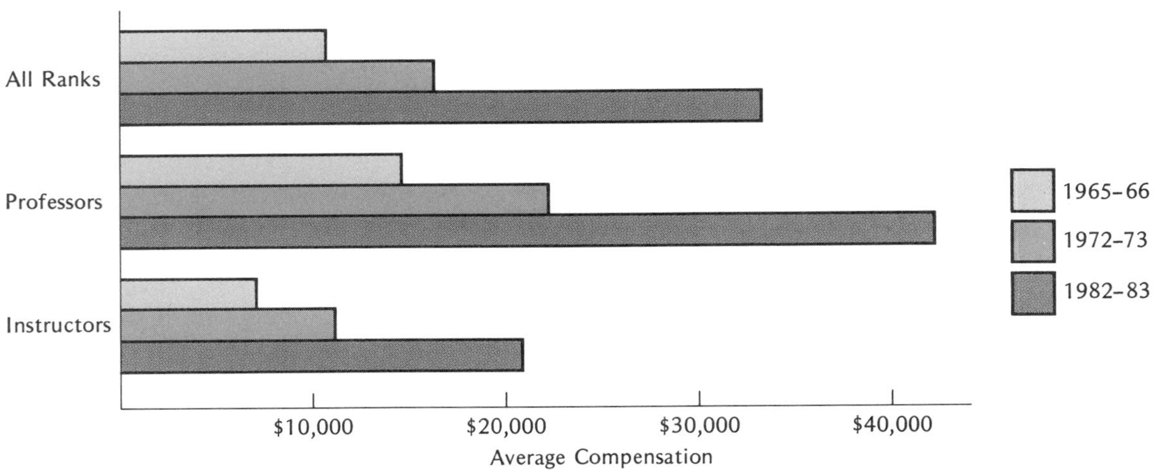

Year	Average Salary[a]	Average Fringe Benefits	Average Compensation	Fringe Benefits as a Percentage of Compensation
			All Ranks[b]	
1965–66	9,816	816	10,632	7.7
1970–71	13,284	1,508	14,792	10.2
1972–73	14,552	1,861	16,413	11.3
1974–75	16,403	2,306	18,709	12.3
1976–77	17,930	2,740	20,670	13.1
1978–79	20,120	3,530	23,650	14.9
1980–81	23,650	4,300	27,950	15.4
1982–83	27,430	5,330	32,760	16.3
			Professor	
1965–66	13,505	1,199	14,704	8.2
1970–71	18,314	2,084	20,398	10.2
1972–73	19,751	2,486	22,237	11.1
1974–75	21,870	3,006	24,876	12.1
1976–77	23,930	3,610	27,540	13.1
1978–79	26,470	4,920	31,390	15.7
1980–81	30,890	5,670	36,560	15.5
1982–83	35,470	6,880	42,350	16.2
			Associate Professor	
1965–66	10,186	847	11,033	7.7
1970–71	13,792	1,538	15,330	10.0
1972–73	14,887	1,884	16,771	11.2
1974–75	16,495	2,329	18,824	12.4
1976–77	18,100	2,790	20,890	13.4
1978–79	20,020	3,400	23,420	14.5
1980–81	23,270	4,300	27,570	15.6
1982–83	26,840	5,280	32,120	16.4
			Assistant Professor	
1965–66	8,429	685	9,114	7.5
1970–71	11,347	1,300	12,647	10.3
1972–73	12,289	1,601	13,890	11.5
1974–75	13,578	1,957	15,535	12.6
1976–77	14,820	2,290	17,110	13.4
1978–79	16,370	2,760	19,130	14.4
1980–81	18,970	3,400	22,370	15.2
1982–83	21,950	4,220	26,170	16.1

(*Continued on next page*)

For footnotes and sources, see next page.

125 Average Faculty Compensation, by Rank, Selected Years, 1965–66—1982–83—*Continued*

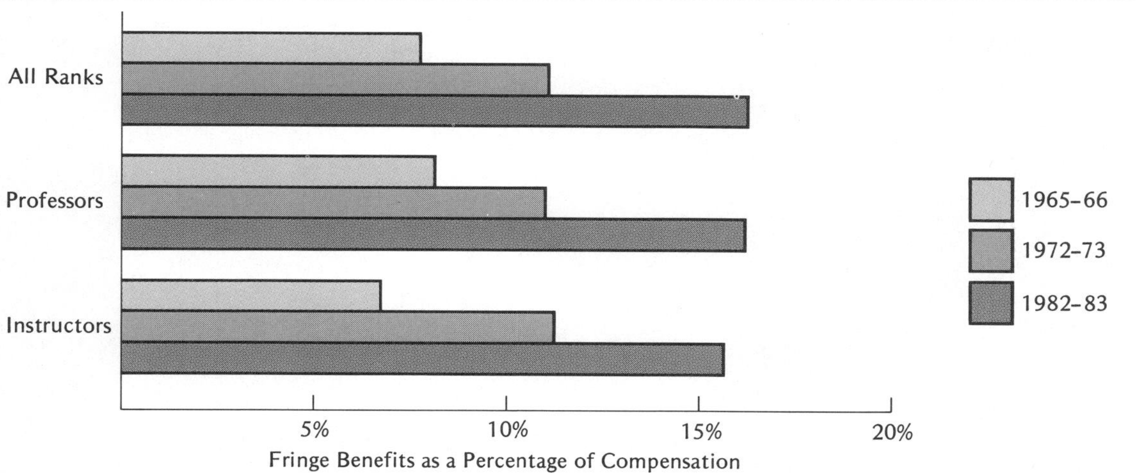

Year	Average Salary[a]	Average Fringe Benefits	Average Compensation	Fringe Benefits as a Percentage of Compensation
			Instructor[b]	
1965–66	6,737	487	7,224	6.7
1970–71	9,084	1,002	10,086	9.9
1972–73	9,873	1,263	11,136	11.3
1974–75	11,005	1,519	12,524	12.1
1976–77	11,920	1,770	13,690	12.9
1978–79	13,420	2,120	15,540	13.6
1980–81	15,140	2,550	17,690	14.4
1982–83	17,640	3,260	20,900	15.6
			Lecturer	
1965–66	8,070	579	8,649	6.7
1970–71	11,113	1,556	12,669	12.3
1972–73	12,168	1,933	14,101	13.7
1974–75	13,334	2,131	15,465	13.8
1976–77	13,830	2,330	16,160	14.4
1978–79	14,890	2,940	17,830	16.5
1980–81	na	na	na	na
1982–83	19,700	4,350	24,050	18.1
			Faculty in Institutions without Professorial Rank[c]	
1965–66	9,198	410	9,608	4.3
1970–71	12,384	927	13,311	7.0
1972–73	13,824	1,313	15,137	8.7
1974–75	15,537	1,877	17,414	10.8
1976–77	16,080	2,060	18,140	11.4
1978–79	17,950	2,750	20,700	13.3
1980–81	21,560	3,560	25,120	14.2
1982–83	24,340	4,240	28,580	14.8

a Salary for full-time faculty on a standard academic year basis.

b Number of institutions supplying data on ranked faculty: 1965–66, 822; 1970–71, 1,161; 1972–73, 1,242; 1974–75, 1,255; 1976–77, 1,885; 1978–79, 1, 743; 1982–83, 2, 572.

c Number of institutions supplying data: 1965–66, 83; 1970–71, 184; 1972–73, 241; 1974–75, 293; 1976–77, 756; 1978–79, 705.

na Not available.

Sources:

1 "The Economic Status of the Profession," *AAUP Bulletin,* American Association of University Professors, June 1966, p. 152; June 1971, p. 240; June 1974, p. 174; August 1975, p. 126; August 1977, p. 152.

2 American Association of University Professors (AAUP), *Annual Report on the Economic Status of the Profession, 1982–83* (Washington: AAUP), 1983.

126 Faculty with Tenure, as a Percentage of All Faculty, by Control of Institution, Region and State, Fall 1981

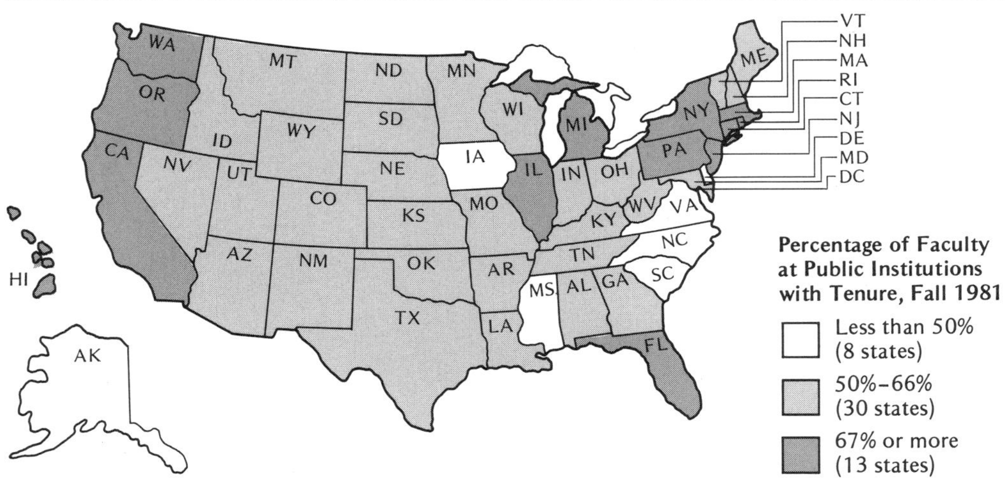

Region and State	Percentage of Faculty[a] with Tenure: Public Insts.	Private Insts.
U. S. & Outlying Parts	**63**	**49**
50 States & D. C.	**63**	**49**
New England	**70**	**48**
Connecticut	76	54
Maine	56	38
Massachusetts	72	48
New Hampshire	61	41
Rhode Island	78	53
Vermont	61	38
Mideast	**69**	**53**
Delaware	49	34
District of Columbia	nr	57
Maryland	64	43
New Jersey	71	61
New York	71	51
Pennsylvania	73	56
Southeast	**54**	**42**
Alabama	63	30
Arkansas	59	41
Florida	69	34
Georgia	58	40
Kentucky	61	48
Louisiana	57	48
Mississippi	31	23
North Carolina	39	48
South Carolina	42	49
Tennessee	62	43
Virginia	47	47
West Virginia	60	42
Great Lakes	**64**	**52**
Illinois	72	55
Indiana	61	55
Michigan	70	46
Ohio	61	52
Wisconsin	50	48
Plains	**56**	**47**
Iowa	47	49
Kansas	61	31
Minnesota	59	49
Missouri	57	51
Nebraska	51	49
North Dakota	54	8
South Dakota	58	42
Southwest	**51**	**48**
Arizona	51	32
New Mexico	55	54
Oklahoma	51	34
Texas	51	52
Rocky Mountains	**60**	**47**
Colorado	60	53
Idaho	59	7
Montana	61	45
Utah	65	54
Wyoming	51	—
Far West	**78**	**49**
Alaska	20	nr
California	82	49
Hawaii	67	38
Nevada	65	nr
Oregon	68	48
Washington	78	53
U. S. Service Schools	**59**	**—**
Outlying Parts	**60**	**26**

— No private institutions.

nr No tenured faculty reported.

a Full-time instructional faculty on nine- and twelve-month contracts.

Source: NCES, HEGIS Fall 1981 computer data tapes with special analysis by ACE's Division of Policy Analysis and Research.

127 Administrative Salaries at Institutions of Higher Education, by Selected Positions, 1967–68, 1975–76, and 1982–83

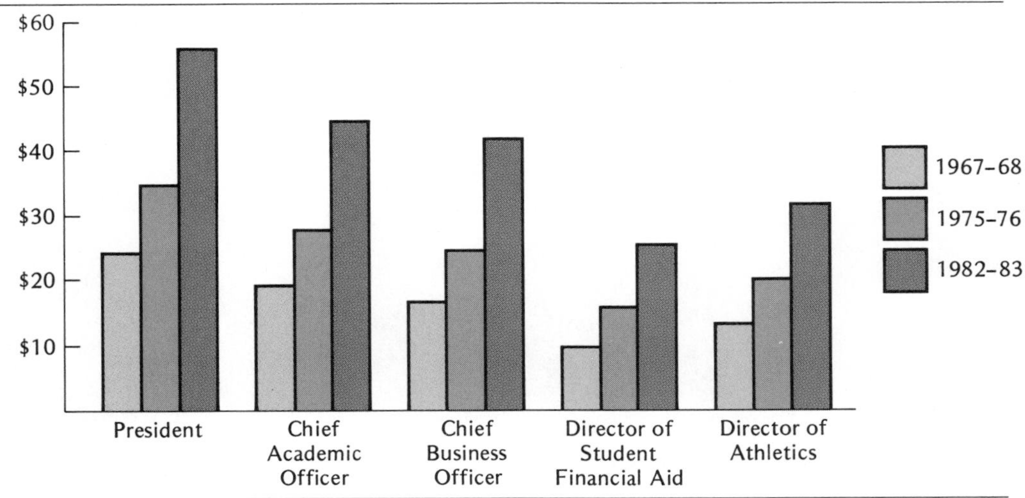

Position	1967–68 Number Reported	1967–68 Median Salary	1975–76 Number Reported	1975–76 Median Salary	1982–83 Number Reported	1982–83 Median Salary
President (Chief Exec. Officer)	415	24,000	864	34,800	1,310	55,624
Chief Academic Officer	400	19,000	974	27,500	1,310	44,136
Registrar	408	11,208	974	17,568	1,192	27,500
Director of Admissions	339	12,000	771	18,500	1,012	28,999
Head Librarian	415	13,000	1,026	19,000	1,129	30,370[a]
Director, Computer Center	260	13,367	626	19,800	901	32,427[e]
Chief Business Officer	392	16,200	1,022	24,378	1,355	41,712
Purchasing Agent	263	10,400	508	15,750	698	25,700[f]
Director, Personnel Services	179	11,976	537	18,430	660	31,500[b]
Director, Physical Plant	383	11,500	904	17,593	1,050	32,000[g]
Director, Food Services	226	10,500	332	16,696	368	26,750
Comptroller	251	11,976	566	19,229	801	33,000
Director, Student Housing	211	10,000	434	15,082	633	22,470
Manager, Bookstore	340	8,000	647	11,693	847	18,740[h]
Staff Legal Counsel	nr	nr	79	25,580	170	43,000[c]
Chief Development Officer	274	15,500	543	22,700	752	37,508
Chief Public Relations Officer	249	12,045	534	17,799	742	27,666
Director, Information Office	245	10,000	421	15,636	367	25,629
Chief Student Life Officer	293	15,500	875	22,750	1,309	36,750[d]
Director, Student Union	210	10,600	428	16,000	420	26,200
Director, Student Placement	259	11,000	605	16,080	860	24,274
Director, Student Financial Aid	285	9,600	842	15,547	1,208	25,100
Director, Student Counseling	219	12,500	621	19,017	814	28,200
Director of Athletics	284	13,200	592	20,000	805	31,710
Director/Dean, Arts & Sciences	nr	nr	416	28,000	371	46,500
Director/Dean, Engineering	nr	nr	186	33,000	230	54,054
Director/Dean, Graduate Programs	nr	nr	279	30,300	364	45,860
Director/Dean, Medicine	nr	nr	63	52,000	81	86,700

nr Not reported.

a Position title: Director, Library Services.

b Position title: Director, Personnel/Human Resources.

c Position title: Director, Legal Services.

d Position title: Chief Student Affairs Officer.

e Position title: Director, Computer Center.

f Position title: Director, Purchasing.

g Position title: Chief, Physical Plant/Facilities Management Officer.

h Position title: Director of Bookstore.

Sources:

1 College and University Personnel Association (CUPA), *1967–68 Administrative Compensation Survey* (Urbana, Il.: CUPA, 1968), p. 10.

2 CUPA, *Administrative Compensation Survey* (CUPA, 11 Dupont Circle, Washington, DC 20036), 1975–76, p. 16; 1980–81, p. 1; 1982–83, p. 1. Copyright © CUPA. Used by permission.

128 Administrative Salaries at Public Institutions, by Selected Positions, 1967–68, 1975–76, and 1982–83

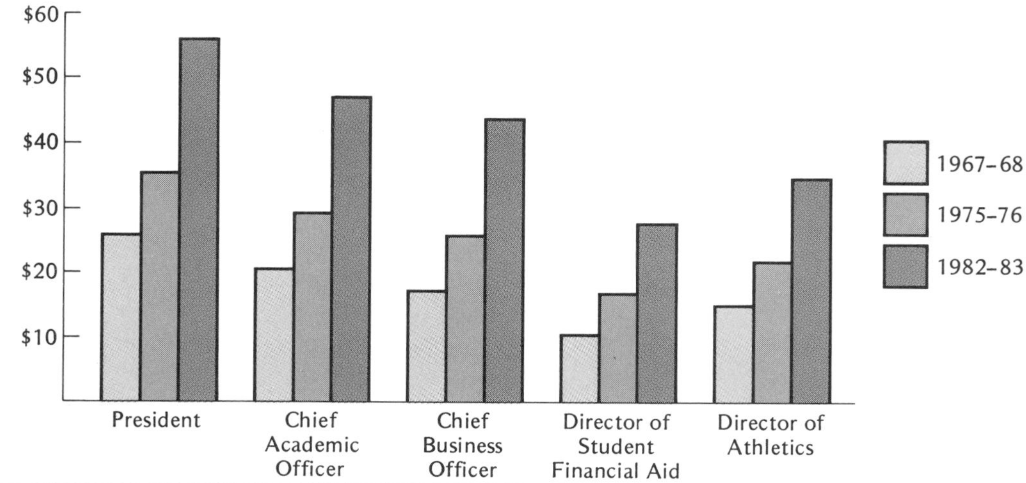

Position	Median Salaries at Public Institutions[a] 1967–68	1975–76	1982–83
President (Chief Exec. Officer)	26,000	35,500	55,693
Chief Academic Officer	20,904	29,229	47,000
Registrar	13,400	19,700	31,000
Director of Admissions	13,200	20,156	30,197
Head Librarian	15,000	21,520	34,469[b]
Director, Computer Center	14,685	21,110	34,740
Chief Business Officer	17,000	25,604	43,500
Purchasing Agent	10,716	16,420	27,224[f]
Director, Personnel Services	12,000	19,500	33,460[c]
Director, Physical Plant	13,200	19,308	34,017[g]
Director, Food Services	11,376	17,300	28,091
Comptroller	13,110	20,200	34,857
Director, Student Housing	10,700	17,140	26,747
Manager, Bookstore	9,568	12,808	21,555[h]
Staff Legal Counsel	nr	25,500	42,420[d]
Chief Development Officer	15,700	24,156	39,234
Chief Public Relations Officer	13,500	20,500	32,000
Director, Information Office	11,628	17,184	26,520
Chief Student Life Officer	17,000	25,346	40,000[e]
Director, Student Union	11,590	17,220	28,830
Director, Student Placement	12,300	17,796	27,307
Director, Student Financial Aid	10,300	16,743	27,800
Director, Student Counseling	13,080	20,182	30,499
Director, Athletics	15,000	21,753	34,750
Director/Dean, Arts & Sciences	nr	28,517	46,500
Director/Dean, Engineering	nr	33,300	52,041
Director/Dean, Graduate Programs	nr	31,500	47,160
Director/Dean, Medicine	nr	50,000	83,968

nr Not reported.

a Number of reporting institutions: 1967–68, 223; 1975–76, 699; 1980–81, 853; 1982–83, 868.

b Position title: Director, Library Services.

c Position title: Chief, Personnel/Human Resources Officer.

d Position title: Director, Legal Services.

e Position title: Chief Student Affairs Officer.

f Position title: Director, Purchasing.

g Position title: Chief, Physical Plant/Facilities Management Officer.

h Position title: Director of Bookstore.

Sources:

1 College and University Personnel Association (CUPA), *1967–68 Administrative Compensation Survey* (Urbana, Il.: CUPA), 1968, p. 10.

2 CUPA, *Administrative Compensation Survey* (CUPA, 11 Dupont Circle, Washington, D C 20036), 1975–76, p. 17; 1980–81, p. 2; 1982–83, p. 2.

129 Administrative Salaries at Private Institutions, by Selected Positions, 1967–68, 1975–76, and 1982–83

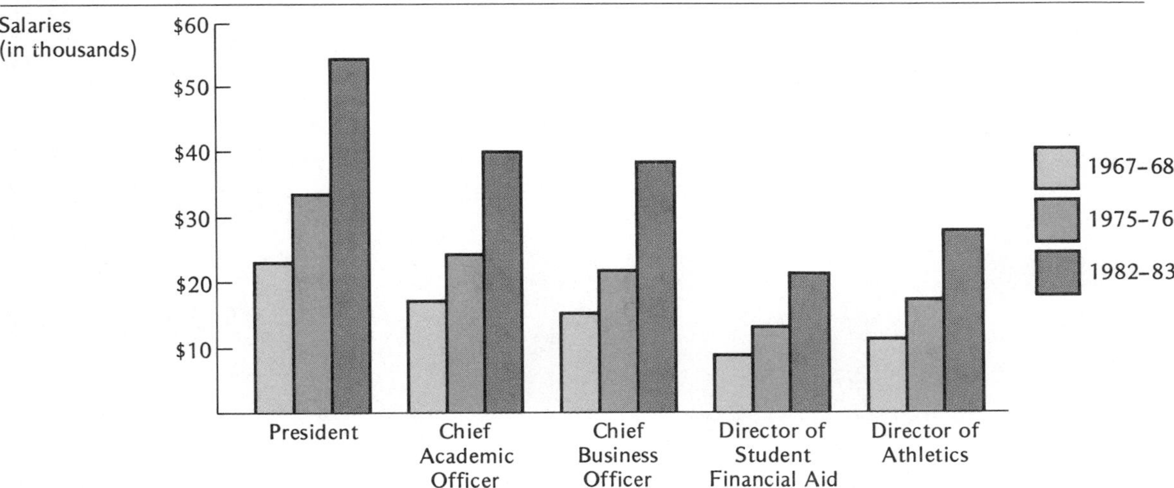

Position	Median Salaries at Private Institutions[a] 1967–68	1975–76	1982–83
President (Chief Exec. Officer)	23,000	33,500	55,400
Chief Academic Officer	17,300	24,150	40,000
Registrar	9,600	14,743	23,165
Director of Admissions	11,000	16,450	27,500
Head Librarian	11,000	15,571	25,641[b]
Director, Computer Center	12,000	16,750	28,250
Chief Business Officer	15,400	21,800	38,500
Purchasing Agent	10,000	14,200	23,000[g]
Director, Personnel Services	11,224	15,550	27,500[c]
Director, Physical Plant	10,000	15,000	28,250[f]
Director, Food Services	10,000	15,185	25,500
Comptroller	11,000	18,180	30,100
Director, Student Housing	8,400	12,500	18,500
Manager, Bookstore	7,000	10,000	15,500[h]
Staff Legal Counsel	nr	25,875	48,400
Chief Development Officer	15,500	22,000	36,000
Chief Public Relations Officer	10,710	15,000	24,250
Director, Information Office	8,770	13,000	23,345
Chief Student Life Officer	12,565	17,902	31,000[e]
Director, Student Union	9,000	12,960	20,100
Director, Student Placement	9,000	13,183	20,950
Director, Student Financial Aid	9,000	13,325	21,200
Director, Student Counseling	10,500	15,845	23,000
Director, Athletics	11,558	17,500	27,950
Director/Dean, Arts & Sciences	nr	26,124	46,119
Director/Dean, Engineering	nr	30,550	59,040
Director/Dean, Graduate Programs	nr	26,000	39,000
Director/Dean, Medicine	nr	53,500	113,000

nr Not reported.

a Number of reporting institutions: 1967–68, 222; 1975–76, 469; 1980–81, 704.

b Position title: Director, Library Services.

c Position title: Chief, Personnel/Human Resources.

d Position title: Director, Legal Services.

e Position title: Chief Student Affairs Officer.

f Position title: Chief, Physical Plant/Facilities Management Officer.

g Position title: Director, Purchasing.

h Position title: Director of Bookstore.

Sources:

1 College and University Personnel Association (CUPA), *1967–68 Administrative Compensation Survey* (Urbana, Il.: CUPA), 1968, p. 13.

2 CUPA, *Administrative Compensation Survey* (CUPA, 11 Dupont Circle, Washington, D C 20036), 1975–76, p. 18; 1980–81, p. 3; 1982–83, p. 3. Copyright © CUPA. Used by permission.

130 Women College Presidents, by Type and Control of Institution, 1975–1982

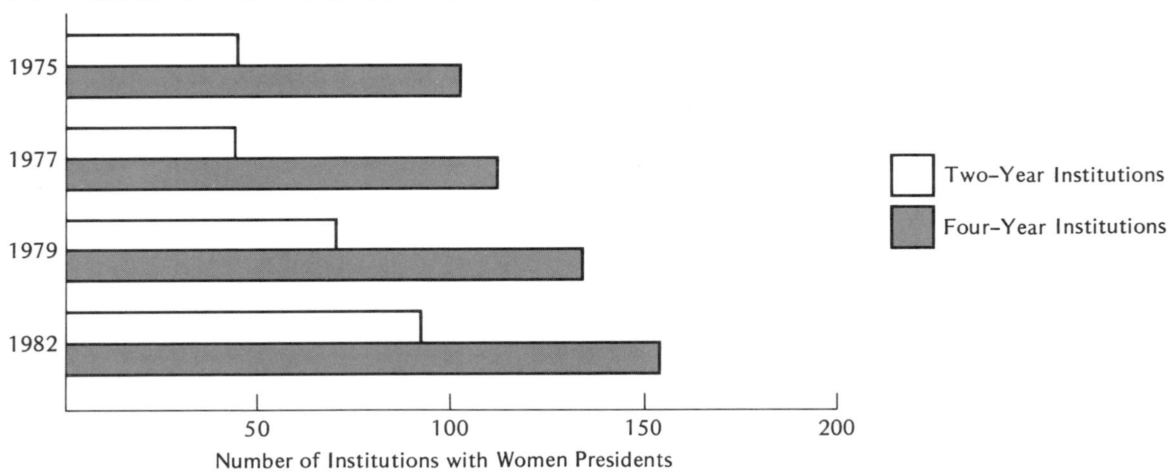

Year and Type of Institution		All Institutions Headed by Women		Public Institutions Headed by Women		Private Institutions Headed by Women		Women's Colleges[a] Headed by Women	
		Number	Percentage[b]	Number	Percentage[b]	Number	Percentage[b]	Number	Percentage[b]
1975	**Total**	**148**	4.8	**16**	1.1	**132**	8.2	na	na
	Four-Year	103	5.4	5	.9	98	7.2	na	na
	Two-Year	45	3.9	11	1.2	34	14.2	na	na
1976	**Total**	**154**	5.0	**16**	1.1	**138**	8.6	**71**	56.8
	Four-Year	110	5.7	3	.5	107	7.8	57	58.8
	Two-Year	44	3.8	13	1.4	31	13.0	14	50.0
1977	**Total**	**156**	5.0	**19**	1.3	**137**	8.3	**87**	71.3
	Four-Year	112	5.7	5	.9	107	7.7	72	75.0
	Two-Year	44	3.7	14	1.5	30	12.0	15	57.7
1978	**Total**	**177**	5.6	**31**	2.1	**146**	8.7	**75**	64.1
	Four-Year	123	6.3	9	1.6	114	8.1	62	66.7
	Two-Year	54	4.5	22	2.4	32	11.3	13	54.2
1979	**Total**	**204**	6.4	**47**	3.2	**157**	9.2	**80**	70.8
	Four-Year	134	6.8	14	2.5	120	8.5	65	71.4
	Two-Year	70	5.8	33	3.5	37	13.0	15	68.2
1982	**Total**	**244**	**7.5**	**78**	**5.2**	**166**	**9.5**	**84**	**75.7**
	Four-Year	152	7.7	25	4.5	127	8.9	62	69.7
	Two-Year	92	7.2	53	5.6	39	11.6	22	100.0

na Not available in source.

a Institutions with enrollment of at least 90 percent women.

b Institutions headed by women as a percentage of all institutions of the type indicated. Annual directories published by NCES are the source of data concerning the "universe" of institutions by type and control.

Sources:

1 "Women Chief Executive Officers in Colleges and Universities," *Comment,* Fall 1976, p. 3; March 1978, p. 5; July 1979, p. 2; June 1980, p. 9.

2 American Council on Education, Office on Women in Higher Education, December 1982, unpublished data.

131 Turnover Rate of Selected Administrative Positions, by Type of Institution, 1975–76 and 1980–81

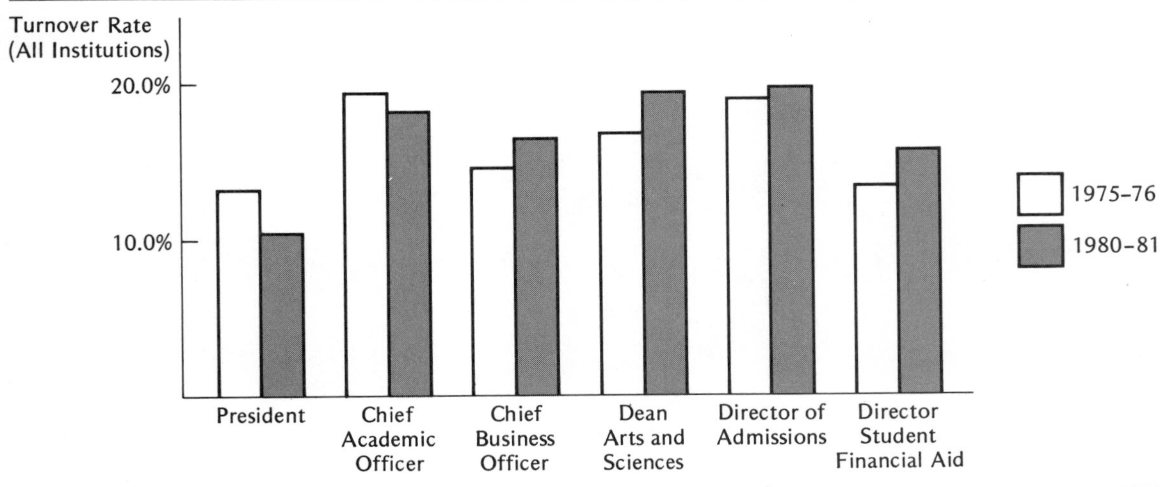

Position	All Institutions 1975–76	All Institutions 1980–81	Four-Year Institutions 1975–76	Four-Year Institutions 1980–81	Two-Year Institutions 1975–76	Two-Year Institutions 1980–81
	Turnover Rate[a]					
President (Chief Exec. Officer)	13.2	10.6	13.6	10.6	12.6	10.7
Chief Academic Officer	19.5	18.2	21.5	18.8	15.9	17.2
Chief Business Officer	14.6	16.1	16.0	16.7	12.0	15.1
Chief Development Officer	10.9	16.6	11.6	16.9	7.6	15.0
Chief Librarian	12.2	13.3	11.6	13.5	13.2	12.7
Registrar	13.2	13.8	13.5	12.6	12.4	13.8
Director of Admissions	19.0	19.7	19.9	22.6	16.3	12.6
Director, Computer Center	10.7	16.3	11.6	17.0	8.4	16.3
Director, Personnel Services	11.5	13.5	12.2	13.4	9.7	13.9
Director, Student Financial Aid	13.6	15.8	13.4	15.8	14.0	15.7
Chief Student Life Officer	14.9	17.0	16.0	17.9	13.2	15.3
Director, Student Placement	10.9	15.8	11.8	15.5	7.5	16.5
Dean of Arts and Sciences	16.9	19.2	17.5	21.0	15.3	14.1
Dean of Graduate Programs	16.8	18.2	16.8	18.2	0.0	0.0
Dean of Engineering	11.2	18.1	11.5	18.3	8.8	17.3

a Data come from the institutional characteristics portion of NCES's Higher Education General Information Survey (HEGIS). The figures show the number of changes from one year to the next in each position as a percentage of the total positions reported.

Source: NCES, *Education Directory, Colleges and Universities* (Washington: GPO), *1975–76,* p. xxxiv; *1980–81,* unpublished data.

132 Trends in Average College Costs by Control of Institution, 1977–78—1984–85

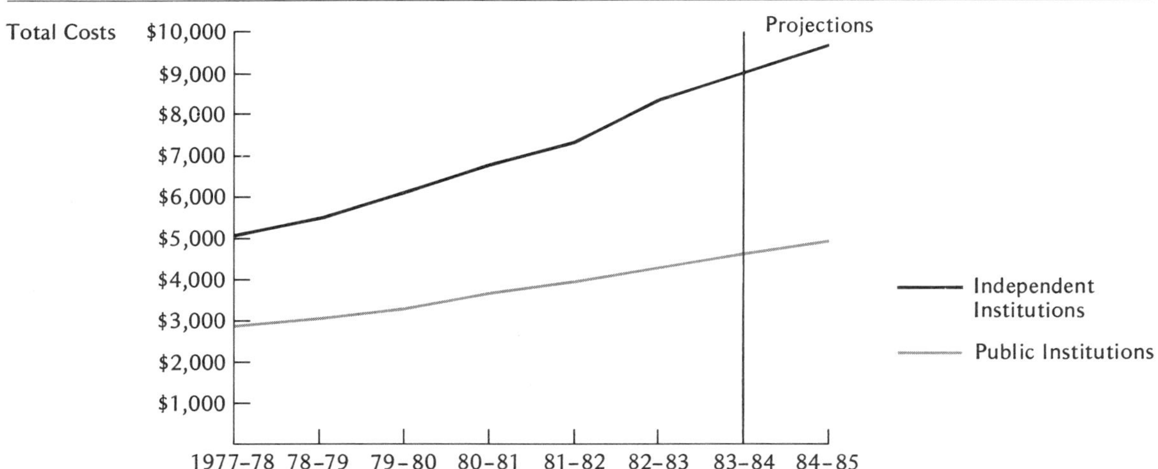

Year	Total Costs[a]			Tuition and Fees			Room, Board, and Other Expenses[a]		
	Total	Public	Independent[b]	Total	Public	Independent[b]	Total	Public	Independent[b]
1977–78	**$3,477**	$2,936	$5,188	**$1,014**	$519	$2,582	**$2,463**	$2,417	$2,606
1978–79	**3,684**	3,067	5,535	**1,114**	554	2,793	**2,570**	2,513	2,742
1979–80	**3,966**	3,280	6,025	**1,217**	581	3,126	**2,749**	2,699	2,899
1980–81	**4,375**	3,601	6,695	**1,350**	634	3,496	**3,025**	2,967	3,199
1981–82	**4,842**	3,993	7,530	**1,505**	719	3,994	**3,337**	3,274	3,536
ACE Projections									
1982–83	**5,266**	4,307	8,296	**1,695**	805	4,513	**3,571**	3,502	3,783
1983–84	**5,678**	4,625	9,012	**1,897**	877	4,964	**3,821**	3,748	4,048
1984–85	**6,057**	4,920	9,652	**2,007**	947	5,361	**4,050**	3,978	4,291

a Total costs combine:
(1) tuition, fee, room, and board charges from the National Center for Education Statistics, and
(2) expenses for transportation, books, supplies, and personal items from the College Scholarships Service survey series.

b Includes a limited number of private proprietary institutions.

Sources: Division of Policy Analysis and Research, American Council on Education, based on data from the National Center for Education Statistics, *Digest of Education Statistics, 1982,* and the College Scholarship Service of The College Board, *The College Cost Book,* selected years.

133 National Norms for Selected Characteristics of Entering Freshmen, by Sex and by Type of Institution, Fall 1982

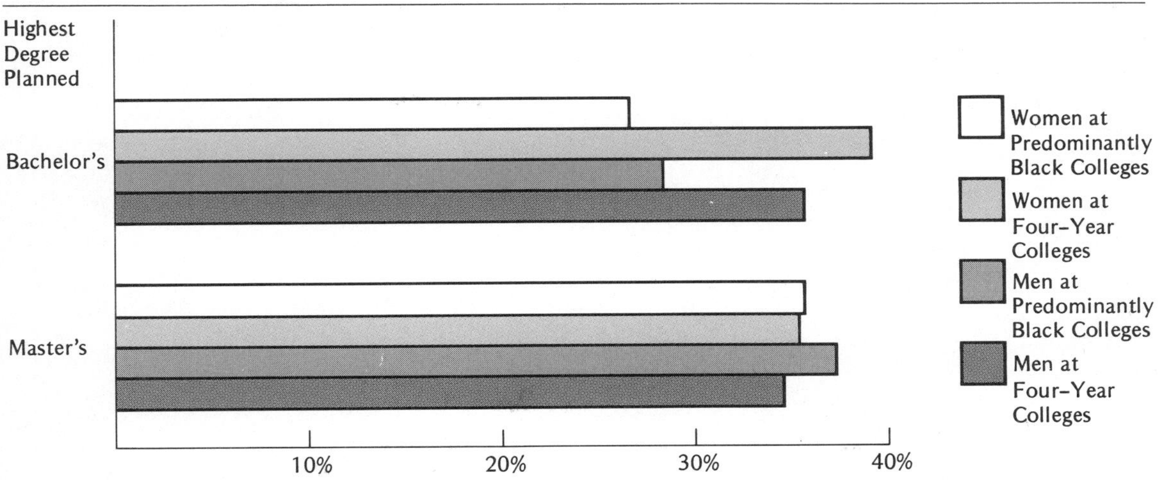

	Percentage of Students[a]					
	All Institutions		Public Univs.		Private Univs.	
Student Characteristics	Men	Women	Men	Women	Men	Women
Highest Degree Planned						
None	2.0	1.7	1.1	.9	.5	.4
Associate Degree (or equivalent)	6.8	9.8	.9	1.3	.2	.2
Bachelor's	37.8	38.8	34.7	38.1	17.4	21.7
Master's	30.8	30.2	34.3	34.6	34.5	36.2
Ph.D. or Ed.D.	8.8	7.6	10.4	9.4	16.7	14.4
M.D., D.O., D.D.S., or D.V.M.	6.3	5.7	10.0	8.8	17.6	15.3
LL.B. or J.D.	4.7	3.8	6.9	5.4	11.4	10.4
B.D. or M.Div.	.6	.3	.4	.2	.4	.2
Other	2.2	2.1	1.3	1.3	1.2	1.2
Racial Background						
White/Caucasian	89.0	87.5	92.6	90.2	83.9	79.8
Black/Negro/Afro-American	7.6	9.4	4.4	7.3	8.5	13.1
American Indian	1.0	.9	.7	.7	.7	.8
Oriental	1.5	1.3	1.8	1.6	4.0	3.8
Mexican-American/Chicano	.9	.9	.8	.8	1.6	1.6
Puerto Rican-American	.9	.9	.5	.4	1.0	1.1
Other	1.5	1.3	1.2	.9	2.9	2.7
Support of $500 or More from						
Parental or family aid	54.9	55.1	66.3	68.9	78.4	78.4
Basic Ed. Opportunity Grant	15.3	16.4	11.4	11.6	15.1	15.4
Supplemental Ed. Opportunity Grant	3.1	3.2	2.1	2.0	7.0	7.1
College Work-Study Grant	6.9	7.7	6.4	6.5	17.4	18.4
State scholarship or grant	7.3	7.8	5.8	6.2	9.9	10.5
College grant	8.0	8.6	5.4	5.0	24.2	24.8
Private grant	3.8	4.2	5.0	5.2	10.5	9.6
Federal Guaranteed Student Loan	19.1	18.8	15.1	13.9	25.8	24.5
National Direct Student Loan	4.6	5.1	4.1	4.5	8.7	9.8
College loan	2.9	2.5	2.3	2.0	4.3	3.7
Other loan	3.3	3.4	3.0	3.3	4.0	4.3
Full-time employment	1.3	.8	.9	.5	.7	.4
Part-time employment	9.2	7.0	8.1	6.2	7.5	6.6
Savings from summer work	25.1	18.1	33.9	24.7	35.4	26.3
Other savings	8.3	7.2	11.1	9.6	12.8	10.0
Spouse	.5	.5	.5	.2	.1	.1
Personal G.I. benefits	.6	.1	.3	—	.1	—
Parent's G.I. benefits	.6	.3	.5	.4	.2	.2
Social Sec. dependent's benefits	1.7	2.0	1.7	2.1	1.5	1.7
Other sources	2.3	1.6	1.5	1.4	3.0	2.5

(Contined on next page)

a Weighted national norms based on data from questionnaire responses from 188,692 full-time, first-time freshmen at 350 institutions in the fall of 1982.

134 National Norms for Selected Characteristics of Entering Freshmen, Fall 1982—*Continued*

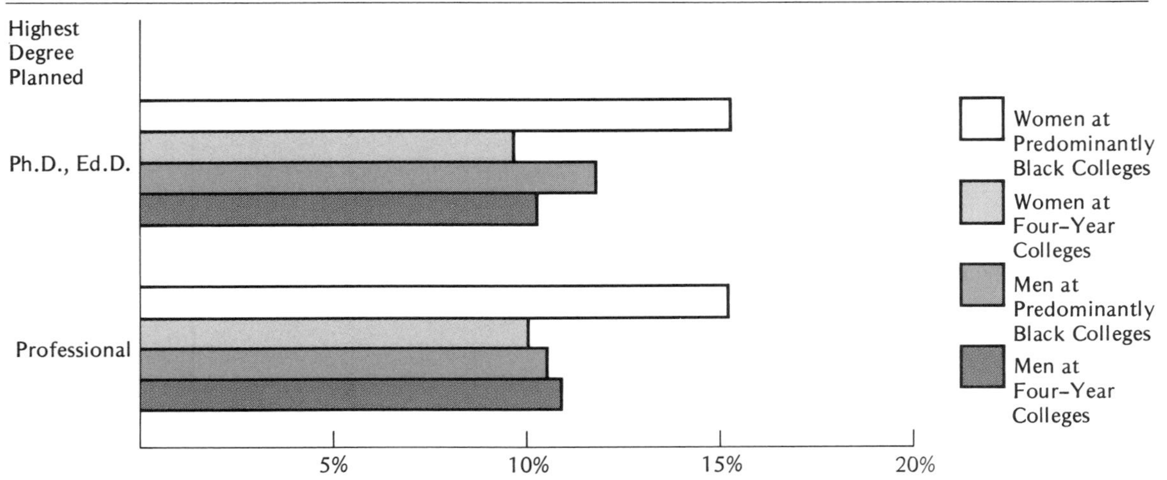

Student Characteristics	Four-Year Colleges Men	Four-Year Colleges Women	Two-Year Colleges Men	Two-Year Colleges Women	Predominantly Black Colleges Men	Predominantly Black Colleges Women
Highest Degree Planned						
None	1.8	1.5	2.9	2.6	1.9	3.4
Associate degree (or equivalent)	2.2	2.3	15.0	23.2	1.5	1.3
Bachelor's	35.8	39.2	44.3	40.9	28.3	26.8
Master's	34.6	35.3	24.9	21.8	37.4	36.8
Ph.D. or Ed.D.	10.6	9.4	5.1	3.8	13.8	15.2
M.D., D.O., D.D.S., or D.V.M.	6.6	5.6	2.6	2.9	6.5	7.9
LL.B. or J.D.	5.3	4.4	2.0	1.6	4.5	5.3
B.D. or M.Div.	.9	.4	.4	.3	2.7	1.1
Other	2.1	1.9	2.8	2.8	3.4	2.4
Racial Background						
White/Caucasian	83.6	81.5	93.0	93.2	4.3	2.8
Black/Negro/Afro-American	12.5	14.6	4.5	4.8	94.3	95.8
American Indian	1.3	1.2	1.0	.7	1.9	1.6
Oriental	1.6	1.5	1.0	.7	1.0	.9
Mexican-American/Chicano	.9	.7	1.0	1.0	.9	.8
Puerto Rican-American	1.3	1.5	.6	.6	1.2	1.0
Other	1.7	1.6	1.3	1.0	2.0	2.1
Support of $500 or More from						
Parental or family aid	55.3	58.2	45.9	43.1	40.1	36.3
Basic Ed. Opportunity Grant	19.0	19.6	13.6	15.5	41.8	43.9
Supplemental Ed. Opportunity Grant	4.3	4.2	2.1	2.2	7.6	8.9
College Work Study Grant	9.3	10.8	3.7	4.0	10.3	11.0
State scholarship or grant	9.1	9.5	6.0	6.2	9.2	8.7
College grant	12.3	13.2	2.9	3.6	8.7	7.8
Private grant	4.2	4.6	2.1	2.7	3.5	4.7
Federal Guaranteed Student Loan	20.8	20.4	18.7	18.8	15.8	16.3
National Direct Student Loan	5.1	5.7	3.6	4.0	5.4	6.6
College loan	3.2	2.9	2.6	2.4	2.4	2.7
Other loan	3.5	3.7	3.1	3.1	4.0	4.5
Full-time employment	1.6	.8	1.3	.8	1.4	1.6
Part-time employment	9.6	6.8	9.5	7.7	3.8	3.5
Savings from summer work	24.3	19.3	20.2	12.9	7.2	5.1
Other savings	7.8	7.1	7.0	5.8	2.6	2.9
Spouse	.5	.4	.5	.6	1.0	.4
Personal G.I. benefits	.4	.1	.9	.2	0.7	.5
Parent's G.I. benefits	.6	.6	.6	.4	1.2	1.3
Social Sec. dependent's benefits	1.9	2.0	1.7	2.0	2.6	2.9
Other sources	3.6	1.8	1.2	1.3	1.4	1.3

Percentage of Students[a]

For footnote, see preceding page.

Source: Alexander W. Astin, Margo King Hemond, Gerald T. Richardson, *The American Freshman: National Norms for Fall 1982* (Los Angeles, Higher Education Research Institute, UCLA), 1982, pp. 15, 19, 26–29, 31, 35, 42–45.

135 Selected Freshman Characteristics, by Sex of Student, 1966, 1972, and 1982

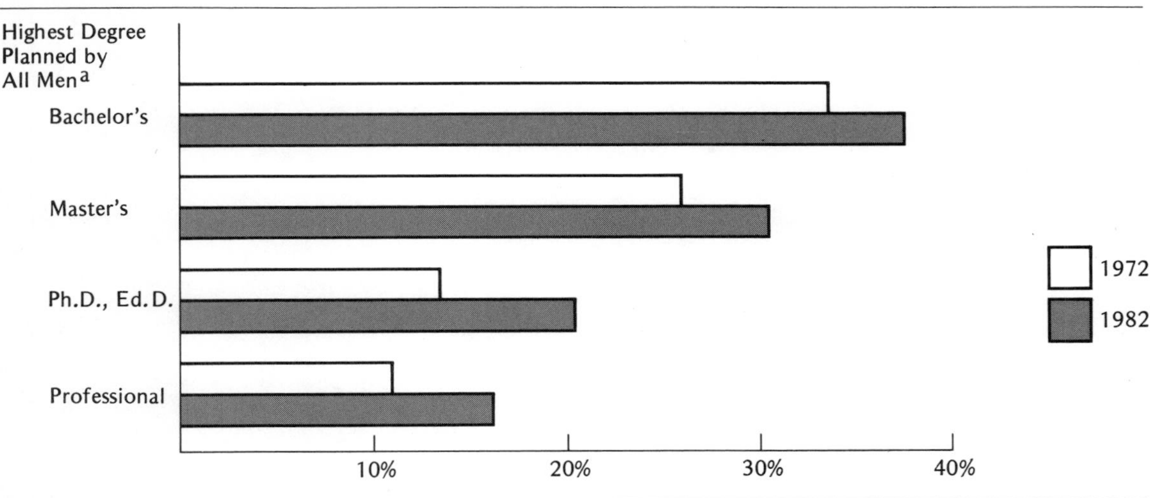

Student Characteristics	Percentage of Students[a] in All Institutions					
	Men			Women		
	1966	1972	1982	1966	1972	1982
Highest Degree Planned						
None	6.1	3.2	2.0	4.8	3.6	1.7
Associate degree	4.1	6.5	6.8	7.3	10.1	9.8
Bachelor's	32.5	33.9	37.8	46.1	41.3	38.8
Master's	31.2	26.0	30.8	32.3	28.9	30.2
Ph.D. or Ed.D.	13.7	10.6	8.8	5.2	6.8	7.6
M.D., D.O., D.D.S., or D.V.M.	7.4	9.7	6.3	1.9	4.3	5.7
LL.B. or J.D.	2.5	6.5	4.7	.3	2.1	3.8
B.D. or M.Div.	.5	.6	0.6	.1	.2	0.3
Other	2.1	2.9	2.2	1.8	2.7	2.1
Racial Background						
White/Caucasian	90.9	88.4	89.0	90.5	85.9	87.5
Black/Negro/Afro-American	4.5	7.6	7.6	5.6	10.0	9.4
American Indian	.5	1.1	1.0	.6	1.2	0.9
Oriental	.8	1.1	1.5	.7	1.1	1.3
Mexican-American/Chicano	—	1.6	0.9	—	1.5	0.9
Puerto Rican-American	—	.6	0.9	—	.7	0.9
Other	3.3	1.8	1.5	2.7	1.8	1.3
Concern about Financing Education						
No concern	34.9	37.3	36.1	35.3	33.5	27.2
Some concern	57.0	48.5	49.0	55.5	50.4	53.4
Major concern	8.1	14.1	14.9	9.2	16.1	19.4
Average Grade in High School						
A−, A, A+	11.3	13.5	17.5	20.2	21.8	24.7
B−, B, B+	49.5	56.3	58.2	59.6	62.3	61.1
C, C+	37.9	29.5	24.1	19.9	15.8	14.2
D	1.3	.7	.6	.3	.2	.1
Objectives Considered to Be Very Important						
Help others in difficulty	59.2	59.4	53.5	79.5	75.1	69.4
Be an authority in my field	70.3	64.8	75.1	60.8	55.7	71.9
Be very well off financially	54.1	50.6	73.1	31.6	30.2	64.9
Raise a family	na	62.2	66.2	na	67.8	67.9
Obtain recognition from colleagues	48.0	41.2	57.1	36.3	31.9	53.6

(*Continued on next page*)

— Item not shown in report.

a Weighted national norms for full-time freshmen based on data from a sample of over 150,000 students each year.

b Listed as "psychology, sociology, anthropology" in 1966. **c** Listed as "clergyman" in 1966.

d Listed as "doctor (M.D.)" in 1966. **e** Listed as "farmer" in 1966. **na** Not available.

136 Selected Freshman Characteristics, by Sex of Student, 1966, 1971, and 1982—*Continued*

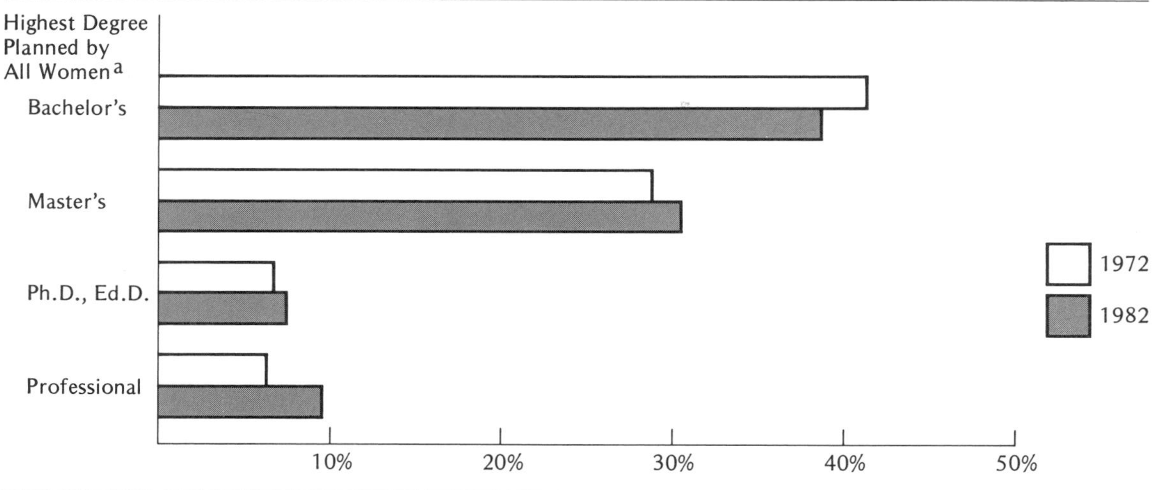

Student Characteristics	Men 1966	Men 1972	Men 1982	Women 1966	Women 1972	Women 1982
	Percentage of Students[a] in All Institutions					
Probable Major Field of Study						
Agriculture (incl. forestry)	3.4	5.3	3.8	.1	.8	1.4
Biological sciences	4.2	4.7	3.7	3.1	3.0	3.8
Business	17.3	17.1	22.3	10.9	13.7	25.7
Education	4.7	3.5	2.4	17.5	11.5	9.0
Engineering	17.9	12.7	22.3	.3	.4	3.6
English	1.9	.9	.6	7.3	2.5	1.0
Fine Arts	6.8	7.9	4.6	10.3	9.8	4.8
Health professional (non-M.D.)	1.5	3.4	1.6	9.8	18.7	13.3
History, political science	7.8	5.0	2.9	5.7	2.7	2.0
Humanities (other)	2.4	2.4	0.9	7.4	4.9	2.8
Mathematics or statistics	4.6	2.2	.6	4.5	2.2	.7
Physical sciences	5.0	3.0	2.6	1.2	.8	1.0
Pre-professional	11.3	13.3	3.2	2.3	5.1	3.0
Social sciences	5.2[b]	4.9	2.0	11.7[b]	11.1	5.5
Other fields	4.0	9.3	22.5	6.1	8.2	15.9
Undecided	1.9	4.4	3.7	1.8	4.8	5.5
Probable Career Occupation						
Artist (incl. performer)	4.6	5.2	3.4	8.9	8.0	4.0
Businessman	18.5	15.4	16.1	3.3	4.8	16.3
Clergy or religious worker[c]	1.2	1.0	.5	.8	.2	.1
Doctor (M.D. or D.D.S.)[d]	7.4	7.9	5.8	1.7	2.8	5.1
Educator (college teacher)	2.1	.7	.2	1.5	.6	.2
Educator (secondary ed.)	10.5	5.0	1.4	18.4	8.4	1.9
Educator (elementary ed.)	.8	.7	.4	15.7	11.1	5.5
Engineer	16.3	9.6	20.6	.2	.3	3.6
Farmer or forester[e]	3.2	4.8	3.3	.2	.7	.9
Health professional (non-M.D.)	3.1	4.6	1.5	6.6	10.4	6.6
Lawyer	6.7	7.1	4.7	.7	2.0	3.9
Nurse	.1	.2	.2	5.3	9.8	7.7
Research scientist	4.9	3.1	1.8	1.9	1.5	1.2
Other occupation	15.8	21.3	32.0	31.0	24.9	32.7
Undecided	5.0	13.4	8.1	3.6	14.4	10.8

For footnotes, see preceding page.

Sources:

1 Alexander Astin, Robert J. Panos, John A. Creager, *National Norms for Entering College Freshmen* (Washington: ACE), *Fall 1966*, pp. 5–9, 12–16.

2 Staff of the Office of Research, *The American Freshman: National Norms for Fall of 1972* (Washington: ACE), 1972, pp. 17, 20–23, 25, 28–30.

3 Alexander W. Astin, Margo King Hemond, Gerald T. Richardson, *The American Freshman: National Norms for Fall 1982* (Los Angeles: Higher Education Research Institute, UCLA), 1982, pp. 15, 19–22, 25, 31, 35–38, 41.

137 Undergraduate Residence and Migration, by State, Fall 1958, 1968, 1975

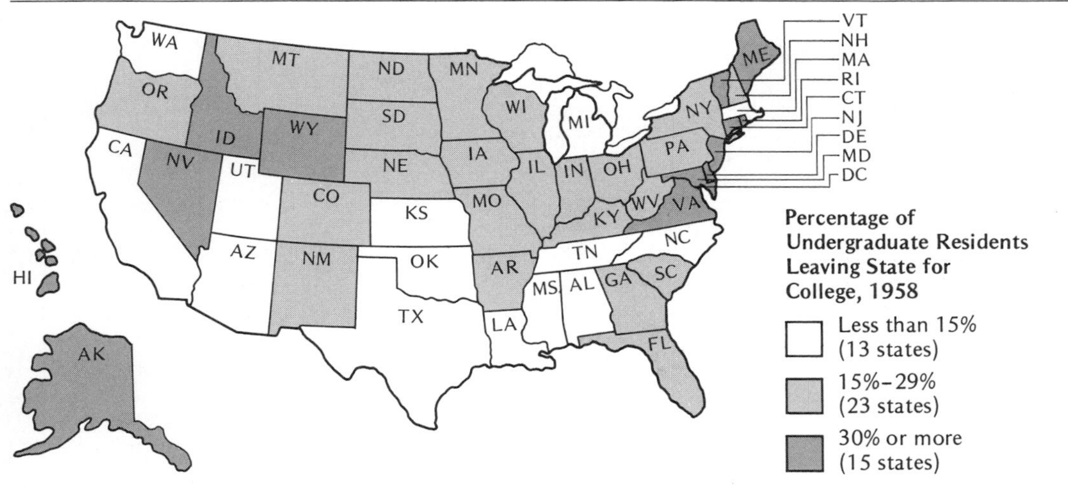

	Undergraduate Student Residents								
				Leaving State for College					
	Total			Number			Percentage[b]		
State of Residence[a]	1958	1968	1975	1958	1968	1975	1958	1968	1975
D. C.	10,629	17,937	26,391	3,506	5,304	11,523	33	44	44
New Hampshire	6,933	16,322	25,593	2,413	6,091	10,336	35	37	40
New Jersey	87,589	207,584	290,890	36,432	98,270	99,880	42	47	34
Connecticut	37,801	97,416	133,489	14,754	36,854	44,686	39	38	33
Vermont	4,426	9,384	16,064	1,526	3,132	5,273	34	33	33
Wyoming	5,475	11,799	13,581	1,832	2,866	4,333	33	24	32
Delaware	4,243	11,709	22,076	2,045	4,929	6,820	48	52	31
Alaska	2,376	4,207	12,805	761	2,001	3,764	32	48	29
New Mexico	12,983	31,843	41,924	2,674	5,298	12,258	21	17	29
Maine	8,627	18,421	28,492	2,643	5,599	7,943	31	30	28
Idaho	10,764	25,089	30,026	4,097	6,011	7,866	38	24	26
Minnesota	50,821	108,397	163,646	8,294	14,158	41,755	16	13	26
Maryland[c]	31,299	99,404	161,696	10,424	25,679	39,005	33	26	24
Virginia	33,766	97,698	149,205	11,818	30,734	35,893	35	31	24
Iowa	41,198	81,036	101,597	9,609	18,522	23,208	23	23	23
North Dakota	12,501	22,815	26,918	2,501	3,646	6,316	20	16	23
Rhode Island	8,930	24,704	37,676	2,793	6,857	8,489	31	28	23
South Dakota	12,335	22,765	24,938	2,230	3,261	5,670	18	14	23
Hawaii	9,696	22,068	40,031	3,696	6,676	8,813	38	30	22
Montana	11,081	23,362	27,075	2,393	3,924	5,952	22	17	22
Nevada	3,258	9,461	26,406	1,290	2,733	5,360	40	29	20
Pennsylvania	135,728	294,698	368,437	26,394	63,598	73,194	19	22	20
Arkansas	21,924	44,682	56,622	4,038	5,835	10,850	18	13	19
Massachusetts	76,934	170,968	253,053	14,714	35,320	47,262	19	21	19
Colorado	25,093	64,229	100,662	4,016	8,665	18,147	16	13	18
Indiana	58,528	121,682	155,578	9,468	17,162	27,474	16	14	18
Georgia	39,091	86,835	133,481	6,741	13,766	22,741	17	16	17
Illinois	143,974	323,353	462,044	34,488	68,928	79,751	24	21	17
Nebraska	23,451	46,025	58,128	4,207	6,051	10,067	18	13	17
West Virginia	25,594	39,615	53,221	4,328	5,022	8,875	17	13	17

(Continued on next page)

For footnotes and sources, see next page.

Undergraduate Residence and Migration, by State, Fall 1958, 1968, 1975—*Continued*

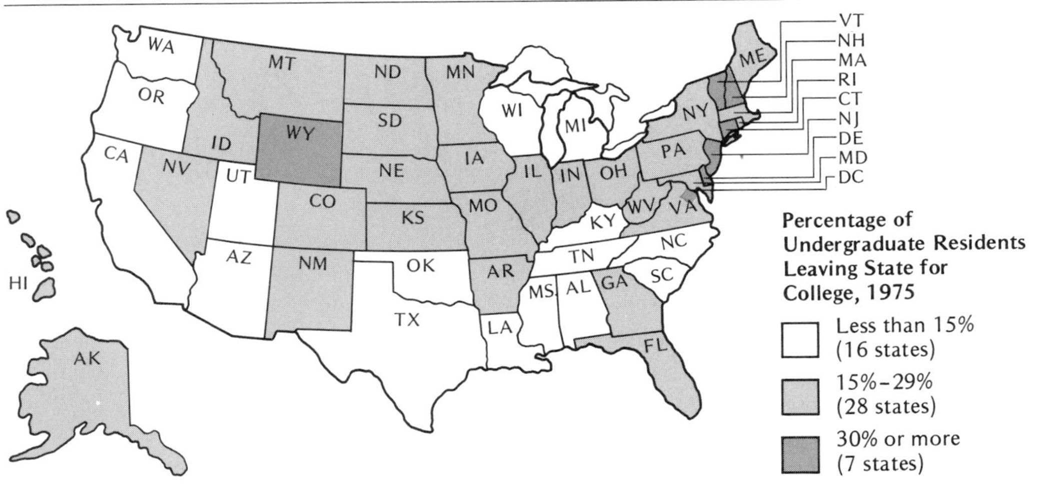

	Undergraduate Student Residents								
				Leaving State for College					
	Total			Number			Percentage[b]		
State of Residence[a]	1958	1968	1975	1958	1968	1975	1958	1968	1975
Kansas	39,010	74,218	91,822	5,503	9,071	14,891	14	12	16
Missouri	49,072	120,211	169,550	10,136	17,561	27,621	21	15	16
Ohio	117,166	271,004	362,273	18,738	41,581	56,359	16	15	16
Florida	53,208	160,444	271,048	11,718	26,175	40,111	22	16	15
New York	268,029	600,626	803,203	50,175	111,331	123,125	19	19	15
Oregon	27,765	66,459	109,815	4,710	7,599	15,781	17	11	14
South Carolina	21,812	49,993	105,606	3,818	9,490	14,333	17	23	14
Kentucky	37,131	71,834	95,683	6,280	9,802	12,670	17	14	13
Tennessee	40,765	86,045	132,927	6,089	10,404	17,928	15	12	13
Alabama	38,897	80,648	126,566	4,876	8,898	15,159	13	11	12
Arizona	22,277	59,898	102,756	2,536	5,829	12,785	11	10	12
Mississippi	26,642	56,435	85,632	3,162	5,022	9,963	12	9	12
Oklahoma	45,560	79,095	110,719	4,533	6,609	13,789	10	8	12
Wisconsin	52,366	122,230	200,638	8,690	12,806	23,420	17	10	12
Louisiana	44,760	94,331	115,673	3,745	6,516	12,197	8	7	11
North Carolina	47,618	90,529	197,014	5,832	9,488	20,423	12	10	10
Washington	44,377	107,227	184,089	5,216	9,564	18,249	12	9	10
Utah	16,844	41,103	57,183	981	1,690	5,361	6	4	9
Michigan	117,019	236,564	378,105	11,147	15,979	30,176	9	7	8
Texas	144,473	302,136	488,321	8,606	16,160	31,870	6	5	7
California	254,111	704,728	1,245,247	16,184	35,405	56,430	6	5	5

Note: Comparability between surveys is limited by differences in survey coverage and because of variations in the definition of **home state.** In 1958, **home state** was defined as "the state in which the student's permanent residence is located." In 1968, **home state** was defined as "state of the student's legal residence as determined at the institution." The 1975 definition of **home state** was changed after the questionnaire was distributed. The questionnaire defined **home state** as "the state in which student completed his secondary education, even though the student may presently be considered a resident of the state in which the institution is located for tuition and fee assessment or other purposes." The revised definition, distributed in August 1975 by letter to all recipients of the original questionnaire package, defined **home state** as the state in which the individual's most recent secondary or postsecondary experience occurred prior to enrolling at the reporting institution.

a In rank order of 1975 percentage of students leaving the home state for college.

b The national percentage for undergraduate students leaving their home state was 17 percent in 1958, 16 percent in 1968, and 15 percent in 1975.

c Figures for 1958 exclude University of Maryland; comparability between years is limited by the extent of this exclusion.

Sources:

1 American Association of Collegiate Registrars and Admissions Officers (AACRAO); *Summary, Home State and Migration of College Students, Fall 1958* (Washington: AACRAO), 1959. Used by permission.

2 NCES, *Residence and Migration of College Students, Fall 1968, Analytic Report* (Washington: GPO), 1970, table 4.

3 NCES, Residence and Migration of College Students, Fall 1975 Survey, preliminary data.

Undergraduate Migration into States, by State, Fall 1958, 1968, 1975

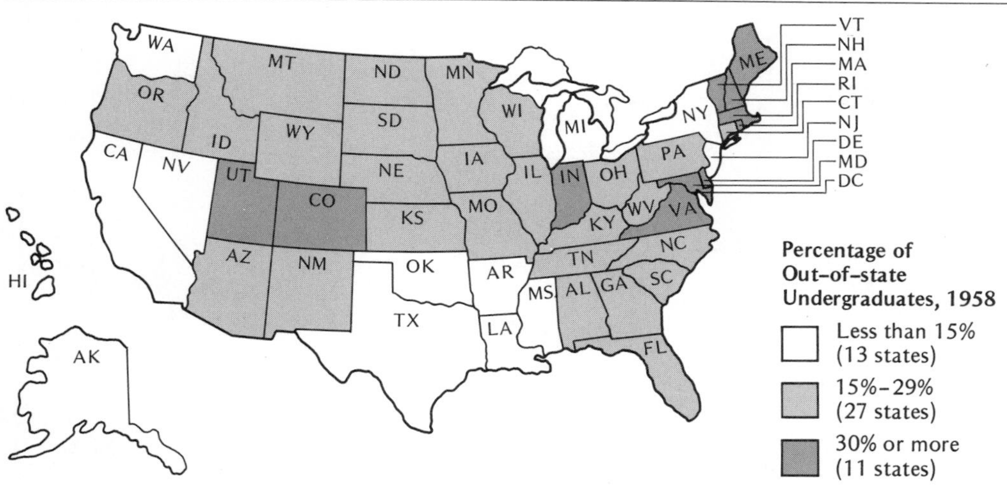

	Undergraduate Students								
	Total Attending College in State			Migrating into State for College[b]					
				Number			Percentage[c]		
State[a]	1958	1968	1975	1958	1968	1975	1958	1968	1975
D. C.	23,153	36,926	44,474	16,030	26,957	29,606	69	73	67
Vermont	8,061	15,954	23,269	5,161	9,702	12,478	64	61	54
New Hampshire	9,456	21,587	32,263	4,936	11,356	17,006	52	53	53
Rhode Island	11,915	28,339	45,317	5,778	10,492	16,130	48	37	36
Idaho	8,629	24,124	33,457	1,962	5,046	11,297	23	21	34
Delaware	3,514	11,290	22,837	1,316	4,510	7,581	37	40	33
Utah	24,426	57,953	77,863	8,563	18,540	26,041	35	32	33
Arizona	24,389	65,048	132,597	4,648	10,979	42,626	19	17	32
Maine	9,613	20,108	29,624	3,629	7,286	9,075	38	36	31
Wyoming	4,299	10,899	13,285	656	1,966	4,037	15	18	30
Colorado	33,367	78,785	116,093	12,290	23,221	33,578	37	29	29
Massachusetts	92,671	196,278	278,449	30,451	60,631	72,658	33	31	26
South Dakota	12,881	24,929	26,125	2,776	5,425	6,857	22	22	26
West Virginia	25,358	49,504	58,876	4,092	14,911	14,530	16	30	25
Indiana	73,116	141,774	165,375	24,056	37,254	37,271	33	26	23
New Mexico	12,948	32,058	38,393	2,639	5,513	8,727	20	17	23
Arkansas	20,436	45,415	54,701	2,550	6,568	11,929	12	14	22
Virginia	32,642	88,209	145,648	10,694	21,245	32,336	33	24	22
Hawaii	6,867	19,036	39,376	867	3,644	8,158	13	19	21
Iowa	42,277	85,588	98,713	10,688	23,074	20,324	25	27	21
Tennessee	46,942	104,054	146,131	12,266	28,413	31,132	26	27	21
Georgia	39,702	90,894	138,097	7,352	17,825	27,357	18	20	20
Nebraska	24,130	52,941	60,086	4,886	12,967	12,025	20	24	20
Connecticut	30,786	76,731	109,138	7,739	16,169	20,335	25	21	19
Montana	10,332	22,613	26,060	1,644	3,175	4,937	16	14	19
Nevada	2,274	8,107	26,062	306	1,379	5,016	13	17	19
Oklahoma	47,543	85,296	119,798	6,516	12,810	22,868	14	15	19
Oregon	28,863	70,509	115,562	5,808	11,649	21,528	20	17	19
North Carolina	52,801	110,724	214,611	11,015	29,683	38,020	21	27	18
North Dakota	12,143	22,411	25,151	2,143	3,242	4,549	18	14	18

(Continued on next page)

For footnotes and sources, see next page.

140 Undergraduate Migration into States, by State, Fall 1958, 1968, 1975—*Continued*

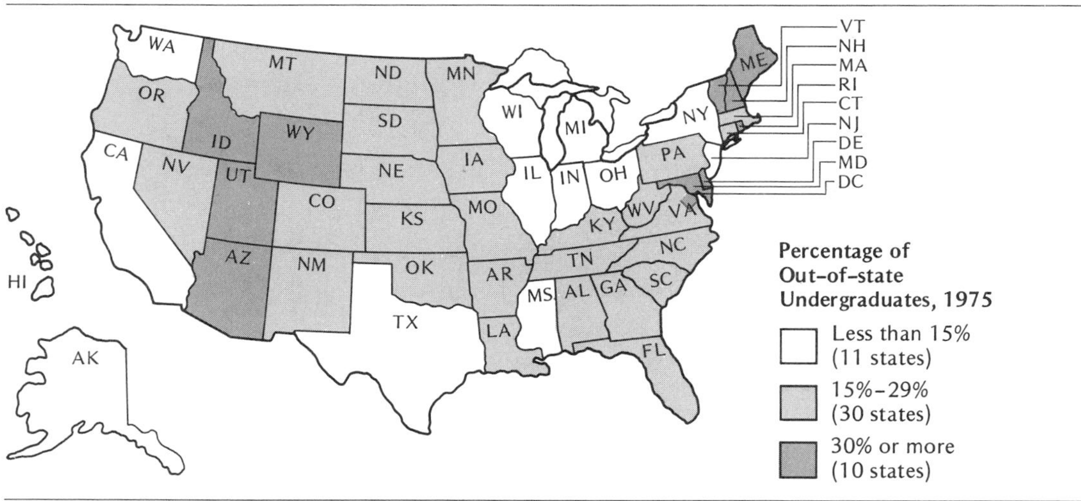

	Undergraduate Students								
	Total Attending College in State			Migrating into State for College[b]					
				Number			Percentage[c]		
State[a]	**1958**	**1968**	**1975**	**1958**	**1968**	**1975**	**1958**	**1968**	**1975**
Alabama	40,209	83,851	133,684	6,188	12,101	22,277	15	14	17
Kansas	40,702	80,974	93,056	7,195	15,827	16,125	18	20	17
Kentucky	37,243	80,155	100,550	6,392	18,123	17,537	17	23	17
Maryland[d]	29,533	88,117	148,390	8,658	14,392	25,699	29	16	17
Florida	50,189	158,612	275,863	8,699	24,343	44,926	17	15	16
Minnesota	51,291	111,218	144,665	8,764	16,979	22,774	17	15	16
Pennsylvania	137,401	284,074	350,852	28,067	52,974	55,609	20	19	16
Louisiana	45,742	97,934	121,714	4,727	10,119	18,238	10	10	15
Missouri	51,036	132,590	167,809	12,100	29,940	25,880	24	23	15
South Carolina	22,984	42,632	108,008	4,990	10,129	16,735	22	24	15
California	261,392	708,614	1,373,851	23,465	39,291	185,034	9	6	13
Michigan	122,224	249,513	398,511	16,352	28,928	50,582	13	12	13
Ohio	122,428	280,634	349,427	24,000	51,211	43,513	20	18	12
Wisconsin	53,796	137,066	202,342	10,120	27,642	25,124	19	20	12
Texas	148,002	313,055	511,539	12,135	27,079	55,088	8	9	11
Washington	45,793	111,579	185,786	6,632	13,916	19,946	14	12	11
Illinois	128,234	294,376	425,313	18,748	30,951	43,020	15	11	10
Mississippi	26,949	58,408	84,213	3,469	6,995	8,544	13	12	10
New Jersey	57,974	122,863	208,870	6,817	13,549	17,860	12	11	9
New York	249,416	544,609	746,836	31,562	55,314	66,758	13	10	9
Alaska	1,786	2,738	9,480	171	532	439	10	19	5

Note: Comparability between surveys is limited by differences in survey coverage and because of variations in the definition of **home state.** In 1958, **home state** was defined as "the state in which the student's permanent residence is located." In 1968, **home state** was defined as "state of the student's legal residence as determined at the institution." The 1975 definition of **home state** was changed after the questionnaire was distributed. The questionnaire defined **home state** as "the state in which student completed his secondary education, even though the student may presently be considered a resident of the state in which the institution is located for tuition and fee assessment or other purposes." The revised definition, distributed in August 1975 by letter to all recipients of the original questionnaire package, defined **home state** as the state in which the individual's most recent secondary or postsecondary experience occurred prior to enrolling at the reporting institution.

a In rank order of 1975 percentage of out-of-state students.

b Includes foreign students and students from outlying parts of the U.S.

c These columns show out-of-state students as a percentage of all undergraduate students attending college in the state.

d Figures for 1958 exclude University of Maryland; comparability between years is limited by the extent of this exclusion.

Sources:

1 American Association of Collegiate Registrars and Admissions Officers (AACRAO), *Summary, Home State and Migration of College Students, Fall 1958* (Washington: AACRAO), 1959. Used by permission.

2 NCES, *Residence and Migration of College Students, Fall 1968, Analytic Report* (Washington: GPO), 1970, table 4.

3 NCES, Residence and Migration of College Students, Fall 1975 Survey, preliminary data.

141 Median Years from Baccalaureate to Doctorate by Field of Study, Selected Years, 1958–1981

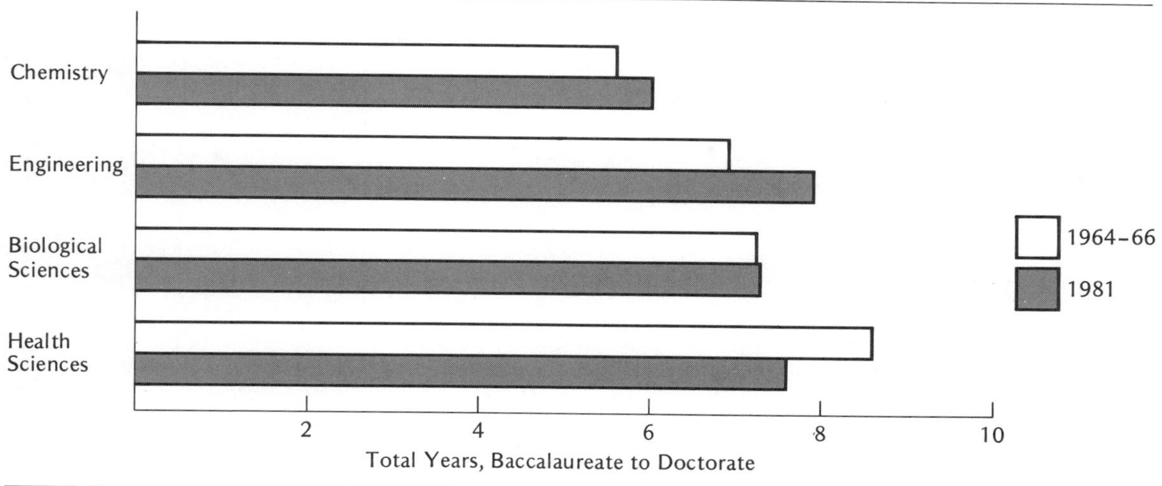

Fields of Study	Total Time[b] 1958–60	Total Time[b] 1964–66	Total Time[b] 1970	Total Time[b] 1981	Registered Time[c] 1958–60	Registered Time[c] 1964–66	Registered Time[c] 1970	Registered Time[c] 1981
	Median Years from Baccalaureate to Doctorate[a]							
All Fields	**8.6**	**8.2**	**7.9**	**8.8**	**5.2**	**5.4**	**5.6**	**6.2**
Physical Science & Engineering	**6.6**	**6.3**	—	**7.2[d]**	**4.9**	**5.1**	—	**5.7[d]**
Mathematics	7.0	5.9	6.0	6.9	5.1	5.0	5.2	7.0
Physics & Astronomy	6.7	6.4	6.4	7.0	5.4	5.6	5.8	6.0
Chemistry	5.7	5.6	5.6	6.0	4.6	4.8	5.0	5.2
Earth Sciences	7.5	7.6	7.7	8.4	4.6	5.5	5.7	6.4
Engineering	7.2	6.9	7.0	7.9	4.9	5.1	5.2	5.6
Biological Sciences	**7.7**	**7.3**	—	**7.3[e]**	**5.1**	**5.3**	—	**5.9[e]**
Agriculture and Forestry	7.4	7.8	7.2	8.1[f]	4.6	5.1	5.2	5.5[f]
Health Sciences	8.0	8.6	8.0	7.6[g]	5.0	5.6	5.2	6.0[g]
Biochemistry, Biophysics, Physiology, Biostatistics	7.3	6.8	6.0 }		5.3	5.3	5.3 }	
Anatomy, Cytology, Entomology, Embryology	7.7	7.3	6.2 }	6.7[h]	5.1	5.3	5.2 }	5.9[h]
Ecology, Hydrobiology	7.8	7.3	6.7 }		5.7	5.3	5.8 }	
Botany, Zoology, General Biology	8.0	7.2	7.0 }	7.5[i]	5.3	5.4	5.6 }	6.3[i]
Social Sciences	**8.7**	**8.0**	—	**8.8**	**5.2**	**5.3**	—	**6.4**
Psychology	7.9	7.1	6.2	8.2	5.6	5.5	5.3	6.2
Anthropology & Archaeology	8.8	9.3	8.2 }	9.9[j]	5.0	5.5	6.3 }	7.4[j]
Sociology	9.6	9.1	8.7 }		5.3	5.8	6.0 }	
Economics & Econometrics	9.0	7.9	7.2	8.0	4.7	4.9	5.2	6.1
Political Science, International Relations	9.8	8.6	8.0	10.2[k]	5.0	5.3	5.6	6.9[k]

(*Continued on next page*)

Note: Between the 1970 and 1981 reports, extensive changes were made in the identification of disciplines. Fields of study were regrouped and reported in broad categories. In order to show general trends, the former categories have been retained as stub-end labels and the 1981 figures footnoted as necessary. Data refer to research doctorates and exclude professional degrees such as M.D., D.D.S., D.V.M. Data in column 1958–60 refer to doctorates awarded in fiscal years 1958 through 1960. Data in column 1964–66 refer to doctorates awarded in fiscal years 1964 through 1966.

For footnotes and sources, see next page.

142 Median Years from Baccalaureate to Doctorate by Field of Study, Selected Years, 1958–1981—*Continued*

	Median Years from Baccalaureate to Doctorate[a]							
	Total Time[b]				Registered Time[c]			
Fields of Study	**1958–60**	**1964–66**	**1970**	**1981**	**1958–60**	**1964–66**	**1970**	**1981**
Arts & Humanities	**9.9**	**9.5**	**—**	**10.4**	**5.7**	**5.7**	**—**	**7.4**
History	9.7	8.9	9.0	10.8	5.7	5.7	6.2	8.2
English & American Language & Literature	9.9	9.7	8.8	10.0	5.8	5.9	6.0	7.3
Modern Foreign Language & Literature	10.2	9.5	8.9	10.7[l]	6.0	5.7	6.0	7.5[l]
Classical Language & Literature	8.0	8.3	7.5		5.3	5.6	5.8	
Philosophy	8.8	7.6	7.9	10.1[m]	5.7	5.4	5.3	7.0[m]
Speech & Dramatic Arts	9.6	10.4	10.2		5.2	5.2	5.2	
Fine Arts & Music	10.9	12.2	12.2		5.3	6.0	6.0	
Professional Fields	**11.3**	**10.8**	**—**	**10.8**	**6.1**	**6.0**	**—**	**6.7**
Business Administration	10.1	9.6	9.0	n	5.1	5.3	5.4	n
Religion & Theology	11.4	11.6	11.9	n	7.1	7.2	8.2	n
Education	**14.0**	**13.8**	**12.8**	**13.0**	**6.6**	**6.8**	**6.2**	**7.1**

a Data refer to doctorates awarded in the one- or two-year periods ending in June 30 of the latest year shown in each column head.

b The total calendar time (in years) elapsed between year of baccalaureate and year of doctorate.

c The total time registered in a university. No distinction is made between full- and part-time study.

d "EMP" fields.

e "Life sciences."

f Agricultural sciences.

g Medical sciences.

h Figure is for "basic medical sciences," which includes all fields listed on the bracketed lines to the left except biostatistics and entomology. Basic medical sciences also include microbiology, immunology, and molecular biology.

i "Other biosciences."

j Anthropology and sociology. Archaeology is included with other arts and humanities.

k Political science, public administration, international relations.

l Foreign language and literature.

m "Other arts and humanities," which include fields listed at the left.

n Not separately identified in the report for this year.

Sources:

1 Research Division of the Office of Scientific Personnel, National Academy of Sciences, *Doctorate Recipients from United States Universities, 1958–1966* (Washington: National Academy of Sciences), 1967, pp. 66–68.

2 Manpower Studies Branch, Office of Scientific Personnel, National Research Council (NRC), *Summary Report 1970, Doctorate Recipients from United States Universities* (Washington: NRC), 1971, pp. 6, 7.

3 Commission on Human Resources, NRC, National Academy of Sciences, *Summary Report 1979, Doctorate Recipients from United States Universities* (Washington: National Academy of Sciences), 1980, pp. 30, 31; 1981 edition, pp. 34–35.

143 Earned Degrees—An Introductory Note

The following pages show data on earned degrees for 1947–48 through 1980–81, the most recent year for which the National Center for Education Statistics (NCES) has released data. Tables show summaries by type of degree, state, and minority status, as well as data for twenty-nine individual disciplines. The historical data come from the earned degree surveys conducted until 1974 by the U. S. Office of Education and since then by NCES. Projections are from NCES.

Data Comparability

A word of caution must be issued regarding comparability of the data over time. Although care has been exercised in tabulating and presenting the figures, several important factors limit the accuracy of comparisons. Differences between institutions' departmental organization and degree-granting traditions tend to reduce comparability.

The most important factors affecting comparability are the questionnaires and reports themselves. Changes in degree definition and the number of fields for which data are required can seriously affect the comparability for two or more years.

In several of the tables on the following pages, degrees in two or more related fields have been combined. This has been done with degrees in the specialized teaching fields and noted above and in other instances in which fields have only recently been separately identified. In each such case, a footnote indicates the component fields. Although such combinations result in totals that do not agree with the recent USOE and NCES figures, they provide a better basis for comparison with earlier data.

Prior to 1960–61, data on bachelor's and first professional degrees were combined and reported as a single figure. Beginning in 1960–61, the degrees were reported separately, and this differentiation is reflected in the following tables.

Strictly limited is the comparability of master's and bachelor's and first professional degree data for 1965–66 and later with earlier figures in certain fields. Prior to 1965–66, those master's degrees that were considered first professional—for example, library science and social work administration—were included with the bachelor's and first professional degree count, not with the master's degrees. Beginning in 1965–66, USOE instructed that all master's degrees be counted as master's degrees even if they were generally considered to be first professional degrees. For a more complete discussion of this change, see Paul L. Mason and Mabel Rice, *Earned Degrees Conferred.* National Center for Education Statistics, Washington, D.C., 1965, p. 1.

Data on the following pages come from the thirteen sources listed on this page. From 1947–48 through 1965–66, figures for all fields except engineering come from the annual survey of earned degrees conducted by the U.S. Office of Education (USOE). They were reported in the publications numbered 1 and 2. During the same period, a separate survey jointly sponsored by USOE and the American Society for Engineering Education provided the engineering degree data. They were reported in publications numbered 8 through 11.

Beginning in 1966–67, data for all fields of study come from the annual earned degree portion of the Higher Education General Information Survey (HEGIS) conducted until 1974 by USOE and since then by the National Center for Education Statistics (NCES). They were reported in the publications numbered 3 through 7.

Projected figures come from publication number 13.

---

1 *Earned Degrees Conferred by Higher Educational Institutions,* issued for each year from 1947–48 through 1957–58.

2 *Earned Degrees Conferred: Bachelor's and Higher Degrees,* issued for each year from 1958–59 through 1965–66.

3 *Earned Degrees Conferred: Part A—Summary Data,* issued for 1966–67, 1967–68 and 1968–69.

4 *Earned Degrees Conferred: 1969–70, Institutional Data.*

5 *Earned Degrees Conferred,* issued for 1970–71, 1971–72, and 1977–78.

6 *Earned Degrees Conferred: Summary Data,* issued for 1972–73 and 1973–74; 1974–75; 1975–76; 1976–77.

7 *Associate Degrees and Other Formal Awards below the Baccalaureate,* issued for 1965–66 through 1978–79.

8 *Engineering Enrollments and Degrees,* issued for each year, from 1950 through 1961.

9 *Advanced Report on Engineering Degrees,* issued for 1961–62 and 1962–63.

10 *Engineering Degrees and Enrollments,* issued for 1963–64 and 1964–65.

11 *Engineering Degrees,* 1965–66.

12 Earned Degree data for 1980–81 are unpublished data tabulations from NCES.

13 Projections of Education Statistics, issued annually.

145 Earned Degrees, by Level, Selected Years, 1949–50—1984–85

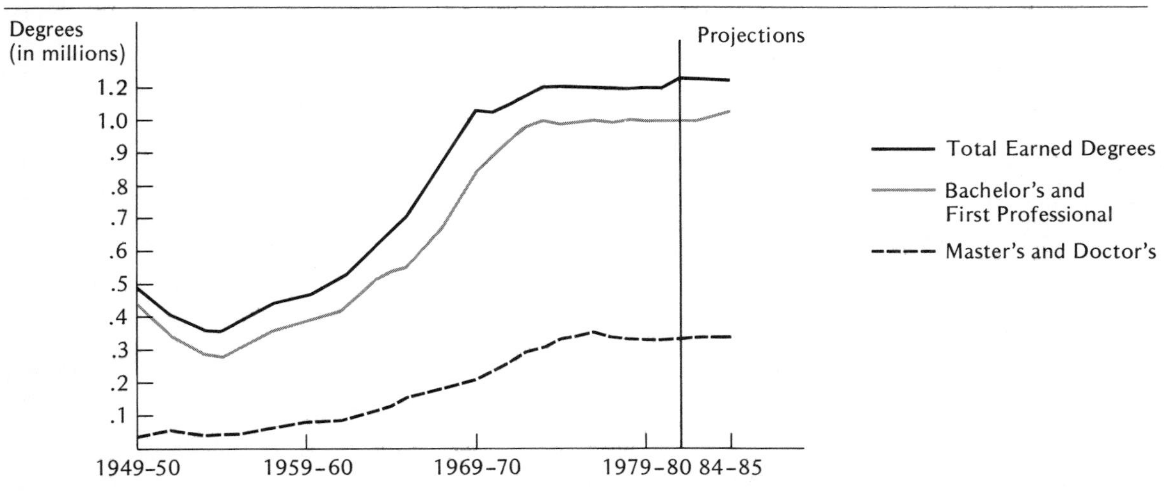

Year	All Earned Degrees	Bachelor's	First Professional[b]	Master's[c]	Doctor's	Bach.'s & First Prof.	Master's	Doctor's
	Earned Degrees							
	Number					Percent Distribution[a]		
1949–50	498,373	433,734		58,219	6,420	87	12	1.3
1953–54	358,699	292,880		56,823	8,996	82	16	2.5
1955–56	379,495	311,298		59,294	8,903	82	16	2.4
1957–58	440,304	365,748		65,614	8,942	83	15	2.0
1959–60	479,215	394,889		74,497	9,829	82	16	2.1
1961–62	516,996	382,822	37,663	84,889	11,622	81	16	2.2
1963–64	617,716	460,467	41,637	101,122	14,490	81	16	2.3
1965–66	714,624	524,117	31,496	140,772	18,239	78	20	2.6
1967–68	871,832	636,863	34,728	177,150	23,091	77	20	2.6
1969–70	1,072,581	798,070	35,252	209,387	29,872	78	20	2.8
1970–71	1,147,985	846,110	38,276	231,486	32,113	77	20	2.8
1971–72	1,224,027	894,110	43,774	252,774	33,369	77	21	2.7
1972–73	1,280,022	930,272	50,435	264,525	34,790	77	21	2.7
1973–74	1,320,739	954,376	54,278	278,259	33,826	76	21	2.6
1974–75	1,315,659	931,663	56,259	293,651	34,086	75	22	2.6
1975–76	1,344,581	934,443	63,061	313,001	34,076	74	23	2.5
1976–77	1,344,493	928,228	64,780	318,241	33,244	74	24	2.5
1977–78	1,342,137	930,201	66,964	312,816	32,156	74	23	2.4
1978–79	1,335,393	931,340	69,222	302,075	32,756	75	23	2.5
1979–80	1,330,244	929,417	70,131	298,081	32,615	75	22	2.5
1980–81	1,335,793	935,140	71,956	295,739	32,958	75	22	2.5
				Projections				
1981–82	1,354,900	945,000	73,600	303,000	33,300	75	22	2.5
1982–83	1,378,700	965,000	73,400	307,000	33,300	75	22	2.4
1983–84	1,403,100	985,000	74,600	310,000	33,500	76	22	2.4
1984–85	1,404,900	985,000	75,300	311,000	33,600	76	22	2.4

Note: Data prior to 1979–80 are for aggregate U. S. (fifty states, D. C., and outlying parts) except where footnoted otherwise; projections are for the fifty states and D. C.

a Percentages for bachelor's and master's degrees are rounded to the nearest unit; those for doctor's degrees, to the nearest tenth. Percentages may not total 100 because of rounding.

b Data showing bachelor's degrees separate from first professional degrees were not gathered prior to 1960–61.

c Second level degrees, i.e., those beyond the bachelor's or first professional but below the doctorate. Until 1965–66, master's degrees that were considered first professional degrees, such as master of library science and master of social work, were excluded. For 1965–66 and later, all master's degrees are included.

For sources, see next page.

146 All Earned Degrees, by Sex of Student and by Control of Institution, Selected Years, 1947–48—1984–85

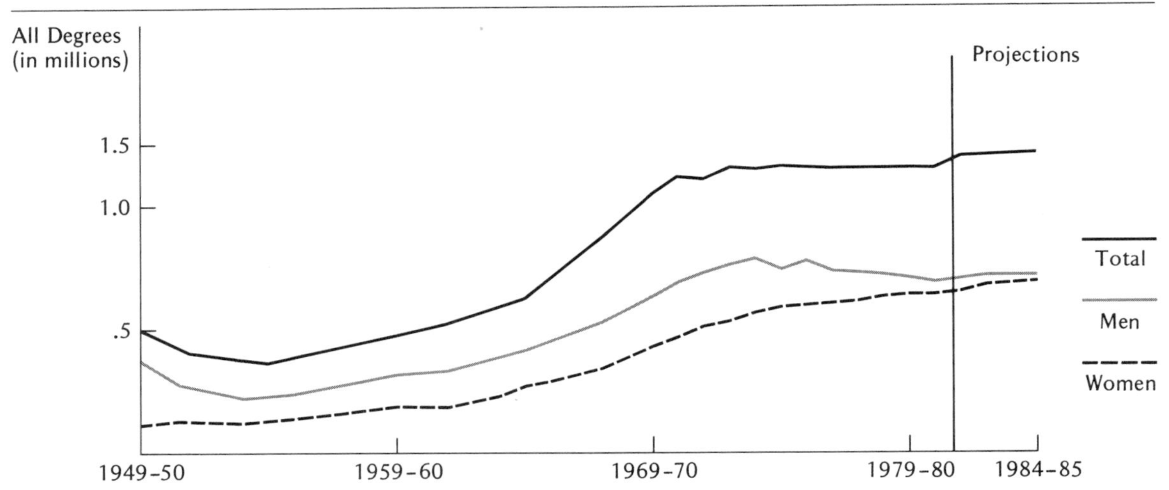

Year	Earned Degrees, All Levels				
	Total	**Men**	**Women**	**Public**	**Private**
1947–48	318,749	208,581	110,168	155,456	163,293
1949–50	498,373	376,860	121,513	246,249	252,124
1951–52	403,194	277,589	125,605	198,852	204,342
1953–54	358,699	233,828	124,871	183,687	175,012
1954–55	354,445	230,356	124,089	184,255	170,190
1955–56	379,495	246,986	132,509	199,915	179,580
1957–58	440,304	295,178	145,126	241,299	199,005
1959–60	479,215	315,242	163,973	262,809	216,406
1961–62	516,996	331,097	185,899	286,346	230,650
1963–64	617,716	381,780	235,936	352,251	265,465
1964–65	667,592	410,573	257,019	384,802	282,790
1965–66	714,624	440,427	274,197	420,595	294,029
1967–68	871,832	526,764	345,068	535,014	336,818
1969–70	1,072,581	638,987	433,594	692,715	379,866
1970–71	1,147,985	680,344	467,641	751,785	396,200
1971–72	1,224,027	722,832	501,195	812,929	411,098
1972–73	1,280,022	751,936	528,086	856,072	423,950
1973–74	1,320,739	765,529	555,210	888,250	432,489
1974–75	1,315,659	746,588	569,071	881,276	434,383
1975–76	1,344,581	755,777	588,804	895,863	448,718
1976–77	1,344,493	745,149	599,344	893,508	450,985
1977–78	1,342,137	728,996	613,141	883,953	458,184
1978–79	1,335,393	711,630	623,763	868,701	466,692
1979–80	1,330,244	700,019	630,225	860,133	470,111
1980–81	1,335,793	692,429	643,364	860,859	474,934
	Projections				
1981–82	1,354,900	701,300	653,600	na	na
1982–83	1,378,700	706,800	671,900	na	na
1983–84	1,403,100	714,500	688,600	na	na
1984–85	1,404,900	708,100	696,800	na	na

Note: Data prior to 1979–80 are for aggregate U. S. (fifty states, D. C., and outlying parts) except where footnoted otherwise; projections are intermediate projections for the fifty states and D. C. Tables showing percent distributions are found on pages 151 and 152.

na Not available.

Sources:

1 USOE/NCES earned degree series. See page 144.

2 NCES, *Projections of Education Statistics to 1990–91* (Washington: GPO), 1982, p. 70.

3 NCES, *Digest of Education Statistics, 1982* (Washington; GPO), 1982, pp. 117, 125.

147 Bachelor's Degrees, by Sex of Student and by Control of Institution, Selected Years, 1947–48—1984–85

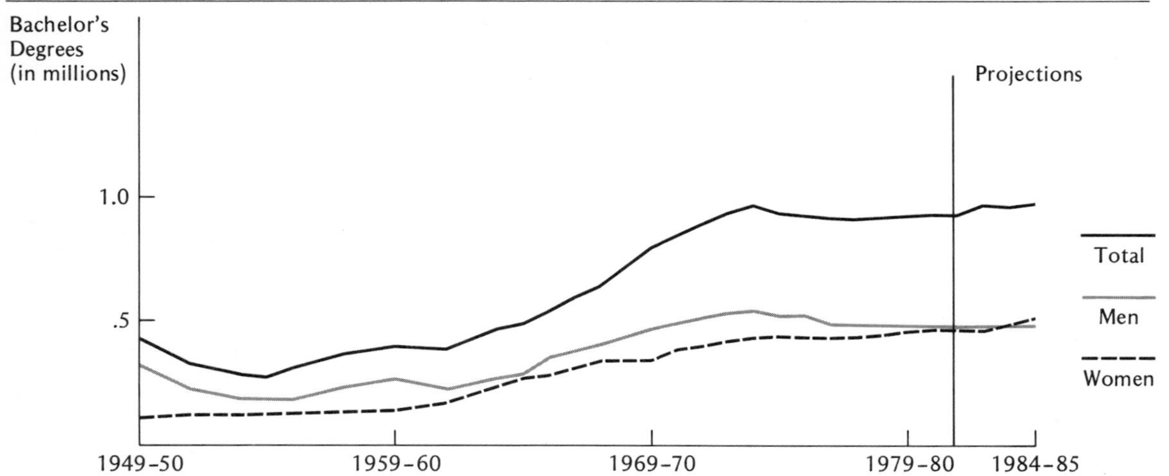

Year	Bachelor's Degrees[a] Total	Men	Women	Public	Private
1947–48	272,311	176,146	96,165	136,180	136,131
1949–50	433,734	329,819	103,915	217,389	216,345
1951–52	331,924	227,029	104,895	163,856	168,068
1953–54	292,880	187,500	105,380	148,330	144,550
1954–55	287,401	183,602	103,799	147,404	139,997
1955–56	311,298	199,571	111,727	162,237	149,061
1957–58	365,748	242,948	122,800	198,731	167,017
1959–60	394,889	255,504	139,385	214,720	180,169
1961–62	382,822	228,445	154,377	216,148	166,674
1963–64	460,467	263,121	197,346	265,821	194,646
1964–65	492,984	279,777	213,207	289,020	203,964
1965–66	524,117	301,051	223,066	313,034	211,083
1967–68	636,863	359,747	277,116	393,707	243,156
1969–70	798,070	453,605	344,465	523,442	274,628
1970–71	846,110	478,423	367,687	562,345	283,765
1971–72	894,110	503,631	390,479	604,471	289,639
1972–73	930,272	521,534	408,738	636,378	293,894
1973–74	954,376	530,907	423,469	657,455	296,921
1974–75	931,663	508,424	423,239	640,524	291,139
1975–76	934,443	508,549	425,894	640,799	293,644
1976–77	928,228	499,121	429,107	635,909	292,319
1977–78	930,201	491,066	439,135	633,183	297,018
1978–79	931,340	481,394	449,946	627,084	304,256
1979–80	929,417	473,611	455,806	624,084	304,333
1980–81	935,140	469,883	465,257	626,452	308,688
			Projections		
1981–82	945,000	475,000	470,000	na	na
1982–83	965,000	480,000	485,000	na	na
1983–84	985,000	485,000	500,000	na	na
1984–85	985,000	480,000	505,000	na	na

Note: Data prior to 1979–80 are for aggregate U. S. (fifty states, D. C., and outlying parts) except where footnoted otherwise; projections are intermediate projections for the fifty states and D. C. Tables showing percent distributions are found on pages 151 and 152.

na Not available.

a Data prior to 1961–62 show bachelor's degrees and first professional degrees combined because USOE did not collect data for the two degrees separately prior to 1960–61. Figures for 1961–62 through 1964–65 show degrees requiring four years of study. Figures for 1965–66 and later show degrees requiring four or five years of study.

Sources:

1 USOE/NCES earned degree series. See page 144.

2 NCES, *Projections of Education Statistics to 1990–91* (Washington: GPO), 1982, p. 70.

3 NCES, *Digest of Education Statistics,* 1982 (Washington: GPO), 1982, p. 121.

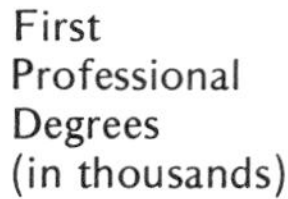

First Professional Degrees, by Sex of Student and by Control of Institution, Selected Years, 1960–61—1984–85

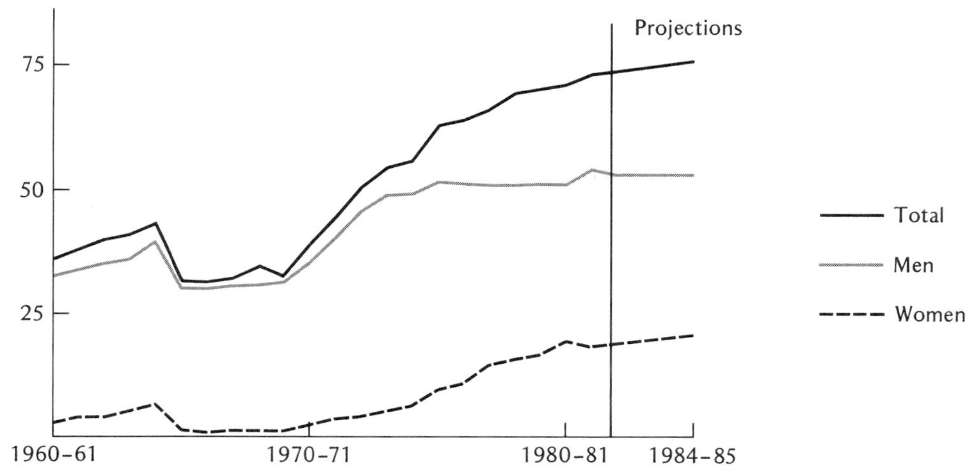

Year	Total	Men	Women	Public	Private
	First Professional Degrees[a]				
1960–61	36,447	32,473	3,974	12,846	23,601
1961–62	37,663	33,570	4,093	13,239	24,424
1962–63	40,171	35,642	4,529	15,029	25,142
1963–64	41,637	36,692	4,945	15,873	25,764
1964–65	45,946	39,893	6,053	18,111	27,835
1965–66	31,496	30,071	1,425	12,474	19,022
1966–67	32,493	31,064	1,429	13,278	19,215
1967–68	34,728	33,083	1,645	14,526	20,202
1968–69	35,681	34,069	1,612	15,038	20,643
1969–70	35,252	33,344	1,908	14,733	20,519
1970–71	38,276	35,797	2,479	16,341	21,935
1971–72	43,774	41,021	2,753	18,727	25,047
1972–73	50,435	46,827	3,608	22,104	28,331
1973–74	54,278	48,904	5,374	23,474	30,804
1974–75	56,259	49,230	7,029	23,907	32,352
1975–76	63,061	53,210	9,851	26,092	36,969
1976–77	64,780	52,668	12,112	26,669	38,111
1977–78	66,964	52,553	14,411	27,408	39,556
1978–79	69,222	52,909	16,313	28,103	41,119
1979–80	70,131	52,716	17,415	27,942	42,189
1980–81	71,956	52,792	19,164	29,128	42,828
	Projections				
1981–82	73,600	54,700	18,900	na	na
1982–83	73,400	53,700	19,700	na	na
1983–84	74,600	53,800	20,800	na	na
1984–85	75,300	53,900	21,400	na	na

Note: Data prior to 1979–80 are for aggregate U. S. (fifty states, D. C., and outlying parts) except where footnoted otherwise; projections are intermediate projections for the fifty states and D. C. Data showing bachelor's degrees apart from professional degrees were not gathered by the U. S. Office of Education prior to 1960–61. Tables showing percent distributions are found on pages 151 and 152.

na Not available.

a For 1960–61 through 1964–65, data are for first professional degrees that required five or more years of study, plus master's degrees that were considered first professional degrees, such as master's degrees in library science, social work, and public administration; for 1965–66 and later, data show only those first professional degrees based on programs which required at least two years of college work for admission and a total of six or more years of work for the degree. For 1965–66 and later, *all* master's degrees, whether or not they were first professional, were to be reported as master's degrees and are excluded from these data.

Sources:

1 USOE/NCES earned degree series. See page 144.

2 NCES, *Projections of Education Statistics to 1990–91* (Washington: GPO), 1982, p. 70.

3 NCES, *Digest of Education Statistics, 1982* (Washington: GPO), 1982, p. 125.

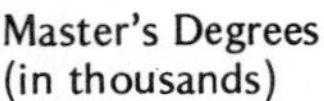

Master's Degrees, by Sex of Student and by Control of Institution, Selected Years, 1947–48—1984–85

Year	Master's Degrees[a] Total	Men	Women	Public	Private
1947–48	42,449	28,939	13,510	17,696	24,753
1949–50	58,219	41,237	16,982	26,192	32,027
1951–52	63,587	43,591	19,996	31,527	32,060
1953–54	56,823	38,147	18,676	30,701	26,122
1954–55	58,204	38,740	19,464	32,291	25,913
1955–56	59,294	39,397	19,897	33,095	26,199
1957–58	65,614	44,252	21,362	37,954	27,660
1959–60	74,497	50,937	23,560	42,991	31,506
1961–62	84,889	58,705	26,184	50,663	34,226
1963–64	101,122	69,012	32,110	62,363	38,759
1964–65	112,195	76,211	35,984	68,199	43,996
1965–66	140,772	93,184	47,588	84,313	56,459
1967–68	177,150	113,749	63,401	112,624	64,526
1969–70	209,387	126,146	83,241	135,351	74,036
1970–71	231,486	138,590	92,896	152,305	79,181
1971–72	252,774	150,085	102,689	167,949	84,825
1972–73	264,525	155,000	109,525	175,220	89,305
1973–74	278,259	158,344	119,915	185,504	92,755
1974–75	293,651	162,115	131,536	194,666	98,985
1975–76	313,001	167,745	145,256	207,209	105,792
1976–77	318,241	168,210	150,031	209,689	108,552
1977–78	312,816	161,708	151,108	202,891	109,925
1978–79	302,075	153,772	148,303	192,683	109,392
1979–80	298,081	150,749	147,332	187,499	110,582
1980–81	295,739	147,043	148,696	184,384	111,355
			Projections		
1981–82	303,000	149,000	154,000	na	na
1982–83	307,000	151,000	156,000	na	na
1983–84	310,000	154,000	156,000	na	na
1984–85	311,000	153,000	158,000	na	na

Note: Data prior to 1979–80 are for aggregate U. S. (fifty states, D. C., and outlying parts) except where footnoted otherwise; projections are intermediate projections for the fifty states and D. C. Tables showing percent distribution are found on pages 151 and 152.

na Not available.

a Figures for 1947–48 through 1964–65 generally exclude those master's degrees that are considered first professional degrees, such as master of library science and master of social work. Data for 1965–66 and later include all master's degrees.

Sources:

1 USOE/NCES earned degree series. See page 144.

2 NCES, *Projections of Education Statistics to 1990–91* (Washington: GPO), 1982, p. 70.

3 NCES, *Digest of Education Statistics, 1982* (Washington: GPO), 1982, p. 117.

150 Doctor's Degrees, by Sex of Student and by Control of Institution, Selected Years, 1947–48—1984–85

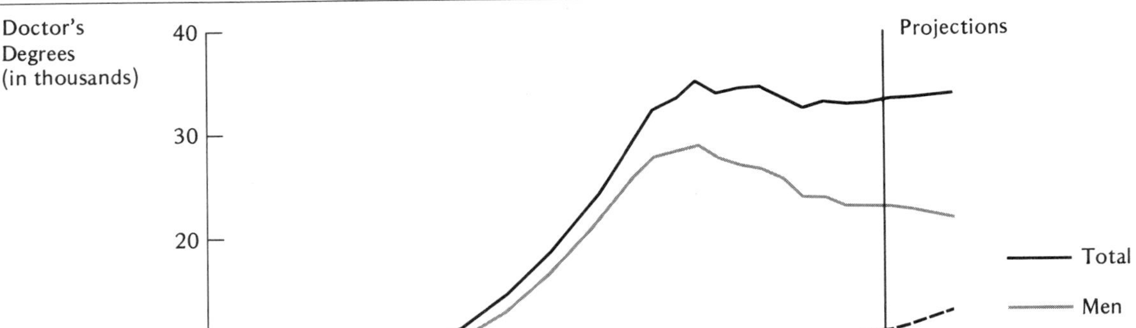

Year	Total	Men	Women	Public	Private
	Earned Doctor's Degrees[a]				
1947–48	3,989	3,496	493	1,580	2,409
1949–50	6,420	5,804	616	2,668	3,752
1951–52	7,683	6,969	714	3,469	4,214
1953–54	8,996	8,181	815	4,656	4,340
1954–55	8,840	8,014	826	4,560	4,280
1955–56	8,903	8,018	885	4,583	4,320
1957–58	8,942	7,978	964	4,614	4,328
1959–60	9,829	8,801	1,028	5,098	4,731
1961–62	11,622	10,377	1,245	6,296	5,326
1963–64	14,490	12,955	1,535	8,194	6,296
1964–65	16,467	14,692	1,775	9,472	6,995
1965–66	18,239	16,121	2,118	10,774	7,465
1967–68	23,091	20,185	2,906	14,157	8,934
1969–70	29,872	25,892	3,980	19,189	10,683
1970–71	32,113	27,534	4,579	20,794	11,319
1971–72	33,369	28,095	5,274	21,782	11,587
1972–73	34,790	28,575	4,215	22,370	12,420
1973–74	33,826	27,374	6,452	21,817	12,009
1974–75	34,086	26,819	7,267	22,179	11,907
1975–76	34,076	26,273	7,803	21,763	12,313
1976–77	32,244	25,150	8,094	21,241	12,003
1977–78	32,156	23,669	8,487	20,471	11,685
1978–79	32,756	23,555	9,201	20,831	11,925
1979–80	32,615	22,943	9,672	20,608	12,007
1980–81	32,958	22,711	10,247	20,895	12,063
	Projections				
1981–82	33,300	22,600	10,700	na	na
1982–83	33,300	22,100	11,200	na	na
1983–84	33,500	21,700	11,800	na	na
1984–85	33,600	21,200	12,400	na	na

Note: Data prior to 1979–80 are for aggregate U. S. (fifty states, D. C., and outlying parts) except where footnoted otherwise; projections are intermediate projections for the fifty states and D. C. Tables showing percent distribution are found on pages 151 and 152.

na Not available.

a Doctorates included in addition to the Ph.D. are degrees such as Ed.D., S.T.D., and Sc.D. Excluded are honorary doctorates and the first professional degrees such as M.D., D.D.S., and D.V.M.

Sources:

1 USOE/NCES earned degree series. See page 144.

2 NCES, *Projections of Education Statistics to 1990–91* (Washington: GPO), 1982, p. 70.

3 NCES, *Digest of Education Statistics, 1982* (Washington: GPO), 1982, p. 117.

151 Percent Distribution of Earned Degrees, by Level of Degree and by Sex of Student, Selected Years, 1947–48—1984–85

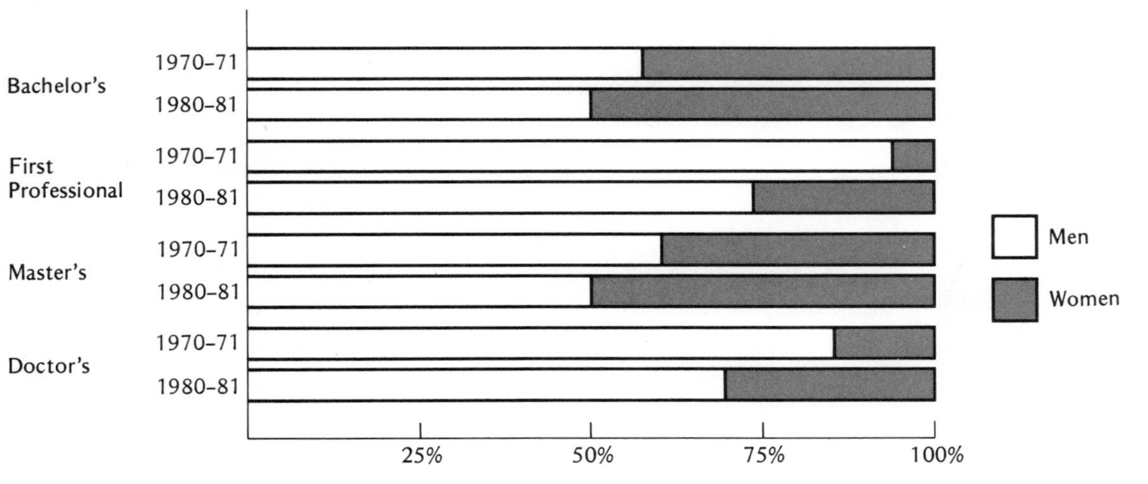

Percent Distribution of Earned Degrees

Year	All Degrees		Bachelor's[a]		First Prof.[ab]		Master's[b]		Doctor's	
	Men	Women	Men	Women	Men	Women	Men	Women	Men	Women
1947–48	65	35	65	35	na	na	68	32	88	12
1949–50	76	24	76	24	na	na	71	29	90	10
1951–52	69	31	68	32	na	na	69	31	91	9
1953–54	65	35	64	36	na	na	67	33	91	9
1954–55	65	35	64	36	na	na	67	33	91	9
1955–56	65	35	64	36	na	na	66	34	90	10
1957–58	67	33	66	34	na	na	67	33	89	11
1959–60	66	34	65	35	na	na	68	32	90	10
1961–62	64	36	60	40	89	11	69	31	89	11
1963–64	62	38	57	43	88	12	68	32	89	11
1964–65	62	38	57	43	87	13	68	32	89	11
1965–66	62	38	57	43	95	5	66	34	88	12
1967–68	60	40	56	44	95	5	64	36	87	13
1969–70	60	40	57	43	95	5	60	40	87	13
1970–71	59	41	57	43	94	6	60	40	86	14
1971–72	59	41	56	44	94	6	59	41	84	16
1972–73	59	41	56	44	93	7	59	41	82	18
1973–74	58	42	56	44	90	10	57	43	81	19
1974–75	57	43	55	45	88	12	55	45	79	21
1975–76	56	44	54	46	84	16	54	46	77	23
1976–77	55	45	54	46	81	19	53	47	76	24
1977–78	54	46	53	47	78	22	52	48	74	26
1978–79	53	47	52	48	76	24	51	49	72	28
1979–80	53	47	51	49	75	25	51	49	70	30
1980–81	52	48	50	50	74	27	50	50	69	31
Projections										
1981–82	52	48	50	50	74	26	49	51	68	32
1982–83	51	49	50	50	73	27	49	51	66	34
1983–84	51	49	49	51	72	28	50	50	65	35
1984–85	50	50	49	51	72	28	49	51	63	37

na Not available.

a Prior to 1961–62, reports combined bachelor's and first professional degrees. Hence, separate figures for the latter degree are not available, and the figures for 1947–48 through 1959–60 are based on the combined total of both types of degree.

b For 1964–65 and earlier, master's degrees that were considered to be first professional degrees, such as a master of library science, were counted as first professional degrees. Beginning in 1965–66, *all* master's degrees are included in the count of master's degrees; none are counted as first professional degrees.

Source: Calculated from data on pp 145–150.

152 Percent Distribution of Earned Degrees, by Level of Degree and by Control of Institution, Selected Years, 1947–48—1980–81

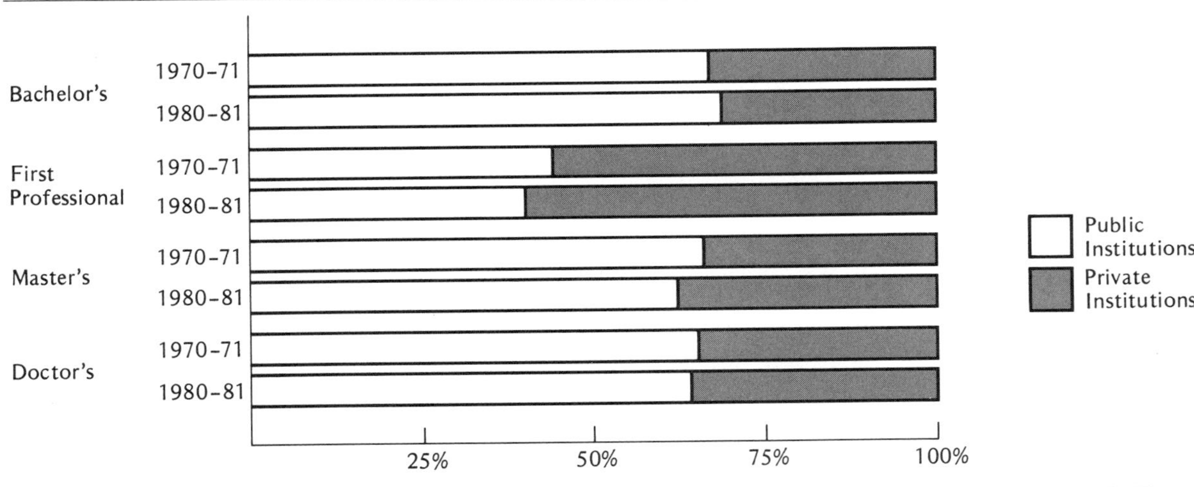

Percent Distribution of Earned Degrees

Year	All Degrees Public	All Degrees Private	Bachelor's[a] Public	Bachelor's[a] Private	First Prof.[ab] Public	First Prof.[ab] Private	Master's[b] Public	Master's[b] Private	Doctor's Public	Doctor's Private
1947–48	49	51	50	50	na	na	42	58	40	60
1949–50	49	51	50	50	na	na	45	55	42	58
1951–52	49	51	49	51	na	na	50	50	45	55
1953–54	51	49	51	49	na	na	54	46	52	48
1954–55	52	48	51	49	na	na	55	45	52	48
1955–56	53	47	52	48	na	na	56	44	51	49
1957–58	55	45	54	46	na	na	58	42	52	48
1959–60	55	45	54	46	na	na	58	42	52	48
1961–62	55	45	56	44	35	65	60	40	54	46
1963–64	57	43	58	42	38	62	62	38	57	43
1964–65	58	42	59	41	39	61	61	39	58	42
1965–66	59	41	60	40	40	60	60	40	59	41
1967–68	61	39	62	38	42	58	64	36	61	39
1969–70	65	35	66	34	42	58	65	35	64	36
1970–71	65	35	66	34	43	57	66	34	65	35
1971–72	66	34	68	32	43	57	66	34	65	35
1972–73	67	33	68	32	44	56	66	34	64	36
1973–74	67	33	69	31	43	57	67	33	64	36
1974–75	67	33	69	31	42	58	66	34	65	35
1975–76	67	33	69	31	41	59	66	34	64	36
1976–77	66	34	69	31	41	59	66	34	64	36
1977–78	66	34	68	32	41	59	65	35	64	36
1978–79	65	35	67	33	41	59	64	36	64	36
1979–80	65	35	67	33	40	60	63	37	63	37
1980–81	64	36	67	33	40	60	62	38	64	36

na Not available.

a Prior to 1961–62, reports combined bachelor's and first professional degrees. Hence, separate figures for the latter degree are not available, and the figures for 1947–48 through 1959–60 are based on the combined total of both types of degree.

b For 1964–65 and earlier, master's degrees that were considered to be first professional degrees, such as a master of library science, were counted as first professional degrees and excluded from the count of master's degrees. Beginning in 1965–66, *all* master's degrees are included in the count of master's degrees; none are counted as first professional degrees.

Source: Calculated from data on pp. 145–150.

153 Bachelor's Degrees, by Region and State, Selected Years, 1961–62—1980–81

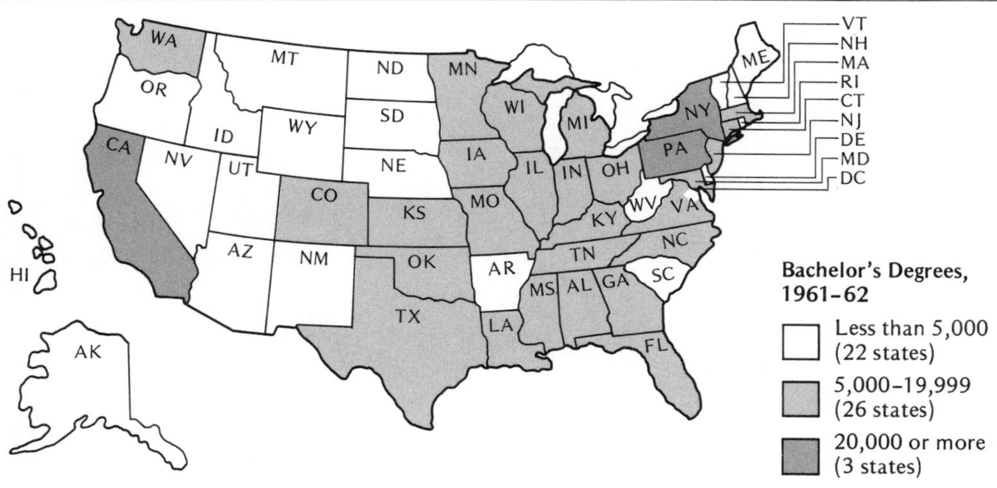

Bachelor's Degrees, 1961–62

- Less than 5,000 (22 states)
- 5,000–19,999 (26 states)
- 20,000 or more (3 states)

	Bachelor's Degrees[a]					
Region and State	**1961–62**	**1964–65**	**1969–70**	**1974–75**	**1978–79**	**1980–81**
U. S. & Outlying Parts	**382,822**	**492,984**	**798,070**	**931,665**	**931,340**	**946,877**
50 States & D. C.	**380,597**	**489,665**	**792,316**	**922,935**	**921,390**	**935,140**
New England	**28,988**	**36,357**	**56,349**	**70,189**	**71,450**	**74,180**
Connecticut	5,176	6,626	10,918	13,647	12,701	13,312
Maine	2,229	2,718	4,118	4,690	4,559	4,817
Massachusetts	15,751	19,462	29,455	36,569	37,803	38,792
New Hampshire	1,875	2,443	4,180	5,023	5,418	6,025
Rhode Island	2,508	3,134	4,793	6,479	7,187	7,263
Vermont	1,449	1,974	2,885	3,781	3,782	3,971
Mideast	**78,629**	**101,923**	**152,266**	**189,318**	**190,523**	**188,599**
Delaware	551	807	1,533	2,776	3,053	3,194
D. C.	2,904	4,103	5,854	6,641	6,833	6,807
Maryland	5,369	7,331	12,076	16,239	15,598	15,901
New Jersey	9,147	12,509	18,007	25,188	25,233	24,474
New York	35,814	46,182	67,481	82,929	85,593	83,777
Pennsylvania	24,844	30,991	47,315	55,545	54,213	54,446
Southeast	**69,475**	**89,154**	**152,336**	**181,305**	**183,661**	**188,080**
Alabama	6,024	7,208	12,868	14,236	16,345	16,534
Arkansas	3,786	4,524	7,287	6,997	6,708	6,955
Florida	6,285	9,179	19,773	26,315	28,523	29,988
Georgia	5,986	7,683	13,911	16,759	16,135	17,014
Kentucky	5,753	7,304	12,018	12,000	11,220	11,509
Louisiana	6,377	7,882	13,617	16,061	14,765	14,821
Mississippi	5,048	5,707	8,784	9,643	8,687	8,982
North Carolina	8,651	11,964	18,587	23,406	23,640	23,712
South Carolina	4,219	5,060	7,835	10,796	11,406	11,358
Tennessee	7,258	9,616	15,916	17,623	17,599	17,409
Virginia	6,320	8,222	13,744	19,056	21,251	22,078
West Virginia	3,768	4,805	7,996	8,413	7,382	7,720
Great Lakes	**74,838**	**97,000**	**158,679**	**173,077**	**166,430**	**171,283**
Illinois	17,462	23,019	38,449	44,447	43,485	44,470
Indiana	12,066	15,026	22,188	24,477	23,677	24,834
Michigan	17,089	21,362	35,295	36,816	36,875	38,647
Ohio	18,925	25,101	41,811	45,602	40,659	41,306
Wisconsin	9,296	12,492	20,936	21,735	21,734	22,026

(*Continued on next page*)

For footnotes and sources, see next page.

154 Bachelor's Degrees, by Region and State, Selected Years, 1961–62—1980–81—*Continued*

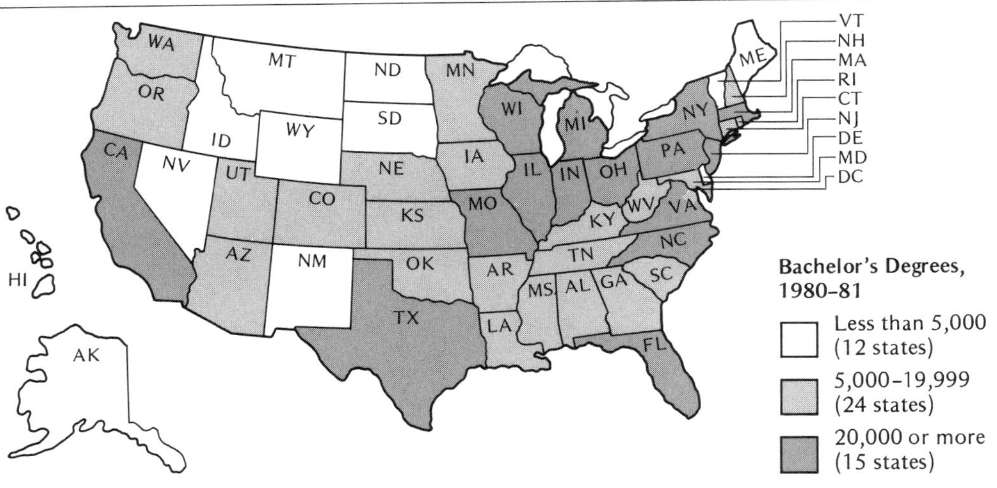

Region and State	Bachelor's Degrees[a] 1961–62	1964–65	1969–70	1974–75	1978–79	1980–81
Plains	**40,577**	**50,223**	**80,780**	**81,632**	**80,365**	**82,613**
Iowa	7,272	9,163	14,312	13,480	13,378	14,441
Kansas	6,395	7,989	12,161	12,198	11,786	11,672
Minnesota	8,883	10,727	18,040	18,429	18,467	19,392
Missouri	8,416	11,244	18,347	21,352	22,034	22,041
Nebraska	4,563	6,174	9,417	8,381	7,398	7,404
North Dakota	1,833	2,367	3,867	3,627	3,613	3,795
South Dakota	2,114	2,559	4,636	4,165	3,689	3,868
Southwest	**30,407**	**37,962**	**64,167**	**77,446**	**81,020**	**81,776**
Arizona	2,926	4,217	7,896	8,994	9,905	10,826
New Mexico	1,496	2,118	4,081	4,727	4,604	4,543
Oklahoma	6,448	7,718	12,012	13,494	12,855	12,818
Texas	19,537	23,909	40,178	50,231	53,656	53,589
Rocky Mountains	**13,248**	**17,027**	**28,606**	**31,170**	**31,008**	**31,907**
Colorado	5,501	6,938	11,923	14,073	13,864	14,677
Idaho	1,251	1,560	2,743	2,805	2,694	2,759
Montana	1,849	2,357	3,746	3,722	3,812	3,815
Utah	3,860	5,313	8,837	9,264	9,349	9,336
Wyoming	787	859	1,357	1,306	1,289	1,320
Far West	**42,165**	**57,485**	**96,306**	**115,777**	**113,702**	**113,433**
Alaska	98	191	315	610	370	465
California	28,824	39,957	67,836	82,878	82,607	81,848
Hawaii	908	1,274	2,612	3,814	3,267	3,212
Nevada	351	516	1,006	1,428	1,391	1,477
Oregon	4,893	6,599	9,923	10,118	10,014	9,783
Washington	7,091	8,948	14,614	16,929	16,053	16,648
U. S. Service Schools	**2,371**	**2,534**	**2,827**	**3,021**	**3,231**	**3,269**
Outlying Parts	**2,225**	**3,319**	**5,754**	**8,730**	**9,950**	**11,737**

Note: Each year's data are for the twelve months ending June 30. The reporting of bachelor's degrees separately from first professional degrees began in 1960–61.

a Data for 1969–70 and later show "bachelor's degrees requiring 4–5 years." The 1964–65 survey defined a bachelor's degree as "requiring 4 but less than 5 years"; the 1961–62 survey defined the term as "all 4-year degrees (bachelor's and first-professional)."

Sources:

1 USOE, *Earned Degrees Conferred, 1961–62, Bachelor's and Higher Degrees* (Washington; GPO), 1963, table 7.

2 USOE, *Summary Report on Bachelor's and Higher Degrees Conferred During the Year 1964–65* (Washington: GPO), 1966, table 2.

3 NCES, *Earned Degrees Conferred, Summary Data* (Washington: GPO), *1969–70,* table 3; *1974–75,* table 3; *1977–78,* table 3.

4 NCES, HEGIS Earned Degrees Conferred, 1978–79, preliminary data; 1980–81, preliminary data.

5 NCES (Washington, 1983), unpublished data.

155 First Professional Degrees, by Region and State, Selected Years, 1961–62—1980–81

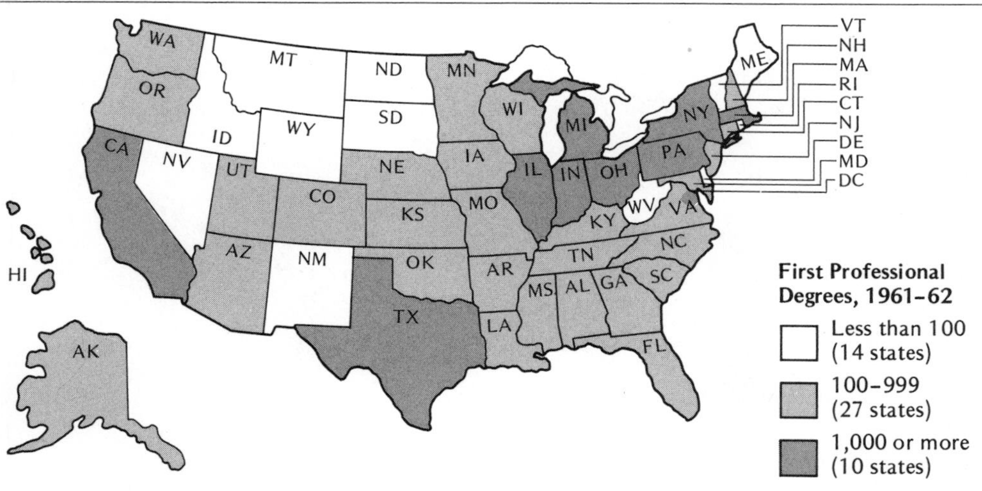

Region and State	First Professional Degrees[a] 1961–62	1964–65	1969–70	1974–75	1978–79	1980–81
U. S. & Outlying Parts	**37,663**	**45,946**	**35,252**	**56,259**	**69,222**	**72,369**
50 States & D. C.	**37,249**	**45,366**	**34,918**	**55,916**	**68,848**	**71,956**
New England	**3,220**	**3,683**	**2,388**	**3,886**	**4,373**	**4,826**
Connecticut	551	721	440	551	725	799
Maine	25	24	45	69	100	83
Massachusetts	2,432	2,710	1,845	3,082	3,157	3,496
New Hampshire	119	144	—	57	169	185
Rhode Island	55	43	—	58	60	67
Vermont	38	41	58	69	162	196
Mideast	**10,253**	**12,293**	**8,639**	**12,778**	**14,694**	**15,115**
Delaware	—	—	—	—	—	—
D. C.	1,290	1,577	1,453	2,267	2,359	2,460
Maryland	587	710	782	940	921	894
New Jersey	707	843	672	1,208	1,454	1,547
New York	4,945	6,050	3,517	5,094	6,203	6,491
Pennsylvania	2,724	3,113	2,215	3,269	3,757	3,723
Southeast	**5,956**	**7,391**	**6,225**	**10,043**	**12,551**	**13,885**
Alabama	273	393	413	838	870	940
Arkansas	115	172	191	228	401	413
Florida	670	998	632	1,187	1,702	1,804
Georgia	777	917	759	1,130	1,355	1,540
Kentucky	655	768	731	1,135	1,352	1,319
Louisiana	864	978	784	1,134	1,377	1,427
Mississippi	143	200	188	294	461	684
North Carolina	750	827	665	1,090	1,384	1,508
South Carolina	185	248	233	541	581	696
Tennessee	732	861	814	1,212	1,387	1,501
Virginia	700	827	657	1,028	1,346	1,715
West Virginia	92	202	158	226	335	338
Great Lakes	**7,400**	**8,911**	**6,859**	**10,562**	**13,098**	**13,173**
Illinois	3,039	3,363	2,254	3,631	4,670	4,471
Indiana	562	914	906	1,206	1,426	1,522
Michigan	1,469	1,742	1,408	2,072	2,702	2,638
Ohio	1,772	2,260	1,769	2,799	3,400	3,584
Wisconsin	558	632	522	854	900	958

(*Continued on next page*)

— No degrees reported.

Note: Each year's data are for the twelve months ending June 30. The reporting of first professional degrees separately from bachelor's degrees began in 1960–61.

For footnotes and sources, see next page.

156 First Professional Degrees, by Region and State, Selected Years, 1961–62—1980–81—*Continued*

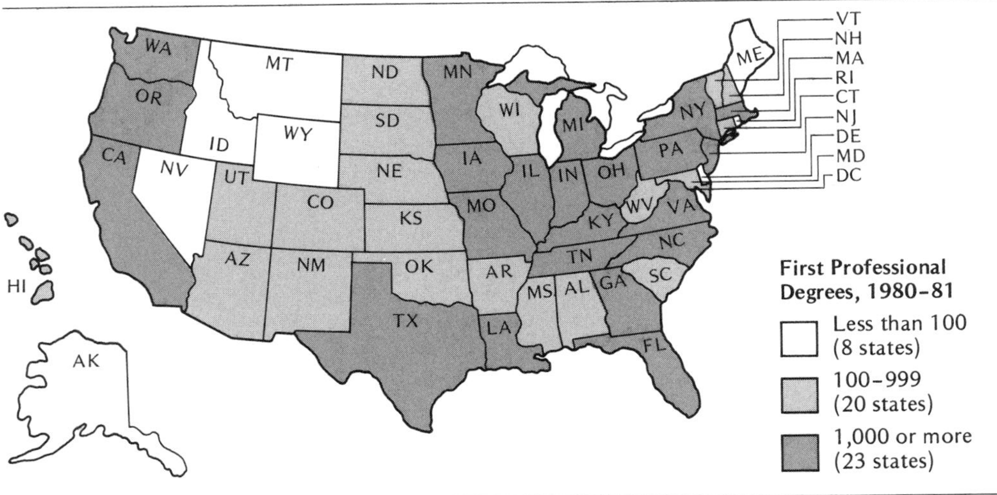

Region and State	1961–62	1964–65	1969–70	1974–75	1978–79	1980–81
	First Professional Degrees[a]					
Plains	**3,461**	**4,475**	**3,573**	**5,762**	**7,148**	**7,074**
Iowa	525	689	526	1,347	1,428	1,587
Kansas	370	441	379	563	725	571
Minnesota	933	1,081	785	1,067	1,654	1,622
Missouri	1,162	1,634	1,391	1,954	2,276	2,321
Nebraska	358	420	407	716	809	721
North Dakota	85	148	37	47	137	118
South Dakota	28	62	48	68	119	134
Southwest	**2,547**	**2,928**	**2,667**	**4,383**	**4,981**	**5,569**
Arizona	338	374	132	284	349	410
New Mexico	18	39	58	162	179	194
Oklahoma	393	501	404	736	857	767
Texas	1,798	2,014	2,073	3,201	3,596	4,207
Rocky Mountains	**783**	**943**	**671**	**1,103**	**1,271**	**1,424**
Colorado	501	525	427	673	722	839
Idaho	16	71	26	75	73	91
Montana	52	54	34	61	74	71
Utah	199	259	153	233	334	360
Wyoming	15	34	31	61	68	63
Far West	**3,629**	**4,564**	**3,896**	**7,399**	**10,732**	**10,823**
Alaska	—	—	—	—	—	—
California	2,855	3,452	3,153	5,784	8,628	8,602
Hawaii	16	22	—	62	121	153
Nevada	—	—	—	—	—	48
Oregon	286	436	397	749	972	1,014
Washington	472	654	346	804	1,011	1,006
U. S. Service Schools	**—**	**178**	**—**	**—**	**—**	**67**
Outlying Parts	**414**	**580**	**334**	**343**	**374**	**413**

a Data for 1961–62 and 1964–65 include those master's degrees, such as master of library science, that were considered first professional degrees. Data for 1969–70 and later exclude all master's degrees and show only first professional degrees requiring at least six years of college work.

Sources:

1 USOE, *Earned Degrees Conferred, 1961–62, Bachelor's and Higher Degrees* (Washington: GPO), 1963, table 7.

2 USOE, *Summary Report on Bachelor's and Higher Degrees Conferred During the Year 1964–65* (Washington: GPO), 1966, table 2.

3 NCES, *Earned Degrees Conferred, Summary Data* (Washington: GPO), *1969–70,* table 3; *1974–75,* table 3; *1977–78;* table 3.

4 NCES, HEGIS Earned Degrees Conferred, 1978–79, preliminary data.

5 NCES (Washington, 1983), unpublished data.

157 Master's Degrees, by Region and State, Selected Years, 1949–50—1980–81

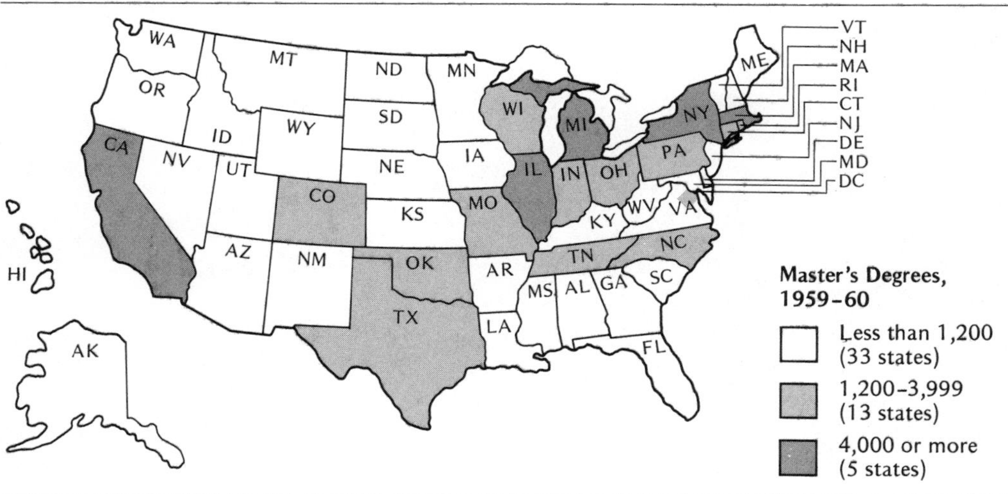

Region and State	Master's Degrees[a] 1949–50[b]	1959–60	1969–70	1974–75	1978–79	1980–81
U. S. & Outlying Parts	**58,219**	**74,497**	**209,387**	**293,651**	**302,075**	**296,798**
50 States & D. C.	**58,217**	**74,435**	**208,291**	**292,450**	**301,079**	**295,739**
New England	**5,362**	**6,852**	**17,621**	**24,140**	**24,239**	**24,416**
Connecticut	673	1,490	3,960	5,863	5,743	6,190
Maine	92	178	595	736	618	527
Massachusetts	4,078	4,588	10,811	13,887	14,243	14,049
New Hampshire	201	221	565	721	882	974
Rhode Island	127	204	1,072	1,787	1,572	1,524
Vermont	191	171	618	1,146	1,181	1,152
Mideast	**17,709**	**18,961**	**50,367**	**71,929**	**65,849**	**64,784**
Delaware	72	144	364	485	453	452
D. C.	1,197	1,327	4,077	5,070	5,187	5,712
Maryland	486	760	3,012	5,015	5,164	5,255
New Jersey	945	1,689	5,048	8,163	7,862	7,737
New York	11,363	11,176	26,811	38,681	33,715	32,457
Pennsylvania	3,646	3,865	11,055	14,515	13,468	13,171
Southeast	**6,514**	**9,839**	**28,969**	**51,844**	**57,260**	**53,908**
Alabama	487	882	2,344	5,180	6,020	5,271
Arkansas	261	612	1,159	1,437	1,716	1,817
Florida	563	993	4,327	7,258	9,435	8,716
Georgia	705	674	3,278	7,360	7,133	6,414
Kentucky	591	877	2,560	4,517	5,006	4,518
Louisiana	575	850	3,086	4,326	4,053	3,925
Mississippi	364	496	1,433	2,850	2,982	2,769
North Carolina	681	1,483	3,216	4,480	5,537	5,289
South Carolina	216	288	769	3,116	3,461	2,985
Tennessee	1,076	1,599	3,054	4,690	4,563	4,662
Virginia	377	579	2,564	4,661	5,178	5,488
West Virginia	618	506	1,179	1,969	2,176	2,054
Great Lakes	**12,800**	**16,278**	**48,870**	**58,848**	**58,428**	**57,799**
Illinois	4,438	4,436	12,712	16,611	16,550	16,423
Indiana	1,763	3,038	8,105	10,046	8,616	8,031
Michigan	3,294	4,565	12,043	14,887	14,896	14,916
Ohio	1,994	2,713	8,761	11,918	13,046	13,229
Wisconsin	1,311	1,526	4,249	5,386	5,320	5,200

(*Continued on next page*)

— No degrees reported.

Note: Each year's data are for the twelve months ending June 30.

For footnotes and sources, see next page.

158 Master's Degrees, by Region and State, Selected Years, 1949–50—1980–81—*Continued*

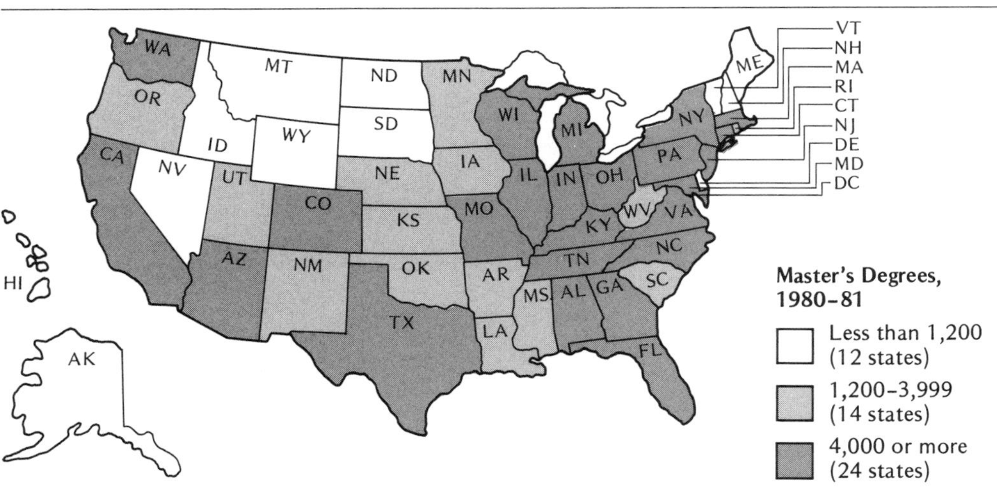

Region and State	1949–50[b]	1959–60	1969–70	1974–75	1978–79	1980–81
	Master's Degrees[a]					
Plains	**4,168**	**5,604**	**15,866**	**17,719**	**19,703**	**19,229**
Iowa	1,062	987	2,244	2,377	2,535	2,511
Kansas	434	1,104	2,883	3,046	3,268	3,202
Minnesota	968	1,099	2,582	2,918	3,317	3,299
Missouri	1,200	1,392	5,308	6,700	7,714	7,464
Nebraska	339	488	1,247	1,517	1,721	1,710
North Dakota	79	221	703	466	465	466
South Dakota	86	313	899	695	683	577
Southwest	**4,512**	**6,123**	**15,460**	**22,881**	**25,553**	**26,129**
Arizona	168	629	2,825	3,866	3,940	4,350
New Mexico	205	455	1,254	1,362	1,710	1,750
Oklahoma	946	1,290	2,892	3,850	3,667	3,508
Texas	3,193	3,749	8,489	13,803	16,236	16,521
Rocky Mountains	**2,197**	**2,627**	**6,469**	**7,797**	**8,912**	**8,873**
Colorado	1,449	1,521	3,330	3,940	4,853	4,811
Idaho	111	183	385	599	613	684
Montana	141	247	586	613	606	669
Utah	362	509	1,827	2,293	2,487	2,376
Wyoming	134	167	341	352	353	333
Far West	**4,955**	**7,898**	**26,776**	**36,316**	**40,234**	**39,675**
Alaska	—	11	174	243	175	190
California	3,950	6,013	19,467	27,584	31,224	30,609
Hawaii	34	63	1,017	1,298	1,105	1,008
Nevada	6	64	222	443	426	461
Oregon	411	869	2,932	3,132	3,259	3,063
Washington	554	878	2,964	3,616	4,045	4,344
U. S. Service Schools	**—**	**253**	**893**	**976**	**901**	**926**
Outlying Parts	**2**	**62**	**1,096**	**1,201**	**996**	**1,059**

a Data prior to 1969–70 exclude those master's degrees, such as master of library science, that were considered first professional degrees. Data for 1969–70 and later include all master's degrees.

b Data for U. S. Service Schools are included in the totals of the states in which they are located.

Sources:

1 U. S. Office of Education, *Earned Degrees Conferred by Higher Educational Institutions* (Washington: GPO), 1949–50, p. xv.

2 USOE, *Earned Degrees Conferred, 1959–60* (Washington: GPO), 1962, p. 14.

3 NCES, *Earned Degrees Conferred, Summary Data* (Washington: GPO), *1969–70,* table 3; *1974–75,* table 3; *1975–76,* table 3; *1977–78,* table 3.

4 NCES, HEGIS Earned Degrees Conferred, 1978–79, preliminary data; 1980–81, preliminary data.

5 NCES (Washington, 1983), unpublished data.

159 Doctor's Degrees, by Region and State, Selected Years, 1949–50—1980–81

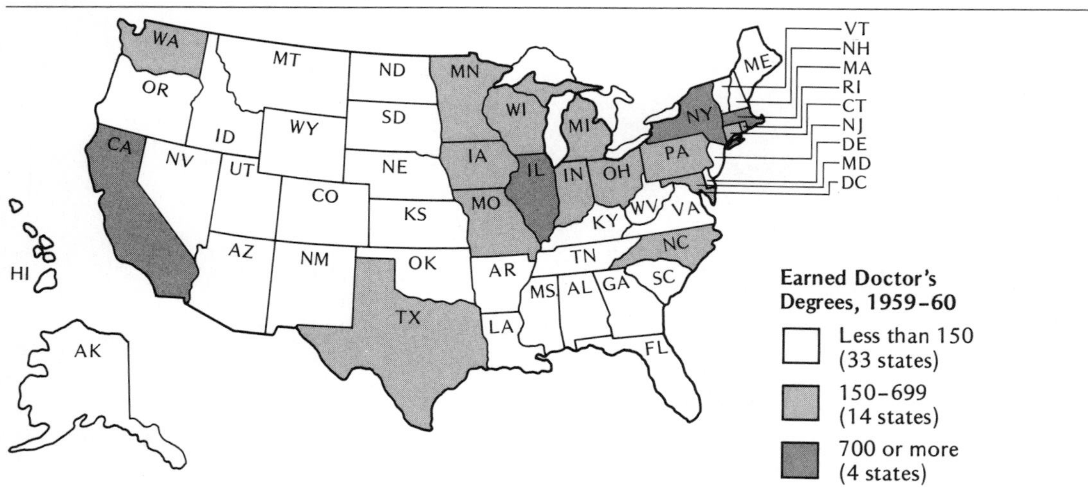

Region and State	Earned Doctor's Degrees[a] 1949–50	1959–60	1969–70	1974–75	1978–79	1980–81
U. S. & Outlying Parts	**6,633[a]**	**9,829**	**29,872**	**34,086**	**32,756**	**32,982**
50 States & D. C.	**6,633**	**9,829**	**29,866**	**34,083**	**32,730**	**32,958**
New England	**857**	**1,116**	**2,480**	**2,935**	**2,669**	**2,791**
Connecticut	197	272	511	584	503	483
Maine	—	1	24	26	22	25
Massachusetts	624	784	1,676	2,018	1,865	2,005
New Hampshire	—	9	49	62	63	68
Rhode Island	34	48	187	204	189	175
Vermont	2	2	33	41	27	35
Mideast	**2,072**	**2,597**	**6,483**	**7,233**	**6,931**	**6,887**
Delaware	23	23	60	76	57	58
D. C.	141	146	498	568	512	535
Maryland	120	210	576	649	587	594
New Jersey	135	249	565	718	719	781
New York	1,290	1,445	3,292	3,451	3,398	3,255
Pennsylvania	363	524	1,492	1,771	1,658	1,664
Southeast	**320**	**806**	**3,707**	**5,036**	**5,407**	**5,122**
Alabama	—	33	221	196	267	254
Arkansas	—	18	124	105	94	106
Florida	16	136	668	1,141	1,517	1,226
Georgia	11	47	345	548	530	553
Kentucky	44	60	173	251	261	264
Louisiana	38	101	348	386	322	269
Mississippi	—	12	178	255	216	241
North Carolina	118	202	634	825	739	714
South Carolina	2	14	115	162	227	196
Tennessee	41	104	452	578	564	603
Virginia	47	73	306	479	555	589
West Virginia	3	6	143	110	115	107
Great Lakes	**1,769**	**2,559**	**6,970**	**7,548**	**6,748**	**6,612**
Illinois	674	823	1,884	2,131	1,943	2,043
Indiana	256	480	1,313	1,300	1,030	1,045
Michigan	244	512	1,577	1,635	1,417	1,310
Ohio	293	371	1,262	1,565	1,551	1,491
Wisconsin	302	373	934	917	807	723

(Continued on next page)

For footnotes and sources, see next page.

160 Doctor's Degrees, by Region and State, Selected Years, 1949–50—1980–81—*Continued*

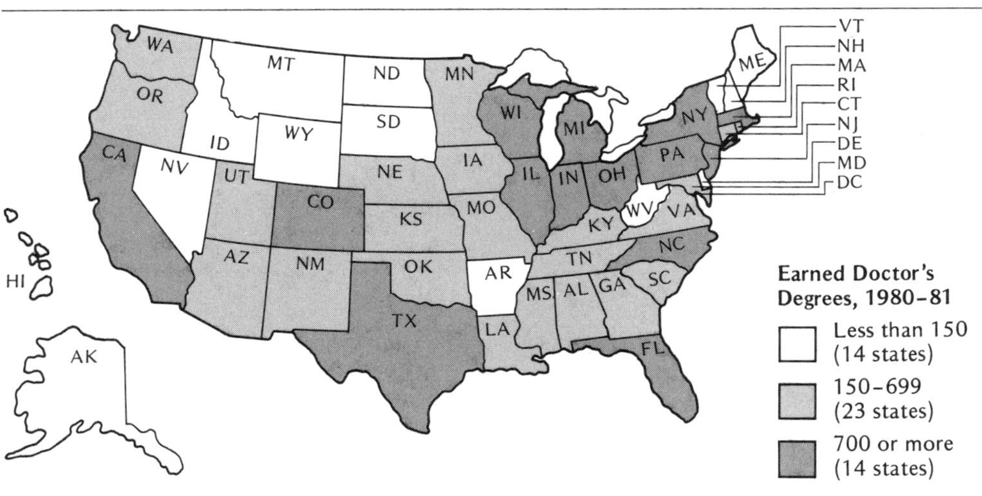

Region and State	Earned Doctor's Degrees 1949–50	1959–60	1969–70	1974–75	1978–79	1980–81
Plains	**616**	**888**	**2,547**	**2,585**	**2,412**	**2,379**
Iowa	253	273	620	551	552	557
Kansas	36	103	389	448	384	369
Minnesota	163	245	546	540	474	535
Missouri	132	183	630	704	688	578
Nebraska	29	70	213	229	200	238
North Dakota	3	8	86	67	69	69
South Dakota	—	6	63	46	45	33
Southwest	**150**	**430**	**2,290**	**2,595**	**2,583**	**2,689**
Arizona	2	31	383	413	392	392
New Mexico	5	10	182	143	158	165
Oklahoma	21	92	484	498	421	379
Texas	122	297	1,241	1,541	1,612	1,753
Rocky Mountains	**95**	**222**	**1,224**	**1,380**	**1,217**	**1,270**
Colorado	61	132	636	701	655	711
Idaho	—	—	45	65	64	60
Montana	—	13	63	81	50	38
Utah	26	66	413	455	393	383
Wyoming	8	11	67	78	55	78
Far West	**754**	**1,210**	**4,153**	**4,754**	**4,748**	**5,196**
Alaska	—	—	7	10	5	2
California	665	949	3,175	3,628	3,716	4,152
Hawaii	—	—	53	97	122	114
Nevada	—	—	11	15	19	30
Oregon	33	98	441	465	375	405
Washington	56	163	466	539	511	493
U. S. Service Schools	**—**	**1**	**12**	**17**	**15**	**12**
Outlying Parts	**—**	**—**	**6**	**3**	**26**	**24**

— No degrees reported.

Note: Each year's data are for the twelve months ending June 30. Doctor's degrees tabulated here include Ph.D.'s, Ed.D's, and their equivalents. Excluded are first professional degrees such as M.D.'s, D.D.S.'s, and so forth.

Sources:

1 U.S. Office of Education, *Earned Degrees Conferred by Higher Educational Institutions* (Washington: GPO), 1949–50, p. xv.

2 USOE, *Earned Degrees Conferred, 1959–60* (Washington: GPO), 1962, p. 14.

3 NCES, *Earned Degrees Conferred, Summary Data* (Washington: GPO), *1969–70,* table 3; *1974–75,* table 3; *1977–78,* table 3.

4 NCES, HEGIS Earned Degrees Conferred, 1978–79, preliminary data.

5 NCES (Washington, 1983), unpublished data.

161 Bachelor's Degrees, by Race, Ethnicity, and Academic Area, 1980–81

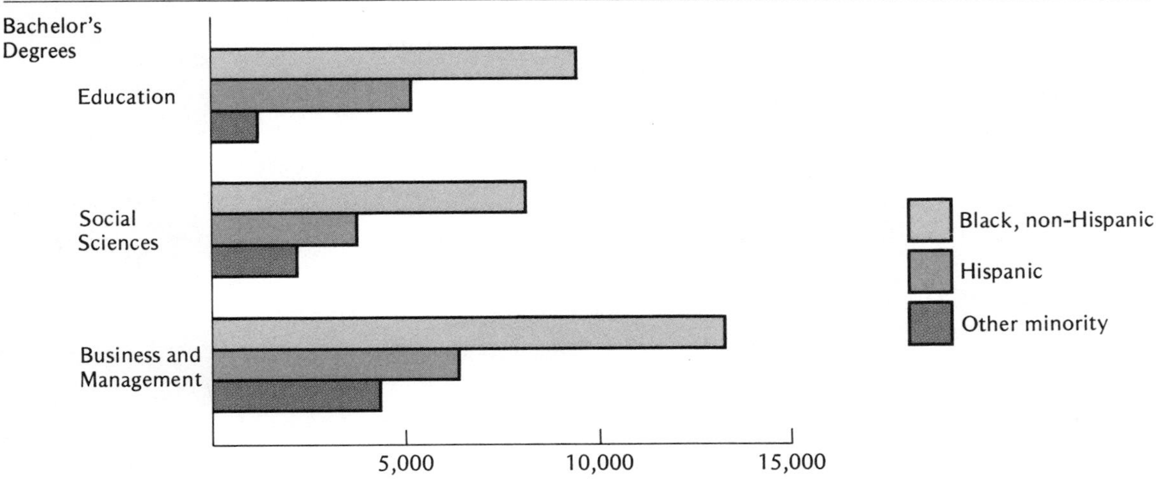

Academic Area	Black, non-Hispanic	American Indian[a]	Asian[b]	Hispanic	Total Minority	White, non-Hispanic	Non-resident Alien	Total
	Bachelor's Degrees Awarded to							
All Academic Areas	**60,589**	**3,584**	**18,807**	**33,066**	**116,046**	**804,659**	**22,615**	**943,320**
Men	(24,388)	(1,692)	(10,053)	(15,010)	(51,143)	(403,609)	(16,320)	(471,072)
Women	(36,201)	(1,892)	(8,754)	(18,056)	(64,903)	(401,050)	(6,295)	(472,248)
Agriculture & nat. resources	380	96	314	390	1,180	20,237	616	22,033
Architecture & environ. design	300	24	296	302	922	8,069	496	9,487
Area studies	67	4	118	104	293	2,242	50	2,585
Biological sciences	2,267	137	1,491	1,950	5,845	37,248	903	43,996
Business & management	13,401	636	3,969	6,934	24,940	174,007	4,577	203,524
Communications	2,405	110	368	607	3,490	27,474	369	31,333
Computer & info. sciences	784	21	669	413	1,887	12,529	777	15,193
Education	9,517	569	767	5,192	16,045	93,750	920	110,715
Engineering	2,432	192	3,038	1,797	7,459	60,074	6,954	74,487
Fine & applied arts	1,835	187	788	863	3,673	35,933	719	40,325
Foreign languages	293	25	210	1,133	1,661	8,615	272	10,548
Health professions	3,603	209	1,312	2,176	7,300	56,791	582	64,673
Home economics	1,125	73	395	404	1,997	16,263	287	18,547
Law	22	2	5	18	47	731	6	784
Letters	1,980	103	465	914	3,462	36,304	477	40,243
Library Science	30	2	2	1	35	339	1	375
Mathematics	583	17	391	275	1,266	9,355	456	11,077
Military science	4	1	1	2	8	140	1	149
Physical sciences	891	64	580	608	2,143	20,961	729	23,833
Psychology	3,303	196	842	1,808	6,149	34,679	486	41,314
Pub. affairs & services	4,872	224	427	1,795	7,318	29,320	316	36,954
Social sciences	8,118	472	1,639	3,904	14,133	85,294	1,982	101,409
Theology	166	5	58	88	317	5,361	138	5,816
Interdisciplinary studies	2,211	215	662	1,388	4,476	28,943	501	33,920

Note: Figures in parentheses show the distribution by sex of all degree recipients. The grand total will not agree with the total bachelor's degree figures for 1980–81 shown elsewhere in this publication because OCR's "universe" of institutions was somewhat different from NCES's.

a Includes native Alaskan.

b Includes Pacific Islander.

Source: Office for Civil Rights (OCR), ED (Washington, 1983), unpublished data.

162 First Professional Degrees, by Race, Ethnicity, and Professional Field, 1980–1981

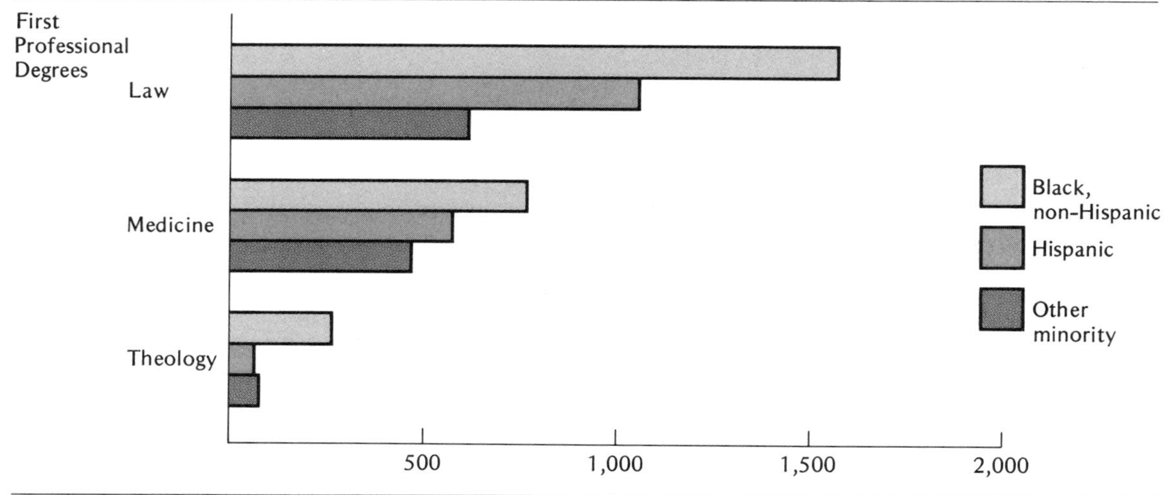

Professional Field	Black, non-Hispanic	American Indian[a]	Asian[b]	Hispanic	Total Minority	White, non-Hispanic	Non-resident Alien	Total
	First Professional Degrees Awarded to							
All Fields	**2,929**	**191**	**1,454**	**1,951**	**6,525**	**64,492**	**669**	**71,686**
Men	(1,771)	(133)	(990)	(1,407)	(4,301)	(47,581)	(537)	(52,419)
Women	(1,158)	(58)	(464)	(544)	(2,224)	(16,911)	(132)	(19,267)
Dentistry	195	10	204	152	561	4,896	69	5,526
Medicine	767	50	444	572	1,833	13,662	121	51,616
Pharmacy	20	3	115	19	157	471	36	664
Veterinary medicine	37	4	17	11	69	1,846	7	1,922
Other health professions[c]	58	14	84	65	221	4,804	151	5,176
Law	1,576	101	530	1,066	3,273	33,111	116	36,500
Theology	276	9	60	66	411	5,702	169	6,282

Note: Figures in parentheses show the distribution by sex of all degree recipients. The grand total will not agree with the total first professional degree figures for 1980–81 shown elsewhere in this publication because OCR's "universe" of institutions was somewhat different from NCES's.

a Includes native Alaskan.

b Includes Pacific Islander.

c Includes optometry, osteopathy, podiatry, chiropractic.

Source: Office for Civil Rights (OCR), ED (Washington, 1983), unpublished data.

163 Master's Degrees, by Race, Ethnicity, and Academic Area, 1980–81

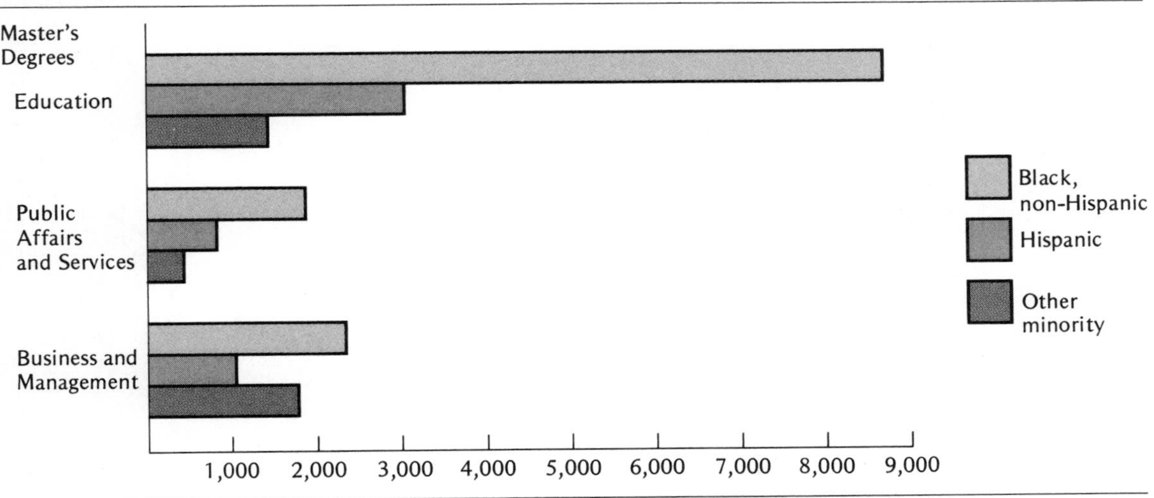

Academic Area	Master's Degrees Awarded to							
	Black, non-Hispanic	American Indian[a]	Asian[b]	Hispanic	Total Minority	White, non-Hispanic	Non-resident Alien	Total
All Academic Areas	**17,152**	**1,034**	**6,304**	**7,439**	**31,929**	**241,254**	**22,058**	**295,241**
Men	(6,161)	(501)	(3,730)	(3,452)	(13,894)	(115,572)	(16,588)	(146,054)
Women	(10,991)	(533)	(2,524)	(3,987)	(18,035)	(125,682)	(5,470)	(149,187)
Agriculture & nat. resources	73	7	67	77	224	3,083	710	4,017
Architecture & environ. design	122	5	112	71	310	2,391	458	3,159
Area studies	14	6	38	39	97	532	89	718
Biological sciences	171	15	145	103	434	5,212	368	6,014
Business & management	2,361	155	1,640	1,029	5,185	47,478	5,052	57,715
Communications	187	9	66	43	305	2,556	244	3,105
Computer & info. sciences	70	12	279	60	421	2,818	904	4,143
Education	8,661	453	981	3,036	13,131	82,801	2,699	98,631
Engineering	260	31	1,079	285	1,655	10,147	4,563	16,365
Fine & applied arts	267	22	160	132	581	7,624	424	8,629
Foreign languages	33	8	26	190	257	1,636	227	2,120
Health professions	889	54	448	421	1,812	14,175	698	16,685
Home economics	132	10	63	31	236	2,191	143	2,570
Law	38	1	37	52	128	1,366	338	1,832
Letters	250	18	114	180	562	7,210	580	8,352
Library science	216	17	69	70	372	4,324	175	4,871
Mathematics	67	7	97	42	213	1,890	464	2,567
Physical sciences	107	11	153	71	342	4,115	786	5,243
Psychology	424	32	77	217	750	7,019	270	8,039
Pub. affairs & services	1,894	92	311	815	3,112	16,440	719	20,271
Social sciences	615	44	235	343	1,237	9,150	1,595	11,982
Theology	71	1	55	50	177	3,282	269	3,728
Interdisciplinary studies	230	24	52	82	388	3,814	283	4,485

Note: Figures in parentheses show the distribution by sex of all degree recipients. The grand total will not agree with the total master's degree figures for 1980–81 shown elsewhere in this publication because OCR's "universe" of institutions was somewhat different from NCES's.

a Includes native Alaskan.

b Includes Pacific Islander.

Source: Office for Civil Rights (OCR), ED (Washington, 1983), unpublished data.

164 Doctor's Degrees, by Race, Ethnicity, and Academic Area, 1980–81

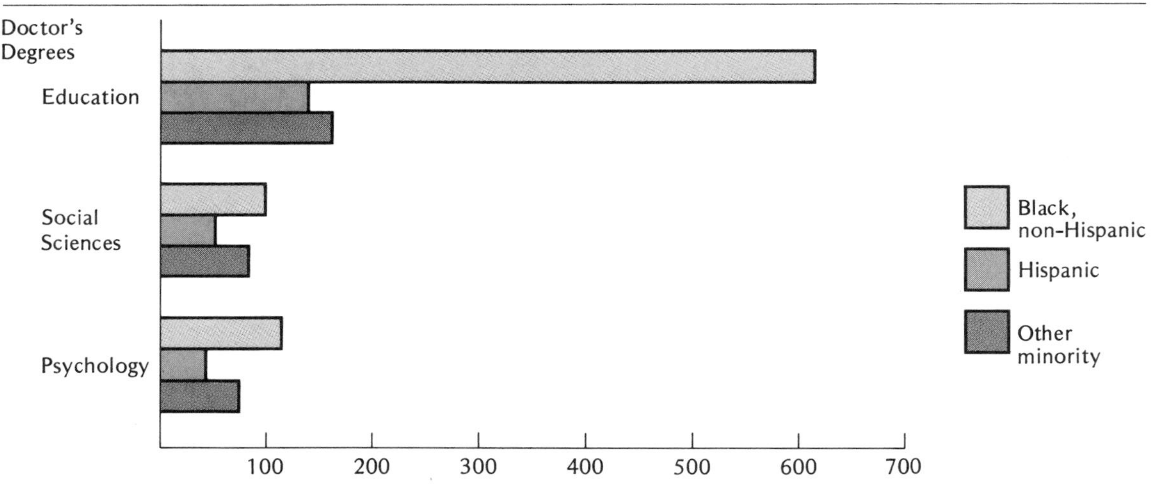

Academic Area	Black, non-Hispanic	American Indian[a]	Asian[b]	Hispanic	Total Minority	White, non-Hispanic	Nonresident Alien	Total
	Doctor's Degrees Awarded to							
All Academic Areas	**1,265**	**130**	**877**	**479**	**2,751**	**25,908**	**4,204**	**32,863**
Men	(694)	(95)	(655)	(286)	(1,730)	(17,310)	(3,565)	(22,605)
Women	(571)	(35)	(222)	(193)	(1,021)	(8,598)	(639)	(10,258)
Agriculture & nat. resources	15	2	29	14	60	664	343	1,067
Architecture & environ. design	6	—	5	2	13	56	24	93
Area studies	6	1	6	1	14	124	19	157
Biological sciences	64	8	140	46	258	3,177	289	3,724
Business & management	32	5	25	2	64	619	161	844
Communications	10	1	2	—	13	147	22	182
Computer & info. sciences	1	1	14	—	16	184	52	252
Education	614	57	105	140	916	6,391	593	7,900
Engineering	24	5	191	23	243	1,352	956	2,551
Fine & applied arts	17	2	7	4	30	587	37	654
Foreign languages	9	1	5	37	52	470	66	588
Health professions	26	6	25	8	65	689	88	842
Home Economics	9	1	6	1	17	206	24	247
Law	1	—	—	1	2	40	18	60
Letters	56	7	22	19	104	1,549	142	1,795
Library science	9	—	3	1	13	51	7	71
Mathematics	9	2	31	6	48	507	173	728
Physical sciences	32	4	106	27	169	2,445	530	3,140
Psychology	116	10	33	73	232	2,637	95	2,964
Pub. affairs & services	52	2	11	10	75	330	28	433
Social sciences	100	12	72	52	236	2,465	418	3,119
Theology	45	1	33	7	86	993	90	1,169
Interdisciplinary studies	12	2	6	5	25	225	29	279

Note: Figures in parentheses show the distribution by sex of all degree recipients. The grand total will not agree with the total doctor's degree figures for 1980–81 shown elsewhere in this publication because OCR's "universe" of institutions was somewhat different from NCES's. Doctor's degrees reported here include Ph.D.'s, Ed.D.'s, and their equivalents; excluded are first professional degrees such as M.D.'s, D.D.S.'s, and so forth.

a Includes native Alaskan.

b Includes Pacific Islander.

Source: Office for Civil Rights (OCR), ED (Washington, 1983), unpublished data.

165 Bachelor's Degrees, by Race, and by Region and State, 1980–81

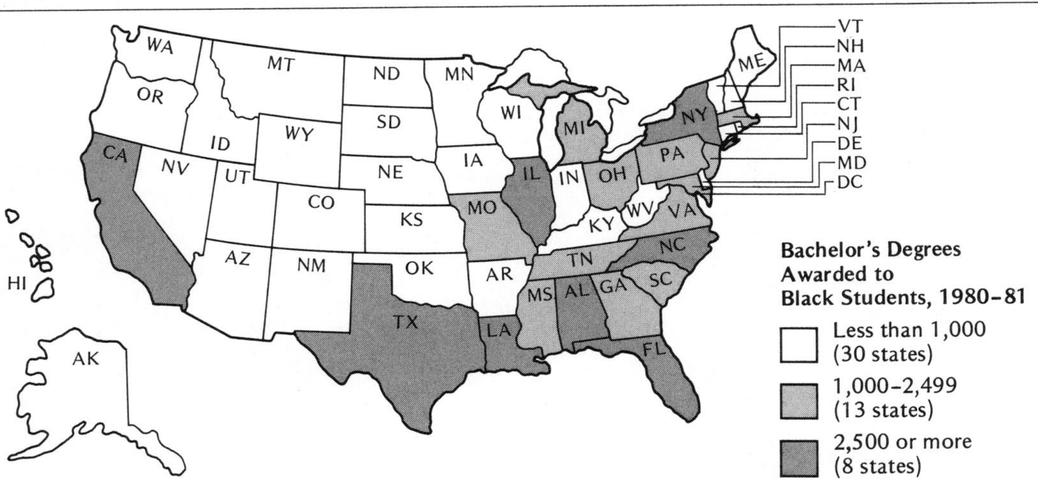

Region and State	Bachelor's Degree Awarded to Black, non-Hispanic	Total Minority	All Races
U. S. & Outlying Parts	**60,589**	**116,046**	**943,320**
50 States & D. C.	**60,533**	**104,541**	**931,583**
New England	**2,176**	**4,023**	**74,180**
Connecticut	357	671	13,312
Maine	26	63	4,817
Massachusetts	1,331	2,517	38,792
New Hampshire	220	289	6,025
Rhode Island	187	376	7,263
Vermont	55	107	3,971
Mideast	**14,134**	**22,171**	**188,599**
Delaware	237	266	3,194
D.C.	1,694	2,021	6,807
Maryland	1,854	2,265	15,901
New Jersey	1,734	2,910	24,474
New York	6,285	11,634	83,777
Pennsylvania	2,330	3,075	54,446
Southeast	**24,722**	**28,839**	**188,075**
Alabama	2,883	3,023	16,534
Arkansas	843	881	6,955
Florida	2,761	4,995	29,988
Georgia	2,309	2,530	17,014
Kentucky	508	662	11,509
Louisiana	2,827	3,142	14,821
Mississippi	2,218	2,290	8,977
North Carolina	3,907	4,211	23,712
South Carolina	1,928	2,019	11,358
Tennessee	1,821	2,042	17,409
Virginia	2,428	2,691	22,078
West Virginia	289	353	7,720
Great Lakes	**9,059**	**12,651**	**171,264**
Illinois	3,254	4,909	44,467
Indiana	785	1,181	24,834
Michigan	2,273	2,963	38,631
Ohio	2,399	2,928	41,306
Wisconsin	348	670	22,026

(Continued on next page)

Bachelor's Degrees, by Race, and by Region and State, 1980–81—*Continued*

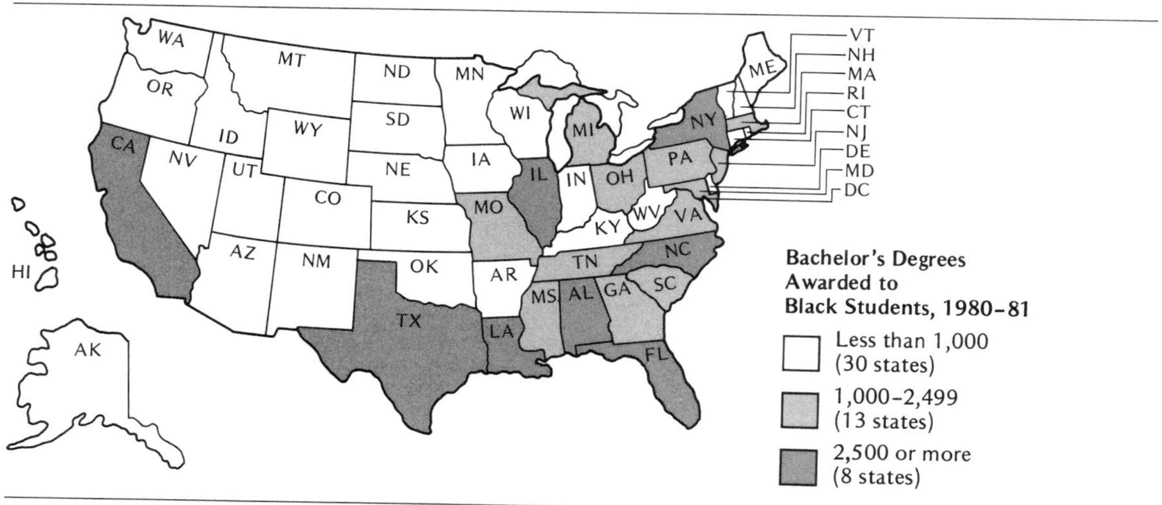

Region and State	Bachelor's Degree Awarded to: Black, non-Hispanic	Total Minority	All Races
Plains	**2,091**	**3,424**	**82,615**
Iowa	241	421	14,441
Kansas	319	537	11,672
Minnesota	160	432	19,392
Missouri	1,151	1,502	22,041
Nebraska	161	343	7,404
North Dakota	28	93	3,795
South Dakota	31	96	3,868
Southwest	**4,005**	**11,812**	**81,776**
Arizona	157	974	10,826
New Mexico	81	1,265	4,543
Oklahoma	506	1,007	12,818
Texas	3,261	8,566	53,589
Rocky Mountains	**387**	**1,634**	**31,907**
Colorado	313	1,073	14,677
Idaho	16	110	2,759
Montana	12	106	3,815
Utah	38	319	9,336
Wyoming	8	26	1,320
Far West	**3,959**	**19,987**	**113,169**
Alaska	17	53	465
California	3,443	15,816	81,584
Hawaii	37	2,128	3,212
Nevada	49	130	1,477
Oregon	87	591	9,783
Washington	326	1,269	16,648
Outlying Parts	**56**	**11,505**	**11,737**

Note: The figures shown here do not agree with data shown elsewhere in this publication because OCR's "universe" of institutions was somewhat different from NCES's.

Source: Office for Civil Rights (OCR), ED (Washington, 1983), unpublished data.

167 Percentage of Earned Doctorates Awarded to Women, by Field of Study, Selected Years, 1949–50—1980–81

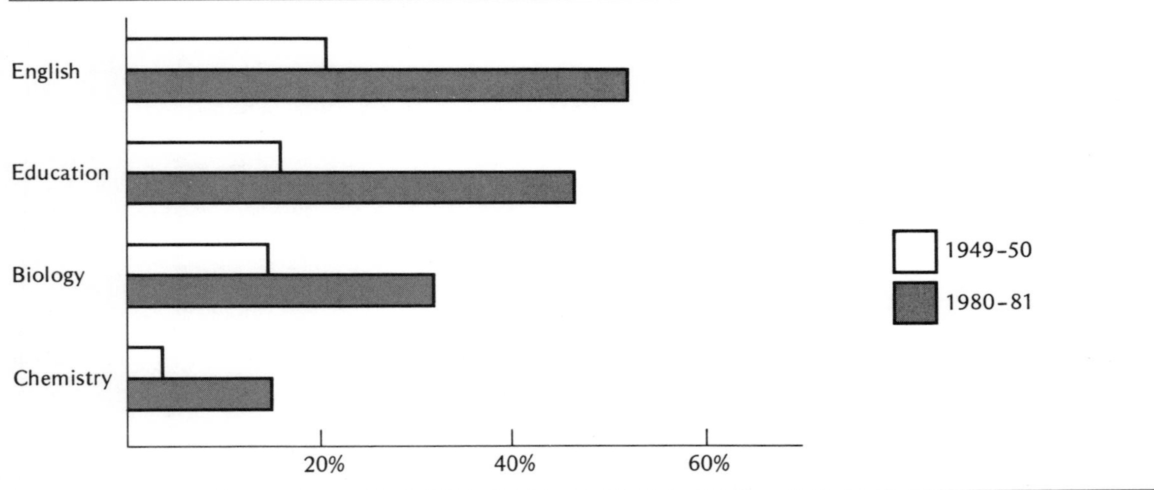

Discipline	Percentage of Doctorates Awarded to Women				
	1949–50	**1959–60**	**1969–70**	**1974–75**	**1980–81**
All Disciplines	**10**	**10**	**13**	**21**	**31**
Humanities					
English	21	21	31	41	54
French	28	38	46	65	70
German	20	33	30	44	53
Philosophy	17	18	12	15	20
Spanish	24	35	39	47	45
Education	**16**	**19**	**20**	**31**	**47**
Social Sciences					
Anthropology	21	17	27	35	39
Economics	4	4	5	8	14
History	11	9	13	22	31
Political Science	8	8	11	16	20
Psychology	15	15	22	31	43
Sociology	18	16	19	30	39
Biological Sciences					
Bacteriology/Microbiology	19	14	21	26	33
Biochemistry	15	13	15	22	31
Biology, General	15	11	20	28	32
Botany	8	7	9	13	22
Zoology	18	14	10	24	26
Physical Sciences					
Chemistry	4	5	8	11	15
Mathematics	6	6	8	11	16
Physics	1	2	3	5	7

Source: USOE/NCES earned degree series.

168 Earned Degrees in the Biological Sciences: Bacteriology, Selected Years, 1947–48—1980–81

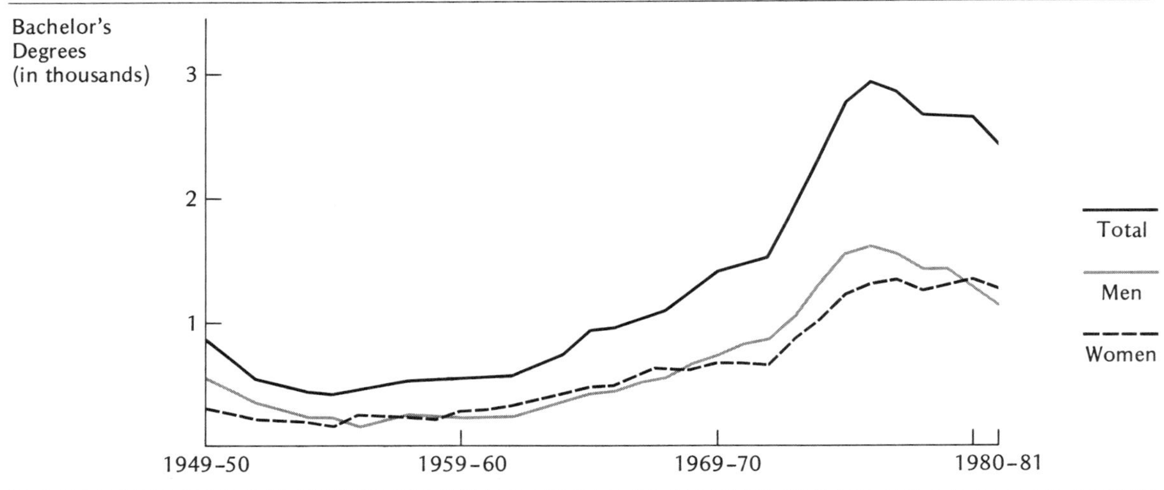

Year	Earned Degrees in Bacteriology[a]				
	Bachelor's			Master's (Second Level)	Doctor's
	Total	Men	Women		
1947–48	624	227	397	174	65
1949–50	870	563	307	327	74
1951–52	566	342	224	321	92
1953–54	439	239	200	242	131
1954–55	414	233	181	233	131
1955–56	426	185	241	249	140
1957–58	515	262	253	249	160
1959–60	533	245	288	248	141
1961–62	570	244	326	323	181
1963–64	763	358	405	350	183
1964–65	938	441	497	341	225
1965–66	996	497	499	385	242
1967–68	1,172	564	608	463	305
1969–70	1,411	741	670	469	359
1970–71	1,475	806	669	458	365
1971–72	1,548	883	665	470	351
1972–73	1,940	1,074	866	518	344
1973–74	2,311	1,305	1,006	509	384
1974–75	2,767	1,538	1,229	554	345
1975–76	2,927	1,606	1,321	588	366
1976–77	2,884	1,557	1,327	662	326
1977–78	2,695	1,419	1,276	617	355
1978–79	2,670	1,409	1,261	597	395
1979–80	2,631	1,281	1,350	596	376
1980–81	2,414	1,130	1,284	482	370

a From 1947–48 through 1954–55, the USOE reports identified the field as "bacteriology"; from 1955–56 through 1959–60, it was listed as "bacteriology, virology, mycology, parasitology"; from 1960–61 through 1969–70, it was listed as "bacteriology, virology, mycology, parasitology, microbiology." In 1970–71 and later, "bacteriology" and "microbiology" are listed as separate fields. Both are included here.

Source: USOE/NCES earned degree series.

169 Earned Degrees in the Biological Sciences: Biochemistry, Selected Years, 1947–48—1980–81

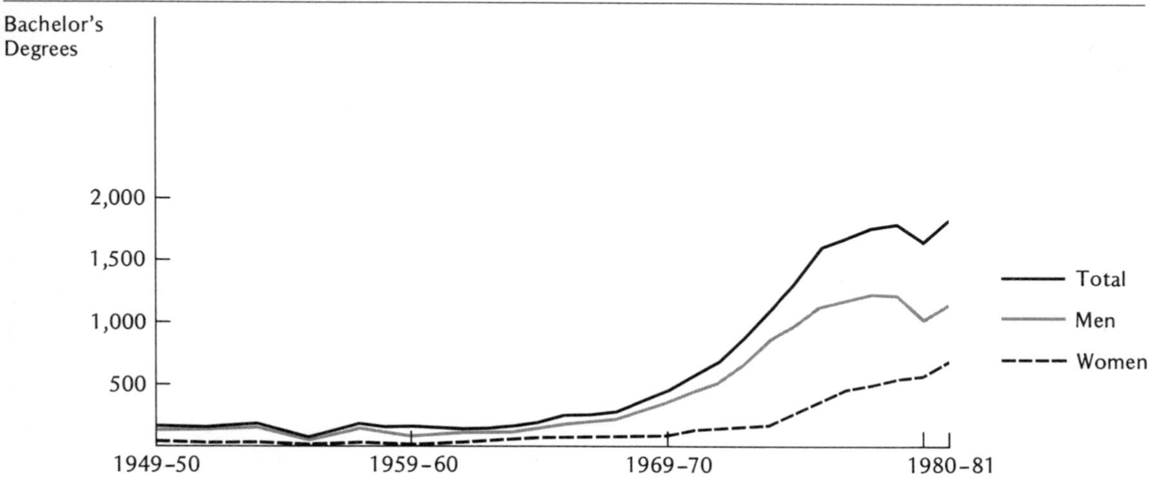

Earned Degrees in Biochemistry

Year	Bachelor's Total	Bachelor's Men	Bachelor's Women	Master's (Second Level)	Doctor's
1947–48	270	226	44	131	65
1949–50	175	160	15	144	116
1951–52	150	129	21	175	99
1953–54	195	173	22	105	145
1954–55	144	124	20	142	147
1955–56	48	39	9	155	146
1957–58	150	127	23	156	149
1959–60	108	84	24	143	165
1961–62	141	101	40	178	183
1963–64	190	141	49	207	264
1964–65	200	143	57	236	290
1965–66	264	195	69	231	315
1967–68	295	213	82	255	442
1969–70	455	332	123	240	449
1970–71	568	430	138	251	517
1971–72	699	524	175	252	462
1972–73	872	677	195	270	501
1973–74	1,101	847	254	249	451
1974–75	1,355	996	359	270	437
1975–76	1,622	1,142	480	254	432
1976–77	1,693	1,198	495	316	447
1977–78	1,752	1,235	517	319	429
1978–79	1,799	1,208	591	301	445
1979–80	1,686	1,090	596	268	475
1980–81	1,837	1,181	656	258	460

Source: USOE/NCES earned degree series.

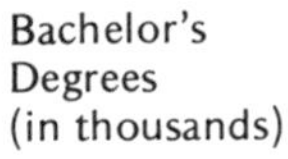

Earned Degrees in the Biological Sciences: Biology, Selected Years, 1947–48—1980–81

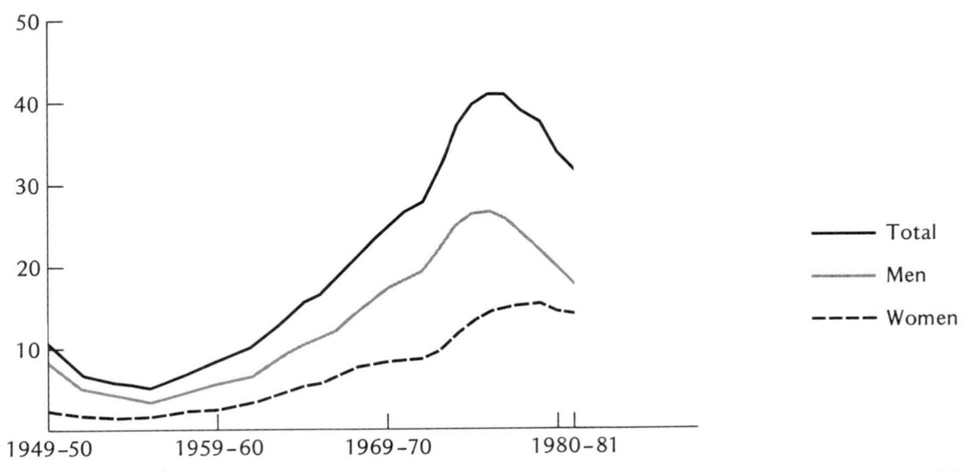

Earned Degrees in Biology[a]

Year	Bachelor's Total	Bachelor's Men	Bachelor's Women	Master's (Second Level)	Doctor's
1947–48	6,739	4,294	2,445	246	65
1949–50	10,428	8,121	2,307	549	81
1951–52	6,960	5,148	1,812	570	132
1953–54	5,847	4,161	1,686	435	147
1954–55	5,493	3,946	1,547	446	150
1955–56	5,007	3,442	1,560	373	121
1957–58	6,821	4,768	2,053	480	145
1959–60	8,426	5,730	2,696	630	159
1961–62	10,018	6,613	3,405	804	178
1963–64	13,766	9,204	4,562	1,149	216
1964–65	15,577	10,316	5,261	1,340	219
1965–66	16,879	11,385	5,494	1,571	282
1967–68	20,963	14,298	6,665	2,352	395
1969–70	24,684	17,037	7,647	2,632	588
1970–71	26,650	18,433	8,217	2,720	669
1971–72	27,886	19,342	8,544	3,017	737
1972–73	31,679	21,910	9,769	3,042	779
1973–74	36,796	24,993	11,803	3,278	797
1974–75	39,289	26,050	13,239	3,210	769
1975–76	40,968	26,615	14,353	3,278	780
1976–77	40,443	25,565	14,878	3,442	759
1977–78	38,639	23,447	15,192	3,195	803
1978–79	37,031	21,829	15,202	3,184	823
1979–80	33,880	19,388	14,492	2,982	1,218
1980–81	31,641	17,457	14,184	2,664	890

a Includes biophysics beginning in 1955–56 and molecular biology beginning in 1968–69, when they were first identified as separate fields on the USOE report form.

Source: USOE/NCES earned degree series.

171 Earned Degrees in the Biological Sciences: Botany, Selected Years, 1947–48—1980–81

Earned Degrees in Botany[a]

Year	Bachelor's Total	Bachelor's Men	Bachelor's Women	Master's (Second Level)	Doctor's
1947–48	353	179	174	169	73
1949–50	494	385	109	299	126
1951–52	346	256	90	254	101
1953–54	293	198	95	197	171
1954–55	302	199	103	173	151
1955–56	285	188	97	186	162
1957–58	334	234	100	236	173
1959–60	385	289	96	248	208
1961–62	430	304	126	320	215
1963–64	469	303	166	372	240
1964–65	503	335	168	433	304
1965–66	501	336	165	415	314
1967–68	655	463	192	537	357
1969–70	597	413	184	528	368
1970–71	569	369	200	430	365
1971–72	558	375	183	452	346
1972–73	736	484	252	495	365
1973–74	918	579	339	429	298
1974–75	1,075	689	386	428	289
1975–76	1,180	676	504	451	305
1976–77	1,228	700	528	471	271
1977–78	1,222	652	570	507	247
1978–79	916	478	438	501	270
1979–80	820	410	410	489	274
1980–81	753	351	402	379	292

a Beginning in 1955–56, includes plant physiology and plant pathology, which were first identified as separate fields on the USOE report form that year.

Source: USOE/NCES earned degree series.

172 Earned Degrees in the Biological Sciences: Zoology, Selected Years, 1947–48—1980–81

Earned Degrees in Zoology

Year	Bachelor's Total	Bachelor's Men	Bachelor's Women	Master's (Second Level)	Doctor's
1947–48	2,306	1,499	807	358	83
1949–50	3,289	2,727	562	551	125
1951–52	2,034	1,574	460	569	151
1953–54	1,696	1,300	396	323	221
1954–55	1,648	1,218	430	264	196
1955–56	1,769	1,324	445	293	148
1957–58	1,980	1,521	459	310	160
1959–60	2,250	1,685	565	364	185
1961–62	2,404	1,736	668	455	222
1963–64	2,488	2,583	905	493	217
1964–65	3,880	2,912	968	575	239
1965–66	4,119	3,198	921	660	293
1967–68	4,825	3,833	992	807	336
1969–70	5,584	4,412	1,172	730	412
1970–71	5,414	4,334	1,080	692	418
1971–72	5,233	4,059	1,174	671	400
1972–73	5,417	4,203	1,214	654	338
1973–74	5,788	4,397	1,391	683	278
1974–75	5,686	4,150	1,536	608	284
1975–76	5,596	3,976	1,620	529	276
1976–77	5,012	3,500	1,512	522	285
1977–78	4,478	2,974	1,504	476	264
1978–79	4,097	2,715	1,382	460	268
1979–80	3,653	2,350	1,303	431	245
1980–81	3,328	2,082	1,246	386	222

Source: USOE/NCES earned degree series.

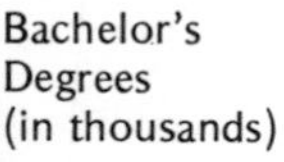

Earned Degrees in Education, Selected Years, 1947–48—1980–81

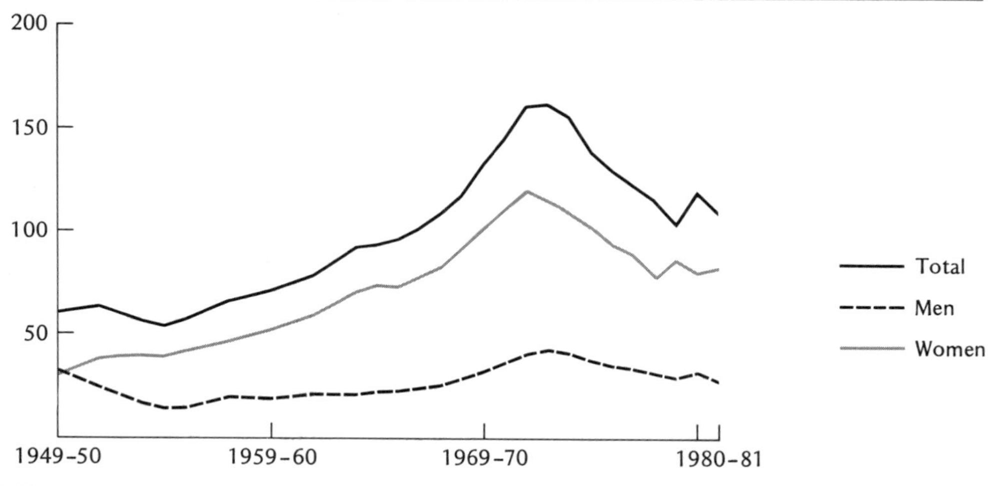

Year	Earned Degrees in Education[a]				
	Bachelor's			Master's (Second Level)	Doctor's
	Total	Men	Women		
1947–48	36,385	12,971	23,414	13,098	521
1949–50	61,725	31,490	30,235	20,069	953
1951–52	62,951	24,599	38,352	26,382	1,146
1953–54	56,817	16,885	39,932	27,785	1,498
1954–55	53,254	14,871	38,383	27,620	1,470
1955–56[a]	56,593	14,874	41,719	27,356	1,438
1957–58	65,571	19,198	46,373	28,223	1,529
1959–60	71,820	19,920	51,900	30,424	1,474
1961–62	78,610	20,357	58,253	32,654	1,737
1963–64	91,389	20,681	70,708	37,186	2,191
1964–65	96,387	21,743	74,644	39,296	2,372
1965–66	95,424	22,783	72,641	45,142	2,711
1967–68	108,531	25,347	83,184	57,119	3,658
1969–70	133,258	32,403	100,855	71,803	5,224
1971–72	160,129	40,764	119,365	90,303	6,333
1972–73	163,549	43,096	120,453	97,455	6,555
1973–74	155,362	41,453	113,909	104,222	6,496
1974–75	139,716	37,615	102,101	111,574	6,714
1975–76	130,232	35,756	94,476	119,943	6,928
1976–77	121,381	33,964	87,417	118,018	7,104
1977–78	115,217	31,697	83,520	111,214	6,806
1978–79	107,815	28,705	79,110	104,739	6,951
1979–80	118,102	30,896	87,206	103,453	7,940
1980–81	108,265	27,069	81,196	98,381	7,900

a Prior to 1955–56, education data are totals of the following fields of study listed in USOE reports: education, industrial arts, and physical education. It was USOE's intent that students preparing to teach in elementary schools be reported under education and those preparing to teach at a higher level be reported under their subject of specialization, such as English, mathematics, or music.

Beginning in 1955–56, a revised USOE report form directed that data for certain specialized teaching fields be counted as degrees in education instead of in the related subject matter areas. In order to increase the comparability of recent data with pre-1955–56 figures, earned degrees in the following specialized teaching fields have been excluded from the table: agricultural education; art education; business, commercial, and distributive education; music education; speech correction; and home economics education.

174 Earned Degrees in Engineering: Chemical Engineering, Selected Years, 1949–50—1980–81

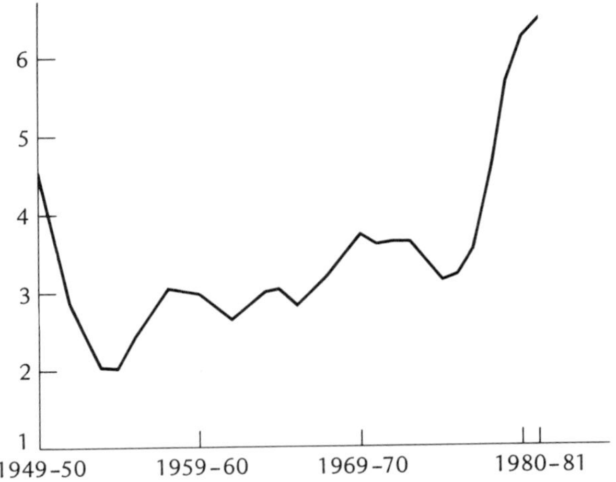

Earned Degrees in Chemical Engineering

Year	Bachelor's[a] Total	Bachelor's[a] Men	Bachelor's[a] Women	Master's[b] (Second Level)	Doctor's
1949–50	4,529	4,509	20	712	178
1951–52	2,859	2,850	9	540	159
1953–54	2,042	2,033	9	448	133
1954–55	2,027	2,014	13	470	139
1955–56	2,466	2,444	22	545	136
1957–58	3,008	2,986	22	561	127
1959–60	2,966	2,935	31	617	170
1961–62	2,677	2,657	20	676	225
1963–64	2,998	2,970	28	762	262
1964–65	3,076	3,050	26	806	364
1965–66	2,848	2,825	23	994	354
1967–68	3,211	3,181	30	1,156	367
1969–70	3,720	3,663	57	1,045	438
1970–71	3,615	3,552	63	1,100	406
1971–72	3,663	3,587	76	1,154	394
1972–73	3,636	3,546	90	1,051	397
1973–74	3,454	3,337	117	1,045	400
1974–75	3,142	3,001	141	990	346
1975–76	3,203	2,927	276	1,031	308
1976–77	3,581	3,152	429	1,086	291
1977–78	4,615	3,899	716	1,237	259
1978–79	5,655	4,649	1,006	1,149	304
1979–80	6,320	5,113	1,207	1,270	284
1980–81	6,527	5,275	1,252	1,267	300

a Includes first professional and bachelor's degrees resulting from four- and five-year programs.

b Includes other "post-graduate, pre-doctoral" degrees.

Source: ASEE/USOE and USOE/NCES earned degree series.

175 Earned Degrees in Engineering: Civil Engineering, Selected Years, 1949–50—1980–81

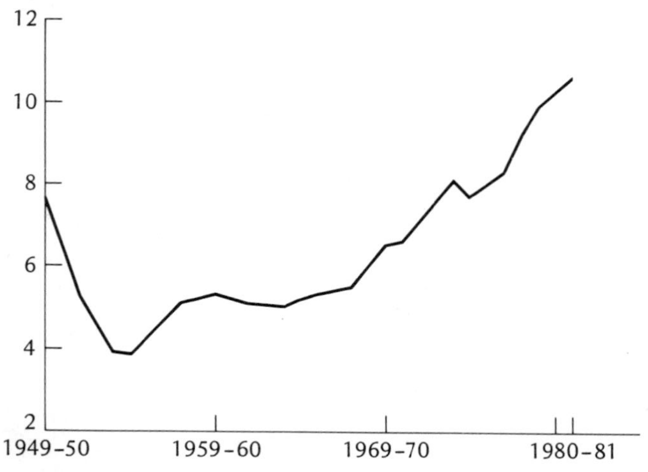

Year	Earned Degrees in Civil Engineering				
	Bachelor's[a]			Master's[b] (Second Level)	Doctor's
	Total	Men	Women		
1949–50	7,772	7,761	11	729	32
1951–52	5,354	5,347	7	586	43
1953–54	3,955	3,948	7	565	43
1954–55	3,868	3,860	8	693	29
1955–56	4,227	4,216	11	822	59
1957–58	5,134	5,121	13	810	60
1959–60	5,287	5,272	15	1,024	73
1961–62	5,185	5,162	23	1,269	142
1963–64	5,077	5,053	24	1,567	217
1964–65	5,200	5,187	13	1,686	252
1965–66	5,335	5,316	19	2,007	283
1967–68	5,508	5,480	28	2,137	376
1969–70	6,524	6,477	47	2,242	411
1970–71	6,613	6,559	54	2,431	446
1971–72	6,909	6,842	67	2,487	415
1972–73	7,502	7,424	78	2,629	397
1973–74	8,145	8,016	129	2,653	368
1974–75	7,790	7,640	150	2,771	356
1975–76	8,059	7,807	252	3,000	370
1976–77	8,376	7,943	433	2,969	309
1977–78	9,265	8,575	690	2,691	277
1978–79	9,941	8,986	955	2,655	253
1979–80	10,326	9,349	977	2,683	270
1980–81	10,678	9,557	1,121	2,891	325

a Includes first professional and bachelor's degrees resulting from four- and five-year programs.

b Includes other "post-graduate, pre-doctoral" degrees.

Source: ASEE/USOE and USOE/NCES earned degrees series.

176 Earned Degrees in Engineering: Electrical Engineering, Selected Years, 1949–50—1980–81

Earned Degrees in Electrical Engineering

Year	Bachelor's[a]			Master's[b] (Second Level)	Doctor's
	Total	Men	Women		
1949–50	13,270	13,258	12	1,168	85
1951–52	6,373	6,367	6	1,017	121
1953–54	4,485	4,475	10	978	111
1954–55	4,860	4,847	13	1,074	141
1955–56	6,222	6,211	11	1,161	136
1957–58	9,567	9,548	19	1,570	144
1959–60	10,631	10,599	32	1,993	203
1961–62	10,263	10,229	34	2,701	295
1963–64	11,261	11,228	33	3,163	460
1964–65	11,730	11,694	36	3,505	511
1965–66	11,007	10,978	29	3,872	569
1967–68	10,725	10,682	43	4,226	723
1969–70	12,288	12,220	68	4,138	882
1970–71	12,288	12,212	76	4,282	879
1971–72	12,181	12,099	82	4,209	824
1972–73	12,377	12,219	158	3,899	791
1973–74	11,419	11,302	117	3,499	705
1974–75	10,246	10,116	130	3,471	701
1975–76	9,874	9,681	193	3,774	649
1976–77	10,018	9,750	268	3,788	566
1977–78	11,213	10,778	435	3,742	503
1978–79	12,440	11,781	659	3,596	586
1979–80	13,821	12,923	898	3,836	525
1980–81	14,938	13,842	1,096	3,901	535

a Includes first professional and bachelor's degrees resulting from four- and five-year programs.

b Includes other "post-graduate, pre-doctoral" degrees.

Source: ASEE/USOE and USOE/NCES earned degree series.

177 Earned Degrees in Engineering: Industrial Engineering, Selected Years, 1949–50—1980–81

	Earned Degrees in Industrial Engineering[a]				
	Bachelor's[b]				
Year	Total	Men	Women	Master's[c] (Second Level)	Doctor's
1949–50	3,369	3,364	5	258	3
1951–52	1,823	1,820	3	271	6
1953–54	1,342	1,338	4	375	6
1954–55	1,448	1,444	4	373	9
1955–56	1,651	1,646	5	354	10
1957–58	2,108	2,105	3	486	9
1959–60	2,242	2,232	10	468	13
1961–62	1,904	1,896	8	508	26
1963–64	2,194	2,186	8	808	32
1964–65	2,236	2,230	6	1,013	61
1965–66	2,335	2,325	10	1,200	45
1967–68	2,727	2,712	15	1,512	79
1969–70	3,199	3,178	21	1,763	126
1970–71	3,210	3,190	20	1,921	139
1971–72	3,713	3,673	40	1,731	168
1972–73	3,508	3,477	31	1,595	130
1973–74	2,921	2,877	44	1,734	146
1974–75	2,583	2,524	59	1,687	119
1975–76	2,241	2,154	87	1,751	121
1976–77	2,264	2,115	149	1,609	104
1977–78	2,712	2,389	323	1,722	118
1978–79	2,804	2,376	428	1,502	149
1979–80	3,175	2,636	539	1,313	116
1980–81	3,833	3,077	756	1,631	166

a Includes administrative, management engineering, and so forth.

b Includes first professional and bachelor's degrees resulting from four- and five-year programs.

c Includes other "post-graduate, pre-doctoral" degrees.

Source: ASEE/USOE and USOE/NCES earned degree series.

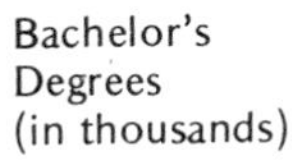

Earned Degrees in Engineering: Mechanical Engineering, Selected Years, 1949–50—1980–81

Earned Degrees in Mechanical Engineering

Year	Bachelor's[a] Total	Men	Women	Master's[b] (Second Level)	Doctor's
1949–50	14,332	14,312	20	835	48
1951–52	7,606	7,597	9	651	68
1953–54	5,419	5,410	9	723	72
1954–55	5,876	5,867	9	759	79
1955–56	6,728	6,717	11	765	61
1957–58	9,060	9,041	19	952	76
1959–60	9,597	9,577	20	1,179	107
1961–62	8,473	8,460	13	1,531	159
1963–64	7,697	7,680	17	1,886	200
1964–65	8,035	8,019	16	2,036	265
1965–66	7,811	7,792	19	2,154	289
1967–68	7,930	7,898	32	2,136	395
1969–70	9,310	9,271	39	2,298	435
1970–71	8,917	8,876	41	2,238	438
1971–72	8,574	8,526	48	2,283	411
1972–73	8,584	8,523	61	2,142	370
1973–74	7,737	7,674	63	1,844	385
1974–75	6,949	6,867	82	1,860	340
1975–76	6,841	6,694	147	1,907	305
1976–77	7,771	7,535	236	1,953	283
1977–78	8,924	8,458	466	1,943	279
1978–79	10,771	9,568	603	1,878	271
1979–80	11,808	10,927	881	2,060	281
1980–81	13,329	12,193	1,136	2,291	276

a Includes first professional and bachelor's degrees resulting from four- and five-year programs.

b Includes other "post-graduate, pre-doctoral" degrees.

Source: ASEE/USOE and USOE/NCES earned degree series.

179 Earned Degrees in the Humanities: English, Selected Years, 1947–48—1980–81

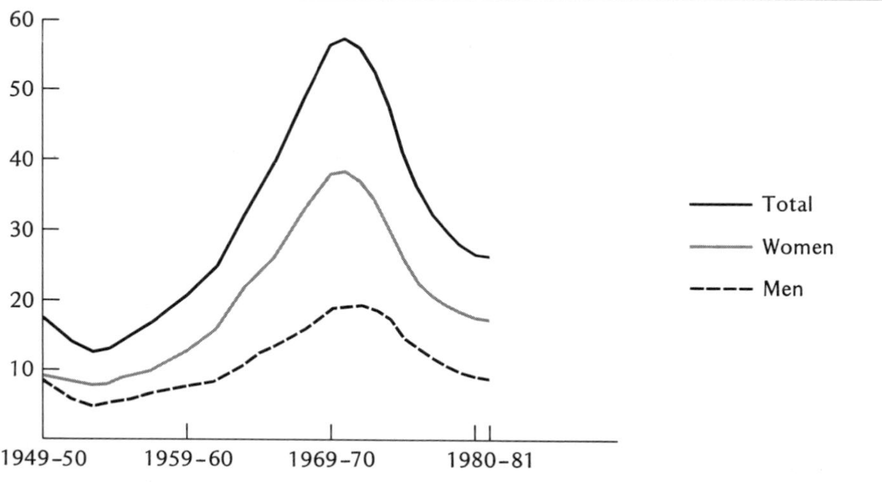

Earned Degrees in English[a]

Year	Bachelor's			Master's (Second Level)	Doctor's
	Total	**Men**	**Women**		
1947–48	12,614	4,392	8,222	2,015	178
1949–50	17,246	8,223	9,023	2,259	230
1951–52	14,087	5,805	8,282	1,922	284
1953–54	12,566	4,729	7,837	1,674	356
1954–55	13,099	5,121	7,978	1,669	341
1955–56	14,406	5,530	8,876	1,892	382
1957–58	16,669	6,755	9,914	2,319	333
1959–60	20,184	7,597	12,587	2,931	397
1961–62	24,413	8,553	15,860	3,514	486
1963–64	32,758	10,987	21,771	4,443	556
1964–65	36,207	12,366	23,841	5,077	689
1965–66	39,192	13,244	25,948	6,265	699
1967–68	48,136	15,735	32,391	7,924	977
1969–70	56,508	18,675	37,833	8,486	1,205
1970–71	57,124	19,020	38,104	8,946	1,441
1971–72	56,094	19,195	36,899	8,717	1,591
1972–73	52,606	18,571	34,035	8,157	1,631
1973–74	47,468	17,133	30,335	7,914	1,616
1974–75	40,387	14,754	25,633	7,414	1,507
1975–76	35,843	13,325	22,518	7,246	1,511
1976–77	32,376	11,878	20,498	6,539	1,318
1977–78	30,069	10,912	19,157	6,380	1,265
1978–79	27,956	9,819	18,137	5,545	1,137
1979–80	26,638	9,032	17,606	5,122	1,131
1980–81	26,006	8,788	17,218	4,948	1,047

a Prior to 1955–56, this field was listed in USOE reports as "English." In reports for 1955–56 through 1966–67, the field is listed as "English and literature," and instructions directed that data for comparative literature be included. Beginning in 1967–68, creative writing and language arts were also specifically included. Data for 1970–71 and later show totals for the following fields: English, general; English literature; comparative literature; classics; and creative writing.

Source: USOE/NCES earned degree series.

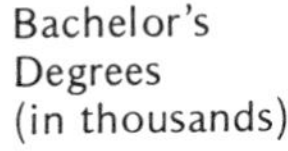

Earned Degrees in the Humanities: Modern Foreign Languages, Selected Years, 1947–48—1980–81

Bachelor's Degrees (in thousands)

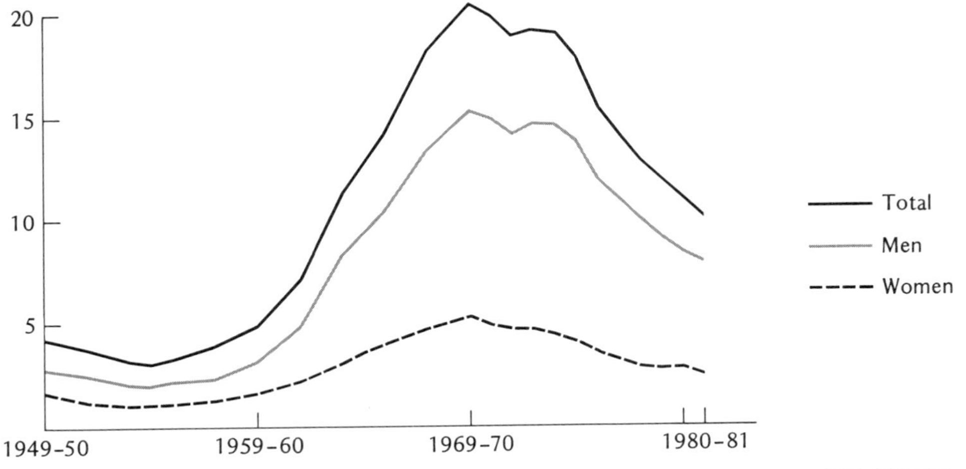

Earned Degrees in Modern Foreign Languages[a]

Year	Bachelor's Total	Bachelor's Men	Bachelor's Women	Master's (Second Level)	Doctor's
1947–48	3,743	902	2,841	700	86
1949–50	4,489	1,752	2,737	921	168
1951–52	3,735	1,230	2,505	800	203
1953–54	3,222	1,075	2,147	682	184
1954–55	3,036	1,043	2,002	647	152
1955–56	3,322	1,078	2,244	669	196
1957–58	3,790	1,353	2,437	695	149
1959–60	4,726	1,618	3,108	892	174
1961–62	7,083	2,218	4,865	1,308	198
1963–64	11,250	3,074	8,176	1,917	277
1964–65	12,924	3,564	9,360	2,390	312
1965–66	14,169	3,855	10,314	3,041	365
1967–68	18,153	4,660	13,493	4,177	521
1969–70	20,363	5,135	15,228	4,548	677
1970–71	19,866	4,917	14,949	4,626	758
1971–72	18,914	4,639	14,275	4,549	819
1972–73	19,149	4,528	14,621	4,252	974
1973–74	19,046	4,425	14,621	3,902	905
1974–75	17,851	4,043	13,808	3,757	853
1975–76	15,293	3,564	11,729	3,470	852
1976–77	14,069	3,295	10,774	3,132	740
1977–78	12,786	2,993	9,793	2,717	640
1978–79	11,823	2,765	9,058	2,396	637
1979–80	10,961	2,640	8,321	2,213	541
1980–81	10,132	2,426	7,706	2,068	582

a Figures for 1947–48 through 1958–59 are totals of degrees identified specifically as "modern foreign languages." Since 1958–59, USOE general category "other languages" does not specify "modern" languages. Even so, the "other languages" included in the data shown for 1959–60 and later, although they may include some degrees in non-modern languages Sanskrit or Aramaic. All figures in this table exclude classical Greek and Latin and linguistics.

Source: USOE/NCES earned degree series.

181 Earned Degrees in the Humanities: Music, Selected Years, 1947–48—1980–81

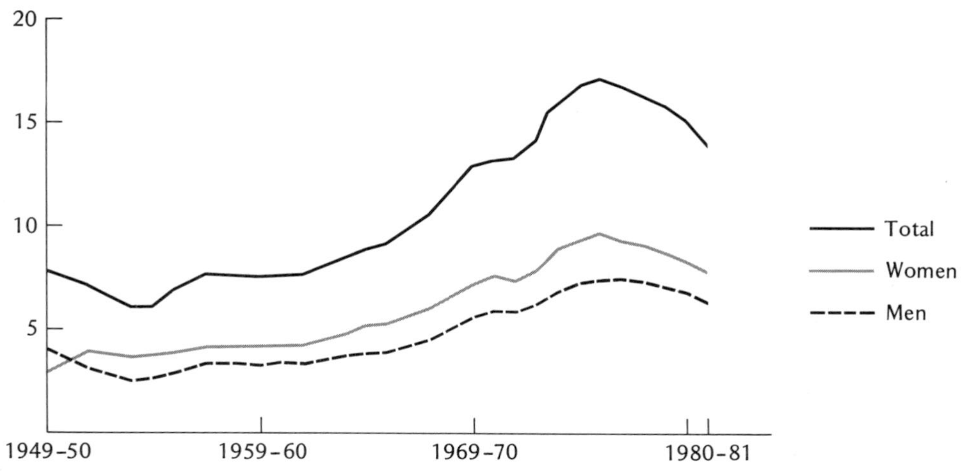

Earned Degrees in Music[a]

Year	Bachelor's Total	Bachelor's Men	Bachelor's Women	Master's (Second Level)	Doctor's
1947–48	5,284	1,766	3,518	1,043	27
1949–50	7,934	4,069	3,865	1,489	34
1951–52	7,015	3,056	3,959	1,738	55
1953–54	6,239	2,545	3,694	1,577	73
1954–55	6,339	2,553	3,786	1,677	68
1955–56	6,995 (3,925)	2,998 (1,715)	3,997 (2,210)	2,069 (994)	122 (41)
1957–58	7,625 (4,753)	3,480 (2,200)	4,145 (2,553)	2,038 (1,028)	115 (41)
1959–60	7,593 (4,605)	3,296 (2,042)	4,297 (2,563)	2,240 (1,069)	157 (38)
1961–62	7,690 (4,749)	3,315 (2,069)	4,375 (2,680)	2,264 (1,112)	172 (62)
1963–64	8,501 (5,245)	3,626 (2,272)	4,875 (2,973)	2,505 (1,214)	220 (61)
1964–65	8,935 (5,466)	3,832 (2,357)	5,103 (3,109)	2,704 (1,241)	208 (67)
1965–66	9,063 (5,498)	3,901 (2,347)	5,162 (3,151)	3,087 (1,392)	212 (48)
1967–68	10,637 (6,464)	4,565 (2,747)	6,072 (3,717)	3,479 (1,581)	266 (81)
1969–70	12,786 (7,353)	5,614 (3,190)	7,172 (4,163)	3,736 (1,606)	368 (90)
1970–71	13,352 (7,283)	5,800 (3,071)	7,552 (4,212)	3,999 (1,564)	435 (109)
1971–72	13,414 (7,107)	5,923 (3,092)	7,491 (4,015)	4,192 (1,529)	433 (177)
1972–73	14,221 (7,459)	6,291 (3,214)	7,930 (4,245)	4,135 (1,483)	461 (95)
1973–74	15,628 (7,752)	6,816 (3,262)	8,812 (4,490)	4,477 (1,472)	472 (87)
1974–75	16,738 (8,063)	7,269 (3,390)	9,469 (4,673)	4,488 (1,384)	467 (64)
1975–76	17,069 (7,937)	7,460 (3,209)	9,609 (4,728)	4,599 (1,382)	448 (80)
1976–77	16,834 (7,666)	7,489 (3,207)	9,345 (4,459)	4,584 (1,437)	476 (74)
1977–78	16,423 (7,412)	7,332 (3,095)	9,091 (4,317)	4,819 (1,355)	461 (66)
1978–79	15,713 (6,714)	7,065 (2,858)	8,648 (3,856)	4,589 (1,282)	533 (90)
1979–80	15,170 (6,220)	6,744 (2,605)	8,396 (3,615)	4,566 (1,149)	507 (105)
1980–81	13,989 (5,332)	6,359 (2,256)	7,630 (3,076)	4,459 (1,127)	449 (68)

a Prior to 1955–56, music education degrees were included in the data for music. Since then, they have been reported as a separate field of study in the academic area "education." In this table, degrees in music education are shown in parentheses and included in the total figures.

Source: USOE/NCES earned degree series.

182 Earned Degrees in the Humanities: Philosophy, Selected Years, 1947–48—1980–81

Earned Degrees in Philosophy[a]

Year	Bachelor's Total	Bachelor's Men	Bachelor's Women	Master's (Second Level)	Doctor's
1947–48	1,726	1,397	329	241	37
1949–50	2,835	2,449	386	277	83
1951–52	2,421	2,124	297	287	102
1953–54	1,845	1,582	263	251	103
1954–55	1,774	1,473	301	231	84
1955–56	2,668	2,343	325	267	82
1957–58	2,981	2,637	344	312	102
1959–60	3,466	3,052	414	383	137
1961–62	3,725	3,254	471	431	123
1963–64	4,810	4,183	627	514	137
1964–65	4,810	4,175	635	581	144
1965–66	5,036	4,306	730	613	203
1967–68	5,768	4,728	1,040	657	278
1969–70	5,717	4,631	1,086	729	359
1970–71	5,790	4,624	1,166	602	394
1971–72	5,953	4,652	1,301	618	364
1972–73	5,934	4,583	1,351	629	409
1973–74	5,809	4,393	1,416	664	413
1974–75	5,348	4,003	1,345	699	375
1975–76	4,766	3,511	1,255	691	382
1976–77	4,451	3,325	1,126	671	330
1977–78	4,035	2,955	1,080	567	283
1978–79	3,799	2,766	1,033	517	258
1979–80	3,695	2,647	1,048	509	246
1980–81	3,643	2,580	1,063	469	280

a Between 1955–56 and 1969–70, figures include data for scholastic philosophy, which was first identified as a separate field of study in the 1955–56 USOE report.

Source: USOE/NCES earned degree series.

183 Earned Degrees in Law, Selected Years, 1947–48—1980–81

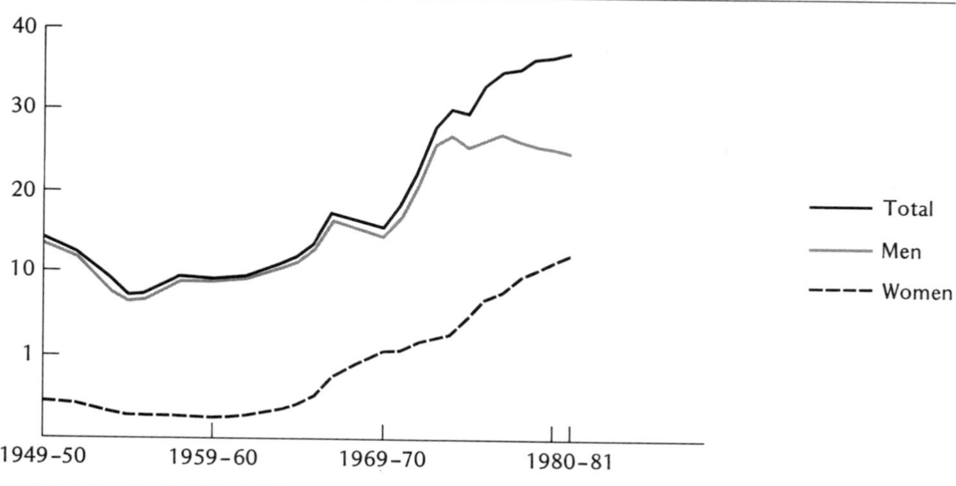

	Earned Degrees in Law				
	Bachelor's[a]				
Year	Total	Men	Women	Master's (Second Level)	Doctor's
1947–48	10,990	10,570	420	394	247
1949–50	14,312	13,891	421	513	27
1951–52	12,558	12,158	400	456	46
1953–54	9,298	8,976	322	341	31
1954–55	8,226	7,937	289	373	22
1955–56	8,285	7,994	291	427	27
1957–58	9,433	9,153	280	458	32
1959–60	9,314	9,073	241	520	24
1961–62	9,627	9,333	294	593	38
1963–64	11,024	10,681	343	641	30
1964–65	12,000	11,596	404	672	29
1965–66	13,687	13,169	518	780	29
1967–68	17,169	16,457	712	724	36
1969–70	15,715	14,837	878	884	35
1970–71	18,197	16,877	1,320	955	20
1971–72	22,520	20,942	1,578	932	40
1972–73	27,958	25,694	2,264	1,071	37
1973–74	30,146	26,686	3,460	1,181	27
1974–75	29,933	25,416	4,517	1,245	21
1975–76	33,066	26,702	6,364	1,553	77
1976–77	34,922	27,023	7,899	1,574	60
1977–78	35,269	26,088	9,181	1,786	39
1978–79	36,065	25,707	10,358	1,647	46
1979–80	36,330	25,265	11,065	1,817	40
1980–81	37,107	24,944	12,142	1,832	60

a Includes first professional degrees.

Source: USOE/NCES earned degree series.

184 Earned Degrees in Medicine and Dentistry, Selected Years, 1949–50—1980–81

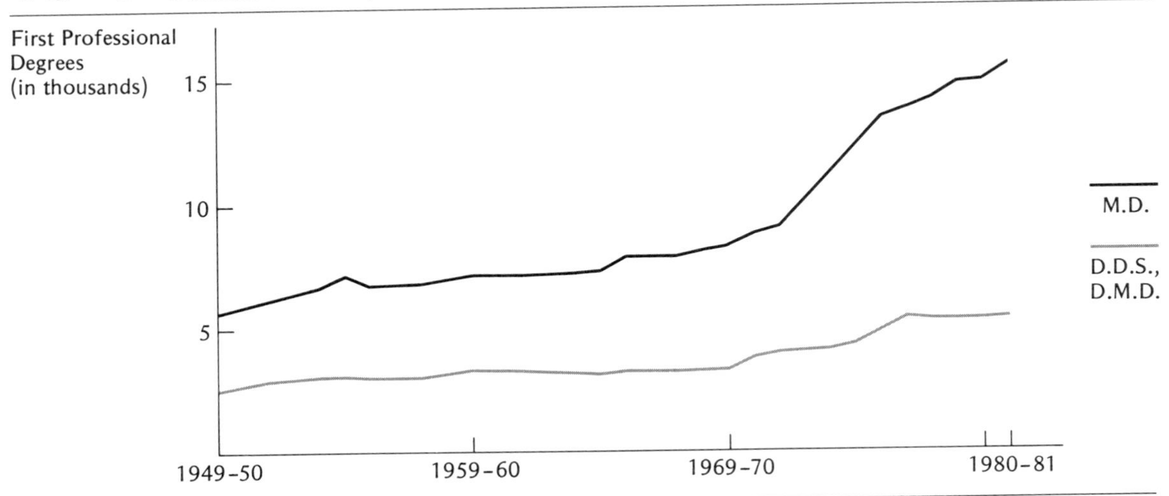

	Earned Degrees in					
	Medicine (M.D. only)			Dentistry (D.D.S. & D.M.D. only)		
Year	Total	Men	Women	Total	Men	Women
1949–50	5,612	5,028	584	2,579	2,561	18
1951–52	6,201	5,871	330	2,918	2,895	23
1953–54	6,757	6,414	343	3,102	3,063	39
1954–55	7,056	6,718	338	3,099	3,071	28
1955–56	6,753	6,498	355	3,009	2,975	34
1957–58	6,861	6,510	351	3,065	3,031	34
1959–60	7,074	6,680	394	3,247	3,221	26
1961–62	7,183	6,791	392	3,209	3,189	20
1963–64	7,342	6,910	432	3,196	3,182	14
1964–65	7,347	6,869	478	3,135	3,112	23
1965–66	7,720	7,204	516	3,264	3,229	35
1967–68	7,987	7,353	634	3,448	3,395	53
1969–70	8,374	7,661	713	3,748	3,712	36
1970–71	8,986	8,157	829	3,777	3,731	46
1971–72	9,331	8,486	845	3,894	3,848	46
1972–73	10,398	9,459	939	4,086	4,028	58
1973–74	11,447	10,167	1,280	4,478	4,390	88
1974–75	12,550	10,896	1,654	4,809	4,660	149
1975–76	13,540	11,340	2,200	5,478	5,229	249
1976–77	13,574	10,974	2,600	5,187	4,804	383
1977–78	14,399	11,299	3,100	5,238	4,652	586
1978–79	14,925	11,473	3,452	5,488	4,836	652
1979–80	14,902	11,416	3,486	5,258	4,558	700
1980–81	15,505	11,672	3,833	5,460	4,672	788

Source: USOE/NCES earned degree series.

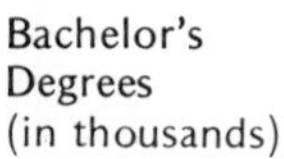

Earned Degrees in Nursing, Selected Years, 1947–48—1980–81

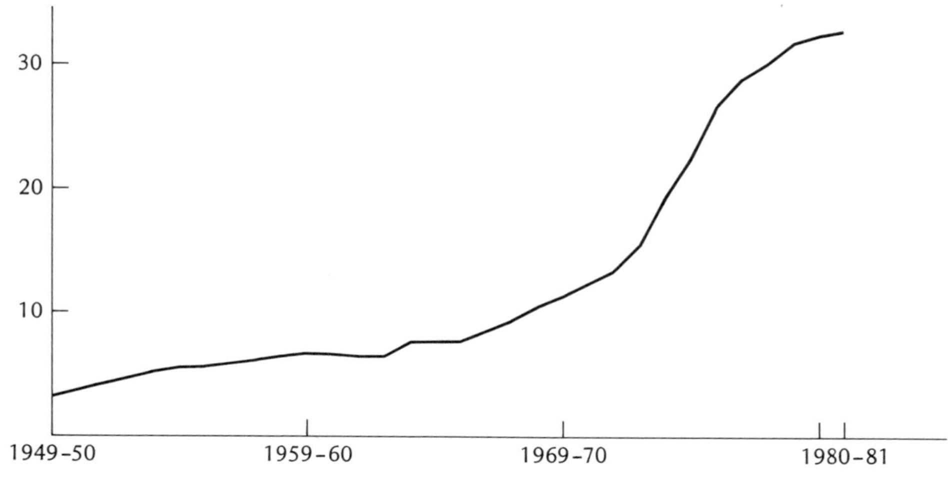

Year	Earned Degrees in Nursing[a]				
	Bachelor's				
	Total	Men	Women	Master's (Second Level)	Doctor's
1947–48	3,351	27	3,324	200	—
1948–49	3,529	20	3,509	246	2
1949–50	3,292	23	3,269	368	2
1951–52	4,137	46	4,091	478	1
1953–54	5,109	62	5,047	482	2
1954–55	5,240	61	5,179	550	3
1955–56	5,315	50	5,265	240	—
1957–58	6,052	49	6,003	479	—
1959–60	6,661	81	6,580	599	—
1960–61	6,574	70	6,504	555	—
1961–62	6,370	65	6,305	504	—
1962–63	6,526	57	6,469	659	—
1963–64	7,363	67	7,296	771	1
1964–65	7,908	77	7,831	809	8
1965–66	7,831	96	7,735	863	1
1966–67	8,334	82	8,252	1,145	1
1967–68	9,186	120	9,066	1,249	4
1968–69	10,380	132	10,248	1,390	3
1969–70	11,280	160	11,120	1,549	11
1970–71	12,283	254	12,029	1,542	7
1971–72	13,245	343	12,902	1,846	10
1972–73	15,526	463	15,063	2,093	17
1973–74	19,409	756	18,653	2,293	14
1974–75	23,813	1,104	22,709	2,220	16
1975–76	26,846	1,362	25,484	3,058	16
1976–77	28,605	1,541	27,064	3,287	24
1977–78	30,307	1,646	28,661	3,812	56
1978–79	31,808	1,806	30,002	4,256	68
1979–80	32,441	1,785	30,656	4,616	118
1980–81	32,794	1,654	31,140	5,096	113

a Beginning in 1955–56, USOE reports include public health nursing. Beginning in 1959–60, USOE report form specified: "include only degrees based on 4 or more years of college work. Include certificates or diplomas based on 4 years of work only."

186 Earned Degrees in the Physical Sciences: Chemistry, Selected Years, 1947–48—1980–81

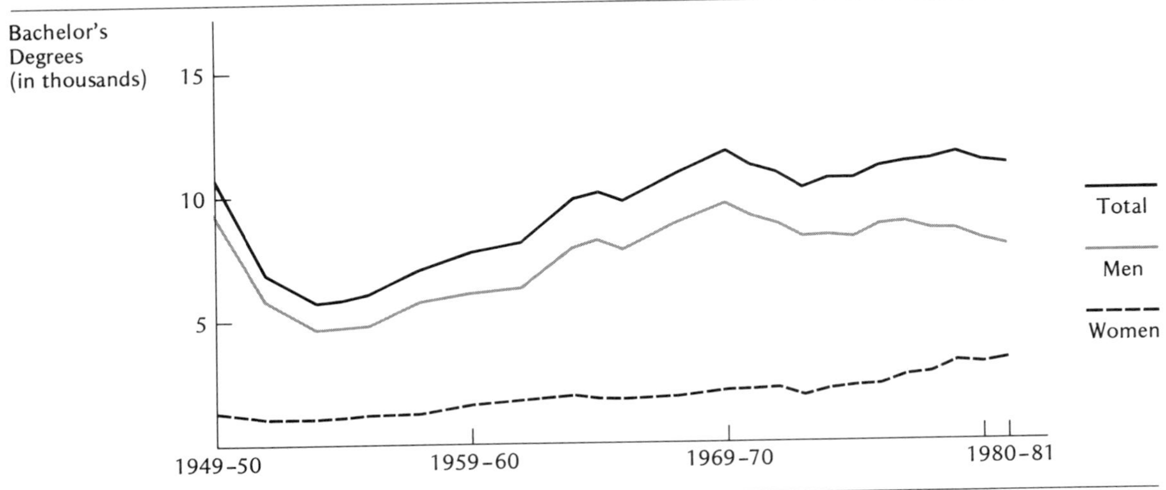

Earned Degrees in Chemistry[a]

Year	Bachelor's Total	Bachelor's Men	Bachelor's Women	Master's (Second Level)	Doctor's
1947–48	7,429	5,361	2,068	1,360	569
1949–50	10,619	9,134	1,485	1,576	953
1951–52	6,819	5,717	1,102	1,409	1,031
1953–54	5,791	4,727	1,064	1,098	1,013
1954–55	5,920	4,781	1,139	1,173	1,005
1955–56	6,178	4,996	1,182	1,164	986
1957–58	7,010	5,705	1,305	1,125	939
1959–60	7,603	6,005	1,598	1,228	1,048
1961–62	8,089	6,374	1,715	1,425	1,139
1963–64	9,724	7,809	1,915	1,586	1,301
1964–65	10,047	8,111	1,936	1,715	1,414
1965–66	9,735	7,934	1,801	1,839	1,571
1967–68	10,847	8,882	1,965	2,014	1,757
1969–70	11,617	9,501	2,116	2,146	2,208
1970–71	11,183	9,088	2,095	2,284	2,160
1971–72	10,721	8,601	2,120	2,259	1,971
1972–73	10,226	8,259	1,967	2,230	1,882
1973–74	10,525	8,413	2,112	2,138	1,828
1974–75	10,649	8,264	2,385	2,006	1,824
1975–76	11,107	8,610	2,497	1,796	1,623
1976–77	11,322	8,720	2,602	1,775	1,571
1977–78	11,474	8,593	2,881	1,892	1,525
1978–79	11,643	8,530	3,113	1,765	1,518
1979–80	11,232	8,050	3,182	1,723	1,545
1980–81	11,347	7,953	3,394	1,654	1,622

a Beginning in 1961–62, pharmaceutical chemisty was identified as a separate field of study in the USOE report. Data for that field are included above. In 1970–71, inorganic chemistry, organic chemistry, physical chemistry, and analytical chemistry were identified as separate fields of study and are included in the figures for 1970–71 and later.

Source: USOE/NCES earned degree series.

187 Earned Degrees in the Physical Sciences: Geology, Selected Years, 1947–48—1980–81

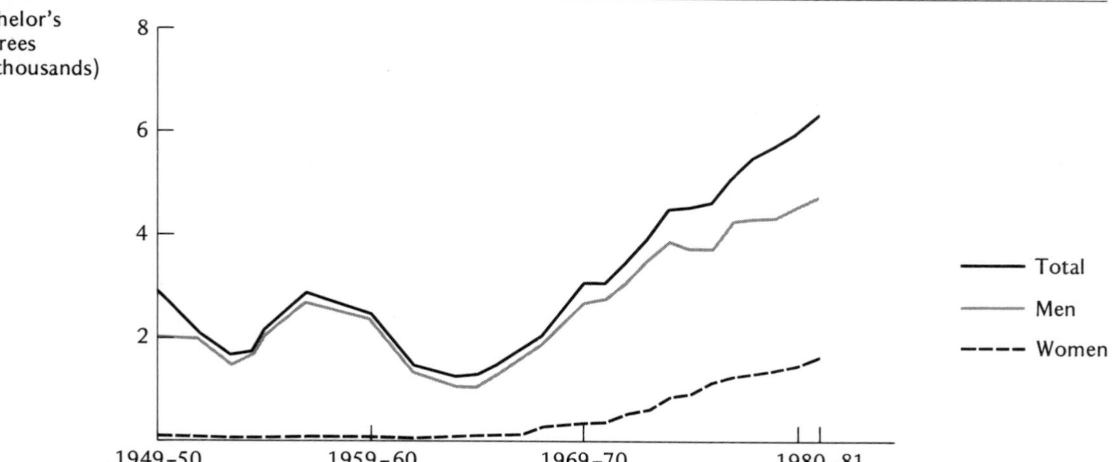

	Earned Degrees in Geology[a]				
	Bachelor's				
Year	Total	Men	Women	Master's (Second Level)	Doctor's
1947–48	1,172	1,037	135	318	57
1949–50	2,043	2,934	109	493	113
1951–52	2,102	2,026	76	486	116
1953–54	1,632	1,553	79	412	136
1954–55	1,795	1,703	92	507	154
1955–56	2,195	2,115	80	517	141
1957–58	2,888	2,783	105	746	154
1959–60	2,564	2,485	79	620	214
1961–62	1,499	1,425	74	639	208
1963–64	1,243	1,136	107	616	245
1964–65	1,258	1,127	131	618	291
1965–66	1,510	1,353	157	594	312
1967–68	2,043	1,819	224	987	316
1969–70	3,002	2,668	334	847	355
1970–71	3,109	2,735	374	937	358
1971–72	3,487	3,006	481	1,098	389
1972–73	3,961	3,436	525	1,227	367
1973–74	4,586	3,801	785	1,376	382
1974–75	4,559	3,738	821	1,314	387
1975–76	4,608	3,705	903	935	390
1976–77	5,390	4,228	1,162	1,420	445
1977–78	5,622	4,335	1,287	1,552	367
1978–79	5,765	4,374	1,391	1,574	355
1979–80	5,924	4,476	1,448	1,566	352
1980–81	6,384	4,741	1,643	1,611	424

a Beginning in 1955–56, "geophysics (including seismology)" and "earth sciences, all other," and, in 1967–68, "earth sciences, general" were identified as separate fields of study in the USOE reports. In 1970–71 the following additional fields were separately identified and are included in these totals: geochemistry, paleontology.

Source: USOE/NCES earned degree series.

188 Earned Degrees in the Physical Sciences: Mathematical Subjects, Selected Years, 1947–48—1980–81

Earned Degrees in Mathematical Subjects[a]

Year	Bachelor's Total	Bachelor's Men	Bachelor's Women	Master's (Second Level)	Doctor's
1947–48	4,266	2,619	1,647	711	128
1949–50	6,392	4,946	1,446	974	160
1951–52	4,721	3,389	1,332	802	206
1953–54	4,090	2,722	1,368	706	227
1954–55	4,034	2,724	1,310	761	250
1955–56	4,660	3,137	1,523	898	235
1957–58	6,924	4,953	1,971	1,234	247
1959–60	11,437	8,312	3,125	1,765	303
1961–62	14,610	10,355	4,255	2,680	396
1963–64	18,677	12,682	5,995	3,603	596
1964–65	19,581	13,132	6,449	4,148	682
1965–66	20,093	13,404	6,689	4,772	782
1967–68	23,625	14,839	8,786	5,533	947
1969–70	27,565	17,248	10,317	5,648	1,236
1970–71	24,918	15,424	9,494	5,201	1,199
1971–72	23,848	14,525	9,323	5,209	1,128
1972–73	23,223	13,878	9,345	5,033	1,068
1973–74	21,813	12,874	8,939	4,840	1,031
1974–75	18,346	10,646	7,700	4,338	975
1975–76	16,085	9,531	6,554	3,863	856
1976–77	14,303	8,354	5,949	3,698	823
1977–78	12,701	7,455	5,246	3,383	805
1978–79	11,901	6,943	4,958	3,046	730
1979–80	11,378	6,562	4,816	2,860	724
1980–81	11,078	6,342	4,736	2,567	728

a Beginning in 1955–56, "statistics" was identified as a separate field of study in USOE reports. In 1970–71, "mathematics, general; applied mathematics; statistics, mathematical and theoretical"; and "other" were identified as separate fields of study. Data for all fields are included above.

Source: USOE/NCES earned degree series.

189 Earned Degrees in the Physical Sciences: Physics, Selected Years, 1947–48—1980–81

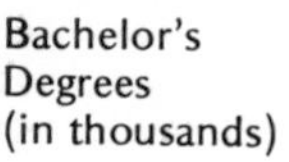

Year	Bachelor's Total	Bachelor's Men	Bachelor's Women	Master's (Second Level)	Doctor's
	Earned Degrees in Physics				
1947–48	2,126	1,962	164	706	198
1949–50	3,414	3,287	127	922	358
1951–52	2,247	2,141	106	886	485
1953–54	1,952	1,877	75	714	485
1954–55	1,996	1,920	76	729	511
1955–56	2,335	2,233	102	742	470
1957–58	3,186	3,042	144	795	464
1959–60	4,338	4,166	172	1,073	487
1961–62	4,812	4,624	188	1,425	667
1963–64	4,956	4,715	241	1,848	778
1964–65	4,954	4,708	246	1,906	942
1965–66	4,609	4,385	224	1,949	973
1967–68	5,045	4,749	296	2,088	1,260
1969–70	5,333	5,004	329	2,205	1,439
1970–71	5,076	4,733	343	2,194	1,482
1971–72	4,645	4,322	323	2,035	1,344
1972–73	4,268	3,955	313	1,755	1,338
1973–74	3,962	3,625	337	1,662	1,115
1974–75	3,716	3,354	362	1,577	1,080
1975–76	3,544	3,156	388	1,451	997
1976–77	3,420	3,062	358	1,319	945
1977–78	3,330	2,961	369	1,294	873
1978–79	3,388	2,939	399	1,319	918
1979–80	3,396	2,962	434	1,192	830
1980–81	3,441	3,009	432	1,296	866

Source: USOE/NCES earned degree series.

190 Earned Degrees in the Social Sciences: Business and Management, Selected Years, 1947–48—1980–81

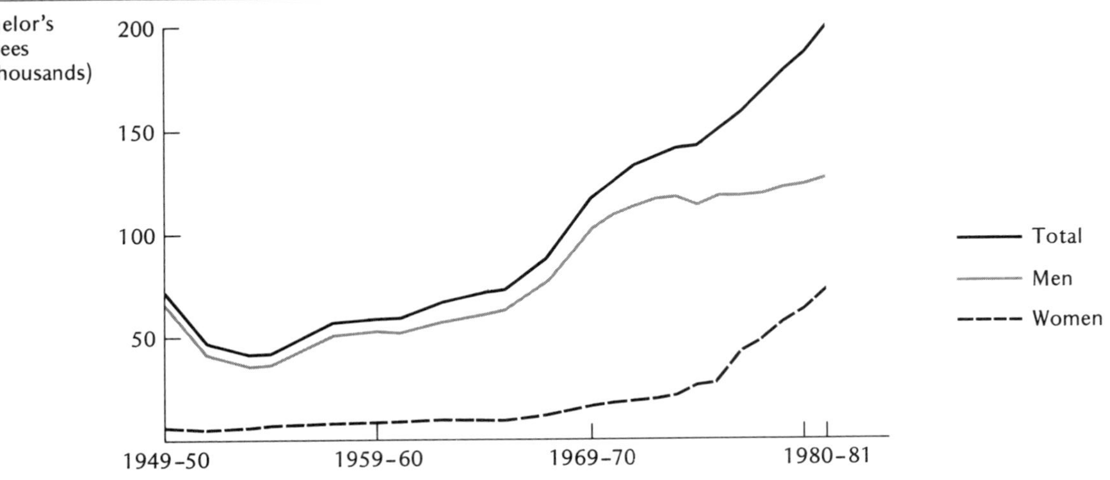

Earned Degrees in Business and Management[a]

Year	Bachelor's[b] Total	Bachelor's[b] Men	Bachelor's[b] Women	Master's (Second Level)	Doctor's
1947–48	38,371	32,260	6,111	2,314	41
1949–50	72,137	65,911	6,226	4,335	58
1951–52	46,683	41,060	5,623	3,826	92
1953–54	40,944	35,255	5,689	3,114	118
1954–55	41,655	35,564	6,091	3,336	144
1955–56	47,203	40,485	6,718	3,854	160
1957–58	57,669	50,427	7,342	4,899	124
1959–60	58,433	50,796	7,637	5,601	157
1961–62	58,622	50,535	8,087	6,166	262
1963–64	66,083	56,956	9,127	7,362	313
1964–65	70,208	60,430	9,778	8,648	359
1965–66[b]	70,708	60,727	9,981	14,402	446
1967–68	88,631	76,062	12,569	19,560	504
1969–70	116,175	100,166	16,009	23,609	692
1970–71	126,505	109,638	16,867	28,878	917
1971–72	131,864	113,941	17,923	32,677	976
1972–73	136,280	116,668	19,612	33,314	1,026
1973–74	141,058	118,099	22,959	34,731	1,053
1974–75	141,732	114,629	27,103	38,408	1,097
1975–76	150,402	117,391	33,011	44,571	1,022
1976–77	158,766	118,551	40,215	48,407	927
1977–78	168,075	119,652	48,423	50,331	930
1978–79	179,886	122,405	57,481	52,110	918
1979–80	186,683	123,964	62,719	55,148	796
1980–81	200,876	127,070	73,806	58,018	845

a Prior to 1970–71, this field was identified as "business and commerce." Prior to 1955–56, data include "business and commerce—accounting," in addition to "business and commerce—all other." Beginning in 1955–56, data include business, commercial and distributive education, and industrial relations, in addition to the major area, business and commerce.

b Until 1965–66, includes first professional degrees. Beginning in 1965–66, USOE directed that all master's degrees be counted as such. Previously, those master's degrees that were considered first professional degrees were included with bachelor's degrees.

Source: USOE/NCES earned degree series.

191 Earned Degrees in the Social Sciences: Economics, Selected Years, 1947–48—1980–81

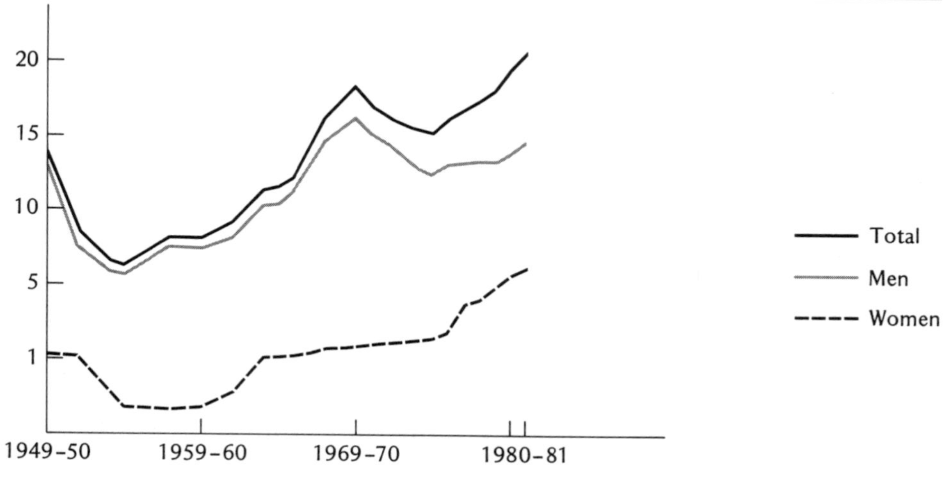

Year	Earned Degrees in Economics[a]				
	Bachelor's				
	Total	Men	Women	Master's (Second Level)	Doctor's
1947–48	9,002	7,684	1,318	922	116
1949–50	14,753	13,471	1,102	921	200
1951–52	8,595	7,520	1,075	695	239
1053–54	6,728	5,938	790	609	245
1954–55	6,364	5,678	686	617	241
1955–56	6,938	6,259	679	753	293
1957–58	8,142	7,535	607	933	310
1959–60	8,101	7,422	679	995	313
1961–62	9,111	8,344	767	1,217	379
1963–64	11,385	10,311	1,074	1,449	500
1964–65	11,538	10,496	1,042	1,597	538
1965–66	12,274	11,130	1,144	1,901	586
1967–68	16,207	14,569	1,638	2,358	752
1969–70	18,352	16,436	1,889	2,396	975
1970–71	17,137	15,214	1,923	2,415	933
1971–72	16,408	14,578	1,830	2,636	960
1972–73	15,848	13,772	2,076	2,662	1,035
1973–74	15,596	13,438	2,158	2,560	953
1974–75	15,160	12,677	2,483	2,522	974
1975–76	16,025	13,032	2,993	2,560	923
1976–77	16,674	13,027	3,647	2,662	898
1977–78	17,443	13,333	4,010	2,549	867
1978–79	18,150	13,383	4,767	2,468	858
1979–80	19,643	13,956	5,687	2,382	841
1980–81	20,644	14,590	6,024	2,494	884

a Includes economics and agricultural economics. The latter field was first identified separately in USOE reports for 1955–56.

Source: USOE/NCES earned degree series.

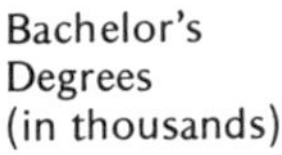

Earned Degrees in the Social Sciences: History, Selected Years, 1947–48—1980–81

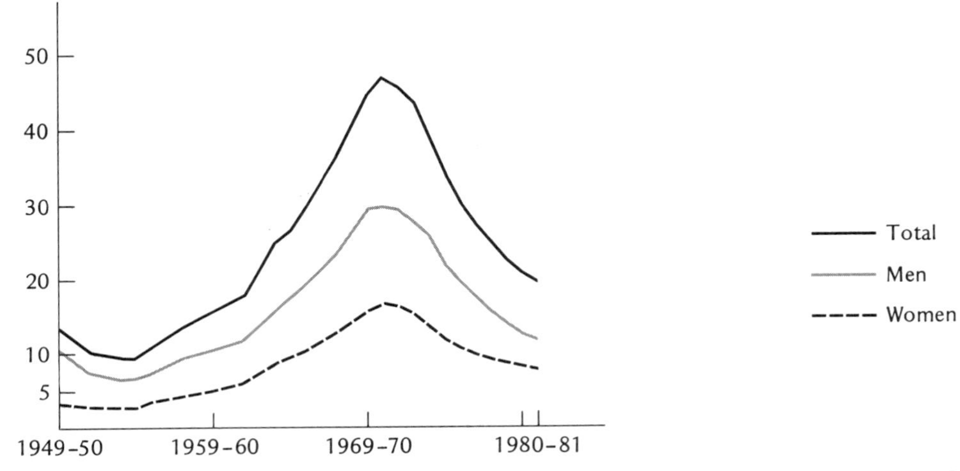

Earned Degrees in History[a]

Year	Bachelor's Total	Bachelor's Men	Bachelor's Women	Master's (Second Level)	Doctor's
1947–48	9,245	5,669	3,576	1,566	162
1949–50	13,567	10,242	3,325	1,801	275
1951–52	10,216	7,285	2,931	1,445	317
1953–54	9,385	6,418	2,967	1,220	355
1954–55	9,540	6,707	2,833	1,199	310
1955–56	10,891	7,584	3,307	1,157	274
1957–58	13,375	9,331	4,044	1,433	313
1959–60	15,227	10,294	4,933	1,861	366
1961–62	17,914	11,720	6,194	2,229	360
1963–64	24,345	15,667	8,678	2,783	533
1964–65	26,421	17,128	9,293	3,234	600
1965–66	29,507	19,217	10,290	4,002	628
1967–68	36,252	23,339	12,913	5,036	726
1969–70	44,784	29,019	15,765	5,287	1,087
1970–71	46,397	29,812	16,585	5,400	1,058
1971–72	45,631	29,570	16,061	5,513	1,207
1972–73	43,009	27,944	15,065	5,309	1,217
1973–74	39,225	25,614	13,611	4,869	1,194
1974–75	33,524	21,653	11,871	4,552	1,192
1975–76	30,351	19,531	10,820	3,972	1,114
1976–77	27,262	17,291	9,971	3,682	1,006
1977–78	24,633	15,405	9,228	3,288	883
1978–79	22,490	13,869	8,621	2,758	623
1979–80	20,589	12,540	8,049	2,566	790
1980–81	19,601	11,855	7,746	2,435	726

a Includes history and "American studies." The latter field was first identified separately in USOE reports for 1955–56.

Source: USOE/NCES earned degree series.

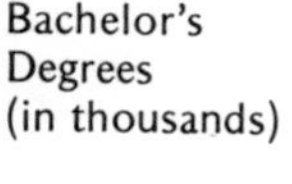

Earned Degrees in the Social Sciences: Political Science, Selected Years, 1947–48—1980–81

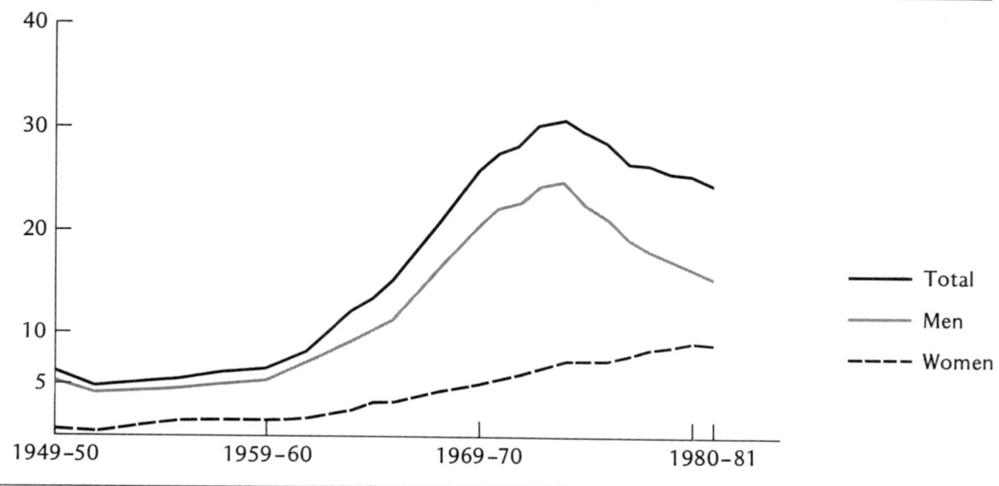

Earned Degrees in Political Science

Year	Bachelor's Total	Bachelor's Men	Bachelor's Women	Master's (Second Level)	Doctor's
1947–48	4,874	3,727	1,147	806	99
1949–50	6,346	5,366	980	710	127
1951–52	4,925	4,016	909	525	147
1953–54	5,332	4,314	1,018	534	153
1954–55	5,500	4,415	1,085	498	181
1955–56	5,670	4,561	1,109	509	203
1957–58	6,167	5,031	1,136	665	170
1959–60	6,657	5,401	1,256	722	201
1961–62	8,390	6,481	1,909	839	214
1963–64	12,206	9,468	2,738	1,163	263
1964–65	13,693	10,655	3,038	1,210	304
1965–66	15,375	11,994	3,381	1,429	336
1967–68	20,522	16,056	4,466	1,937	457
1969–70	25,856	20,698	5,158	2,105	525
1970–71	27,636	22,072	5,564	2,318	700
1971–72	28,317	22,979	5,338	2,451	758
1972–73	30,246	24,327	5,919	2,399	747
1973–74	30,932	24,733	6,199	2,448	766
1974–75	29,314	22,704	6,610	2,333	680
1975–76	28,515	21,310	7,205	2,192	723
1976–77	26,576	19,079	7,497	2,223	641
1977–78	26,245	18,077	8,168	2,070	636
1978–79	25,817	17,197	8,620	2,038	563
1979–80	25,457	16,315	9,142	1,938	535
1980–81	24,977	15,796	9,181	1,875	484

Source: USOE/NCES earned degree series.

194 Earned Degrees in the Social Sciences: Psychology, Selected Years, 1947–48—1980–81

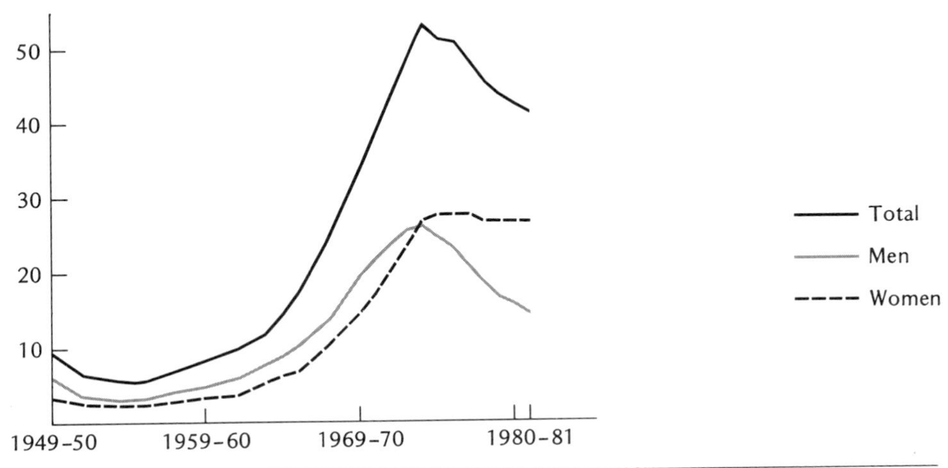

Earned Degrees in Psychology[a]

Year	Bachelor's Total	Bachelor's Men	Bachelor's Women	Master's (Second Level)	Doctor's
1947–48	6,402	2,808	3,594	1,200	154
1949–50	9,582	6,058	3,524	1,316	283
1951–52	6,622	3,783	2,839	1,406	540
1953–54	5,758	3,085	2,673	1,254	619
1954–55	5,532	3,009	2,523	1,293	688
1955–56	5,665	3,108	2,557	973	634
1957–58	6,930	4,063	2,867	1,235	572
1959–60	8,111	4,785	3,326	1,406	641
1961–62	9,638	5,817	3,821	1,832	781
1963–64	13,359	7,834	5,516	2,059	939
1964–65	14,771	8,729	6,042	2,708	1,004
1965–66	17,065	10,069	6,996	3,117	1,206
1967–68	24,095	13,908	10,187	4,328	1,447
1969–70	33,927	19,148	14,779	5,167	1,962
1970–71	38,469	21,318	17,151	5,724	2,144
1971–72	43,862	23,488	20,374	6,768	2,277
1972–73	48,341	25,251	23,090	7,670	2,550
1973–74	52,574	26,012	26,562	8,824	2,875
1974–75	51,693	24,427	27,266	9,432	2,913
1975–76	50,733	23,053	27,680	10,234	3,157
1976–77	48,282	20,766	27,516	10,878	3,386
1977–78	45,377	18,591	26,786	10,316	3,174
1978–79	43,248	16,725	26,523	10,165	3,240
1979–80	42,093	15,440	26,653	9,938	3,395
1980–81	41,068	14,332	26,736	10,223	3,576

a Beginning in 1964–65, USOE reported educational psychology degrees in two major areas—education and psychology. The figures above include both sets of data.

Source: USOE/NCES earned degree series.

195 Earned Degrees in the Social Sciences: Sociology, Selected Years, 1947–48—1980–81

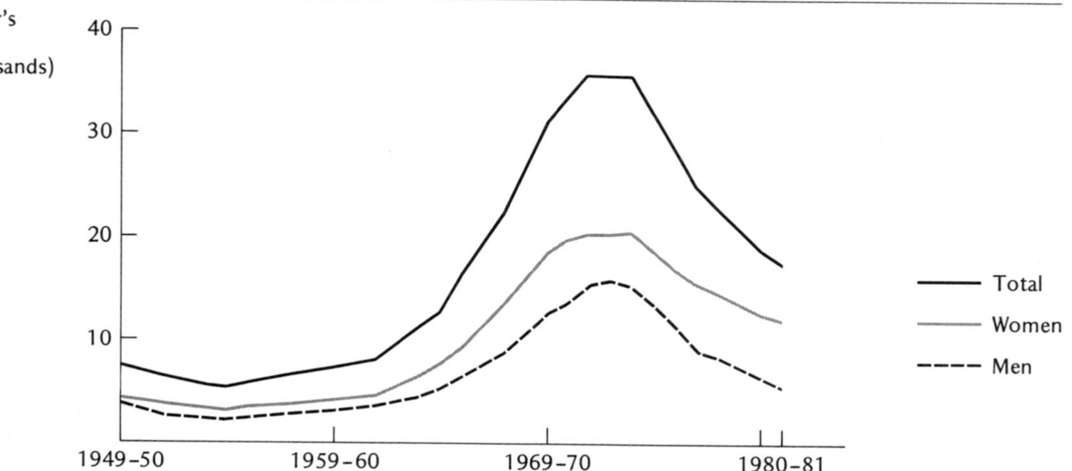

Earned Degrees in Sociology

Year	Bachelor's Total	Bachelor's Men	Bachelor's Women	Master's (Second Level)	Doctor's
1947–48	6,271	1,787	4,484	430	66
1949–50	7,887	3,848	4,039	552	98
1951–52	6,697	2,986	3,711	517	141
1953–54	5,702	2,387	3,315	440	184
1954–55	5,533	2,333	3,200	474	167
1955–56	5,916	2,553	3,363	402	170
1957–58	6,583	2,977	3,606	397	150
1959–60	7,182	3,171	4,011	440	161
1961–62	8,183	3,629	4,554	578	173
1963–64	11,053	4,466	6,587	646	198
1964–65	12,896	5,123	7,773	789	230
1965–66	15,203	6,139	9,064	981	244
1967–68	22,062	8,577	13,485	1,193	367
1969–70	30,848	12,445	18,403	1,716	534
1970–71	33,662	13,703	19,959	1,809	574
1971–72	35,626	15,332	20,294	1,945	636
1972–73	35,994	15,745	20,249	1,923	583
1973–74	35,896	15,314	20,582	2,196	632
1974–75	31,817	13,330	18,487	2,112	693
1975–76	27,970	11,379	16,591	2,010	729
1976–77	24,989	9,802	15,187	1,830	714
1977–78	22,991	8,423	14,568	1,611	599
1978–79	20,545	7,155	13,390	1,415	612
1979–80	18,881	6,270	12,611	1,341	583
1980–81	17,272	5,247	12,025	1,240	610

Source: USOE/NCES earned degree series.

196 Associate Degrees, by Sex of Student and by Control of Institution, 1965–66—1979–80

Year	Total	Men	Women	Public	Private
	Degree-Credit Associate Degrees[a]				
1965–66[b]	111,740	63,861	47,879	82,419	29,321
1966–67	139,731	78,505	61,226	105,528	34,203
1967–68	160,054	90,483	69,571	125,202	34,852
1968–69	184,113	105,879	78,234	148,402	35,711
1969–70	206,753	117,657	89,096	171,278	35,475
1970–71	188,784	107,233	81,551	154,081	34,703
1971–72	227,459	128,460	98,999	192,550	34,909
1972–73	242,290	133,581	108,709	206,414	35,876
1973–74	253,875	138,409	115,466	216,147	37,728
1974–75	264,335	139,514	124,821	226,410	37,925
1975–76	281,570	149,816	131,754	238,644	42,996
1976–77	284,488	146,293	138,195	237,792	46,696
1977–78	287,724	141,955	145,769	239,131	48,593
1978–79	282,119	132,725	149,394	232,340	49,779
1979–80	282,261	128,425	153,836	231,867	50,394
	Percent Distribution				
1965–66	100	57	43	74	26
1966–67	100	56	44	76	24
1967–68	100	57	43	78	22
1968–69	100	58	42	81	19
1969–70	100	57	43	83	17
1970–71	100	57	43	82	18
1971–72	100	56	44	85	15
1972–73	100	55	45	85	15
1973–74	100	55	45	85	15
1974–75	100	53	47	86	14
1975–76	100	53	47	85	15
1976–77	100	51	49	84	16
1977–78	100	49	51	83	17
1978–79	100	47	53	82	18
1979–80	100	45	55	82	18

a Except where footnoted otherwise, figures show associate degrees awarded as a result of work creditable wholly or chiefly toward a bachelor's degree. Figures may vary from those showing data by state and region inasmuch as the latter data include degree-credit associate degree and other awards.

b The 1965–66 questionnaire did not specify degree-credit awards only; hence, these data include non-degree-credit associate degrees.

Source: USOE/NCES earned degree series.

197 Associate Degrees, by Type and Control of Institution, Selected Years, 1965–66—1979–80

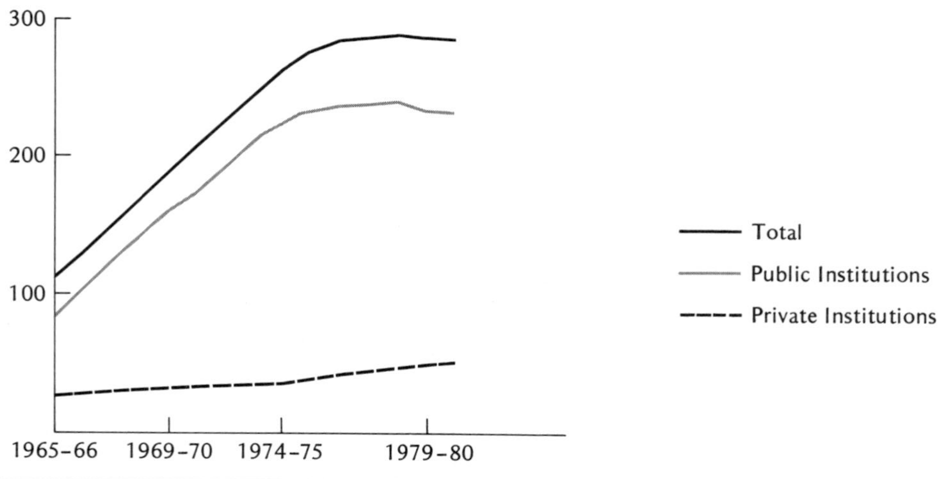

Year	Associate Degrees Awarded[a]						
	Number				Percent Distribution[b]		
	All Institutions	Universities	Other Four-Year	Two-Year Insts.	Universities	Other Four-Year	Two-Year Insts.
	All (Public and Private) Institutions						
1965–66	111,740	7,546	10,507	93,687	7	9	84
1969–70	206,753	11,889	14,167	180,697	6	7	87
1974–75	264,335	10,587	29,054	224,694	4	11	85
1975–76	281,570	10,861	36,595	234,114	4	13	83
1976–77	284,488	10,674	40,143	233,671	4	14	82
1977–78	287,724	10,799	41,708	235,217	4	14	82
1978–79	282,119	9,899	41,670	230,550	4	15	81
1979–80	282,261	10,010	41,118	231,133	4	15	82
	Public Institutions						
1965–66	82,419	5,795	3,318	73,306	7	4	89
1969–70	171,278	10,322	4,316	156,640	6	3	91
1974–75	226,410	7,731	14,621	204,058	3	6	90
1975–76	238,644	8,270	17,653	212,721	3	7	89
1976–77	237,792	7,953	19,425	210,414	3	8	88
1977–78	239,131	8,480	20,830	209,821	3	9	88
1978–79	232,340	7,733	19,606	205,001	3	8	89
1979–80	231,867	7,950	19,459	204,458	3	8	88
	Private Institutions						
1965–66	29,321	1,751	7,189	20,381	6	25	70
1969–70	35,475	1,567	9,851	24,057	4	28	68
1974–75	37,925	2,856	14,433	20,636	8	38	54
1975–76	42,926	2,591	18,942	21,393	6	44	50
1976–77	46,696	2,721	20,718	23,257	6	44	50
1977–78	48,593	2,319	20,878	25,396	5	43	52
1978–79	49,779	2,166	22,064	25,549	4	44	52
1979–80	50,394	2,060	21,659	26,675	4	43	53

a Figures for 1965–66 show all associate degrees. Figures for 1969–70 and later show associate degrees awarded as a result of work creditable wholly or chiefly toward a bachelor's degree.

b Percentages total across and may not add to 100 percent because of rounding.

Source: USOE/NCES earned degree series.

198 Associate Degrees, by Region and State, Selected Years, 1965–66—1980–81

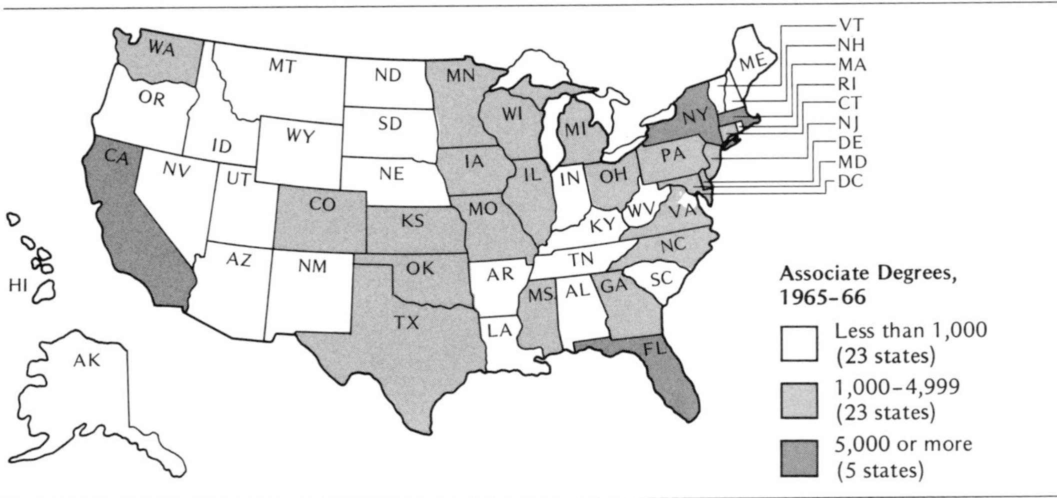

Region and State	Associate Degrees				
	1965–66	1969–70	1974–75	1975–76	1980–81
U. S. & Outlying Parts	**111,740**	**206,753**	**267,815[a]**	**281,570**	**na**
50 States & D. C.	**111,607**	**206,023**	**265,589[a]**	**278,762**	**416,377**
New England	**8,812**	**14,439**	**17,627**	**21,229**	**28,159**
Connecticut	1,389	2,650	4,070	4,311	5,381
Maine	293	336	965	1,116	1,731
Massachusetts	5,403	9,133	8,804	10,401	14,632
New Hampshire	375	461	1,066	1,700	1,980
Rhode Island	551	1,041	1,648	2,533	3,150
Vermont	801	818	1,074	11,168	1,285
Mideast	**23,734**	**42,615**	**63,633**	**66,020**	**83,403**
Delaware	379	1,026	1,102	943	1,195
D. C.	593	694	980	928	639
Maryland	1,279	2,494	3,480[b]	4,653	6,778
New Jersey	1,264	3,461	5,763	6,051	9,834
New York	16,428	27,158	44,120	45,446	48,679
Pennsylvania	3,791	7,782	8,188	7,999	16,278
Southeast	**19,477**	**35,352**	**48,385**	**51,895**	**86,088**
Alabama	438	1,772	2,520	3,515	4,839
Arkansas	253	422	884	995	1,785
Florida	8,596	17,096	20,907	22,334	31,503
Georgia	1,780	3,052	4,300	4,814	5,978
Kentucky	690	1,440	2,926	3,230	4,818
Louisiana	28	310	636	1,037	2,066
Mississippi	2,464	3,258	2,952	2,812	4,190
North Carolina	1,910	3,210	3,832	3,299	10,608
South Carolina	867	1,056	2,110	1,813	5,501
Tennessee	481	1,020	2,730	3,466	5,659
Virginia	1,530	1,891	3,280	2,978	6,755
West Virginia	440	825	1,308	1,602	2,386
Great Lakes	**10,239**	**25,239**	**38,941**	**39,669**	**69,720**
Illinois	3,751	8,382	13,065	12,934	21,173
Indiana	503	1,887	3,231	3,346	6,932
Michigan	3,355	8,050	11,593	12,270	18,938
Ohio	1,491	4,633	8,928	8,804	15,455
Wisconsin	1,139	2,287	2,124	2,315	7,222

(Continued on next page)

For footnotes and sources, see next page.